A GUIDE TO NATIONAL MONUMENTS AND HISTORIC SITES

A GUIDE TO NATIONAL MONUMENTS AND HISTORIC SITES

Jill MacNeice

PRENTICE HALL
New York

Copyright© 1990 by Jill MacNeice
First edition, first printing
All rights reserved, including the right of
reproduction in whole or in part in any form.

Published by Prentice Hall Trade Division
A division of Simon & Schuster, Inc.
15 Columbus Circle
New York, NY 10023

Produced by Menasha Ridge Press
Design by Barbara E. Williams
Manufactured in the United States of America

Library of Congress Cataloging-in-Publication Data:
MacNeice, Jill, 1956–
    A guide to national monuments and historic sites / Jill
MacNeice.—1st ed.
        p.   cm.
    Includes index.
    ISBN 0-13-611682-5 : $14.95
        1. National parks and reserves—United States—
Guide-books.   2. National monuments—United States
—Guide-books.   3. United States—Description and
travel—1981– —Guide-books.   I. Title.
E160.M26   1990
917.304'928—dc20   90-7509
                                                      CIP

ISBN 0-13-611682-5

CONTENTS

LIST OF MAPS

A map of each state appears on the first page of each chapter. Other maps included are:

U.S. MAP OF NATIONAL MONUMENTS AND HISTORIC SITES

ACKNOWLEDGMENTS

I'd like to thank Ed Bearss, Chief Historian of the National Park Service, who reviewed my manuscript and worked with me through the early stages of this book. Thanks also to Mary Ingels of the National Park Service Public Information Office, Tom DuRant of the Historic Photograph Collection, and editors Julia Leigh and Marshall Messer for their invaluable assistance. And, although they are too numerous to mention by name, I offer a special thanks to all the National Park Service rangers and historians in the field who took the time to read my articles, check for accuracy, and make comments.

INTRODUCTION

Some of the most interesting and exotic vacation spots in the country can be found among the National Park Service's monuments, historic sites, and battlefields. These sites cover the country from Arkansas to Alaska, from Georgia to Guam, and they span American history from Indian pueblos of the 12th century to the Vietnam Veterans Memorial built in 1982. They include well-known American icons such as the Statue of Liberty and Mount Rushmore; the remnants of frontier forts and Spanish missions, the homes of President John F. Kennedy, Dr. Martin Luther King, Jr., Eleanor Roosevelt, and other great Americans; the spectacular natural scenery of Death Valley, Rainbow Bridge, and Buck Island Reef. Taken together, these sites weave a rich tapestry of time and place that brings American history in its natural environment to life.

Most sites offer a wide range of free interpretive activities for visitors. There are excellent orientation films and slide shows, thoughtful exhibitions describing the area's unique culture and wildlife, guided nature and historical walks, living-history programs, and campfire talks. Some sites have concessions that offer exciting outdoor activities—spelunking tours of crystalline caves, rafting trips down wild rivers, or cross-country horseback treks with Indian guides. The larger parks have beautiful, inexpensive campgrounds; backcountry camping, when available, is usually free of charge.

Whatever the site, bring your imagination with you. Some sites are well documented while others consist of little more than a few crumbling walls and interpretive plaques. A little imagination can help you conjure the heat of the colonial blast furnace in Hopewell, Pennsylvania, the acrid smell of gunpowder at a Civil War battlefield, or the vision of Edgar Allan Poe writing a chilling story in his drafty Philadelphia row house.

Feel free to ask questions. The Park Service personnel and volunteers know their sites intimately and have a special affection for them. They know the landscape and the natural life, the histories and the mysteries, and they can tell you more about the parks than you can learn from any book. It won't take much to get them talking. "We do this because we love it," said one Park Service employee who stands guard as a Continental soldier at Saratoga National Historical Park in Stillwater, New York. "If people learn something new while they're here, then we have done a good job. That's our reward."

Take care not to disturb a site. The buildings and artifacts, earthworks and ruins, plants and animals, even the stones on the ground are precious national resources, part of the physical and historical environment that these parks preserve for generations to enjoy.

"I hear America singing, the varied carols I hear," wrote Walt Whitman, one of the country's greatest poets. In the historic sites, monuments, and battlefields of the National Park Service, the great American chorus heralded by Whitman resonates through time and space, from prehistoric pueblos to the homes of contemporary presidents, from the Caribbean to the Klondike.

Jill MacNeice

HOW TO USE THIS BOOK

The sites in this book are arranged alphabetically by state. Each entry contains a short description of the site with information about its history, natural life, tours, and special festivals. Entries end with important visitor information: hours of operation, fees, mailing address, telephone number, and directions. Dates for summer hours and times for tours and festivals vary from year to year, depending on weather, visitation, and financing, so you may want to call or write before your arrival. Always make reservations where indicated as access to some sites, particularly fragile ruins or historic homes, is strictly limited. Address all mail to the Site Superintendent.

With some advance notice, park rangers generally will tailor their interpretive programs to school, professional, religious, and family groups. Often such groups can gain admittance to little-visited sections of the sites. Call at least two weeks in advance to make the necessary arrangements.

Some sites have spectacular natural features such as sheer cliffs, switchback trails, rough terrain, and blazing hot deserts. Dress appropriately and carry proper equipment. This may include long pants and good hiking boots to guard against poisonous snakes; jackets, hard hats, and lamps for underground caves; sunscreen and extra water for desert areas; and cold weather gear and emergency rations for camping in Alaska. Many parks open their backcountry areas to hiking and camping. If you plan to wander off the established trails, register at the visitor center, leave a copy of your itinerary with the ranger if requested, and respect any restrictions on fires.

For the sites in this book that charge entry fees (generally $1.00 to $3 a person), the Park Service offers three types of passes. Since all of them apply to the permit holder and an accompanying carload of people (or the immediate family if entry is by bus), these passes are ideal for families and groups that plan to visit several sites during the year.

The Golden Eagle Passport, available for $25 to people under age 62, is good from January 1 to December 31. This pass may be purchased in person or by mail from the National Park Service headquarters in Washington, D.C., at regional offices, or at the sites that charge entrance fees. The Golden Age Passport, a free lifetime entrance permit for senior citizens and permanent residents age 62 or older, provides a 50-percent discount on fees for camping, boat launching, and parking, but does not apply to concession services. Golden Age passes must be picked up in person and require proof of age such as a driver's license, a birth certificate, or a Medicare card. Golden Access Passports, free lifetime permits for handicapped people who are receiving federal benefits, provide a 50-percent discount for facilities and services; they do not apply to park concessions. Golden Access cards are available only in person to people who can show proof of medical disability and who receive federal benefits. For further information, contact the National Park Service Headquarters, Room 1013, U.S. Department of the Interior, 18th and C streets, N.W., Washington, D.C. 20013-7127.

The Park Service headquarters, regional offices, and sites also offer free brochures about individual parks in English and other languages and a guide and map to the parks. Write to the Park Service at the above address, or contact the individual sites at the addresses provided in this book.

Most sites are open year-round. While many visitor centers are closed on major holidays, it is often possible to walk or drive through the larger sites on your own. Smaller sites, like a single historic house or building, however, may be completely closed. If you plan to visit on a major holiday, call ahead to determine which facilities will be open.

Happy Trails!

A GUIDE TO NATIONAL MONUMENTS AND HISTORIC SITES

ALABAMA

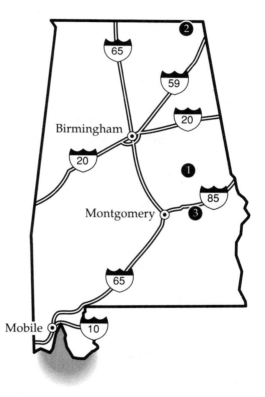

1. Horseshoe Bend National Military Park
2. Russell Cave National Monument
3. Tuskegee Institute National Historic Site

‖ Horseshoe Bend National Military Park

The last major campaign of the Creek Indian War, a defeat that spelled the end of Native American culture in the South, was fought at Horseshoe Bend on the Tallapoosa River on March 27, 1814. The battle marked a turning point in the fortunes of both Andrew Jackson and the Indians he subdued with 3,000 troops. Jackson went on to become the seventh president of the United States in 1829; the Indians eventually were relocated to Oklahoma and ceded much of their land in the south to settlement.

There is a paved, three-mile loop road through the battlefield that leads by the Creek Indian encampment called Tohopeka. Here 350 Indian women and children huddled during the fighting.

The museum in the visitor center contains exhibits, weapons, maps, bullet molds, and a diorama of the battle. A ten-minute slide show gives an overview and description of the Creek War. In all, the park has ten miles of hiking trails, including a 2.8-mile nature trail through the surrounding pine and hardwood forest. In spring these woods blossom with dogwood and a riot of wildflowers. Rangers will give guided tours and nature walks when arrangements are made beforehand.

The park has picnic facilities but no food is available. There is a ramp for boating on the Tallapoosa. Fishing in the Tallapoosa, which requires a state license, is excellent—catfish, bass, bluegill, and brim are common catches.

Open: 8 a.m. to 4:30 p.m. daily. Closed Christmas Day.
Fees: None.
Mailing Address: Horseshoe Bend National Military Park, Route 1, Box 103, Daviston, AL 36256.
Telephone: 205-234-7111.
Getting There: From Montgomery, take I-85 north and turn north on Rt. 49 (left) through Dadeville to the park, which will be on your right.

|| Russell Cave National Monument

About 4,000 years before the Egyptians built the Great Pyramid, a small band of Indians sought refuge from the harsh North American winters in northern Alabama's Russell Cave. The artifacts they and their descendants left behind chronicle 9,000 years of Native American civilization. A visit to this vast earthen shelter offers a thrilling glimpse into the past and a unique insight into the daily lives of prehistoric Indians.

Russell Cave has yielded one of the richest caches of prehistoric artifacts in the country—over two tons. In the park's museum you can see the spearheads these ancient people used in hunting and the fishhooks they used for fishing. Samples of the pottery from which they ate and drank are displayed as well as beautiful shell ornaments worn as jewelry.

Rangers, who are schooled in early survival skills, make arrowheads and stone tools, drill holes in shells, and throw darts and spears. During the summer, a garden teems with corn, beans, squash, and other vegetables cultivated by the Indians. Using stones excavated from local fields, park personnel will grind corn and crack nuts Indian-style. (Samples are available.)

According to the fossil record found in the cave, the Indians who lived here hunted deer, wild turkey, coyote, porcupine, and peccary —a wild pig now found only in the Southwest. From the Tennessee River, they gathered mussels and snails. They also ate nuts, primarily hickory, walnuts, acorns, and buckeyes. (Food preparation was so sophisticated that the Indians devised a way to leach the poison out of buckeyes so they could be consumed.)

The cavern where these Indians lived was excavated in the 1950s through the combined efforts of the Tennessee Archeological Society, the Smithsonian Institution, and the National Geographic Society. In 1962 the National Park Service joined the effort. The cavern's main chamber measures 107 feet wide by 258 feet deep, with a 29-foot ceiling.

With a permit, adventurous spelunkers can explore the 1.8-mile water cave below the main chamber. Required equipment: a hard hat, three sources of light, good shoes, a towline, knife, and first-aid kit.

The cave, which contains few mineral formations, may be closed due to flooding during heavy rains.

A slide program in the cave shelter provides information about the excavations. Audio-visual programs are available upon request in the visitor center. Other facilities include nature and hiking trails and a small picnic area.

Open: 8 a.m. to 5 p.m. daily. Closed Christmas, New Year's, and Thanksgiving Day and during heavy snow.

Fees: None.

Mailing Address: Russell Cave National Monument, Route 1, Box 175, Bridgeport, AL 35740.

Telephone: 205-495-2672.

Getting There: From Chattanooga, TN, take I-24 west about 33 miles to U.S. 72. Turn left (west) on U.S. 72 to Bridgeport, turn right onto County Road 91 to Mt. Carmel, and turn right on County Road 75. The monument is about four miles from this turnoff, on the left.

‖ Tuskegee Institute National Historic Site

Take a good look at the buildings on the campus of the Tuskegee Institute. They were built by the students. In fact, the students even made the bricks used in construction.

Founded in 1881 by black educator and philosopher Booker T. Washington, Tuskegee Institute was the first institution of higher learning dedicated to vocational training for blacks. Washington, a former slave who struggled for his education, founded Tuskegee in a dilapidated church in 1881. From this modest beginning, the school has grown to a modern, accredited college with 161 buildings and nearly 5,000 students, faculty, and staff.

Today the red and brown bricks are sun-bleached and mottled with age, but they still embody Washington's philosophy of working with both mind and body to build a better future. The bricks were assembled into buildings under the direction of architect Robert Robertson Taylor, a Tuskegee faculty member and the first black graduate of the Massachusetts Institute of Technology (1892). The students erected a total of 26 buildings including Washington's house, a Queen Anne-style mansion known as "The Oaks" built in 1899.

The earliest structures are Band Cottage (the foundry and blacksmith shop) built in 1889, Phelps Hall (the Bible training school) built in 1892, and Thrasher Hall (the science building) constructed in 1893.

In 1896, Washington invited plant scientist George Washington Carver, another former slave, to join the Tuskegee staff. During his 47 years at the Institute, Carver conducted his famous experiments on peanuts and sweet potatoes. Exhibits about Carver's work, artifacts from his library, and samples of his knitting, crocheting, and artwork are on display. Of special note are the beautiful watercolors Carver painted including his still life of a yucca plant, which was exhibited at the Chicago World's Fair in 1893. The museum also displays products —including face creams and massage oils—that Carver made from peanuts and sweet potatoes.

Standing near the main campus is Grey Columns, an antebellum mansion built by slave craftsmen in the Greek Revival style with some Italianate features. Theodore Roosevelt stayed at Grey Columns when he visited Tuskegee Institute in 1905. The mansion is not open to the public.

In spring, the park and the Macon County Council hold the George Washington Carver Craft Festival. Dates vary, so check with the Park Service for details.

Open: George Washington Carver Museum: 9 a.m. to 5 p.m. daily. Closed Thanksgiving, Christmas, and New Year's Day.

The campus historic district is always open for self-guided walking tours, but the school requests that visitors not interfere with the students' privacy or academic pursuits. Requests to sit in on classes are handled by the University administration.

Fees: None.

Mailing Address: Tuskegee Institute National Historic Site, 399 Old Montgomery Road, Tuskegee, AL 36088.

Telephone: 205-727-6390.

Getting There: From Montgomery, take I-85 north to Rt. 81 south. Turn right at the intersection of Rt. 81 and Old Montgomery Road (Rt. 126). The entrance to Grey Columns is 2½ blocks from this turn on the left. The Institute's campus is just beyond.

ALASKA

1. Cape Krusenstern National Monument
2. Klondike Gold Rush National Historical Park
3. Sitka National Historical Park

| Cape Krusenstern National Monument

Along the coast of the the Chukchi Sea in northwestern Alaska lies Cape Krusenstern National Monument, a traditional Eskimo hunting ground for marine mammals. This undeveloped wilderness area, thought to be a resting point during prehistoric migrations to the Western Hemisphere, holds 6,000 years of Eskimo artifacts.

This is a wild and undeveloped park, a place where moose and caribou graze, where grizzly bears lumber through the Arctic tundra and walrus frolic in the frigid northern waters. Each summer wildflowers bloom and insects blanket the area.

The 560,000-acre monument has beaches, estuaries, lakes, coastal bluffs, and upland tundra. Here berries grow wild and birds and fur-bearing animals abound. Fishing for whitefish, grayling, and arctic char is excellent and requires a state license, which can be purchased in nearby Kotzebue. A $15 license is good for ten days; a $30 license is good for one year. Sport hunting is not permitted within monument boundaries.

In summer, the Eskimos set up beach camps, hunt seals and other marine animals, and catch salmon in the rivers. Archeologists have found the remains of earlier Eskimo camps—some dating back thousands of years—in the 114 beach ridges at Cape Krusenstern. The record in these ridges represents every cultural period that has been identified in Arctic prehistory.

Located 600 miles from the nearest road and 35 miles from the small town of Kotzebue, Cape Krusenstern is an isolated monument. There are no facilities, no trails, and no visitor services. Visitors are on their own and cannot expect to be looked for if they get lost. Bring extra food in case bad weather delays your return by boat or airplane.

Camping in this harsh but beautiful environment is primitive and demands survival skills. Make noise while hiking to warn off grizzly bears and keep food outside the tent. Winter camping, when the temperatures regularly reach −20 degrees, is not advised for the inexperienced. The summers are wet so bring adequate rain gear, and be prepared for 40- to 65-degree temperatures. To combat the insects, which are particularly fierce in June and July, bring a head net and good insect repellent. The best backpacking is along the west coast of the monument and in the hills that run east and west.

Each year during the first week in July, Kotzebue holds a native trade fair with competitions and displays of Eskimo handicrafts. Kotzebue has a hotel and several small stores where visitors can purchase basic goods.

Open: Visitor Center in Kotzebue: 8 a.m. to 5 p.m. Monday through Friday and on weekends during the summer.

Fees: None.

Mailing Address: Cape Krusenstern National Monument, P.O. Box 1029, Kotzebue, AK 99752.

Telephone: 907-442-3760.

Getting There: Northwestern Alaska cannot be reached by road. Daily commercial flights serve Kotzebue from Anchorage and Fairbanks. From Kotzebue, access to the monument is by chartered aircraft or chartered boat. Planes land on primitive air strips, on beaches, or on lagoons. Charter flights from Kotzebue cost between $180 and $310 an hour. Contact park headquarters for a list of licensed carriers.

‖ Klondike Gold Rush National Historical Park

From downtown Skagway, with its boardwalks and honky-tonk saloons, to the beautiful but brutal northern wilderness beyond, Klondike Historical Park tells the story of Alaska's gold rush days. This newly established park includes the second leg of the arduous trek prospectors made to the Yukon gold fields in 1897–98, passing through historic Skagway, the ruins of nearby Dyea, and the Chilkoot and White Pass trails to Bennett and the Klondike beyond. Another section of the park is in Seattle, Washington, the jumping off point for ambitious prospectors.

Paved streets and false-fronted buildings help preserve the brawling, bawdy atmosphere of gold rush Skagway. The city's historic district contains many buildings from these early days, some of which may be under renovation. An hour-long walking tour leaves twice daily from the visitor center.

The visitor center shows a 29-minute film about the Klondike gold rush. A museum, still in the planning stages, will eventually exhibit artifacts of the bygone era.

Skagway is nestled in the narrow tidewater plain between Taiya Inlet and the surrounding 5,000-foot-high mountains. Founded in 1888 by Captain William Moore, a resourceful seaman who realized its location was important for access to the Alaskan interior, Skagway was for a brief time the largest city in Alaska.

Dyea, which rivaled Skagway for prominence, is located at the head of Taiya inlet, nine miles to the north. During the race to the Alaskan gold fields, more than 30,000 prospectors passed through the two cities. Dyea was abandoned after the White Pass and Yukon Route Railroad was opened between Skagway and Bennett. Today all that is left of Dyea are overgrown building foundations and the rotting stubs of the once active wharf.

The Chilkoot trail from Dyea to Bennett, where prospectors boarded boats to reach the Yukon River, is open to hikers. The White Pass Trail parallels the Klondike Highway out of Skagway. The Chilkoot trail, which is 33 miles long and takes three to five days to complete, runs through breathtaking terrain—the dense forests of the Pacific Coastal plain, the subarctic tundra near the summit of Chilkoot peak, and the stands of alpine fir beyond. Along the way are ruins of camps, rusting cans, old horseshoes, and animal bones—grim reminders of the prospectors who braved wilderness and weather in search of riches.

The terrain is rough, so be prepared for steep climbs, ankle-turning trails, torrential rains, heavy snows, biting winds, and bitter cold even in the summer. This is not an outing for the inexperienced. Hikers should dress warmly and bring plenty of supplies, including emergency rations. There are ten primitive campgrounds along the way, many of them with outhouses, shelters, and historic ruins. You cross an international border on the Chilkoot Trail, and must report your presence in Canada at Fraser in British Columbia. You can call in at 403-821-4111.

Brown and black bear are found along the route. Black bears—Ursus americanus—weigh 200 to 475 pounds and live below the timberline. Brown, or grizzly bears—Ursus arctos—weigh up to 1,000 pounds and live above the treeline. Both species range in color from blonde to black and both are very dangerous. To avoid confrontations with bears, stay on the trails, keep food outside of tents, and carry bells or noisemakers to announce your presence. Moose, porcupine, and other small animals can also be sighted along the route.

Open: 8 a.m. to 8 p.m. daily, June to Aug.; 8 a.m. to 6 p.m. mid-May to Sept. Check for exact dates. Closed Thanksgiving, Christmas, and New Year's Day and all federal holidays. Travel on the Chilkoot Trail during off-season requires a registration, obtainable from the visitor center.

Fees: None.

Mailing Address: Klondike Gold Rush National Historical Park, P.O. Box 517, Skagway, AK 99840.

Telephone: 907-983-2921.

Getting There: Skagway is located north of Juneau, Alaska. Scheduled and chartered air service is available from Juneau, Haines (B.C.) and Whitehorse (B.C.). Cars and buses can reach Skagway via the Alaska and Klondike Highways. Boats bound for Skagway leave from Seattle (WA), Prince Rupert (B.C.), Ketchikan, Wrangell, Petersburg, Sitka, Juneau, and Haines (B.C.).

‖ Sitka National Historical Park

The Alaskan island of Baranof, once the headquarters of a 19th-century Russian fur-trading settlement now known as Sitka, is an exotic combination of Indian totem poles and Russian Orthodox architecture. The 106-acre park on Sitka is on the site of an Indian fort which Alexander Baranov, head of the Russian-American Company, successfully attacked in 1804. After this skirmish, the Tlingit Indians withdrew and the Russians established a thriving fur trading colony in the area until the United States purchased Alaska for $7.2 million in 1867.

Two miles of walkways lead through the island's fragrant forests. Ferns and berry bushes line the grounds and elaborate totem poles rise among the shaggy trees. Against this primitive backdrop is the graceful cupola of St. Michael's Russian Orthodox cathedral and the Russian Bishop's House, a 16-room log structure built in 1842.

At the visitor center is an Indian Cultural Center, an organization that helps preserve native crafts and heritage. Tlingit teachers demonstrate silverwork, beadwork, and woodcarving. Russian artifacts from the days of the colony are displayed in the Russian Bishop's House.

A half-mile walk from the park, in Sitka proper, is Saint Michael's, a Russian cathedral with a bell tower and traditional Slavic cupola. This wooden church has an interesting collection of icons, robes, and other reminders of the Russian population that once thrived here.

Open: Park grounds: 7 a.m. to 10 p.m. daily, June 1–Sept. 30, closing at 8 p.m. during the rest of the year. Visitor Center: 8 a.m. to 5 p.m. daily, June 1-Sept. 30; open weekdays only Oct. 1–May 31. Russian Bishop's House: 8 a.m. to 5 p.m. daily, June 1–Sept. 30, by appointment during the rest of the year. Call the Visitor Center at 907-747-6281. Southeast Alaska Indian Cultural Center: 8 a.m. to 5 p.m. daily, June 1–Sept. 30. Closed Thanksgiving, Christmas, and New Year's Day.

Fees: None.

Mailing Address: Sitka National Historical Park, P.O. Box 738, Sitka, AK 99835.

Telephone: 907-747-6281.

Getting There: The Visitor Center is located at 106 Metlakatla Street and the Russian Bishop's House is at Lincoln and Monastery streets. Sitka can be reached by commercial airline direct from Seattle (WA), Juneau, and Anchorage; it is a port of call on the Alaska Marine Highway System. For more information about transportation, contact Alaska State Division of Tourism, Pouch E, Juneau, AK 99811. Telephone: 907-465-2010.

ARIZONA

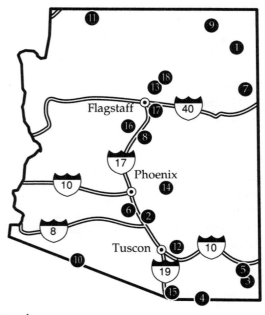

1. Canyon de Chelly National Monument
2. Casa Grande Ruins National Monument
3. Chiricahua National Monument
4. Coronado National Memorial
5. Fort Bowie National Historic Site
6. Hohokam Pima National Monument
7. Hubbell Trading Post National Historic Site
8. Montezuma Castle National Monument
9. Navajo National Monument
10. Organ Pipe Cactus National Monument
11. Pipe Spring National Monument
12. Saguaro National Monument
13. Sunset Crater National Monument
14. Tonto National Monument
15. Tumacacori National Monument
16. Tuzigoot National Monument
17. Walnut Canyon National Monument
18. Wupatki National Monument

Canyon de Chelly National Monument

Sheer red cliffs, prehistoric Indian ruins, and spectacular sandstone spires make Canyon de Chelly (pronounced de-Shay) one of the most beautiful and interesting monuments in the Southwest, a combination of unique geological formations and Indian ruins spread over 83,840 acres.

Alongside the crumbling villages and pueblos of the prehistoric Anasazi Indians, present-day Navajo still live in circular log hogans, vivid reminders of more than 1,600 years of Indian habitation in the region. The Navajo fought many battles with Spanish and federal forces—including a bloody skirmish with Indian fighter Kit Carson in 1864—for control of these canyon lands.

Two roadways, punctuated with scenic overlooks, hug the rims of the V-shaped monument. The 32-mile road along the north rim of the Canyon del Muerto leads to Mummy Cave Ruin, a pueblo perched atop a ledge that was occupied from approximately 350 to 1300. Another site, Standing Cow Ruin, contains Navajo pictographs of a blue-and-white cow and a Spanish cavalry unit. The 36-mile route along the south rim of Canyon de Chelly follows cliffs that reach from 40 to 1,000 feet in height. This road leads by Spider Rock, an enormous sandstone spire that rises 800 feet from the canyon floor.

From White House Trail Overlook on the south rim drive, a 2.5-mile round-trip trail leads to White House Ruin. This is the only trail within the canyon that visitors can hike on their own. All other excursions must be accompanied by a ranger or an authorized guide.

During the summer, rangers lead regular hikes into the canyons. Check at park headquarters for schedules and for information about commercial tours and traveling in four-wheel-drive vehicles in the monument. A small exhibit in the park's visitor center displays tools and artifacts of the Navajo and Anasazi Indians.

Thunderbird Lodge and Canyon de Chelly Motel near park head-quarters offer accommodations. The Lodge offers guided trips up the canyon floors from spring through fall, depending on the weather. Check for details. It is advisable to make reservations well in advance of your visit. For more information, contact Thunderbird Lodge, Chinle, Arizona 86503. Cottonwood Campgrounds, also near park headquarters, has campsites with fireplaces, tables, and restrooms. Cottonwood is open year-round.

Open: 8 a.m. to 5 p.m. daily, extended to 6 p.m. from mid-May to Oct.

Fees: None.

Mailing Address: Canyon de Chelly National Monument, P.O. Box 588, Chinle, AZ 86503.

Telephone: 602-674-5436.

Getting There: The monument is located in northeastern Arizona near the New Mexico border. From Flagstaff, take I-40 east through the Painted Desert and turn north on Rt. 191 at Chambers. Continue along Rt. 191 to Ganado, and turn west on Rt. 264. After five miles, pick up Rt. 191 north and follow it toward Chinle. The park is just east of Chinle at the intersection of Rt. 191 and Rt. 7.

‖ Casa Grande Ruins National Monument

The Casa Grande, an immense earthen structure that towers above the ruins of a prehistoric Indian village in southern Arizona, is a remarkable example of primitive engineering. It is the only structure of its type known to exist.

The monument, located in the Gila (pronounced Hee-la) River valley, covers 472 acres of flat southern Arizona desert. The highly developed Hohokam Indians lived in villages here, tended crops, and even played a kind of court ball game until they abandoned the region in the late 1300s. These Indians, thought to be related to the present day Pima, are known for creating a vast network of irrigation canals to water their crops.

Without the guidance of a written record, archeologists can only guess what role the four-story Casa Grande played in this complex Indian culture. The positions of window-like openings in the structure's thick earthen walls indicate that it could have been an astronomical observatory. But there is no proof. One thing is certain: This unusual building served a special purpose.

The first European to record the existence of this extraordinary ruin was Eusebio Kino, a Jesuit priest who explored the region in the late 17th century. He was led to the site by local Indians in 1694.

Visitors can wander unguided among the ruins of the prehistoric sites. The visitor center has exhibits about the Hohokam and their ancient pottery and tools. Picnic tables are available but there are no camping facilities in the park. Overnight accommodations are available less than a mile away in Coolidge, Arizona. Wildlife in the area includes quail, roadrunners, rabbits, rattlesnakes, and scorpions.

Open: 7 a.m. to 6 p.m. daily.

Fees: $1 per person over 16 years of age.

Mailing Address: Casa Grande Ruins National Monument, 1100 Ruins Drive, Coolidge, AZ 85228.

Telephone: 602-723-3172.

Getting There: The monument is in southern Arizona, halfway between Phoenix and Tucson. From Coolidge, take Rt. 87 north one mile to the monument.

‖ Chiricahua National Monument

Precariously balanced monoliths, towering pinnacles, and extraordinarily lush vegetation make Chiricahua National Monument a geological and biological wonderworld. The 16,000-acre park, located in the southeastern Arizona grasslands on a once-active volcano bed, is full of grotesque rock formations created by erosion. Chiricahua means "people of the mountain" in Apache.

Over 20 miles of hiking trails wind through beds of volcanic ash, ledges strewn with marble-like pellets, and cliffs with columns created by erosion. Some formations resemble creatures, others form natural bridges and battlements.

An eight-mile paved mountain road leads up Bonita Canyon to the Massai Point overlook, which offers an expansive view of the entire park. Nearby is the 7,310-foot-high Sugarloaf Mountain, with a foot path leading to the top. The 31.5-mile loop through Echo Canyon is one of the most scenic trails in the park and takes about three hours to complete. The seven-mile Heart of Rocks trail leads visitors to the Punch and Judy and the Big Balanced Rock formations. Allow five to six hours for this trip and carry plenty of water.

The Chiricahua Mountains have an abundance of greenery. In the canyon bottoms and on the cool northern slopes of the mountain, seasonal springs and streams supply water to the sycamores, Arizona cypress, scrub oak, and flowering herbs. The hotter southern exposures have more typical desert vegetation—yuccas, cactuses, and agaves.

This wide variety of plantlife in turn attracts large numbers of birds and animals. White-tailed deer are especially abundant. The visitor center has an eight-minute slide presentation on the park's natural and cultural features, including the early settlers and the Apaches who lived in the region. Cochise and Geronimo, two famous Indian warriors, were Chiricahua Apaches. Rangers offer daily walks and campfire talks about the region's unique features. Check for times.

Faraway Ranch was opened to the public in August 1988. This early cattle and guest ranch was started in 1888 by two Swedish immigrants, Neil and Emma Erickson, and was run by their daughter Lillian and her husband Ed Riggs until Lillian's death in 1977. The grounds of the ranch are open all year and a trail guide is available. Tours of the house are conducted daily in spring and summer and on weekends during the rest of the year.

There is a 27-site campground at the monument, which is available for 14-day stays during the summer tourist season for $5 a night. Chiricahua has neither hot water nor hookups. Wood gathering in the park is prohibited so bring fuel. Lodging, gas, and groceries are available in Willcox, 37 miles to the north.

Open: Visitor Center: 8 a.m. to 5 p.m. daily. Closed Christmas Day.

Fees: $3 per car, $1 per person.

Mailing Address: Chiricahua National Monument, Dos Cabezas Route, Box 6500, Willcox, AZ 85643.

Telephone: 602-824-3560.

Getting There: From Tucson, go east on I-10 to Willcox, then southeast on Rt. 186 for 33 miles. At Rt. 181 go east approximately four miles to the visitor center.

|| Coronado National Memorial

This mountainous park on the border between Arizona and Mexico lies within sight of the valley through which Francisco Vasquez de Coronado, the Spanish explorer searching for gold and riches in the New World, led the first European expedition into southwest America in 1540. The short trail to Coronado Peak in the Huachuca (pronounced wha-choo-ka) Mountains gives an expansive view of the countryside through which the Coronado expedition marched. This trail, marked with quotes from the journals of the men who participated in that early enterprise, snakes to the top of the 6,864-foot-high mountain.

In his search for the fabled "Seven Cities of Cibola," Coronado wandered for two years in North America without success. But the legacy he left—horses for the Indians and the Hispanic influence which still flavors the Southwest—was an important contribution to the region's cultural development.

Other trails in the park offer stunning views of the San Rafael Valley, the Patagonia Mountains, and the Santa Rita Mountains. From perches atop the high trails, you can also see Montezuma Canyon and Sonora, Mexico.

Be sure to bring binoculars as Coronado Memorial is an excellent birding ground. There are about 50 different species of resident birds and as many as 160 kinds of birds have been sighted in the park. They include the elegant coppery-tailed trogon, the gray-breasted jay, the painted redstart, and the golden eagle. The visitor center has a special alcove with a 14-foot window wall for bird watchers to take pictures. Exhibits in the visitor center include armor, swords and equipment from the days of the Spanish conquistadors, and paintings of Coronado's expeditions.

The park is full of flowering plants such as the white-blooming mountain yucca and the vibrant cholla cactus, and of animals including the raccoon-like coati, white-tailed deer, and bobcat.

There is no camping in the park but picnic sites are available. The nearest accommodations are to the east in Bisbee, Arizona, or to the north in Sierra Vista.

Open: Visitor Center: 8 a.m. to 5 p.m. Closed Thanksgiving, Christmas, and New Year's Day.

Fees: None.

Mailing Address: Coronado National Memorial, Rural Route 2, Box 126, Hereford, AZ 85615.

Telephone: 602-366-5515.

Getting There: From Tucson, take I-10 east to Rt. 90, exiting to Rt. 92 south at the Sierra Vista turnoff. Continue south along Rt. 92 through the Sierra Vista, then turn right onto an unnamed access road to the Visitor Center. A sign for the memorial is posted one-half mile before the turnoff onto the access road.

‖ Fort Bowie National Historic Site

Built in 1862 to protect Apache Springs, a vital water supply at Apache Pass in the Chiricahua Mountains of Arizona, Fort Bowie was the base for bloody military operations against the Apache Indians and their famous leaders Cochise and Geronimo. It was here that Geronimo was brought after his final surrender in 1886.

The park consists of the adobe ruins of Fort Bowie, the stage station that was part of the old Butterfield Overland Trail from Missouri to San Francisco, the once important Apache Spring, and a cemetery. To get to the crumbling walls and foundations of the fort's 37 buildings, you'll have to drive 13 miles down a dirt road, then hike another 1.5 miles through the scrubby blue-green grasslands of this secluded valley.

The visitor center contact station contains photographs of the fort's early days and displays of Indian clothes, tools, and a 19th-century sword.

Plantlife in the park includes desert grasslands and chaparral, with scattered stands of evergreen and mountain mahogany. On the higher slopes are oaks, juniper, and piñon pines along with willow, walnut, and cottonwood trees in the less arid areas. After a rain, the wild-flowers bloom, blanketing the landscape in vibrant color. Gray foxes, coyotes, mountain lions, bobcats, rattlesnakes, lizards, and many birds inhabit the area.

On the weekend following Labor Day each year, the site hosts a Fort Bowie Days Festival, which features reenactment camps of cavalry, Apaches, and other groups who played a role in the historic Apache pass. There are also musical performances and exhibitions of crafts and foods. Contact the ranger for details.

If you plan to spend a day hiking around the site, bring plenty of water. The park gets extremely hot and dry in the summer. There is no camping but overnight accommodations are available in Bowie, Willcox, and at the nearby Chiricahua National Monument.

Open: Visitor contact station: 8 a.m. to 4:30 p.m. daily. Closed Christmas Day.

Fees: None.

Mailing Address: Fort Bowie National Historic Site, P.O. Box 158, Bowie, AZ 85605.

Telephone: 602-847-2500.

Getting There: From Tucson, take I-10 east; exit at Bowie and go through town following the brown national park signs. Continue south on this road 13 miles to Fort Bowie. The road is mostly unpaved.

‖ Hohokam Pima National Monument

Ruins of many prehistoric pit houses distinguish the place called Snaketown in the Hohokam Pima National Monument, where the region's Hohokam (pronounced Ho-ho-KAM) Indians lived between A.D. 200 and the 1400s. Hohokam means "those who have gone before" in the Pima Indian language. These people were skillful farmers who devised sophisticated irrigation techniques to raise crops in the barren Arizona desert. Their houses were made of shallow pits dug into the ground and covered with brush and mud.

Today's Pima Indians consider the Snaketown site closed to the public and do not want non-Indian visitors admitted to the archeological part of the reservation. However, non-Indian visitors are welcome on other parts of the reservation and at the Gila River Indian Arts and Crafts Center.

For further information, contact the Director of Economic Development, Gila River Indian Community, Sacaton, AZ 85247.

Telephone: 602-562-3311.

‖ Hubbell Trading Post National Historic Site

This still-operating trading post established on the Navajo reservation by frontier businessman John Lorenzo Hubbell has changed little since it opened in 1878. Indians still sell their crafts and still buy groceries and manufactured products here, though "Don Lorenzo," whose respect and influence among the Navajo was legendary, is long gone.

The 160-acre site commemorates the heyday of trading posts on the southwestern frontier, and it includes Hubbell's original trading post structure and several related buildings. Hubbell's restored trading post, one of the largest on the reservation, retains the feel of a 19th-century frontier general store. Guns line the walls, baskets hang from the ceiling, and there is a wide selection of woven Navajo rugs (ranging from about $70 to $2,400 in price), exquisite turquoise and silver jewelry, Hopi dolls, and pottery made by the Pueblo Indians. Visitors can try their hand at weaving on a demonstration loom. In summer, you can watch an Indian silversmith and Navajo weavers at work.

A keen businessman with an eye for quality, Hubbell and his sons once owned a total of 24 trading posts and a wholesale house in Winslow, Arizona. Hubbell encouraged Indian weavers to create only the finest products and many of their rugs were based on his own designs—patterns he knew would be marketable in the East. Hubbell's deep respect for Indian culture won him the affection of the Navajos during their difficult adjustment to life on the reservation.

In addition to the trading post, Hubbell's five-room residence has been restored. Tours of the house are offered hourly in summer, less frequently in winter. The other buildings, which are not open to visitors, include a barn, the manager's residence, a chicken coop, a bunk house, and an eight-sided guest "hogan" designed after Indian homes.

When he died in 1930, Hubbell was buried on Hubbell Hill between his wife, Lina Rubi, and his dear friend the Navajo chief Many Horses. According to a pact made by the two men, whoever died first would be buried on the hill with a rock over the grave to keep his spirit down. This rock would be removed only when the other died so the two could ascend heavenward together.

Open: Visitor Center: 8 a.m. to 5 p.m. in winter, hours extended to 6 p.m. in summer. Closed Thanksgiving, Christmas, and New Year's Day.

Fees: None.

Mailing Address: Hubbell Trading Post National Historic Site, P.O. Box 150, Ganado, AZ 86505.

Telephone: 602-755-3475.

Getting There: The site is located in northeastern Arizona on the Navajo Indian Reservation. From Winslow take I-40 east to Chambers and turn left onto Rt. 63 north (also known as Rt. 191) to Ganado. Turn left, west, onto Rt. 264. The site is one mile on the left.

❚❚ Montezuma Castle National Monument

Built into a yellow limestone cliff over 800 years ago by the Sinagua Indians, this 20-room dwelling is one of the best-preserved prehistoric structures in the country. The name Montezuma comes from the early settlers who mistakenly believed the ruin was of Aztec origin.

The building was once part of a thriving Indian community of multi-room dwellings, a sort of ancient garden-apartment complex, that grew up around Beaver Creek. Unfortunately, the six-story 45-room "Castle A" located nearby did not fare as well over the centuries; it is now a badly deteriorated ruin. A smaller eight-room structure near a pair of storage caves is nothing but a pile of yellow rubble.

It is not possible, however, to tour the Montezuma Castle—in fact, there aren't even ladders to take visitors 150 feet up the side of the cliff to the dwelling's entrance. But visitors can tour the 850-acre site on a one-third mile loop trail.

Although the Sinagua Indians who lived here between 1100 and 1400 left no written record of their activities, archeologists have gleaned much about their lifestyle from rummaging around in an enormous trash heap at the base of the cliff. The evidence shows that the Indians ate corn, beans, squash, and small game, that they fashioned fairly complex tools of bone and stone, and that they wove handsome cotton garments and crafted ornaments of shells and turquoise.

A museum in the visitor center exhibits pottery, textiles, and other Sinagua artifacts.

Not far from Montezuma Castle is the Montezuma Well, a spring-fed limestone sinkhole formed when an underground cave collapsed. Despite the region's arid climate, the well remains a source of water. The early Indians built irrigation ditches from the well to water their crops.

To get to the well, return to I-17 North and go to the McGuireville exit. Watch for signs. Because the approach to the site is unpaved and can be extremely slick after rains, contact the ranger before you go.

Open: 8 a.m. to 5 p.m. daily, extended hours during summer.

Fees: $1 per person.

Mailing Address: Montezuma Castle National Monument, P.O. Box 219, Camp Verde, AZ 86322.

Telephone: 602-567-3322.

Getting There: The monument is located in central Arizona between Phoenix and Flagstaff, just north of Camp Verde on I-17.

‖ Navajo National Monument

Three extraordinarily well-preserved Indian cliff dwellings make Navajo National Monument one of the best places in the country to tour prehistoric pueblos. Unlike sites with more fragile ruins, visitors can actually walk through the remains of Betatakin and Keet Seel.

Guided tours of Betatakin, which means "ledge house" in Navajo, are offered at least twice daily from May through September. Constructed from 1267 to 1286 by the Anasazi (from the Navajo for "ancient ones"), this pueblo lasted only about 50 years and housed about 125 people throughout its brief lifespan. The five-to-six hour round-trip hike is arduous—the equivalent of walking up a 70-story building—and is not recommended for people with heart or respiratory problems. Places on the 5-mile excursion are offered on a first-come, first-served basis on the day of the tour.

Keet Seel, the Navajo expression for "broken pieces of pottery," is bigger than Betatakin. Tucked into an alcove in the orange cliffs of the Arizona desert, Keet Seel is one of the best preserved cliff dwellings

The Betatakin House Ruins at Navajo National Monument are among the largest and most elaborate cliff dwellings in the country.—*Fred E. Mang, Jr., National Park Service (NPS) photograph*

in the Southwest. Rangers give tours of this pueblo from Memorial Day to Labor Day, but access is strictly limited to only 20 a day.

The route to Betatakin is as strenuous as the one to Keet Seel and considerably longer—1,000 feet down, 16 miles round trip. Schedule at least eight to ten hours for hiking the eight-mile trail and touring the site. Groups are limited to five people at a time, so plan to arrive early. A primitive campground nearby is available for overnight stays.

A local Navajo family will lead ten people at a time on day-long horseback trips to Keet Seel. Reservations for a horse and a ruin-entry permit must be made no later than 4:30 p.m. on the day before the trip, and no earlier than two months in advance of the day. For more information, contact Virginia Austin, c/o Navajo National Monument, HC-71 Box 3, Tonalea, Arizona 86044. Telephone: 602-672-2366.

Another dwelling in the monument is Inscription House, a fragile pueblo built against a cliff. But it has been closed to visitors since 1968.

The Navajo Indians, who now live on the reservation surrounding the park, are not related to the Anasazi Indians who built these dwellings and cultivated corn, beans, and squash in the once fertile valleys of the area. It is believed that the Pueblo and Hopi Indians descended from the Anasazi, while the Navajo migrated to the Southwest from northern Canada in the 1400s.

Navajo National Monument is located several hours drive from Flagstaff and Page, the nearest major cities. The park has a picnic area and a 30-unit campground with toilets but no hot water. For a back-country permit to use undeveloped areas, make reservations no more than two months in advance of the date you plan to arrive. You must pick up your permit from the visitor center by 9:00 a.m. of the day of your hike or your reservation will be cancelled. When arranging a guided tour, keep in mind that the monument is on Mountain Daylight Savings Time, which means it is one hour ahead of Phoenix and other Arizona cities of the Navajo Reservation. Kayenta, a town 30 miles to the east, has stores and accommodations.

Open: 8 a.m. to 5 p.m. in winter, hours extended to 6 p.m. in summer. Closed Thanksgiving, Christmas, and New Year's Day.

Fees: None.

Mailing Address: Navajo National Monument, Tonalea, AZ 86044

Telephone: 602-672-2366.

Getting There: From Flagstaff, take Rt. 89 to Rt. 160. Follow Rt. 160 east for 70 miles to Rt. 564 north. Turn left, and go nine miles into the park.

|| Organ Pipe Cactus National Monument

The sparse, open desert of this monument on the Arizona-Mexico border has one of the most most varied collections of cactus in the country. Here, the tubular stems of the rare organ pipe cactus grow up to ten feet high.

Scenic drives and hikes take visitors through a unique combination of Sonoran desert environments. The Arizona Upland Division contains chollas, saguaros, and organ pipe cactus along with trees such as paloverde, mesquite, and ironwood. The second major division in Organ Pipe is the Lower Colorado Division, the hottest and driest part of the Sonoran Desert. Encompassing most of the northern and western portions of the Monument, this division's dominant plants are the creosote bush and bursage. In the Central Gulf Coast Division, the elephant tree abounds.

Ajo Mountain Drive, a 21-mile loop which takes about two hours to complete, leads by sheer canyon walls and cuts through impressive stands of organ pipe cactus. A longer drive, the Puerto Blanco, parallels in part the routes early explorers and desert travelers took through the area. The southern portion of Puerto Blanco Drive, along the International Boundary, parallels the old desert route known as *El Camino del Diablo* (the Devil's Highway). Some portions of the drive follow roads originally established by 19th- and early 20th-century settlers. This 53-mile trip takes about half a day. Driving in the hot desert is hard on cars so check tire pressure and carry enough water.

Hikers can trek to the Victoria Mine, an early gold and silver mine, or travel other self-guided trails to ridges with impressive desert overlooks. Cross-country hiking is especially good in the open terrain of the park and park rangers can suggest good routes. To walk or camp in the backcountry, you will need a permit.

With its stark, hilly landscape and unusual stands of cactus, Organ Pipe Monument is an excellent place for nature photography. But beware: Desert heat can spoil film and concentrated light can cause overexposure. The best time to shoot is in the early morning or late afternoon, when the contrast is strongest.

Wildlife in the park includes foxes, coyotes, tortoises, and six species of rattlesnake, so watch your step. Birds are particularly abundant, with 35 resident species including cactus wrens and roadrunners and another 260 migratory species. To escape the searing heat of the desert day, many animals are active during the night. A short walk after dark with a flashlight reveals a completely different world. In May and June, the organ pipe cactus produces white, lavender-tinged blossoms that open after dark and close near sunrise.

The park has numerous picnic areas and a campground with 208 sites for tents and trailers. No showers or hookups are available. A small fee is charged. Check with the ranger for details. Accommodations, groceries, and gas are available in Lukeville, five miles from park headquarters.

Open: Visitor Center: 8 a.m. to 5 p.m. daily.

Fees: $3 per vehicle, $1 per person arriving by bus, foot, or bicycle.

Mailing Address: Organ Pipe Cactus National Monument, Route 1 Box 100, Ajo, AZ 85321.

Telephone: 602-387-6849.

Getting There: The monument lies in south central Arizona on the Mexican border. From Phoenix, take I-10 west to Rt. 85. Follow Rt. 85 south to Why, AZ, which is just south of Ajo. At Why, continue on Rt. 85 into the park.

Pipe Spring National Monument

At a spring-fed oasis in the northern Arizona desert, where the Vermillion Cliffs rise majestically in the distance, Mormon pioneers established a cattle ranch in 1870. The ranch at Pipe Spring was a welcome stop-over for travelers who braved the rugged terrain.

Today the Pipe Spring ranch is a memorial to the early southwest frontier, the Mormon church that helped to settle it, and the cowboys and cattle trade for which it was famous. Visitors to the 40-acre site can tour Windsor Castle, the small fort that forms the nucleus of the settlement, as well as the ranch's workshops, outbuildings, corrals, and gardens. The corrals, made of typical unfinished cedar posts, give the site an authentic ramshackle look.

Windsor Castle, the main building at Pipe Spring, is composed of two, two-story houses enclosed by connecting walls. Built of red sandstone quarried from nearby cliffs, Windsor housed the kitchen, parlor, offices, bedrooms, and the area's first telegraph. The cold waters of the spring, which well up through a fault in the earth directly under the ranch, feed two ponds and water the orchards.

When Pipe Spring was at its peak in 1879, the ranch had 2,269 head of cattle and 162 horses worth over $54,000, and produced 60 to 80 pounds of cheese a day. Cowboys worked the range, tending the animals and caring for the property. Meat and dairy products were delivered to the Southern Utah Tithing Office for the workers building the Saint George Temple in Saint George, Utah.

The trail by the fort became known as the Honeymoon Trail because young Mormon couples traveled it on their way home from being married in the Saint George Temple. The church sold Pipe Spring in 1888, during a time of turmoil between the U.S. government and the Mormons over polygamy.

The visitor center museum has original cooking utensils, plows, and water barrels. Outside, a grapevine that has been bearing fruit since 1870 still flourishes. Costumed guides interpret life at Pipe Spring by demonstrating pioneer activities. On Memorial Day, a special festival features cattle branding and other activities.

There is no camping at the park but the nearby Kaibab Indian Reservation has picnic and overnight facilities, including hookups for trailers.

Open: 8 a.m. to 4:30 p.m. daily. Closed Thanksgiving, Christmas, and New Year's Day.

Fees: $1 a person, ages 16–62.

Mailing Address: Pipe Spring National Monument, Moccasin, AZ 86022.

Telephone: 602-643-7105.

Getting There: The monument in north central Arizona is near the Utah border. From Flagstaff, take Rt. 89 north to Rt. 89A; follow that west about 40 miles to Jacob Lake. Continue north on Rt. 89A to Fredonia and take Rt. 389 west to the site, just outside of Kaibab in the Kaibab Indian Reservation.

‖ Saguaro National Monument

Giant saguaro (pronounced sa-WAR-oh), the picturesque cactus which dominates southern Arizona's Sonoran desert, is preserved in the Saguaro National Monument. This stately cactus, with its tall trunk and bent elbow limbs, is a familiar background in many old cowboy movies.

Like all the plants that live in arid environments, the saguaro are well adapted to desert life. By storing vast amounts of water in its tissues, a single saguaro can survive 200 years of desert heat and can grow to heights of 50 feet. The cactus blooms in May with creamy white flowers.

Saguaro National Monument consists of two separate stands of saguaro that flank Tucson on the east and west. The Rincon Mountain District to the east stretches from desert scrub and grasslands to the pine and fir forests of the Santa Catalina mountains. The visitor center offers a spectacular view of thousands of stately saguaro with the blue stripe of the mountains hovering in the background.

Visitors can drive into the heart of the saguaro stand on the nine-mile Cactus Forest Drive, or hike through the desert to the mountains on several trails. There are six campgrounds and a ranger station along the hiking trails of the 62,836-acre district.

The Tucson Mountain District, to the west of Tucson, is smaller than the Rincon District and its saguaro population is younger. More of the park is accessible by car and more picnic facilities are available for day use. Rangers conduct daily nature walks and talks covering topics such as desert birds, rattlesnakes, cactuses, and local wildflowers and animals. The Rincon Unit visitor center shows a ten-minute slide show throughout the day and a 30-minute film on weekends at 1 p.m.

Other cactuses in the monument include the stocky barrel cactus, the shrub-like cholla, and the prickly pear with its flat pads. After a good rain in spring, the desert blooms with vibrant red, orange, and yellow flowers. At higher altitudes, the desert scrub and grasslands give way to oak and pine trees.

The park's wildlife includes reptiles (some 50 species), tarantulas (not poisonous), and scorpions (poisonous). The peccary, a boar-like beast, and coyote are present. Bird watching at Saguaro is excellent.

The giant saguaro cactus, which can reach a height of 50 feet, is unique to the Sonoran Desert.—*National Park Service photograph*

Hawks, owls, road-runners, quail, and gila woodpeckers, which nest in the saguaro cactus, live in the monument.

Open: Rincon Mountain District and Tucson Mountain District Visitor Centers: 8 a.m. to 5 p.m. Closed Christmas and New Year's Day.

Fees: $1 per car for Rincon District; no fee for Tucson District.

Mailing Address: Saguaro National Monument, 3693 S. Old Spanish Trail, Tucson, AZ 85730.

Telephone: Rincon Mountain District (East) 602-296-8576; Tucson Mountain District (West) 602-883-6366.

Getting There: The monument's two sites in south central Arizona are east and west of Tucson. From downtown Tucson, take 22nd Street or Broadway East to Old Spanish Trail, and proceed to the park headquarters of the Rincon Mountain District. To get to the Tucson Mountain District, take Speedway Boulevard west to Kinney Road, turn right (north) and follow signs to the Visitor Center.

‖ Sunset Crater National Monument

This black volcanic mountain, rising out of the pine lands north of Flagstaff like a giant overturned bowl, glows with the red and orange of a perpetual mineral sunset. The volcano, the most recent member of the San Francisco Mountain Range, first erupted sometime around 1064 forcing the region's Sinagua Indians to flee until the volcano quieted. More recently, this harsh, rugged terrain was a training ground for the astronauts on the *Apollo 17* crew.

Visitors can tour this 3,000-acre field of volcanic rubble. A short nature trail and a paved loop road cuts through the lava flows for visitors who want to explore the bizarre landscape at Sunset Crater on their own. Along the nature trail are various volcanic formations, from "squeeze-ups," created when lava squeezes through a crack in the rock, and spatter cones, formed by escaping gases to the razor sharp aa (pronounced ahh-ahh) lava and rope-like pahoehoe (pronounced pa-hoy-hoy) lava.

Sunset Crater is a two-tiered park. Beneath the thick lava crust that overlays the park is a hollow lava tube, formed when lava cooled at different rates. To explore this 225-foot-long cave, bring a good flashlight, sturdy shoes, a hard hat, and a warm jacket. The tube is so cold that it contains ice throughout most of the year. Check with the ranger for current conditions.

The park offers several programs, including occasional guided hikes, campfire programs, and other non-scheduled activities. Check for details. A popular activity is the bus tour to O'Leary Peak, from which you get a great view of the crater of Sunset Crater volcano and the entire San Francisco volcanic field. Sign up at the visitor center for the bus tour.

There is no food or camping in the monument but accommodations and groceries are available in nearby Flagstaff.

Open: 8 a.m. to 5 p.m. daily; hours may be extended in summer. Call for exact times. Closed Christmas and New Year's Day.

Fees: $3 per car, also good for nearby Wupatki National Monument.

Mailing Address: Sunset Crater National Monument, Route 3, Box 149, Flagstaff, AZ 86004.

Telephone: 602-527-7042.

Getting There: From Flagstaff, take Rt. 89 north 15 miles to the visitor center. An access road connects Sunset Crater and the Wupatki Monument.

‖ Tonto National Monument

These cliff dwellings, built in the scrubby central Arizona desert by the Salado Indians more than 600 years ago, are among the few prehistoric ruins in the Southwest you can actually walk through.

The Lower Ruin is located on a plateau 1,000 feet above the irrigated valley where the Salado Indians raised corn, beans, and squash. Some of the rooms are preserved intact, giving visitors a feel of the pueblo in the 14th century when the village supported a community of 40 to 60 people. Other ruins in the monument are in varying states of disintegration, especially those at the Lower Ruin Annex where exposure to the elements is extreme. The Lower Ruin, a complex of about 19 rooms, is nearly a mile's walk from the visitor center. A paved, self-guided trail to the Lower Ruin leads by many of the desert plants that the Salado used for food, clothing, and construction materials. The trail is steep, with a vertical climb of 350 feet, and it closes by 4 p.m. each day. Visitors must begin the trail no later than one hour before the scheduled park closing.

To visit the Upper Ruin (open from October through April), you will need to make a reservation with the ranger. This trip, over three miles of extremely rough terrain, takes about three hours. It is possible to enter some of the rooms and peek in through the windows and openings of the others.

The Salado Indians lived in the Salt River Valley (Salado comes from the Spanish word for "salty") between 1100 and 1400. They abandoned the area in the 15th century for reasons that remain obscure. These early inhabitants of the Sonoran desert were masons, known for their pottery and beautiful textiles. Some of the walls in the pueblos they built still have fingerprints left in the wet clay during replastering.

The Indians were also skilled farmers who engineered irrigation ditches that remained in the area until Roosevelt Lake was formed around 1910. The Salado were excellent craftsmen as well. They wove fine cotton cloth, painted dramatic geometric designs on their red clay pottery, and fashioned beautiful jewelry from shells and turquoise. Cotton cloth, tools, and several pottery bowls dating from the 14th century are on display in the visitor center. The visitor center also features a 12-minute slide program on the ruins and the Salado Indians.

There are no camping facilities in the 1,120-acre monument but camping is available in nearby Roosevelt Lake, a 23-mile man-made reservoir with fishing and boating. Accommodations are available in Globe and Miami, AZ, 30 miles to the east.

Open: 8 a.m. to 5 p.m. daily. Hours may be extended in summer. Closed Christmas day.

Fees: $3 per car.

Mailing Address: Tonto National Monument, P.O. Box 707, Roosevelt, AZ 85545.

Telephone: 602-467-2241.

Getting There: The park is located near Roosevelt Lake, five miles east of Roosevelt Dam. From Globe, take Hwy 88 about 30 miles to the park entrance. Hwy 188, which joins the Beeline Highway (Hwy 87) south of Payson, provides the main access from the north. A third alternative is the Apache Trail that starts at Apache Junction. This is rated as one of the most scenic drives in Arizona, but allow plenty of time as 22 miles are on unpaved mountain road. Regardless of route, the trip from Phoenix takes 2½ to three hours.

‖ Tumacacori National Monument

The ruins of the Spanish mission at Tumacacori, with its bell tower topped by a simple cross, recall the time when explorer-priests roamed the American Southwest, converting the Indians and holding mass in the desert.

Built in stages from 1803 to 1825, San Jose de Tumacacori stands near the spot visited by Father Eusebio Kino, an Italian Jesuit who explored and mapped much of the Mexican Sonora and southern Arizona countryside in the 17th century. The Spanish priest Ramon Liberos supervised the late stages of construction and was responsible for the look of the structure that remains today. Liberos was forced to leave in April 1828 as a result of the expulsion of most Spaniards from Mexico.

At one time, the partially-finished chapel at Tumacacori was the center of a bustling mission with living quarters, classrooms, workshops, granaries, an orchard, and a cemetery. The site was abandoned in 1848 when a change in Mexican policy towards far-flung missions left Tumacacori without funding and at the mercy of Apache raiders.

The museum in the visitor center, a Sonora mission-style building near the parking lot, has a 15-minute video tape about the site and exhibits on early Indian culture and life in the Southwest. A self-guided tour through the grounds takes about 30 minutes. The church still stands but many other buildings have fallen into ruins. In the cemetery lie the vandalized graves of Indians who helped to build the mission.

Native Indians and Mexicans participate in the park's living history programs, demonstrating the Spanish-Indian culture of the old Southwest. On the first Sunday in December each year, Tumacacori hosts a fiesta with an outdoor Mariachi Mass, music, crafts, and native food. Picnic tables are provided at the site but no overnight camping is allowed. Overnight accommodations are available at Nogales, 18 miles to the south, or at Tucson, 45 miles to the north.

Open: 8 a.m. to 5 p.m. daily. Closed Christmas Day.

Fees: $3 per car; $1 per person on bus.

Mailing Address: Tumacacori National Monument, P.O. Box 67, Tumacacori, AZ 85640.

Telephone: 602-398-2341.

Getting There: The monument is located in southern Arizona, near the Mexican border. From Tucson, take I-19 south 45 miles, or from Nogales, take I-19 north 18 miles to the park.

‖ Tuzigoot National Monument

Between 1125 and 1400, prehistoric Indians piled rock upon rock to build this 110-room apartment atop a limestone ridge overlooking the Verde Valley. The Apaches who came later called it Tuzigoot (pronounced TOO-zi-goot) for the "crooked water" of the Verde River that meanders through the scrublands of the central Arizona desert.

The ruins of this pueblo indicate there were 77 rooms on the ground floor, each measuring about 12 by 18 feet, and that the structure rose two or three stories high. A one-third mile trail takes visitors on a self-guided tour from the visitor center through the ruins at Tuzigoot.

Excavated in the 1930s by the University of Arizona, Tuzigoot is one of the largest agricultural communities of the Sinagua Indians found to date. These farmers built complex masonry dwellings atop mesas and in cliffs. The Indians entered their dwellings from the roof by using ladders.

A trash heap at the base of the site has yielded tools, bits of pottery, the uncremated remains of pueblo inhabitants, and finely crafted ornaments—thought to be grave offerings—of turquoise mosaics, shells, and beads. Archeologists have found the remains of children buried in the walls and floors of the pueblo, a practice which suggests that the Sinaguans believed that young souls would be born again into the next generation.

An excellent museum in the visitor center tells the story of this Sinaguan farming village, from its beginnings as a small pueblo of 15 to 20 rooms to its height in the 13th century, when extended drought brought farmers from nearby regions closer to the river. Pottery, jewelry, stone axes, arrows, and fire-making equipment are on display. No one knows why Tuzigoot and other pueblos in the Arizona valleys were abandoned in the 1400s.

There are no camping facilities at the monument, but Flagstaff is less than 50 miles away and nearby Cottonwood has accommodations and restaurants. Dead Horse Ranch State Park, three miles to the south, has tent sites and hookups.

Open: 8 a.m. to 5 p.m., hours extended in summer. Check for details.

Fees: $1 per person.

Mailing Address: Tuzigoot National Monument, c/o Montezuma Castle National Monument, P.O. Box 219, Camp Verde, AZ 86322.

Telephone: 602-634-5564.

Getting There: The monument is located on U.S. 89A in central Arizona between Phoenix and Flagstaff. From Phoenix, take I-17 north to Camp Verde, and turn west onto Rt. 279 through Cottonwood. Take U.S. 89A west through Cottonwood. Shortly before Clarkdale, take the access road north to Tuzigoot.

‖ Walnut Canyon National Monument

The ruins of more than 25 cliff dwellings, built in the sheer walls of this hidden canyon during the 12th century, are a reminder of the Sinagua Indians who farmed the pockets of fertile soil and hunted the abundant wildlife of Walnut Canyon.

Today, the 24 cliff dwellings at Walnut Canyon are accessible to visitors along the Island Trail. The visitor center has an excellent view of the many cliff dwellings. A route leading around the canyon rim, which is at an elevation of 7,000 feet, gives another overview.

For a closer look, take the Island trail that leads directly into the canyon. This .9-mile route traverses a total of 480 steps, a strenuous hike that should be avoided by people with heart or respiratory problems.

In all, the Sinagua built 300 rooms of stone and mud measuring roughly 12 by 14 feet. They raised corn, beans, and squash and took advantage of the canyon's considerable natural resources. Less than 150 years after they arrived, the Sinagua mysteriously abandoned the canyon.

Because of its unique curved shape, Walnut Canyon has a climate that is congenial to an unusually wide range of plants and animals. For this reason, both the Black Walnut, which generally grows at lower elevations, and the Douglas-fir tree, which is normally found on higher ground, thrive in the canyon. Numerous animals—including mule deer, coyote, bobcat, fox, porcupine, bear, cougar, and many birds—live in the lush foliage.

The visitor center has exhibits of Indian pottery, textiles, and tools as well as information about the region's geology and ecology. In summer, the rangers conduct scheduled interpretative talks and off-trail hikes. Check for details. There are no accommodations in the 2,250-acre park but Flagstaff, which is located less than ten miles to the west, has numerous hotels and restaurants.

Open: 8 a.m. to 5 p.m. Summer hours extended 7 a.m.–7 p.m. The trail into the canyon closes at 4 p.m. during winter and at 5 p.m. in summer. Closed Christmas and Thanksgiving Day.

Fees: $1 per person age 16 and over, $3 maximum per family.

Mailing Address: Walnut Canyon National Monument, Walnut Canyon Road, Flagstaff, AZ 86004.

Telephone: 602-526-3367.

Getting There: The monument, in north central Arizona, is just on the eastern outskirts of Flagstaff. Take the Walnut Canyon exit off I-40 east.

‖ Wupatki National Monument

The remains of a prehistoric ball court, amphitheater, and hundred-room pueblo make Wupatki one of the most unusual of the Indian ruins in the Southwest. Located in the once fertile land created by the volcanic San Francisco Mountains of central Arizona, Wupatki lies near what is believed to be a major prehistoric trade route between Mexico and North America. There are over 200 ruins in 2,600 archeological sites in the monument and more than 100 sites within one square mile.

The main ruin, a three-story pueblo, was built of carefully stacked red sandstone bricks during the 1100s by the Sinagua Indians. Several excavated rooms reveal clay firepits that the Sinagua Indians used to cook and heat their homes. The word "Wupatki" means "tall house" in the Hopi Indian language.

The amphitheater, with its pleasing oval shape, has a smooth earthen floor that could have been used for ceremonial dances. Nearby is a "blow hole," a crack in the ground that serves as a natural barometer, blowing out air from deep below the earth or sucking it in as the pressure dictates. But perhaps most interesting is a circular structure that archeologists think is a ball court used for some kind of ritual game.

Short hiking trails in the western part of the monument lead to Lomaki and Citadel, an 800-year old ruin atop a butte overlooking the countryside. Another 800-year-old ruin, Nalakihu, is near the parking area. All visits to the pueblos at Wupatki are self-guided. Occasionally, talks are given. Bring plenty of water if you plan to go in summer as temperatures in the high desert can reach 100 degrees. Sunset Crater National Monument is located to the south along the 36-mile loop trail that connects Wupatki to Route 89.

During the summer, the park has daily demonstrations of tool and pottery making and other Indian crafts.

Wupatki has no campgrounds. The nearest accommodations, food, and gas are in Flagstaff, 40 miles south.

Open: 8 a.m. to 5 p.m. Summer hours extended 7 a.m.–7 p.m. Closed Christmas and New Year's Day.

Fees: None.

Mailing Address: Wupatki National Monument, HC 33 Box 444A, Flagstaff, AZ 86001.

Telephone: 602-774-7000.

Getting There: The monument is located north of Flagstaff. From Flagstaff, take Rt. 89 north 15 miles to the access road for Sunset Crater and Wupatki.

ARKANSAS

1. Arkansas Post National Memorial
2. Fort Smith National Historic Site
3. Pea Ridge National Military Park

‖ Arkansas Post National Memorial

From one log cabin built in 1686 by French fur traders to a bustling 19th-century river port, Arkansas Post on the Arkansas River represents more than two centuries of American frontier life.

This was the first settlement by Europeans in the lower Mississippi River valley. Originally intended to be the linchpin in a trade route connecting French holdings in Canada and Louisiana, Arkansas Post became U.S. territory through the Louisiana Purchase in 1803. As settlers moved westward, the post became a frontier boom town populated by pioneers and professionals, educators and adventurers.

But in 1821, just as the city was beginning to blossom, Arkansas Post lost its position as territorial capital to the newly established town of Little Rock. Three years later, the Quapaw Indians, who supplied Arkansas Post with much of its business, were relocated to Oklahoma. In the second half of the 19th century, railroad transit adversely affected river trade. Arkansas Post was abandoned, its buildings left to rot.

Today, signs along a two-mile trail down old Main and Front streets mark the sites where factories, warehouses, and residences once stood. The 389-acre park has a museum with artifacts from the past—old bullets, farming implements, spurs, and spoons—and a movie about the area's history.

A pond in the park is stocked with largemouth bass and catfish. An Arkansas license is required for fishing. The park has a picnic area with tables and grills. Facilities for launching boats on the Arkansas River are located one-half mile outside the park.

Hikers inclined to wander into the wooded areas of the park should beware of Japanese Honeysuckle. Planted during World War II to help control erosion, the vine grows in thick tangles, creating impasses on some trails. Also beware of ticks and other insects, poisonous plants such as poison ivy, and snakes—both copperheads and cottonmouths are found in the park.

Open: 8 a.m. to 5 p.m. daily, with grounds open from 8 a.m. until dark. Closed Christmas Day.

Fees: None.

Mailing Address: Arkansas Post National Memorial, Route 1, Box 16, Gillett, AR 72055.

Telephone: 501-548-2432.

Getting There: From Little Rock, take Rt. 65 south to Dumas; turn left onto Rt. 165 and cross over the Arkansas River to Country Road 169. The memorial is two miles down this road.

| Fort Smith National Historic Site

A re-created 12-man gallows stands in the courtyard of Fort Smith, a grim reminder of justice in the American Wild West and of the infamous "Hanging" Judge Isaac Parker. From 1817 until it was abandoned 80 years later, the fort was a buffer between Indian territory and the white man's world, a lonely outpost of civilization during a time of rampant lawlessness.

The Barracks-Courthouse-Jail complex, once known as "Hell on the Border" for its unbearable conditions, still stands. Here Parker tried 13,000 cases, sentenced 160 men to hang, and carried out 79 executions.

But if Parker had a reputation as a harsh and unforgiving arbiter of the law, the men he tried were equally nefarious. Many of the lawbreakers were hardened criminals seeking refuge from the law in Indian territory. The job of controlling them was a tough one. During Parker's tenure at Fort Smith, 65 deputy marshals were murdered in the line of duty.

Although Parker is remembered today as an unforgiving hanging judge, he was known in the community as a kind and gentle man. He was a "good citizen" with a winning smile, a way with the ladies, and an interest in education. He was also indefatigable in his efforts to bring law and order to a chaotic region and he was respectful of the Indians. "People have said that I am a cruel, heartless and bloodthirsty man, but . . . I have ever had the single aim of justice in view. . . . Do equal and exact justice has been my motto," he said. In fact, Parker used his powers as judge to control exploitation of the Indians at a time when many Americans were out to do exactly that. Possibly, it was Parker's protection of the Indians that sullied his reputation as a fair and honest judge. Parker is buried in the Fort Smith National Cemetery.

The Initial Point Marker, a small stone monument set in 1858, marks the boundary between the Arkansas Territory and lands belonging to the Choctaw Indians. For 65 years after the boundary was established, no white men were allowed to settle west of the line.

The 46-acre park at Fort Smith is still under restoration. The visitor center in the courthouse shows a slide program about the fort and displays deputy marshal badges, handcuffs, leg irons, and guns. The site's landscaping is not complete and as yet, there are no picnic facilities and few shade trees. Western Arkansas is hot and humid in summer, when temperatures can rise above 100 degrees. Park rangers suggest visiting the site in spring and fall, when the weather is cooler.

Fort Smith is located at the confluence of the Arkansas and Poteau Rivers. Swimming and water sports are not recommended. Tourists should watch for snakes in the grounds.

Each year around Memorial Day, the normally quiet city of Fort Smith, population 70,000, holds one of the biggest rodeos in the country. The high-stakes prize money attracts some of the nation's top rodeo performers.

Open: 9 a.m. to 5 p.m. daily. Closed Christmas Day.

Fees: None.

Mailing Address: Fort Smith National Historic Site, P.O. Box 1406, Fort Smith, AR 72902.

Telephone: 501-783-3961.

Getting There: Fort Smith is located on Rogers Avenue between Second and Third streets in downtown Fort Smith. Take Rt. 64 and turn south onto Rogers Ave.

‖ Pea Ridge National Military Park

On March 7–8, 1862, the battle of Pea Ridge, one of the most important Civil War battles west of the Mississippi River, gave the Union control of Missouri.

Pea Ridge is the only major battle in the Civil War in which Indians participated as regular troops. The Confederates recruited about 1,000 Cherokees from the Indian Territory, now Oklahoma. But the Indians, having never before seen field cannon, were so awed by the power of the artillery that they eventually took to the woods.

The 4,300-acre park preserves the ground over which the battle was fought. It has changed little since the days of the Civil War. Markers along a seven-mile, self-guided tour indicate the sites of major importance.

One of the battlefield's most interesting sights is the reconstructed Elkhorn Tavern. The tavern was occupied by Union troops, captured by Confederates, and later recaptured by Union soldiers. It is open from 10 a.m. to 4 p.m. daily from mid-May through mid-October.

The park grounds, which are mostly covered with eastern mixed hardwood forests, has picnic tables, grills, and water fountains. Camping and hunting is not permitted.

The visitor center presents a brief slide program on the battle and the role Arkansas and Missouri played in the Civil War. The museum displays guns, cannon, cannon balls, and bullets from the battle. From the visitor center, you can walk along the Old Telegraph Road, so called because telegraph wire was strung along it. Stage coaches took this road west to California in the late 1850s.

Occasionally the park hosts special festivals.

Open: 8 a.m. to 5 p.m. daily. Closed Thanksgiving, Christmas, and New Year's Day.

Fees: $1, ages 17–61.

Mailing Address: Pea Ridge National Military Park, Pea Ridge, AR 72751.

Telephone: 501-451-8122.

Getting There: The park is northeast of Rogers, AR, on U.S. 62.

CALIFORNIA

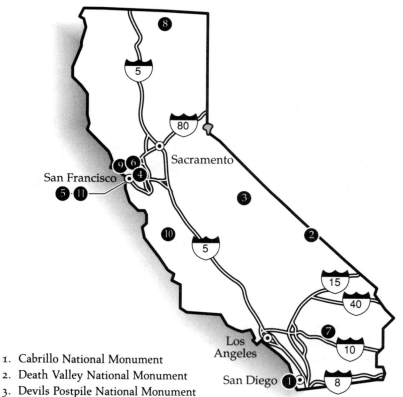

1. Cabrillo National Monument
2. Death Valley National Monument
3. Devils Postpile National Monument
4. Eugene O'Neill National Historic Site
5. Fort Point National Historic Site
6. John Muir National Historic Site
7. Joshua Tree National Monument
8. Lava Beds National Monument
9. Muir Woods National Monument
10. Pinnacles National Monument
11. San Francisco Maritime National Historical Park

‖ Cabrillo National Monument

San Diego's Cabrillo National Monument, overlooking the Pacific Ocean from beautiful Point Loma, offers the shore lover everything from crustaceans to cetaceans.

One cetacean you won't want to miss is the California Gray Whale, a major attraction at the monument. Each year thousands of these behemoths, which measure 42 to 46 feet and weigh about 45 tons, pass by Point Loma from December through February on their migrations to the lagoons of Baja. The best place to watch for the waterspouts —the clue that allows you to distinguish a whale from a bed of kelp heaving in the ocean waves—is the whale overlook.

On a smaller scale, the tidal pools at the water's edge teem with crustaceans—limpets, anemones, starfish, crabs, and microscopic plant and animal life. These are best seen at low tide during the fall, winter, and spring. Check with the park ranger for times and dates.

The 144-acre park commemorates the landing of the Portuguese explorer Juan Rodriguez Cabrillo, the first European to set foot on California soil. Cabrillo sailed into what is now San Diego harbor on September 28, 1542. After naming the place San Miguel, Cabrillo continued up the coast to Oregon. A larger-than-life statue of Cabrillo in conquistador regalia stands near the visitor center. Inside are exhibits about the man and the expedition he led.

By all accounts, Cabrillo was a good sailor with a keen sense of observation. When he reached the next major harbor on the California coast, he called it *Bahia de los Fumos* for the smoke and fumes caused by Indian campfires. Now known as Los Angeles, the area is still enveloped in a shroud of haze but the smog is caused by cars, not campfires.

At the park, the Old Point Loma Lighthouse, a small white sandstone structure with an elaborate iron-and-brass housing for the light, guided ships into San Diego harbor from 1855 to 1891. The Bayside Trail, a short walk around the promontory, is open from 9 a.m. to 4 p.m. This trail has remnants of artillery that guarded San Diego harbor during World Wars I and II. There are no picnic facilities at the park.

Fishing from the point is excellent and requires a state fishing license. Perch, opal eye, and bass are caught in the area. Or sample the local seafood in the delightful marine community at Point Loma, six miles away. This Navy community has docks and wharves and plenty of seafood restaurants.

On September 29–30, San Diego holds the annual Cabrillo Festival, which features a re-enactment of the historic landing along with food and folk dancing from Portugal, Spain, and Mexico. A parade ends in Point Loma.

Open: Visitor Center: 9 a.m. to 5:15 p.m., with extended hours in summer.

Fees: $3 per vehicle, seniors free.

Mailing Address: Cabrillo National Monument, P.O. Box 6670, San Diego, CA 92106.

Telephone: 619-557-5450.

Getting There: The monument is located within the city limits of San Diego at the southern end of Point Loma. Take Rosecrans Street, turn right on Canon Street, turn left onto Catalina Blvd. and proceed through the Naval Ocean System Center gates to the end of the point. Public buses make several trips each day to the monument.

Death Valley National Monument

Death Valley. This legendary desert, with its wrinkled gray mountains, crusty yellowed canyons, blazing white salt flats, and rippled sand dunes, is one of the most colorful natural areas in the country. The unique combination of landscape, history, natural life, and heat is unforgettable.

Extending more than two million acres along the bed of an ancient lake, Death Valley chronicles the geological history of the earth with an astonishing array of formations. The lowest points in the Western Hemisphere—Badwater, at 279 feet below sea level, and a nearby spot at 282 feet below—are found here. Telescope Peak, with an elevation of 11,049 feet, is here as well.

At that altitude, the summit of Telescope Peak is cool year-round. The rest of the park, however, is oven-hot, especially in summer. From May through September, temperatures regularly rise above 100 degrees, so hot that hiking on the valley floor is not recommended. Little wonder that the Indian name for Death Valley is *Tomesha*, meaning "ground afire." Safe and comfortable hiking can be done in the mountains, however. The winter months are more bearable, with temperatures ranging from the 60s to the 80s in the day and dipping into the 40s at night.

A trip in this uncommonly hot, dry climate calls for careful planning. Be sure to carry protective clothing and take enough water for your car and all the members of your party.

Death Valley has nine campgrounds and two resorts. Three of the campgrounds—Furnace Creek, Mesquite Spring, and Wildrose—are open year-round. The Texas Spring, Sunset, and Stovepipe Wells sites are open from October to April, and Emigrant, Thorndike, and Mahogany are open from April to October. The resorts at Stovepipe Wells and Furnace Creek are run by Fred Harvey Inc., P.O. Box 187, Death Valley, CA 92328. Telephone: 619-786-2345. Food and supplies are available at Furnace Creek and Stovepipe Wells.

Among the most interesting natural features of the park are Telescope Peak, which takes six to eight hours to hike, Devil's Golf Course, a salt bed with a surface so hard it "pings" underfoot, and the multicolored canyon walls near Dante's View Road.

Racetrack Playa is a dry lake bed about three miles long and two miles wide with a 1,000-foot-deep layer of beige-colored mud. Loose rocks that have fallen into the area skid on the surface when it is wet, leaving a trail in the soft mud. Nearby is Ubehebe Crater, a volcanic basin 500 feet deep and half a mile across, walled by layers of colorful rocks.

Rising out of the northern part of the monument like some fantastic desert mirage is Scotty's Castle, a provincial Spanish-style vacation estate constructed during the 1920s for millionaire Albert M. Johnson. It takes its name from a colorful man known as Death Valley Scotty, a friend of Johnson's and a valley resident for more than 30 years. Visitors can tour this extraordinary luxury lodging, taking time out for a bite and a cold drink in the castle's fast food restaurant.

Hundreds of springs underlie Death Valley and provide the desert with delightful oases. There is a spring near park headquarters at Furnace Creek and another at the Mesquite Spring campground near Scotty's Castle. In the southern end of the park, Saratoga Springs feed a 15-acre lake and marsh that supports geese, ducks, and herons. Lake swimming is not recommended but swimming pools are available at the Furnace Creek Ranch and the Stovepipe Wells Village.

It was in 1849, during the Gold Rush era and the push to settle California, that Death Valley got its name. A group of pioneers known as the Bennett-Arcane party became stranded in the desert with few provisions and no water. When they finally emerged from the ordeal, Mrs. Bennett bid goodbye to the place she called Death Valley. The name stuck.

After the settlers came the miners, men with their burros in search of gold. The gold did not pan out, but borax, an ingredient in glass and fiberglass, was discovered. Refined borax, some 20 tons at a time, was hauled by teams of up to 20 mules—the famed "twenty mule teams"—to a train depot 100 miles away. Ruins of the Harmony Borax Works and the Eagle Borax Works still stand.

Despite its name, Death Valley contains abundant wildlife. There are rodents such as ground squirrels, kangaroo rats (big-footed rodents), and pocket mice along with jack rabbits, kit foxes, coyotes, bobcats, and desert bighorn sheep. There are 17 different kinds of lizards, 19 kinds of snakes, and 230 different birds that pass through the area on their migrations.

Some 900 different kinds of plants live in the harsh, dry environment, including 20 species that are found nowhere else in the world. Look out for the Panamint daisy, a large sunflower, and the Death Valley Monkey Flower, which has a "face" and can be found near the Ubehebe Crater. During the infrequent rains of spring, the park is awash with the vibrant pinks, whites, and greens of the desert in bloom. Thirteen species of cactus grow in the monument, but none grow on the floor of Death Valley. Cottontop, strawtop, cholla, beavertail, and grizzly bear cactuses are most common.

For information about the historical, natural, and geological features of the park, check the Furnace Creek visitor center. The Furnace Creek area also has a post office, the Death Valley Museum, and the Borax Museum.

Each year in November, the park commemorates the '49ers, the gold prospectors who came to California and Death Valley during the Gold Rush of 1849. Check for details.

Open: Visitor Center: 8 a.m. to 5 p.m. in summer. Hours are extended in winter until 8 p.m. The park itself is always open.

Fees: $5 per single private car for a seven-day permit; $2 per person for motorcyclists, bicyclists, pedestrians, and bus passengers for a seven-day pass. Permanently disabled U.S. citizens and those age 62 and over are admitted free. Campsites are $4 to $8 a night; some are free.

Mailing Address: Death Valley National Monument, Death Valley, CA 92328.

Telephone: 619-786-2331.

Getting There: Route 395 passes west of Death Valley and connects with Rt. 178 and 190 to the park. Rt. 95 passes east and connects with Rts. 267, 374, and 373 to the park. I-15 passes southeast and connects with Rt. 127.

‖ Devils Postpile National Monument

Hot lava cracked as it cooled almost 100,000 years ago, forming the unique 60-foot-high basalt columns of Devils Postpile. The monument is located along the Middle Fork of the San Joaquin (pronounced wah-KEEN) River, high on the western slope of the Sierra Nevada mountain range in eastern California.

It is a hiker's paradise, a rough and rugged landscape with quiet pine forests. The park's most striking feature is the Devils Postpile formation, a pipe-organlike stand of hexagonal gray columns two to three feet in diameter. Over 10,000 years ago, glaciers scraped and polished the top of the columns to resemble an intricately tiled floor.

Hike two miles to the south to Rainbow Falls, where the San Joaquin River drops 101 feet over a sheer cliff. A stairway and short trail lead to the bottom of the falls, where numerous flowers and grasses form an enchanting garden.

The John Muir Trail passes through the monument, and several other trails lead by the park's many natural features. Open only during the summer, the 798-acre park has a 23-site campground that operates from about July 1 to October 15, depending on the weather. If you are planning to visit the area, call to check on the dates.

On most days during the summer, park rangers lead nature walks at 11 a.m. and 2 p.m. and they offer campfire programs with singing and natural history talks on Wednesday and Saturday nights.

With a California fishing license, visitors can angle for rainbow trout, brook trout, and German brown trout in the San Joaquin River. Hunting is prohibited.

Shuttle buses operated by the Mammoth-June Mountain ski areas carry visitors from Mammoth Mountain to Devils Postpile for a nominal fee. For more information about the shuttle bus system, contact the Mammoth Visitor Center, P.O. Box 148, Mammoth Lakes, CA 93546. Telephone: 619-934-2505.

Open: From mid-June to mid-Oct. Closed in winter, depending on snow conditions. The ranger station is open from 8 a.m. to 5 p.m. daily during the summer.

Fees: None. There is a small fee for the shuttle bus. Check for details.

Mailing Address: Devils Postpile National Monument, P.O. Box 501, Mammoth Lakes, CA 93546.

Telephone: 619-934-2289 in summer; 209-565-3341 in winter.

Getting There: The monument is located north of Bishop, CA and is surrounded by the Inyo National Forest. The monument is reached by a 17-mile drive west from U.S. Highway 395 or by State Route 203 to Minaret Summit and an eight-mile paved but narrow mountain road with turnouts.

‖ Eugene O'Neill National Historic Site

"Before O'Neill, there was American theater; after O'Neill, there was American drama," said a critic of Eugene O'Neill. The Nobel- and Pulitzer-prize-winning playwright lived on this isolated property east of the San Francisco Bay area from 1937 to 1944. The recently opened site includes Tao House, where O'Neill lived with his wife Carlotta, and 14 acres of his estate. Here he found the solitude he needed to write his greatest plays—*Long Day's Journey Into Night, Moon for the Misbegotten,* and *The Iceman Cometh.*

Access is limited at this 14-acre site, which opened in January 1985. The gate is locked and only visitors who have made reservations with the National Park Service can view the house.

The house, an austere Spanish-mission-style structure with white concrete walls and Mexican floor tiles, is set against the Las Trampas ridge at an elevation of 700 feet. A 1½-hour guided tour takes visitors through the main building and into the extensive, beautifully landscaped grounds. You can see the swimming pool, with its original bath house, and the grave of Blemie, the O'Neill's beloved dalmation.

Two rooms of Tao House have been refurnished and photographs in each room show the O'Neills in their custom-built home. One of the rooms, known as Rosie's room, was built especially for the O'Neills' pea-green player piano with painted roses. Most interesting of all is the playwright's study, an inner sanctum so isolated you have to pass through three doors and a closet to reach it. The view overlooking the San Ramon Valley from the window is spectacular. O'Neill worked five to eight hours a day in this splendid study.

O'Neill and his wife landscaped the grounds with an oriental influence. The pathways are curved rather than straight. The abundant oaks, fruit trees, and shrubbery made a serene cloister for the eccentric writer, who worked at Tao House until ill health forced him to quit.

No picnicking or camping is allowed on the site, and only a limited number of visitors are granted entrance to the area each day. For more information, contact the ranger at the address listed below.

Open: By reservation only.
Fees: None for entry to site.
Mailing Address: Eugene O'Neill National Historic Site, P.O. Box 280, Danville, CA 94526.
Telephone: 415-838-0249.
Getting There: Contact the site for directions.

▌ Fort Point National Historic Site

At Fort Point, rangers and volunteers in period U.S. Army costumes interpret the life of the garrison soldier during the Civil War by leading tours and demonstrating cannon firing. This fort, which guarded the entrance to San Francisco Bay at the Golden Gate, is the only casemated, mid-19th century coastal defense fortification ever constructed on the West Coast.

Fort Point is one of about 30 brick and granite forts constructed as part of a national system of coastal defense between the end of the War of 1812 and the end of the Civil War. The system included such posts as Fort Sumter, Fort Monroe, and Fort Pulaski on the Atlantic Coast along with Fort Jefferson, Fort Massachusetts, and Fort Pike on the Gulf Coast.

Historians refer to these posts as "third system" forts. Many of them were influenced by Simon Barnard, a French engineer brought to the United States, and Joseph Totten, who would become the chief engineer of the United States Army. Other coastal defense forts built on the West Coast during this time period include Alcatraz Island and Fort Stevens. But only Fort Point was part of the national system of coastal defense.

The fort's irregular quadrangle, enclosed by brick walls, granite cornices, and sills, was built between 1853 and 1861 on the site of an earlier Spanish fort known as the Castillo de San Joaquin. During the Civil War, California and Fort Point remained in Union hands. The soldiers there, although never attacked, stood ready throughout the conflict to repel both foreign and Confederate naval intervention in San Francisco Bay.

Exhibits in the fort include displays of artillery, soldiers' gear, a restored powder magazine, lighthouses, and shipwrecks. On the second floor of the fort, two special photographic exhibits, "Ready and Forward" and "Women at War," portray the contributions of black soldiers and women in defense of their country.

Sutler Store, operated by the Golden Gate National Parks Association, sells a variety of publications and other materials related to the site's historical and natural themes. Two slide programs, "Fort Point—Cornerstone of Coastal Defense" and "Building the Golden Gate Bridge," are shown in the fort theater daily at 11:30 a.m. and 3:30 p.m. A fishing pier near the fort extends into San Francisco Bay for crabbing and fishing.

The weather in the San Francisco area may be mild but it is uniformly windy and cold at Fort Point, so dress warmly when visiting.

Open: 10 a.m. to 5 p.m. daily. Closed Thanksgiving, Christmas, and New Years Day.

Fees: None.

Mailing Address: Fort Point National Historic Site, P.O. Box 29333, Presidio of San Francisco, CA 94129.

Telephone: 415-556-1693.

Getting There: Fort Point can be reached by riding the San Francisco MUNI buses #28 and #29 or Golden Gate Transit to the Golden Gate Bridge toll plaza. From there, walk one-fourth mile down the hill to the fort. For information on bus schedules and boarding stops, call MUNI at 415-673-6864 or Golden Gate Transit at 415-332-6600. Ample parking is available at the fort.

❙ John Muir National Historic Site

John Muir, naturalist and father of the national park system, often went hiking with President Theodore Roosevelt. Muir's indefatigable defense of the environment led to the establishment of Yosemite, Petrified Forest, the Grand Canyon, and Mt. Rainier national parks. He also started the Sierra Club in 1892, a vocal environment group that remains active today. When Muir paused from his famous treks across the country, he came to his Victorian house just north of San Francisco.

Here, the bearded man of the mountains wrote many of the articles and books that inspired Americans to treasure their nation's natural areas and protect them from wanton development. Muir's works include *Our National Parks, Travels in Alaska,* and more than 300 magazine articles.

Muir's 8.5-acre estate in the rolling hills of Martinez, California, is unchanged since the conservationist lived and worked here between 1890 and 1914. Stately palm trees flank the entrance to the 17-room Victorian house, and the house's bay windows and porches look out on the orchards. The house is furnished in period antiques and a few original pieces, including an oil painting of Muir painted by his sister.

Born in 1838 in Scotland, Muir was ten years old when he and his family moved to the Wisconsin frontier of America. In 1880, Muir moved into the house in Martinez, originally home to the parents of Muir's wife Louie Strentzel. It was in Muir's study on the second floor that he wrote some of his most influential books and articles about conservation. Muir called the study "Scribble Den." True to form, the original oak desk is strewn with papers and the floor littered with manuscript pages. When a book or article was finished, Muir would roll it up and insert it in the orange crate near his desk to differentiate it from the other papers in the room. His wife and daughter would then edit and type the manuscript.

Visitors to the Muir house can see a half-hour movie about the celebrated naturalist and wander on their own around the grounds and the house.

On the last Saturday in April each year, the park celebrates Muir's birthday (April 21) with bagpipe music and dancing. At Christmas, the house hosts a Victorian tea with cookies and caroling. Call for time and tickets.

Open: 10 a.m. to 4:30 p.m. daily. Closed Thanksgiving, Christmas, and New Year's Day.

Fees: None.

Mailing Address: John Muir National Historic Site, 4202 Alhambra Ave., Martinez, CA 94553.

Telephone: 415-228-8860.

Getting There: The house is located at the intersection of John Muir Parkway, Rt. 4, and Alhambra Ave. From Berkeley, take I-80 and turn right on Rt. 4. If you get to Rt. 680, you've missed the site.

‖ Joshua Tree National Monument

Boulders and granite monoliths rise above the flatlands like towering sculptures, jagged mountains cut the clear skies, and 20-foot-tall Joshua trees stand upright and outstretched in the unrelenting sun. This is Joshua Tree National Monument, a unique desert park near Palm Springs.

Located between the Pinto Mountains and the Little San Bernadino range, the monument stretches for over half a million acres in the arid southern California landscape. Here is a magnificent stand of Joshua trees, a yucca plant with spiked leaves and greenish white flowers.

Mormon pioneers who passed through the area gave the tree its name because it reminded them of Joshua reaching to God. They were part of a procession of people entering the region, from prehistoric Indians searching for food and miners looking for gold to today's visitors, who revel in the sights of this striking desert.

Nine campgrounds, equipped with tables, fireplaces, and toilets, and several picnic areas serve the half-million-acre park. There are no electricity, water, or sewer connections for trailers and no stores for visitors. Groceries, gasoline, hotels, and restaurants are located within five miles north of the park.

Camping is limited to 14 days between October 1 and June 1, and to 30 days during the summer months. Two of the campgrounds allow horses, and only two campgrounds, Cottonwood and Black Rock Canyon, charge a fee for camping.

Two different desert ecosystems come together at Joshua Tree. In the east, there is the dry Colorado Desert at an altitude below 3,000

The early settlers thought the tree-like *Yucca brevifolia* resembled the out-stretched arms of the prophet Joshua in prayer, and so named it the Joshua tree.—*NPS photograph*

feet; in the west, there is the higher Mojave Desert. The Joshua tree thrives in the Mojave's cooler and more moist environment. This slow-growing plant, which stores water in its trunk and does not transpire moisture, is well suited to desert life. Unlike regular trees, Joshua trees do not have rings, making it impossible to date them. But biologists believe some of the park's specimens are 400 to 450 years old.

Five oases, with fan palms and abundant wildlife, dot the desert. In spring, the entire park blooms in a brilliant mosaic of short-lived wild flowers. Elsewhere in the park sparse vegetation reveals the region's bare terrain. Gulches, pediments, alluvial plains, granites, and rock and mineral deposits are all plainly visible.

Wildlife in the park includes coyotes, roadrunners, rattlesnakes, tarantulas, and kangaroo rats, beguiling large-footed rodents that live entirely on metabolically produced water.

Like all deserts, Joshua Tree is hot and dry and the sky is clear some 259 days a year. Temperatures top 100 degrees on an average of 80 days, with heat in the 90s from June through September. When it rains, flash flooding often occurs.

The park has three visitor centers: the Twentynine Palms Oasis, Black Rock Canyon, and Cottonwood Springs. Exhibits explain the natural and historical aspects of the monument and include displays of plants and insects. Rangers conduct nature walks and evening campfire programs in the fall and spring.

Open: Visitor Center: 8 a.m. to 4:30 p.m. daily. Closed Christmas Day.

Fees: $5 for one to seven days. The Cottonwood and Black Rock campgrounds charge $6 and $10 respectively per night and both have flush toilets and running water. Black Rock is available also through the Ticketron reservation system.

Mailing Address: Joshua Tree National Monument, 74485 National Monument Drive, Twentynine Palms, CA 92277.

Telephone: 619-367-7511.

Getting There: The monument is 140 miles east of Los Angeles. You can approach it via I-10 (Rt. 60) and 29 Palms Highway (Rt. 62). The park has entrances at the towns of Joshua Tree, Twentynine Palms, and Cottonwood Springs.

Lava Beds National Monument

The landscape of Lava Beds National Monument is so rugged that it was used by Indians as a natural fortress during the Modoc Indian War in 1872–73. Lava tube caves, created by volcanic activity over 30,000 years ago, make this 72-square-mile monument in the northern California mountains an immense subterranean playground.

You will discover an amazing array of basalt and cinder and splatter cones, lava flows, and tubes. Here prehistoric man sought shelter, and left pictographs and petrographs—simple geometric drawings and carvings—on the dark rock walls.

Visitors can explore more than 200 lava tube caves. These low, rounded passages wriggle underground for thousands of feet. Lamps are provided free by the Park Service. Because the tubes are one-way formations, it is virtually impossible to get lost in them. But rangers do go out looking for those who do not return their flashlights. The mile-long Catacombs Cave has branching passageways. There are also wild caves in the monument as well as seldom-visited formations that may require rock-climbing skills. To explore the wilderness caves, you will need adequate climbing gear including rope, sturdy shoes, hard hats, and a good flashlight. Protective head gear is on sale in the visitor center. In the summer, rangers lead afternoon walks in the caves. Evening campfire programs focus on the area's history, geology, and wildlife.

Above ground, there are extensive lava flows called pahoehoe (pronounced pah-hoy-hoy) and aa (ah-ah)—named ostensibly for the noise a barefoot person might make when negotiating this rougher formation. Cinder cones, formed when frothy lava cooled in the air, dot the monument.

The three-quarter-mile trail to Schonchin Butte leads to a panoramic view of the monument and a glimpse of the unique plants that blanket the crater.

The monument's history was a bloody one. In 1872, the Modoc Indians made their last stand, a battle between 53 Indians and 1,000 federal troops. The Modoc leader, known as "Captain Jack," held the troops at bay for six months. He was hanged when he surrendered.

Most of the fighting took place in Captain Jack's Stronghold, near the northern part of the monument. Canby's Cross marks the spot where the two sides negotiated their numerous peace agreements, and where General E. R. S. Canby was assassinated during one of the meetings.

Situated at elevations of 4,000 to 5,493 feet, the monument has plant life ranging from grassland and sagebrush at lower levels to chaparral in the mid-range to ponderosa pine at higher elevations. Wildlife varies with the vegetation and includes squirrel, rabbit, bobcat, coyote, mule deer, and eagle.

Near the visitor center is a 40-unit campground with sites suitable for tents and small trailers. Water and toilets are available year-round. From September 15 to May 15, water must be carried from the visitor center. Restrooms also are available at the visitor center during the winter season.

Temperatures in summer are moderate, from 75 to 90 degrees during the day and from 40 to 60 degrees at night. In winter, expect daytime temperatures in the 40s and nights below freezing. Cold weather is possible at any time and snow has been recorded in the monument in all months.

From Memorial Day weekend through Labor Day, rangers conduct evening programs to explain the natural features of the park. Check for times and topics.

Open: The monument is open 24 hours throughout the year. The Visitor Center is open from 8 a.m. to 5 p.m., and from 9 a.m. to 6 p.m. from Memorial Day to Labor Day. Closed Thanksgiving and Christmas Day.

Fees: $3 a car.

Mailing Address: Lava Beds National Monument, P.O. Box 867, Tulelake, CA 96134.

Telephone: 916-667-2282.

Getting There: Park headquarters is 30 miles from Tulelake, CA, and 58 miles from Klamath Falls, OR, off Rt. 139. A 1.3-mile section of road between Tulelake and the park are not paved. Airlines serve Medford and Klamath Falls, where rental cars are available.

‖ Muir Woods National Monument

Just north of San Francisco is the V-shaped canyon of Muir Woods, a tranquil forest of gargantuan redwood trees dedicated to America's best known conservationist, John Muir. Six miles of trails lead through trees that tower 250 feet and range from 400 to 800 years old. The ground below them is blanketed with evergreen swordferns, a common companion of these giant trees.

Over 150 million years ago giant Sequoias grew throughout the Northern Hemisphere but today they can be found only in northern California. Redwoods, a species of sequoia which thrives in damp climates, live in the foggy coastal zone between Monterey, California, and the southwestern corner of Oregon.

Muir, who lived from 1838 to 1914 and is considered the father of the conservation movement, only visited the 550-acre site twice. But each year more than 1.5 million people tour the primeval redwood

Sun filtering through a virgin stand of coastal redwoods at Muir Woods National Monument. —*George A. Grant, NPS photograph*

forest, paying homage to the outdoorsman and the natural world he labored so hard to preserve.

At the turn of the century, conservationist William Kent raised $45,000 to buy the woods, saving the redwoods in what is now Muir Woods from the axe. He donated the land to the U.S. government in 1907 to save the site from being flooded for a reservoir.

One of the earliest attractions in the area was a train known as

"The Crookedest Railroad in the World." This train, which operated from 1907 to 1930, took sightseers from Mill Valley to a tavern at the top of Mount Tamalpais. The route had 281 curves. "Gravity cars," four-wheeled vehicles that coasted down the mountain side using only gravity, brought people from the summit to Muir Woods.

Redwoods may be the main reason for visiting Muir Woods but the park offers many other natural delights. Red alder, azalea, and California laurel thrive in the park. Black-tailed deer, Western gray squirrels, and Sonoma chipmunks scamper about. In winter, silver salmon and steelhead trout spawn in Redwood Creek. The creek and fish are protected so fishing is not allowed.

Easily accessible from San Francisco, Muir Woods is an extremely popular spot. So popular, in fact, that the 200-space parking lot fills up early in the day. For this reason, park rangers recommend that visitors arrive before 11 a.m. or after 4 p.m.

There is no picnicking in the park but tourists can purchase food at a concession stand. Camping is available in Mount Tamalpais State Park, which surrounds Muir Woods.

Open: 8 a.m. to dusk.

Fees: None.

Mailing Address: Muir Woods National Monument, Mill Valley, CA 94941.

Telephone: 415-388-2595.

Getting There: Muir woods is 17 miles north of San Francisco. Greyline Tours and Dolphin Tours run charter bus service from San Francisco. By car from San Francisco, cross the Golden Gate Bridge and take Rt. 101 to Shoreline Highway. Following the signs, turn right onto Panoramic Highway and travel north to Muir Woods Road, which leads into the park.

‖ Pinnacles National Monument

Above the scrub brush and chaparral south of Salinas rise the jagged outcroppings of Pinnacles National Monument. Pinnacles' peaks and spires, remnants of ancient volcanos, make the park a favorite place for rock climbing and exploring the talus caves. The park's rock outcroppings, some of them 600 feet high, are connected by 26 miles of trails.

There are two separate sections in the 16,221-acre park. Bear Gulch is on the east and Chaparral on the west, and no road links them. The east side has a visitor center and facilities while the west side has only a ranger station.

Wildlife in the park includes mule deer, bobcats, golden eagles, prairie falcons, and hawks. The visitor center has an exhibit illustrating the movement of the volcanic formations along the San Andreas fault. The fault itself lies east of the monument.

Vegetation is sparse in the arid, hardscrabble lands one finds here, and fires are a constant hazard. For this reason, no backcountry camping is allowed. Competition for the park's 23 walk-in sites on the west side is intense, especially during weekends, and reservations are not accepted so plan to arrive early if you want a space. There is no parking for motor homes or trailers. Pinnacles Campground Incorporated, a private campground, is located in the east side off Route 146 and has family and group sites with some electrical hookups. Other amenities include showers, a swimming pool, and a store.

The Monument is open all year, although most visitors go to the park in fall and spring, when the climate is mild. Summers are so hot that daytime temperatures can reach 100 degrees or more; hikers should bring at least two quarts of water per person and a flashlight, which is essential for going through the caves. Winters are rainy.

Caves are closed occasionally after earthquakes and heavy rains for monitoring of rock movement. Prior training and proper equipment are strongly recommended for any rock climbing. The park does offer occasional talks on local geology and wildlife.

Open: The monument is open 24 hours. The east-side Visitor Center is open daily, hours subject to change. The west-side ranger station is open weekends and holidays and occasionally during the week.

Fees: $3 per car, $1 a person.

Mailing Address: Pinnacles National Monument, Paicines, CA 95043.

Telephone: 408-389-4485.

Getting There: From San Jose, take Rt. 101 south to Soledad, and exit on Rt. 146 to the Chaparral ranger station on the west side. Or turn off onto Rt. 25 south through Hollister, continue 30 miles south from Hollister to Rt. 146. Follow Rt. 146 to the Bear Gulch visitor center on the east side. [There is no road connecting the two sides of the monument.]

|| San Francisco Maritime National Historical Park

This new park, which interprets West Coast maritime history, boasts the largest (by tonnage) collection of historic ships in the United States. Originally part of the Golden Gate National Recreational Area, the unit was recently established at the western edge of Fisherman's Wharf in San Francisco so the staff could concentrate on preserving historic ships. The vessels in the collection include the *Eureka, C.A. Thayer, Balclutha, Hercules, Eppleton Hall, Alma,* and *Wapama.*

The *Eureka*, a ferry built by the North Pacific Rail Road Company in 1890, is a 300-foot-long boat used to transport passengers and rail cars across San Francisco Bay. It was refitted to carry cars in 1922. The *Thayer* is a West Coast lumber schooner built in 1895 to carry lumber from the Pacific Northwest to the growing cities of California. It was also used for cod fishing in the Barents Sea.

Perhaps the most beautiful ship in the collection is the *Balclutha*, a square-rigged Cape Horn sailing ship launched from Scotland in 1886. It is typical of the "Deep Waterman" vessels that sailed to San Francisco bringing coal, wine, and hardware from Europe, returning with California grain.

Also part of the park is the Maritime Museum, which has a collection of ship models and artifacts from the California whaling and gold rush days and an art and photo gallery. The J. Porter Shaw Library collection, located in the museum, has 14,000 volumes of maritime history, oral history, and historic documents relating to ships and shipping.

Located just across the street from Ghiradelli Square, the Maritime Museum building was built in 1939 by the Works Progress Administration and is a classic example of 1930s art deco architecture.

Open: 10 a.m. to 5 p.m. daily, November to May, extended to 6 p.m. in summer. Closed Christmas and New Year's Day.

Fees: $2 ages 17–61.

Mailing Address: San Francisco Maritime National Historical Park, Building 201, Fort Mason, San Francisco, CA 94123.

Telephone: 415-556-3002.

Getting There: The park is located at the corner of Jefferson and Hyde streets, at the western edge of Fisherman's Wharf. Fisherman's Wharf is a prime tourist attraction in San Francisco.

COLORADO

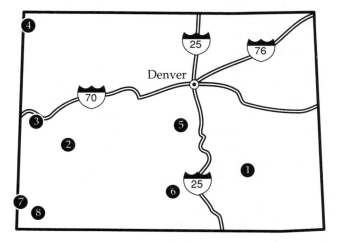

1. Bent's Old Fort National Historic Site
2. Black Canyon of the Gunnison National
   Monument
3. Colorado National Monument
4. Dinosaur National Monument
5. Florissant Fossil Beds National Monument
6. Great Sand Dunes National Monument
7. Hovenweep National Monument
8. Yucca House National Monument

‖ Bent's Old Fort National Historic Site

This reconstructed adobe fort in southeastern Colorado was an important stop along the Santa Fe Trail in the early 1800s and a gathering point for the merchants who traded on the Southwestern frontier. During that bygone era, Bent's Old Fort was a bustling commercial center and a friendly meeting ground where rival Indian tribes could come together in peace.

In the frontier days, full-time workers at the fort numbered 15 to 60 people, including cooks, craftsmen, and Hispanic and Native American women. Visitors can tour rooms that have been refurnished—some with replica period furniture—to look as it did in 1846. There is even a billiard room, considered an extraordinary luxury at the time.

Today, a living history program operates year-round to preserve this early atmosphere. Between Memorial Day and Labor Day, interpreters dress in period costumes to demonstrate adobe making, blacksmithing, carpentry, trading, cooking, and other frontier skills. An antique Conestoga wagon and a reproduction of the same wagon convey the feel of life on the Santa Fe Trail.

The video film room has a 20-minute film on the site's history, including the three entrepreneurs—the brothers Charles and William Bent and Ceran St. Vrain—who founded the fort. These men traded manufactured goods from around the world for animal pelts, Indian tanned buffalo robes, and Mexican mules. William Bent was on such good terms with the Cheyenne Indians that he married Owl Woman, the daughter of Chief Gray Thunder, keeper of the tribe's medicine arrows. In 1846 Susan Magoffin, the first white women to travel the Santa Fe Trail, passed through the fort. The business prospered until the U.S. army moved into the area in the late 1840s.

Bent's Old Fort celebrates July 4th with authentic speeches, period games, demonstrations, and an old-time supper. During early September there is a Fur Trade Encampment. The four-day festival, open to the public, features lectures, demonstrations, historical vignettes, and hundreds of authentically clad volunteers to help you take a step back in time.

Open: 8 a.m. to 4:30 p.m. from Labor Day to Memorial Day, extended to 6 p.m. in summer.

Fees: $3 per car, $1 per person in bus, on foot, or on horseback.

Mailing Address: Bent's Old Fort National Historic Site, 35110 Highway 194 East, La Junta, CO 81050.

Telephone: 719-384-2596.

Getting There: The site is located in southeast Colorado, six miles from La Junta. From Pueblo, take Rt. 50 east about 60 miles to La Junta. Go through the town following signs for Highway 109. Follow 109 north to Highway 194 east and go six miles to the park entrance, which will be on your right.

‖ Black Canyon of the Gunnison National Monument

Black Canyon of the Gunnison, a savage gash through the high mesas of western Colorado, is one of the most rugged, dramatic, and breathtaking canyons in the country.

Sheer walls of dark gray rock descend half a mile into the earth, blocking the sun and leaving much of the gorge in perpetual shadow. The roaring, churning Gunnison, one of the nation's few remaining unspoiled wild rivers, snakes below while eagles, hawks, and peregrine falcons circle in the updrafts above. In natural beauty, if not scope, this formation rivals the Grand Canyon.

The monument follows the course of the Gunnison River for 12 miles, encompassing the most spectacular parts of the canyon. At its narrowest point, the canyon's north and south rims are only 1,300 feet apart and the floor of the canyon is only 40 feet wide.

From Dragon Point at the south rim, you can view the extraordinary Painted Wall—a bare outcropping of dark rock with pink intrusions that look like Chinese dragons.

Campgrounds, visitor centers, and hiking trails are available at both the north and south rims. Although it is possible for experienced rock climbers to descend into the bottom of the canyon, there are no marked trails. Anyone attempting the arduous climb down the gorge should be in excellent physical condition and have all the necessary equipment. All climbers must register with the park before and after climbs and all hikers must obtain a permit.

Both the north and south rims have roads that lead to the very edge of the canyon. On the south rim there are 12 overlooks with interpretive signs. Rangers conduct three nature walks daily in the summer and demonstrate rock climbing techniques on Sundays. In the evenings, there are campfire programs about the region's unique geology.

The monument's two campgrounds have over 100 sites (most of them are on the south rim) and take visitors on a first-come, first-served basis. Fees are collected during spring, summer, and fall. Water is shut off when the freezing weather arrives in October. The campground on the south rim has facilities for trailers and recreational vehicles. Wood gathering is not permitted in the park, so bring your own cooking fuel. Be sparing with the water, which must be hauled into the monument by truck.

Wildlife in the 20,700-acre monument includes everything from weasels and badgers to black bears, bobcats, and cougars. Fishing requires a state license.

The gaping chasm of the Black Canyon was formed as the Gunnison River cut its way through the mesas over the past two million years. Ute Indians had long lived near the canyon rims, but white men did not discover the chasm until 1874.

Open: Visitor Centers: 8 a.m. to 4:30 p.m. daily, from Labor Day to Memorial Day. The north rim is closed all winter. The south rim is open all year. Check with ranger for exact dates.

Fees: $3 per car and $1 per person.

Mailing Address: Black Canyon of the Gunnison National Monument, P.O. Box 1648, Montrose, CO 81402-1648.

Telephone: 303-249-7036.

Getting There: The monument is located in west central Colorado, 15 miles east of Montrose via Rt. 50 and Rt. 347. Airlines and buses serve Montrose. To get to the north rim, use either Rt. 50 or Rt. 92 west through Curecanti National Recreation Area, a 90-mile drive. Or use Rt. 50 west and Rt. 92 east through Delta to Crawford and take the graveled road from there to the north rim, an 80-mile trip.

‖ Colorado National Monument

Colorado National Monument, in western Colorado, is one of the finest examples of canyon land in the country, with 20,450 acres of canyons, unusual rock formations, dinosaur fossils, and prehistoric Indian relics.

A wide variety of hiking trails vein the scrub-stippled canyons and mesas. One of the most interesting trails is the Serpents Trail, which slowly ascends into the high country over 54 switchbacks. Another favorite is the short trek to Devils Kitchen, a name that was inspired by the area's curious rock formations. For those who prefer the comfort of a car, there is Rim Rock Trail. This paved road skirts the edge of the highland and affords striking views of striped orange canyons and ribbed gulches.

One of the more popular attractions here is Independence Monument, a 350-foot-tall, free-standing rock that rises out of the canyon like a giant stalagmite. The red sandstone rock is held together by a hard cap of Kayenta sandstone. An easy-to-hike, 5.5-mile trail winds past Kissing Couple, Squaw Fingers, and other interesting formations and leads to Independence Monument.

Colorado National Monument is a favorite among amateur and professional geologists because its display of rock layers is similar in scope to that of the Grand Canyon and considerably more accessible. In addition to the spectacular geology, visitors can also see carvings and rock paintings, known as petroglyphs, created by prehistoric Indians who lived in the region. The visitor center has an exhibit of dinosaur fossils quarried from the surrounding areas, including a replica of an eight-foot legbone from an 80-foot Brachiosaurus.

Most of the park is backcountry, open to all for camping and exploration with few restrictions. Open fires are prohibited. Free passes to use the park's undeveloped areas are available from the ranger. There is also an 84-site campground near the visitor center.

Park wildlife includes mule deer, elk, mountain lions, and bighorn sheep. Plants range from sagebrush and cactus in the more arid sections to pine and juniper at higher elevations. Elevations range from 4,700 to 7,100 feet. The monument is at an average elevation of 5,000 feet. In winter, when dry snow covers the ground, the cross-country skiing is excellent.

Open: Visitor Center: 8 a.m. to 4:30 p.m. in winter, extended to 8 p.m. in summer. Check for dates. The park is open year-round.

Fees: $3 per car, $1 per person.

Mailing Address: Colorado National Monument, Fruita, CO 81521.

Telephone: 303-858-3617.

Getting There: The park is located in west central Colorado near

Grand Junction. From Grand Junction, follow signs west on Grand Avenue to Highway 340 and Monument Road to the East entrance, about four miles. From Fruita, follow Highway 340 South across Colorado River to the West entrance, about 2.5 miles.

‖ Dinosaur National Monument

The largest known Jurassic Period dinosaur quarry in the world is in the high desert of northeastern Utah, where the Yampa and Green Rivers meet in a spectacular swirl of white water. Fossil bones from ten species of these enormous ancient beasts have been found preserved in the park's sandstone quarry. Dinosaur fossils exhibited at the monument include the bony-plated Stegosaurus, the long-necked Brontosaurus, and the meat-eating Allosaurus.

The Dinosaur Quarry visitor center in northeastern Utah abuts one side of a bone-bearing cliff and provides an uncommonly close look at the natural bas-relief of bone in stone.

Beyond the quarry, the park covers more than 211,000 acres of some of the most spectacular canyon land in the country. Over the centuries, the Yampa and Green rivers cut their way through the layers of rock, creating rapids, whirlpools, and breathtaking overlooks.

Seven hiking trails, ranging in length from less than a mile to 8½ miles, wind through the rugged terrain offering spectacular views. Harpers Corner Scenic Drive goes to the heart of the Y-shaped park at the confluence of the Green and Yampa. There are also challenging primitive roads accessible only to high-clearance vehicles. Check with the ranger about local conditions before exploring on your own.

The Green and Yampa rivers are great for rafting. Local outfitters offer one- to six-day trips from late spring to early fall, depending on the river level. Contact the park for a list of outfitters. For those who like to arrange their own rafting adventures, the park holds a lottery for the 300 free permits they give out each year. To apply, send an application to Park Service headquarters between December 1 and January 15. Motorized boats are prohibited. If you plan to run your own rafting trip, you'll need to submit a list of your party members and an itinerary. Carry drinking water and fuel with you.

There are six drive-in campgrounds with a total of 175 sites that are available for overnight use. The Green River and Split Mountain camping areas are located about four miles east of the Dinosaur Quarry. Gas, food, supplies and lodging are available in nearby Jensen (UT), Dinosaur (CO), Rangely (CO), and Vernal (UT).

Wildlife in the area includes bighorn sheep, mule deer, black bears, and mountain lions as well as prairie dogs, rattlesnakes, eagles, and peregrine falcons. Catfish and pike can be caught in the rivers but a license is required. Throughout the summer, rangers conduct quarry talks, guided walks, and Young Naturalist activities for children.

Open: The park is open year-round. The Headquarters Visitor Center is open 8 a.m. to 4:30 p.m. in winter. Closed weekends and daily in summer. The Dinosaur Quarry Visitor Center is open 8 a.m. to 4:30 p.m. daily, extended to 7 p.m. in summer. Closed Thanksgiving, Christmas, and New Year's Day.

Fees: $5 per vehicle, good for seven days.

Mailing Address: Dinosaur National Monument, P.O. Box 210, Dinosaur, CO 81610.

Telephone: 303-374-2216.

Getting There: The monument is located in the northwestern corner of Colorado and the northeastern corner of Utah. Take Rt. 40 west from Craig, CO. Monument Headquarters is located on the right just outside of Dinosaur, CO. To get to the Dinosaur Quarry and campgrounds, continue on Rt. 40 to Jensen, UT, and turn right onto Rt. 149, which leads into the park.

‖ Florissant Fossil Beds National Monument

Florissant Fossil Beds, located in the mountains of central Colorado, is one of the world's richest sources of insect fossils. The shale—part of an immense ancient lake bed formed from volcanic activity—has yielded more than 80,000 fossils of extinct insects and plants. Among these are detailed "carbon copies" of the delicate dragonflys, beetles, spiders, and plants that inhabited the ancient lake bed at Florissant 35 million years ago.

Most of Florissant's fossils are in museums and research institutions, but about 400 of them are on display in the visitor center. In addition to these fossil impressions, formed when ash and cinders from nearby volcanoes swept the insects into the lake-bottom silt, seven petrified trees were unearthed in the park. Although Florissant was once a commercial business where people could dig their own fossils, visitors are no longer allowed to take artifacts from the area.

Florissant comes from the French for "flowering," and it is little wonder. In spring and summer, Florissant explodes in a riot of wild-flowers: Indian paintbrush, locoweed, senecio, scarlet gilia, wild iris, shooting stars, and columbines bloom among the grasses. In summer, rangers conduct one-hour tours. Mule deer, rabbits, coyotes, bobcats, and smaller mammals inhabit the park, and, in winter, roaming herds of elk can be seen.

Facilities are still being developed at this relatively recent addition to the park service. Currently, there are two self-guided trails: The "Walk Through Time Trail" runs .4 miles through a forest with petri-fied tree stumps and the one-mile "Petrified Forest Loop" goes through a wooded area and meadow. In addition to the self-guided trails, other trails include the "Sawmill Trail," which is an easy two-mile hike (the sawmill, however, is gone); and the "Hornbek Wildlife Loop," which includes the Hornbek Homestead built in 1875 by Adeline Hornbek. The homestead consists of the Hornbek house, hired hands' quarters, a stable and barn, and a fantastic root cellar built into the side of a hill. Check at the visitor center for information about tours.

The park visitor center has an excellent display of fossils, including delicate impressions of prehistoric bees in shale along with early fern, pinecone, hickory nut, and sequoia fossils. You cannot buy or collect fossils at Florissant.

There are no overnight facilities here, but several campgrounds are within ten miles of the monument. Check with the ranger if you plan to hike in the backcountry. Fires are prohibited. Cross-country ski-ing is excellent in winter, when the snow cover is about a foot deep. During spring visits to the monument, beware of ticks that can carry Rocky Mountain Spotted Fever.

Open: 8 a.m. to 4:30 p.m. from mid-Sept. to mid-June, extended to 7 p.m. in summer. Closed Thanksgiving, Christmas and New Year's Day.

Fees: $3 per vehicle.

Mailing Address: Florissant Fossil Beds National Monument, P.O. Box 185, Florissant, CO 80816.

Telephone: 303-748-3253.

Getting There: From Denver, go south on I-25 to Colorado Springs, and 35 miles west on Highway 24. Follow this road to Florissant, then turn south onto Teller County Road. Follow signs for two miles to the park entrance.

| Great Sand Dunes National Monument

America's biggest sandbox is not along the Atlantic or Pacific Ocean but at Great Sand Dunes National Monument in south central Colorado. This land-locked sea of sand at the foot of the rugged Sangre de Cristo Mountains covers 155 square miles. Visitors can trek through the dunes, wander in nearby prairie flats, rumble over rough country in four-wheel drive vehicles, or hike in the surrounding snow-capped mountains.

Debris from the glacier that covered the area in the last Ice Age, along with debris left by the Rio Grande as it changed its course, created this extraordinary sand pile. The southwesterly winds that have barreled through the Sangre de Cristos for the past 15,000 years continue to shape it, sculpting the surface of the ever-shifting field of dunes.

Sometimes the winds, which can reach 120 miles per hour, blow with such force that the sand literally screams. According to local lore, the screaming is made by a lonely shepherd looking for the shepherdess and the flock that were buried during a sandstorm.

A hike from the visitor center to the tallest dune and back takes 1½ to 3 hours. Beware of the heat. In midday, the summer sun can heat the sand to 140 degrees, hot enough to blister unprotected feet and inflict heat and sun stroke. Plan your exploring for early morning or late in the day. Bring boots, sunscreen, and plenty of water to drink. And watch children closely.

Wildlife in the park includes camel crickets, deer, eagles, and songbirds. The park is a favorite among bird-watchers. Piñon pines, juniper, and shrubs grow in the high valley and tufts of grasses grow in the dunes. Fishing in the Mendano Creek requires a state license.

The shifting sands of Great Sand Dunes National Monument create striking landscapes.—*NPS photograph*

The park's one campground has a total of 88 sites available for two-week stays. Two additional backcountry sites are reserved for hikers. Get a free backcountry permit from the ranger for access to these spots. Firewood gathering is not allowed, so bring fuel or buy it from a concessionaire during summer.

The rangers offer guided nature hikes daily and nightly campfire programs, lasting from one to two hours, from Memorial Day to Labor Day.

Open: Park is open year-round. Visitor Center: 8 a.m. to 8 p.m. in summer (subject to change), and 8 a.m. to 5 p.m. in winter. Closed federal holidays in winter.

Fees: $3 per vehicle, $1 a person ages 16 to 61, from May 1 to Sept. 30.

Mailing Address: Great Sand Dunes National Monument, 11500 Highway 150, Mosca, CO 81146.

Telephone: 719-378-2312.

Getting There: The park is located 38 miles northeast of Alamosa in south central Colorado. From Denver, take I-25 to Walsenburg, turn right onto U.S. 160, and right onto State 150 to the dunes.

‖ Hovenweep National Monument

Ruined pueblos, 20-foot-high walls, and tumbled piles of masonry are all that remain of the pueblos built by the pre-Columbian Indians who farmed Hovenweep's canyons in southern Colorado's "Four Corners" area 700 years ago.

Named for the Ute Indian word meaning "deserted valley," Hovenweep is made up of six clusters of ruins, four in Colorado and two in Utah. Mostly, these ruins are square and circular towers made of Dakota sandstone and mortar. (Most of the original mortar is gone. New mortar was added over the years.) The best preserved and most extensive of these are at the Square Tower Unit, reachable by a self-guided trail.

Similar ruins in Colorado—Holly, Hackberry/Horseshoe Canyon, Cutthroat Castle, and Goodman Point—as well as Cajon in Utah are isolated and can be reached by car. Four-wheel drive vehicles may be necessary in mud or snow.

The Anasazi Indians, hunter-gatherers who became increasingly reliant on agriculture, started to farm the area 2,000 years ago. They raised corn, beans, squash, and domestic turkeys. In the late 1200s, a severe drought struck the region and by 1300, the sites were abandoned. Pioneer photographer William H. Jackson visited the area in 1874 and named it Hovenweep.

Wildlife in the park includes rodents, coyotes, rattlesnakes, and birds. Temperatures are extreme and variable. In summer, temperatures can range from the 100s during the day to the 50s at night; in winter, temperatures can dip below zero.

Monument headquarters at the Square Tower Group has a 31-site campground with only a few sites filled each night. The campground has comfort stations and will accommodate trailers, but it does not have hookups or supplies. The closest sources of supplies are at Hatch Trading Post, 16 miles west, and Ismay Trading Post, 14 miles south. The dirt roads through the monument are often impassable after storms. For a daily road report, call 303-529-4461.

Open: 8 a.m. to 5 p.m. all year.
Fees: None.
Mailing Address: Hovenweep National Monument, McElmo Route, Cortez, CO 81321.

Telephone: No phone.

Getting There: The monument is located in southwestern Colorado. From Durango, take Rt. 160 west to Cortez, turn south on Rt. 666, and turn right onto the McElmo Canyon Road that leads to the monument. It is 43 miles to the monument on paved, dirt, and gravel roads. An alternative route goes north from Cortez on Rt. 666 and turns left on a gravel road one mile south of Pleasant View, CO. Follow gravel and dirt roads for 25 miles to the monument. Both routes are well marked by signs.

‖ Yucca House National Monument

The unexcavated ruins of this prehistoric Indian village, now open to the public, are but a collection of mounds with no visible man-made features. It is believed that this monument will yield much archeological information when it is developed. You can get directions to the ten-acre site from the superintendent at Mesa Verde National Park.

Discovered by Professor William H. Holmes in 1877, the monument has lain fallow since it became part of the Park Service in 1919. The most prominent mound rises 15 to 20 feet above its foundation and is surrounded by the smaller mounds. A spring provided water to the village. To build their settlement, the Indians hauled limestone from the surrounding area.

Yucca House is located 15 miles south of Cortez, Colorado, on a dirt road that is virtually impassable when wet.

For more information, contact the superintendent at Mesa Verde National Park, Mesa Verde, CO 81330. Telephone: 303-529-4465.

DISTRICT OF COLUMBIA

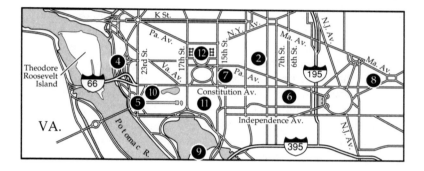

1. Bethune Museum and Archives National Historic Site—*see map on p. 80*
2. Ford's Theatre National Historic Site
3. Frederick Douglass Home—*see map on p. 80*
4. John F. Kennedy Center for the Performing Arts
5. Lincoln Memorial
6. National Mall
7. Pennsylvania Avenue National Historic Site
8. Sewall-Belmont House National Historic Site
9. Thomas Jefferson Memorial
10. Vietnam Veterans Memorial
11. Washington Monument
12. White House

|| Bethune Museum and Archives National Historic Site

Mary McLeod Bethune, political activist, presidential advisor, and educator, lived and worked in this four-story, second-empire Victorian town house in Washington, D.C. The house also served as the headquarters of the National Council of Negro Women, which Bethune founded in 1935. She was unanimously elected the group's first president.

Bethune was born in 1876, the 15th of 17 children, on the McLeod Plantation in Mayesville, South Carolina. Beginning her career as an educator, she established the Daytona Normal School for Negro Girls, which later become Bethune-Cookman College.

From this start, Bethune went on to become involved in national politics through the National Child Welfare Commission under Presidents Calvin Coolidge and Herbert Hoover. She was director of President Franklin D. Roosevelt's Division of Negro Affairs from 1939–1944 and was a friend of Eleanor Roosevelt. Although particularly interested in the rights of black women in America, Bethune fought for the rights of all disenfranchised peoples in America and abroad.

The tradition of awareness, education, and activism that Bethune helped cultivate is enshrined and carried on by the historic site. You will not find Bethune's personal belongings and furniture on display. Instead, the exhibits feature black women who have made major contributions to American society, the Civil Rights movement, and to the solidarity of black women. These exhibits are designed to enlighten and awaken the same sense of activism that motivated Bethune.

The carriage house in the backyard contains the Bethune Archives, the world's largest collection of materials documenting the accomplishments and political activity of black women in America. Open for scholarly research only, the archives hold the records of national black women's organizations that made valuable contributions.

Visitors may wander through the museum exhibits on their own. Guided tours for groups can be arranged.

Open: 10 a.m. to 4:30 p.m., Monday through Friday. Closed some major holidays. Access to the Archives is by appointment only.

Fees: General Membership, contact the site for information.

Mailing Address: Bethune Museum and Archives National Historic Site, 1318 Vermont Ave, N.W., Washington, DC 20005.
Telephone: 202-332-1233.
Getting There: The house is located near the White House in downtown Washington, DC, between Logan and Thomas circles.

‖ Ford's Theatre National Historic Site

This 19th-century theater, forever remembered as the place where President Abraham Lincoln was shot by John Wilkes Booth on April 14, 1865, has been historically re-created, right down to the wallpaper. The box in which Lincoln and his party sat is arranged exactly as it was on that fateful day: The railings are festooned with flags, the balustrade is adorned with an original engraving of George Washington, and a reproduction of the rocking chair in which the president sat is empty.

Abraham Lincoln had been enjoying a performance of "Our American Cousin" when assassin John Wilkes Booth fired the fatal shot. Pandemonium broke out in the theater as Booth, a Southern sympathizer, leaped to the stage shouting *"Sic semper tyrannis"* ("Thus always to tyrants"). Booth broke his leg as he jumped from the stage. He hobbled out of the theater, mounted a horse, and fled to Maryland. Lincoln, who lay unconscious in his box, was carried across the muddy street to the home of William Petersen, where he died the next morning.

After the Lincoln assassination the theater closed and was converted to a government office space. A second tragedy occurred on June 9, 1893, when the third floor collapsed, killing and injuring many government workers. The building seemed jinxed. It was used for storage until it was refurbished in 1968 and opened to the public as an active theater and a shrine to Abraham Lincoln.

Today Ford's Theatre is an extremely popular spot with more than 500,000 visitors each year, so expect crowds and arrive early. Six times daily, rangers give 15-minute historical talks on the building and the assassination. Visitors may also wander on their own through the orchestra area and presidential box upstairs, which is cordoned off.

The House Where Lincoln Died is directly across from the theater

President Abraham Lincoln was assassinated in Ford's Theatre on April 14, 1865. The theater has been restored and is still operating today. —*NPS photograph*

at 516 Tenth Street, N.W. Three rooms on the first floor are open: the bedroom where the unconscious president lay, the back parlor where Secretary of War Edwin M. Stanton interviewed witnesses, and the front parlor, where Mary Todd Lincoln and her son Robert waited through the grim night. Like Ford's Theatre, the small rooms of this modest house have been restored as accurately as possible.

In mid-April and mid-September, the Surratt Society, which preserves the house of Mary Surratt, a Marylander who was convicted as Booth's co-conspirator and hanged, leads tours of John Wilkes Booth's attempted escape route through southern Maryland. The 12-hour tours are booked months in advance. Contact the Surratt Society at 9110 Brandywine Road, Clinton, Maryland 20735. Telephone: 301-868-1121.

Another organization offering escape-route tours during April and

September is Marker Tours. Marker runs several excellent tours, including a historical night tour of the city; a visit to Washington's old cemeteries; a trip along Route 40, the Old National Road in Maryland; and the Lincoln Heritage Trail tour to Lincoln sites in Kentucky, Illinois, and Indiana. Contact: Joan Chaconas, Marker Tours, 9102 Cheltenham Drive, Brandywine, Maryland 20613. Telephone: 301-372-6945.

Open: 9 a.m. to 5 p.m. daily. Closed Christmas Day and during performances and rehearsals on Thursdays, Saturdays, and Sundays. Call before coming.

Fees: None. The Surratt tour (not a Park Service offering) costs about $22 a person; Marker Tours cost about $25 a person.

Mailing Address: Ford's Theatre National Historic Site, 511 Tenth Street, N.W., Washington, DC 20004.

Telephone: 202-426-6924; TDD 202-426-1749.

Getting There: The theater is on Tenth Street in downtown Washington. From the Metro Center subway stop, walk south on 11th Street to F Street, then east along F Street one block to Tenth Street. The theater is located on Tenth between E and F streets.

‖ Frederick Douglass Home

Abolitionist, statesman, and former slave Frederick Douglass lived in his Victorian house overlooking the U.S. Capitol from 1877 until he died in 1895. Douglass' second wife, Helen Pitts Douglass, a white woman, worked to preserve the house intact and most of the furnishings are original.

Born Frederick Augustus Washington Bailey, a slave in Talbot County, Maryland, Douglass escaped to freedom in Massachusetts in 1838. He then married under the name Johnson, later changing his surname to Douglass from a character in Sir Walter Scott's *Lady of the Lake*. An active abolitionist, Douglass fled to England in 1845 after revealing he was an escaped slave in his book *Narrative of the Life of Frederick Douglass, An American Slave*. The move was fortunate: Friends helped buy his freedom, enabling Douglass to return to the United States and continue his anti-slavery activities.

During the turmoil of reconstruction after the Civil War, Douglass

1. Bethune Museum and Archives National Historic Site
3. Frederick Douglass Home

worked to give blacks a political voice. He became one of the most respected blacks of his time. He served in numerous public offices in Washington, D.C., and was appointed counsel-general to Haiti. When he moved into his D.C. home, called Cedar Hill, Douglass was the first black man in the neighborhood. He died here on February 20, 1895.

Cedar Hill is little changed from the time when Frederick Douglass lived here. Tours of the house, given as guests arrive, last 30 minutes and take visitors through 14 rooms, including Douglass' library of 1,200 books. Much of the furniture is original, and there are several unique photographs and lithographs. In the backyard is the "Growlery," a quiet place where Douglass retreated to think and write. The visitor center has a film about Douglass' life and contributions; a museum features exhibits on people—like Harriet Tubman and Ulysses S. Grant—who influenced Douglass' philosophy. Other exhibits include Douglass' walking stick, deathmask, and quotes from his speeches. "To those who have suffered in slavery I can say I, too, have suffered . . . to those who have battled for liberty, brotherhood, and citizenship I can say, I, too, have battled," is one of his best known utterances.

During Christmas and on the weekend nearest September 15, Douglass' wedding anniversary, the house is open for refreshments and evening candlelight tours. A wreath-laying ceremony commemorates his birthday on February 14. (After his death, Douglass was buried in Rochester, New York, where he once lived and published a newspaper.)

Open: 8 a.m. to 4 p.m. daily in winter and 9 a.m. to 5 p.m. from April 15 to Labor Day. Closed Thanksgiving, Christmas, and New Year's Day.

Fees: None.

Mailing Address: Frederick Douglass Home, 1411 W Street S.E., Washington, DC 20020.

Telephone: 202-426-5960.

Getting There: From downtown Washington, cross the 11th Street Bridge and go south on Martin Luther King, Jr. Avenue to W Street. Turn left and continue four blocks to the Visitor Center. From I-295, take the Pennsylvania Avenue exit and go east two blocks to Minnesota Avenue. Turn right on Good Hope Road, then left at 14th Street and continue to W Street. The B5 Mount Rainier Metrobus also stops by the site.

‖ John F. Kennedy Center for the Performing Arts

Each time the lights dim and the performance begins at this national cultural center, it is a living tribute to former President John F. Kennedy. The Kennedy administration was dedicated to enriching the country's cultural life. Since its opening in 1971, the Kennedy Center has hosted performances of classical and avant-garde art by some of the finest actors, dancers, and musicians in the world, as well as by emerging young artists from across the country.

Each of the Kennedy Center's six theaters is unique in style and bears the gifts of the many nations who contributed to the project. The Opera House has a red-and-gold silk stage curtain from Japan and a star-burst chandelier from Austria; the Concert Hall, known for its excellent acoustics, is decorated in a frosty gold and white and contains crystal chandeliers from Norway; the Eisenhower Theater curtain was a gift from Canada. Upstairs, the intimate Terrace Theater donated by the Japanese government is decorated in warm pinks and purples. The American Film Institute Theater near the Hall of States entrance shows classic American and foreign movies. The Grand Foyer, where theater-goers relax between acts, is adorned with mirrors from Belgium, chandeliers from Sweden, a bronze bust of President Kennedy sculpted by American artist Robert Berks, and marble from Italy.

Designed by Edward Durell Stone, the Kennedy Center is an enormous building, measuring two football fields long and 300 feet wide, with an overall height of 142 feet. Ceilings on the main floor are 65 feet high. In the Hall of States, the names of donors are inscribed on the walls, and the flags of the United States and its territories hang in the order in which they entered the Union. In the Hall of Nations, the flags of countries recognized diplomatically by the United States are hung in alphabetical order.

The very best way to see the Kennedy Center is to attend a performance. There are also free 45- to 50-minute tours of the building offered daily from 10 a.m. to 1 p.m. Tours leave from Parking Level A as groups form. No reservations are necessary. Visitors can also obtain passes for a special 9:30 tour from their congressmen. The tours take visitors through the major halls, and the auditoriums and reception rooms if no performances or rehearsals are underway. The broad roof terrace offers a terrific panorama of the Washington skyline, the Potomac River, and the northern Virginia palisades. Four restaurants —The Roof Terrace, Hors d'Oeuverie, Curtain Call Cafe, and Encore Cafeteria—accommodate all types of diners, from those seeking an elegant, formal meal to those wishing a quick, inexpensive snack. Hours vary. For information and reservations, call 202-416-8555.

Open: 10 a.m. until half an hour after last performance ends, daily.

Fees: None for tours; ticket prices for performances vary; check with the box office.

Mailing Address: The John F. Kennedy Center for the Performing Arts, Washington, DC 20566.

Telephone: General information, 202-467-4600. Instant Charge: 202-467-4600 or 800-444-1324.

Getting There: The Kennedy Center is in Washington, DC, near the Watergate complex. Parking is available for a fee. Or take the subway to the Foggy Bottom Metro stop, walk south along 23rd Street for 3 blocks and northwest along Virginia Avenue for 1½ blocks.

‖ Lincoln Memorial

Perched on a bluff above the Potomac River is the Lincoln Memorial. Inside this white marble monument, modeled after the Parthenon in Athens, Greece, is a seated statue of Abraham Lincoln, 16th president of the United States. His expression is one of deep contemplation, as if he were musing on the words of his Gettysburg Address which are carved into the walls of the memorial chamber. Delivered during the Civil War on November 19, 1863, the speech was an eloquent plea for unity, "that government of the people, by the people, and for the people shall not perish from the earth."

Part temple, part monument, the Lincoln Memorial combines grandeur and simplicity into one of the most impressive memorials in the country. The harmony and unity of its classical design symbolizes the Union that Lincoln struggled to preserve. Thirty-six Doric marble columns surrounding the walls represent the 36 states of the Union at the time of Lincoln's death; state names are carved into the frieze.

The 19-foot-high seated statue of Abraham Lincoln, which dominates the Lincoln Memorial, was sculpted by Daniel Chester French.
—*NPS photograph*

Above these are the names of the 48 states in the Union when the monument was built in 1922.

The statue of Lincoln himself, sculpted of Georgia white marble by Daniel Chester French, sits in the monument's center with Lincoln gazing toward the Washington Monument. His proportions are enormous. He measures 19 feet by 19 feet; if he were standing, his figure would be 28 feet tall. Flanking the great man are marble inscriptions of his two best-known speeches, the Gettysburg Address and the Second Inaugural Address, along with allegorical murals that portray national unity and the freeing of the slaves. In the foreground, a 2,000-foot-long, 160-foot-wide reflecting pool stretches like a carpet of water.

Although Congress incorporated the Lincoln Monument Association in 1867, two years after Lincoln's death, the ground was not broken until 1914. The spot was chosen on dredged land known as West Potomac Park, which lay on an axis with the Washington Monument and the Capitol Building. The site symbolically connects Lincoln to the major institutions and influences in American history. The memorial was dedicated on Memorial Day, May 30, 1922, when Chief Justice (and former President) William Howard Taft presented the memorial to President Warren G. Harding. Since its opening, the Lincoln Memorial has become one of the most popular sites in the park system. Some two million people from around the world visit the memorial each year.

One of the best times to see the site is at night, when the crowds are thin, the city is still, and the white marble glows under the spotlights. From the base of the monument, one can look east over the reflecting pool towards the obelisk of the Washington Monument, or west over the Potomac River to the Virginia skyline. Rangers give short historical talks about the monument and its construction on request.

Over the years, water dripping through minute cracks in the limestone has formed stalactites and stalagmites in the cavity underneath the monument. Visitors can see them, along with rusting tools and charcoal drawings left by the workmen, by joining free "Looking Under Lincoln" tours given daily in spring and fall. The stalactites, called soda straws, are thin hollow tubes that resemble the fringe of a spaghetti mop. They are most common under the front steps to the monument, where waters drain into the foundation. Because the tours are limited to 15 people, they are booked months in advance. For a reservation, call 202-426-6841. The memorial observes Lincoln's birthday, February 12, with an honor guard, speeches, and a military band. A souvenir shop and public restrooms are open when rangers are on duty.

Open: The memorial is always open. Rangers are on duty from 8 a.m. to midnight daily, except Christmas Day.

Fees: None.

Mailing Address: Lincoln Memorial, c/o National Park Service, National Capital Parks-Central, 900 Ohio Drive, S.W., Washington, DC 20242.

Telephone: 202-426-6841.

Getting There: The memorial is located between Constitution and

Independence avenues, at 23rd Street, N.W. Arlington Memorial Bridge leads right to the memorial from Virginia. Two-hour parking is available along West Basin Drive and Ohio Drive, near Independence Avenue; there is all-day parking at West Potomac Park and Sunday parking on Constitution Avenue. Or take the subway to the Foggy Bottom Metro Stop; walk south along 23rd Street (past the State Department) to the memorial, about 8 long blocks.

|| National Mall

One of the most striking features of the nation's capital is the National Mall, a swath of green that sweeps across the city's midsection from Capitol Hill to the Potomac River. This grassy, tree-lined boulevard, flanked by the Smithsonian Museums and the National Gallery of Art, is a favorite spot for joggers, picnickers, and tourists.

Technically, the Mall extends from First to 14th streets N.W., between Constitution and Independence avenues, after which the land is occupied by two other parks, the Washington Monument Grounds and West Potomac Park. But to the visitor, all three parks meld into one, and the unbroken vista from the Capitol Building to the Potomac River seems part of a unified park covering 545 acres of downtown Washington.

When French engineer Pierre L'Enfant laid out Washington in 1791, the area that is now the Mall was a forbidding swamp. Along this swamp, which formed the base of a triangle linking the White House with the Capitol Building, he proposed a canal linking the Potomac and Anacostia rivers. Bordered by gardens, the canal paralleled Constitution Avenue and dipped southward to the Anacostia just before reaching the Capitol grounds.

In the 1850s, landscape architect Andrew Jackson Downing attempted to turn the Mall into a romantic park with serpentine carriage lanes and an assortment of American evergreens. But in mid-project, Downing died in a steamboat accident and the park that remains today more nearly resembles L'Enfant's proposal.

A final phase in the evolution of the Mall took place in the late 19th and early 20th centuries, when the canal was drained, earthworks were constructed to level the ground throughout, and trains were rerouted to Union Station. During the same time period, the land that became West Potomac Park was dredged from the Potomac River to create more sites for parks and monuments, and the Tidal Basin was built.

On the south side of the Mall, near the Capitol, stands the U.S. Botanic Garden Conservatory, a delightful Victorian greenhouse with high arching cupolas and a lush collection of greenery and exotic flowers. Something is always blooming here, whatever the time of year. The permanent plant collection consists of some 1,800 different species from around the world, including palms, cacti, bromeliads (related to the pineapple family), cycads (prehistoric plants), and orchids. During Christmas, Easter, and early fall, there are seasonal flower displays.

One interesting section of the Conservatory re-creates an American desert, with cactuses and succulents growing in tasteful arrangements. The Conservatory is free and offers free lectures and classes for laypersons on topics such as lawn care and holiday plants. For information, contact the U.S. Botanic Garden Conservatory, 245 1st Street, S.W., Washington, D.C. 20024. Telephone: 202-225-8333 or 202-225-7099 (for recordings about upcoming events).

Perhaps the most visited attractions on the National Mall are the nine museums of the Smithsonian Institution: the National Air and Space Museum, the National Museum of Natural History, the National Museum of American History, the Smithsonian Institution Building (known as the Castle), the Hirshhorn Museum and Sculpture Garden, the Arts and Industries Building, the Freer Gallery of Art, the Arthur M. Sackler Gallery, and the National Museum of African Art. Other Smithsonian museums—the National Zoological Park, the National Museum of American Art, the Renwick Gallery, the National Portrait Gallery, and the Anacostia Neighborhood Museum —are located elsewhere in the city.

The Smithsonian originated in 1838 when the English chemist James Smithson (who discovered the mineral smithsonite, used as a source of zinc) left his fortune of half a million dollars to the United States. The money was "to found, at Washington, under the name of the Smithsonian Institution, an establishment for the increase and diffusion of knowledge among men."

Although Smithson never visited this country during his lifetime, his remains are buried in a crypt in the Castle, a red Norman castle-like building on the south side of the Mall. Today the institution has an active research division and a collection of more than 100 million pieces, including items of scientific, archeological, historical, and artistic interest. Most of the museums and galleries are free. For information about all museums, call 202-357-2700.

The Castle, at 1000 Jefferson Drive, S.W., once housed the entire Smithsonian collection. Now it is an orientation center with information and displays about the institution's various buildings. Upstairs are administrative offices and the Woodrow Wilson International Center for Scholars, where academics and scholars in all fields pursue special projects.

To the west of the Castle is the Freer Gallery of Art, which contains Charles Lang Freer's collection of Oriental Art. This museum has everything from Japanese screens and Persian miniatures to Egyptian glasswork. The gallery also has the largest collection of James McNeill Whistler paintings in the country.

The Arts and Industries Building, east of the Castle, is a delightful red brick Victorian structure with a diverse collection of 19th-century objects. Inside is a re-creation of exhibits from the 1876 Centennial Fair in Philadelphia, including a full-sized steam locomotive and an Otis elevator.

The two newest museums on the Mall are the National Museum of African Art and the Arthur M. Sackler Gallery. Located side by side, these structures are largely underground and both offer unique collections. The African art museum, the only one of its kind in the country, has an extensive collection of sub-Saharan art, including sculpture, textiles, household objects, architectural elements, and decorative arts. Items of particular interest include a mask from the Chokwe Peoples of Angola and an exquisite wooden sculpture of a woman and child made by the Kongo Peoples, Yombe Group, Zaire.

The Sackler Gallery was named after Dr. Arthur M. Sackler, who donated his private collection of 1,000 Asian masterworks to the Smithsonian. These include a group of ritual bronze vessels from ancient China, jade carvings of beasts from the 3rd millenia B.C., and scrolls by 20th-century Asian painters.

The Hirshhorn Museum and Sculpture Garden is an excellent museum of contemporary art. The doughnut-shaped building allows plenty of natural light and lots of room to view the more than 1,000 pieces on display, including works by Henry Moore, Auguste Rodin, Thomas Eakins, Henri Matisse, Pablo Picasso, and René Magritte. The Special Exhibition Gallery in the basement has featured shows on the avant-garde in Russia and on utopian visions in Modern Art. On evenings and weekends, the Hirshhorn offers free lectures and films in the auditorium. Don't miss the Sculpture Garden, a beautifully land-scaped park in a depression in the mall. Despite its small size, the sculpture garden has an astonishing variety of vistas.

The National Air and Space Museum is touted as the most popular museum in the world. In 1984, over ten million people visited the extensive collection of airplanes, rockets, astronaut paraphernalia, and displays of space-age technology. The museum tells the story of flight, from hot-air balloons and the Wright Brothers to satellites and moon shots. There is a moon rock to touch, full-scale space vehicles that visi-tors can inspect, and displays that explain the mysteries of astronaut hygiene in outer space. Films, among the most popular attractions, are shown on a five-story screen in the Samuel P. Langley Theater.

The National Gallery of Art, on the north side of the Mall, is not a part of the Smithsonian. It was donated by industrialist and art col-lector Andrew W. Mellon. The main building was designed by John Russell Pope, the architect of the Jefferson Memorial, and the stunning East Wing was designed in the 1970s by I. M. Pei. At any given time, the National Gallery exhibits at least 600 works of art from its pro-digious collection. The Gallery's holdings range from gilded religious works of the Middle Ages to abstract works by Picasso, and include many fine paintings by Turner, El Greco, Rembrandt, and da Vinci. Concerts are occasionally held in the neoclassical garden of the de-lightful central rotunda. The gift shop on the ground floor has a vast selection of inexpensive postcards, prints, and posters.

A motorized underground walkway connects the National Gallery to the East Wing building. This structure is as much a masterpiece as the artwork it houses. Walkways, stairways, escalators, and balconies cross the main chamber at different angles and levels. An immense Calder mobile hangs down from the skylight and a Miró tapestry, also of impressive proportions, is on permanent exhibition. Other works include art by Picasso, Rothko, and Miró. Recent special exhibits have featured shows on Rodin, Munch, and Cycladic art.

A 13-foot-high stuffed African elephant, bagged in Angola in 1955, greets visitors to the National Museum of Natural History. There are more than 84 million specimens in the museum's collection of biologi-cal, geological, archeological, and anthropological treasures. Less than one percent are on display. The biggest attraction by far is the Hope

Diamond in the Gem Hall; the most disturbing is a kitchen covered with roaches, illustrating what would happen if all the progeny of one roach survived for three generations. Other permanent displays include a model of a 92-foot-long blue whale suspended from the ceiling and the fossil remains of a 70-foot-long Diplodocus dinosaur.

The National Museum of American History is home of the "Star Spangled Banner." This 30-by-42-foot American flag, which flew over Fort McHenry in Baltimore and withstood a British bombardment during the War of 1812, inspired Frances Scott Key to write the poem that became the national anthem. The museum also has the famous Foucault Pendulum illustrating the earth's rotation. The earth moves while the pendulum swings in place, knocking down flags that pass beneath it. There are more than 17 million objects in this collection, 15 million of them stamps, but only a small fraction are ever exhibited. Among the most popular attractions are the Hall of Transportation, which has antique bikes and carriages and a 1923 black Packard; the First Ladies' gowns; a room full of model ships; and an old-fashioned ice-cream parlor that serves "Star Spangled" banana splits.

In early July, the Smithsonian holds its annual Festival of American Folklife in tents on the Mall. Activities include food, music, and performances by the country's different cultural groups. Past festivals have featured old-time vaudeville and medicine man shows, steel bands and calypso music, oriental dance and music, story-telling, and country crafts. The food is always exotic and excellent. In April the Smithsonian holds a kite festival with workshops on kite-making and flying competitions.

On the Fourth of July, the city puts on a dazzling display of fireworks over the Mall. The evening begins with a free concert by the National Symphony Orchestra at an outdoor theater on the Capitol grounds. Pyrotechnics begin at dark and continue for an eye-popping hour. By the time the show starts, the Mall is crowded with spectators, so arrive well before dark to stake out some turf.

Open: The Mall is always open. The Botanic Garden Conservatory is open 9 a.m. to 5 p.m. daily, extended to 9 p.m. from June through August. Closed Christmas Day. All Smithsonian buildings are open 10 a.m. to 5:30 p.m. daily. Closed Christmas Day.

Fees: None for the Mall or museums. Tickets for movies and the planetarium show at the Air and Space Museum are $1.50 for adults and $.75 for chidren. (Get tickets on arrival and look at exhibits while waiting.) Free tickets for some special exhibitions are required.

Mailing Address: National Mall, c/o National Park Service, National Capital Parks-Central, 900 Ohio Drive, S.W., Washington, DC 20242.

Telephone: 202-426-6841.

Getting There: By subway, take the Mall exit at the Smithsonian Metro station. Most buildings are within a 5- to 15-minute walk.

‖ Pennsylvania Avenue National Historic Site

When Pierre L'Enfant designed the national capital in 1791, he envisioned a broad boulevard linking the White House and the Capitol. These two greats seats of American democracy would be separate but within sight of each other, symbolizing the discrete yet interrelated roles of the nation's executive and legislative branches. That visual bond was lost when the Treasury Building, erected while Andrew Jackson was president, obstructed the view. But Pennsylvania Avenue between the White House and Capitol Hill still maintains its role as the nation's main street, a route for parades and protests. The buildings along this avenue are some of the most beautiful, and important, in the nation.

Since 1965, when the Kennedy administration decided to make the street a showcase, Pennsylvania Avenue has been getting a massive face-lift. Under the auspices of the Pennsylvania Avenue Development Corporation, old buildings such as the Willard Hotel, which has been around since the Civil War, and the Romanesque-style Post Office Building, designed by Henry Hobson Richardson, are being refurbished. New parks, like Pershing Park with its summer pond and winter ice rink, have opened. Companies like Sears have moved into old buildings while others have built impressive new structures. A Navy Memorial with a bandstand for concerts is planned. And statues, such as the winged sculpture near the National Gallery honoring General George Gordon Meade, who defended Washington during the Civil War and who commanded Union forces at Gettysburg, have been taken out of storage. With all this development, the pedestrians have not been forgotten. New sidewalks, benches, and tree-skirts give the street a unified look despite differing architectural styles.

The National Visitor Center, in the Commerce Building on 14th Street, has brochures about Washington's tourist sites and activities. The Commerce Building also houses the National Aquarium, which features a stunning array of fresh- and saltwater fish.

The elegantly restored Willard Hotel and Pershing Park, honoring General John J. "Black Jack" Pershing, commander of U.S. forces in World War I, are nearby. The ice rink is open daily in the winter. In summer, the park with its fountain and pond is a delightful place to lunch or relax. A second ice rink is located at the Sculpture Garden near the Smithsonian's National Gallery. For information, call 202-889-3800.

One of the most popular sites along Pennsylvania Avenue is the Old Post Office. An intensive preservation campaign saved this turn-of-the-century building from the wrecker's ball. Now the inside has been converted into a vast public space with more than a dozen restaurants and a stage for free performances. On New Year's Eve, the Post Office holds a giant bash with live jazz and late-night revelries. For an excellent view of the city, take the elevator to the carillon in the tower, where Park Service interpreters are on duty to answer questions.

Between 14th and Sixth streets on the south side of Pennsylvania Avenue stand government buildings constructed in the 1930s. Many of them have interesting façades with bas-reliefs, inscriptions, and art deco motifs. The Federal Bureau of Investigation's J. Edgar Hoover Building, a forbidding concrete structure, is between Ninth and Tenth streets. It offers a fantastic 1¼-hour tour that includes presentations on famous public enemies, an introduction to anti-crime technology and to the FBI's labs, and a sharp-shooting demonstration that will scare the crime right out of you. This is a great excursion for kids. Arrive early for tours, or ask your member of Congress to reserve a spot. For FBI information, call 202-324-3447.

Open: The National Visitor Center from 9 a.m. to 5 p.m., Tuesday to Saturday. Hours for other sites may vary. Closed government holidays.

Fees: Contact individual sites for fees.

Mailing Address: Pennsylvania Avenue National Historic Site, c/o

National Capital Parks-Central, 900 Ohio Drive, S.W., Washington, DC 20242.

Telephone: 202-426-6740.

Getting There: The historic area is along Pennsylvania Avenue between 14th and First streets N.W. The Federal Triangle Metro station is the nearest subway stop.

‖ Sewall-Belmont House National Historic Site

Between the Dirksen and Hart Senate Office Buildings on Capitol Hill stands a 17th-century brick house, headquarters of the National Woman's Party. The purple, gold, and white suffrage banners that hang here, once worn by women demonstrating for the right to vote, are a reminder of the early, and ongoing, struggle for women's rights. From this building Alice Paul led the fight for the adoption of the Equal Rights Amendment to the Constitution.

Of the women who have worked for equal rights, Alice Paul was one of the most formidable. Founder of the National Woman's Party in 1913, she organized a march to the White House of some 5,000 women suffragists on the night before President Woodrow Wilson's inauguration. More marches followed. When she was jailed in 1917, she staged a hunger strike and had to be force-fed. After her release, Paul gave jail-door pins to the women who were incarcerated with her. (Visitors to the Sewall-Belmont House can buy the pins.) Paul's activism helped convince Congress in 1920 to ratify the 19th amendment to the constitution, which granted women the right to vote. Three years later, Paul wrote the first version of the controversial Equal Rights Amendment, which read: "Men and women shall have equal rights throughout the United States and in every place subject to its jurisdiction." This amendment is yet to be adopted and remains a subject of hot debate.

In 1929 the Woman's Party bought the two-and-a-half story Sewall House, one of the oldest and most historic on Capitol Hill, and named it for the party's benefactor, Mrs. Alva Belmont. The structure was built by Robert Sewall in 1800 and remained in the family for the next 123 years. Albert Gallatin, secretary of the treasury under Presidents Thomas Jefferson and James Madison, rented the house and, it is believed, worked out the details of the Louisiana Purchase here. In the 20th century, the Sewall-Belmont House has been a headquarters for lobbying and political actions against sex discrimination. Congress declared it a national historic landmark in 1972. Architecturally, it is a combination of Federal and Queen Anne styles with Classical Revival, Victorian, and French Mansard influences.

The house has memorabilia from the suffragist movement, including posters, flags, and photographs of the early marches. There are sculptures of Susan B. Anthony, Elizabeth Cady Stanton, and Lucretia Mott, who led the fight for equality in the mid-19th century, and items used by the early leaders, including a tea set, desks belonging to Anthony and Paul, and Stanton's chair. The Florence Bayard Hilles Library, the first feminist library in the country, dates from 1943 and has a microfilm collection of the suffrage campaign and more than 450,000 pages of related history. A tour guide is available at all times.

On the Sunday nearest August 26, the day American women were granted the right to vote, the house holds a special commemoration with members of Congress, women celebrities, speakers from women's groups, and refreshments. Near January 11, the house commemorates Alice Paul's birthday with speeches and refreshments. Dates and times vary.

Open: 10 a.m. to 3 p.m. Tuesday through Friday; 12 p.m. to 4 p.m. on weekends. Closed Mondays, Thanksgiving, Christmas, and New Year's Day.

Fees: None.

Mailing Address: Sewall-Belmont House National Historic Site, 144 Constitution Avenue, N.E., Washington, DC 20002.

Telephone: 202-546-3989.

Getting There: The house is on Capitol Hill near the Capitol Building. From the Union Station subway stop, walk south along First Street for three long blocks and turn left (east) on Constitution Avenue and go two blocks to the site, which is on the left side of the street. Street parking is metered and difficult to find.

|| Thomas Jefferson Memorial

This circular, colonnaded monument to Thomas Jefferson, philosopher, author of the Declaration of Independence, and third president of the United States, is built in an architectural style that Jefferson himself introduced to this country. Jefferson's designs for his home, Monticello, in Charlottesville, Virginia, and for the University of Virginia nearby also reflect his fondness for classical buildings.

As befits one of the seminal thinkers of American political theory, the memorial occupies a symbolically important site in the national capital. Together with the White House it forms one axis of a giant cross that is completed by the axis extending from the Capitol Building to the Lincoln Memorial. This arrangement not only preserves the symmetry Pierre L'Enfant envisioned when he laid out the District of Columbia in 1791, it also links Jefferson's influence to the major institutions and ideas upon which the nation was built.

Jefferson was only 33 years old in 1776 when he wrote the Declaration of Independence in Philadelphia, Pennsylvania. This eloquent document declared that "All Men are created equal, that they are endowed by their Creator with certain unalienable Rights, that among these are Life, Liberty, and the Pursuit of Happiness." From this beginning as Virginia's delegate to the Constitutional Convention, Jefferson's political rise was meteoric. After the Revolutionary War, he served as a foreign minister to Europe, helping gain support for the newly established United States. He returned to become George Washington's secretary of state then John Adams' vice president. He was elected president in 1801, the first of two terms during which he doubled the size of the country with the Louisiana Purchase (1803).

National politics was not the only arena for Jefferson's genius. He was active in state politics, he was also a gentleman farmer, a naturalist, and an inventor fond of technology and gadgets. He even wrote his own version of the Bible, which he published as *Jefferson's Bible*. Jefferson died on July 4, 1826, one year after his final project, the University of Virginia, opened near his home in Charlottesville, Virginia.

In Washington, the white marble memorial honoring this great man was dedicated in 1943 on reclaimed marshland at the edge of the Tidal Basin. Inside the domed structure, a pedestal of black Minnesota granite supports a gleaming 19-foot-high statue of Jefferson by Rudolph Evans. Above the entrance is a group of sculptures by Adolph A. Weinman depicting Jefferson before the Continental Congress with Benjamin Franklin, John Adams, Roger Sherman, and Robert Livingston. Inscriptions from Jefferson's writings are carved into the wall panels. The outside terrace affords spectacular views of the White House, the Washington Monument, the Lincoln Memorial, and the Capitol. Rangers are on duty to answer questions and give talks about the memorial on request.

One of the most popular times to visit the Jefferson Memorial is in early April, when the 650 Oriental Flowering Cherry Trees that ring the Tidal Basin burst into a glorious display of pink popcorn blooms. The annual Cherry Blossom Festival, a week-long celebration with beauty pageants and parades, begins on Easter Monday. Jefferson's birthday is commemorated at noon on April 13 with a wreath-laying ceremony, speeches, a color guard, and music.

From spring through fall, paddle boats are available for rent at a concession stand near the Tidal Basin. The stand operates daily.

Open: The memorial is open daily, except Christmas Day. Rangers are on duty from 8 a.m. to midnight daily. Summer concerts begin at 8 p.m., dates vary. Paddleboat concession open from 9 a.m. to dusk daily in season.

Fees: None for monument or concerts; paddleboat rentals, about $3.75 an hour.

Mailing Address: Thomas Jefferson Memorial, c/o National Park Service National Capital Parks-Central, 900 Ohio Drive, S.W., Washington, DC 20242.

Telephone: 202-426-6841.

Getting There: Take 15th Street south past the Washington Monument and the Bureau of Engraving toward the 14th Street Bridge. Keep to the right around the the Tidal Basin to avoid taking the bridge into Virginia. There is free parking at the site.

‖ Vietnam Veterans Memorial

Since it was dedicated on Memorial Day, 1982, 10,000 people a day come to the Vietnam Veterans Memorial. Some leave a flower or tape a letter by one of the 58,156 names on the memorial, a silent tribute to friends and family members who died in Vietnam. Some run their hands over the inscriptions, trying, perhaps, to catch the essence of the person. Others weep openly before the monument that has become America's "wailing wall." The purpose of this solemn memorial, according to founder Jan C. Scruggs, is to heal the wounds the Vietnam War caused to the national psyche and to allow Vietnam veterans a rightful place beside others who have fought—and died—for their country.

Designed by Maya Ying Lin, the Yale University student who in 1980 (then only 21) won a nationwide design competition, the monument is strikingly simple. Two 247-foot-long walls of black granite from India meet at a 125 degree angle, tapering from a height of ten feet to a few inches. One end points to the Washington Monument, the other to the Lincoln Memorial, thus giving a historical context to the ultimate sacrifice these names represent. These walls have been polished so they reflect the faces and city around them like a dark mirror. They are inscribed with the names of those who were killed in Vietnam, died of wounds received there, or are missing. The names are arranged by date, starting in 1959 with panel 1 on the east wall, and ending in 1975 with panel 1 on the west wall. A sculpture by Frederick Hart of three servicemen in combat gear stands nearby, a graphic reminder of the Vietnam experience.

As early as 1959, two military advisors to Vietnam were shot. By 1964, when Congress authorized full-scale U.S. participation with its "Gulf of Tonkin Resolution," 20,000 troops were there. At the height of American involvement, in 1969, American military personnel numbered 550,000. When the Republic of Vietnam surrendered to the North Vietnamese in 1975, the United States evacuated the country, ending one of the longest and most unpopular wars in American history.

Jan C. Scruggs, the monument's founder, was a 19-year-old native of Washington, D.C., who served with the Army's 199th Light Infantry Brigade. Half of his company was killed or injured in the fighting, and Scruggs himself was hospitalized when he was wounded in the back with shrapnel from an exploding grenade.

In April 1979, Scruggs, who had earned a graduate degree in psychological counseling, incorporated the Vietnam Veterans Memorial Fund to raise money for a national memorial. The money would come from the people, a sign that ambivalence over the war had ended. Within three years more than 250,000 donors, most of them individuals, had contributed $6 million.

It took five months to "gritblast" the names, which were taken from official Vietnam casualty lists, into the monument's 19 marble panels using a photographic process that had been specially developed for the task. A diamond beside a name indicates the person died; a cross indicates the person is missing or a P.O.W. Visitors can watch new names being added to the monument each year near Memorial Day.

Park Service personnel are stationed at the monument from 8 a.m. to midnight every day except Christmas. Volunteers, many of them Vietnam veterans, are also there during that time to help visitors locate specific names. Even before the monument was lighted at night, a surprising number of people would come with flashlights and Coleman lanterns. Memorial Day and Veterans Day events at the monuments have become very popular, and sometimes feature congressmen and the President as speakers. Posters, books, statues and other souvenirs are available at the kiosk near the base of the Lincoln Memorial, across the Reflecting Pool from the Vietnam Veterans Memorial, and in the Lincoln Memorial bookstore.

Open: Always open.

Fees: None.

Mailing Address: Vietnam Veterans Memorial, c/o National Park Service National Capital Parks-Central, 900 Ohio Drive, S.W., Washington, DC 20242.

Telephone: 202-426-6841.

Getting There: The memorial is located in Constitution Gardens, between the Reflecting Pool and Constitution Avenue. From the Smithsonian subway stop, the Mall exit, walk west through the Washington Monument Grounds to 17th Street and north to Constitution Avenue. The monument is near 20th and 21st streets and Constitution Avenue, but is set into the ground and cannot be seen easily from the street.

‖ Washington Monument

Tennessee Senator Howard Baker once wrote that the Washington Monument ". . . soars above the city as nothing else—as I suspect Washington soared above his time." This white marble obelisk honoring George Washington is the premier monument in a city of monuments. It stands at the center, more or less, of two visual and symbolic axes formed by the city's layout—one extending south from the White House, the other extending west from the Capitol. That, at least, is how Pierre L'Enfant envisioned the monument when he laid out the nation's capital in 1791. But the site he chose turned out to be too marshy to support a monument, so it was moved to more solid ground 360 feet east and 120 feet south of the original position. The true center of the axes is marked today by a small stone pier.

As every American school child knows, George Washington was commander-in-chief of the Continental Army and first president of the United States. With the help of great statesmen such as Thomas Jefferson, John Adams, Alexander Hamilton, and Benjamin Franklin, he managed to gain the respect of European nations, restore public credit, and steer a mid-course between the powers of the federal government and the states. Washington retired to his Mount Vernon estate just south of the District of Columbia on the Virginia side of the Potomac River in March 1797 after serving two terms as president. He died two years later.

The Continental Congress considered erecting a monument to Washington as early as 1783, but it was not until 1847 that the Washington Monument Society had raised sufficient public funds to hire an architect. The design, by Robert Mills, called for a 600-foot-high Egyptian obelisk projecting from a circular colonnaded Greek temple, 100 feet high and 250 feet in diameter. This structure was to be an American pantheon, with statues of presidents and national heroes.

Fortunately, that grandiose plan was never realized. The monument today conforms to the proportions of a classical obelisk, with its height measuring ten times its base. It is a simple, elegant statement of Washington's greatness. It stands 555 feet, 5⅛ inches high, with walls that are 15 feet thick at the base of the shaft tapering to 18 inches at the top. The structure weighs 90,054 tons and is held together without any mortar. (Some mortar was used for fitting but it was not necessary for structural support.) The cornerstone was laid on July 4, 1848, amid great fanfare and with the same trowel Washington used to lay the cornerstone of the Capitol in 1793.

But the project was plagued with difficulties. In 1854, after a stone donated by Pope Pius IX was stolen by The American Party, an anti-Catholic, xenophobic political group called the "Know-Nothings," contributions flagged. The Know-Nothings also took over the Monument Society and controlled it from 1855 to 1858, when they turned it over to the proper officials. As a result of Know-Nothing control, Congress tabled action on a $200,000 appropriation, bringing construction on the monument to a halt.

By the time Monument Society officials regained their grip on the project, the Civil War was imminent and the monument remained a 154-foot-high marble stub. "It has the aspect of a factory chimney with the top broken off," observed Mark Twain.

Construction resumed in 1880—with work on the foundation starting somewhat earlier—this time with public financing. But the marble used in the renewed construction did not come from the same vein as the original marble. The result: A darkish ring 150 feet up the monument demarcates the later construction. Work was completed when the structure was topped with an 8.9-foot aluminum pyramid. The monument was dedicated in 1885.

An elevator whisks visitors to the top of the monument in 70 seconds for one of the best views in the city. (By law, no buildings in Washington, D.C., can be taller than 150 feet; the actual limit is 110 to 130 feet.) Inside, at the monument's top, there are two windows in each of the four walls with diagrams explaining the buildings that can be glimpsed in the background. Visitors can stay as long as they like. But come early as waiting time can last for up to two hours during the peak tourist season.

It is no longer possible to walk up the monument's 897 steps, but the Park Service leads special guided tours down the monument, which are available by reservation only. The staircase route reveals the 192 memorial stones including the Pope's Stone, engraved with *A Roma Americae*, which was added in 1982. The stones were donated by state and local governments, foreign countries, fire departments, professional organizations like the American Medical Association, and even temperance groups. Some have elaborately carved bas-reliefs, others are simple engravings on indigenous stones such as the petrified wood donated by the state of Arizona. Rangers lead free, 1½-hour tours daily when staffing permits. For a reservation, call the day you plan to visit. Telephone: 202-426-6841.

Special activities and festivals are held throughout the year on the monument grounds. Washington's birthday is celebrated on February 22 with a wreath-laying ceremony. On the Mall, the Smithsonian hosts the annual kite festival in March and the Festival of American Folklife, with performances, crafts, and food, in early July. Dates and themes vary. There are also free music and dance concerts at the Sylvan Theater just south of the monument. (Public restrooms are located nearby.)

Open: 9 a.m. to 5 p.m. daily in winter; 8 a.m. to midnight from mid-April to Labor Day. Free tours conducted at 10 a.m. and 2 p.m. daily.

Fees: None.

Mailing Address: Washington Monument, c/o National Park Service, National Capital Parks-Central, National Park Service, 900 Ohio Drive, S.W., Washington, DC 20242.

Telephone: 202-426-6841.

Getting There: The monument is between 15th and 17th streets and Constitution and Independence avenues. There is some parking on the grounds, and limited free parking is available evenings and weekends on the Ellipse to the north. Nearby West Potomac Park has all-day parking between the Tidal Basin and the Potomac River. The nearest subway stop is the Smithsonian (Mall), a ten-minute walk from the site.

▌ White House

The White House has been the official residence of every president of the United States except George Washington. Designed by James Hoban, an Irishman who won $500 for his proposal in the design competition, the three-story building has the harmonious proportions of a late 18th-century English country mansion. Some say the White House resembles the house of the Duke of Leinster in Dublin; others dispute the comparison. Whatever the architectural influence, the name "White House" is unique: It comes from the coat of white paint used to cover the charred limestone after the British burned the building in 1814. Mansion features include a characteristic circular portico, graceful Ionic columns, tall windows with alternating arched and triangular pediments, and a sweeping balustrade.

The cornerstone was laid on October 13, 1792, on a spot selected by George Washington, but the building was still not complete in 1800 when President and Mrs. John Adams moved in. Mrs. Adams used to hang laundry in the East Room, where balls, receptions, and weddings are held today. Each succeeding president has made his mark at the residence: Thomas Jefferson opened the White House to the public and kept grizzly bears brought by explorer Meriwether Lewis on the grounds; James and Dolley Madison brought the dazzle of high society to the reception rooms; John Quincy Adams planted a garden; James Polk added gas lighting; and Benjamin Harrison introduced electricity. Theodore Roosevelt expanded the office space and in 1948, Harry S Truman added a balcony. By that time the floors were sagging and the original foundations were so weak that Margaret Truman's piano fell partially through the floor. A major renovation was ordered and the Trumans moved into Blair House across the street—where visiting dignitaries now stay—while the White House skeleton was rebuilt with steel girders and concrete floors. In the 1960s, Mrs. John F. Kennedy was responsible for restoring many of the famous rooms to their original French decor.

Continuing a tradition started by Thomas Jefferson, the White House is open to visitors in the mornings for free, self-guided tours. (Rangers are stationed in every room to answer questions.) The tour goes by the Library, which contains more than 2,700 volumes on American life and a chandelier once owned by the family of author James Fenimore Cooper. Then there is the East Room, an elegant reception hall with white enameled wood paneling, cut glass chandeliers, and oak parquet floors. The Gilbert Stuart portrait of George Washington, which Dolley Madison saved from flames when the British burned the White House during the War of 1812, hangs in this room. The tour continues to the Green Room, named for the moss-green silk wall coverings. Refurbished as a Federal-style parlor from 1810, the Green Room has Duncan Phyfe furniture, a coffee urn owned by John Adams, and a pair of Dolley Madison's silver candlesticks. Thomas Jefferson, who used to dine here, would take trays of food from a revolving door he designed and would serve his guests himself.

The elliptical Blue Room, considered one of the most beautiful rooms in the White House, is where presidents receive official guests. Despite its name, the walls of the Blue Room are white, covered in cream-colored silk wallpaper with classical scenes. The room contains French Empire furnishings and looks as it did when James Monroe moved into the White House in 1817. Seven of the original Monroe chairs and one original sofa, upholstered in blue silk and decorated with American eagles on the back, still remain and are in excellent shape.

The intimate Red Room where John Adams used to breakfast is now a favorite reception area for First Ladies. These walls are covered in red twill satin with a border of gold scrolls. Nearby is the State Dining Room, a sumptuous setting for formal luncheons and dinners. This room has oak paneling installed by Theodore Roosevelt, an elaborate gilded chandelier, and a portrait of Abraham Lincoln by G. P. A. Healy hanging above the marble mantle. Also above the mantle is the White House motto, written by John Adams in a letter to his wife: "I pray to heaven to bestow the best of Blessings on this House and all that shall hereafter inhabit it. May none but honest and wise men ever rule under its roof."

Visitors are not permitted into the presidential offices and living quarters on the second and third floors. Famous rooms closed to the public include the Lincoln Bedroom, with an eight-foot-long bed that dates from the Civil War, the Treaty Room next door, which has furniture purchased by Ulysses S. Grant, and the famous Oval Office, the main presidential office.

With special tickets, available only from members of Congress, visitors can beat the crowds and take an early-morning guided tour. This tour covers all the stops of the regular tour plus the Diplomatic Reception Room, an oval parlor with a rug containing the symbols of all fifty states. In this room Franklin Roosevelt broadcast his famous fireside chats.

Lines for both tours form by the East Gate on East Executive Avenue across from the Treasury Building. The White House is occasionally closed for official events, so call before coming. From Memorial Day to Labor Day, pick up free tickets for tours (one to a person) at the booth on the Ellipse south of the White House. Arrive early. Each ticket will be stamped with a tour time, freeing tourists to visit other sites during the wait.

On Easter Monday each year, the White House holds its annual Easter Egg Hunt. Children eight and under, and their parents, are invited to scavenge on the grounds for hidden Easter eggs. Tours of the garden, which has trees planted by every president from James Madison to Ronald Reagan, are offered on one weekend in fall and spring. Dates vary. These tours take visitors through the South Grounds, the

East Garden, known as the First Lady's Garden, the Rose Garden, and on through the White House. Candlelight tours are conducted near Christmas.

Open: 10 a.m. to 12 p.m. daily; guided tours given from 8 a.m. to 10 a.m. with special tickets. Easter egg hunt from 10 a.m. to 2 p.m., Easter Monday. Occasionally closed for official purposes.

Fees: None.

Mailing Address: White House, c/o National Parks Service, National Capital Parks Central, 900 Ohio Ave., S.W., Washington, D.C. 20242.

Telephone: 202-456-1414.

Getting There: The White House is at 1600 Pennsylvania Avenue, between the Old Executive Office Building and the Treasury Building. The subway stops at McPherson Square, Farragut Square, and Metro Center (13th Street) are all within a five-minute walk. Line up for tours at the East Gate on East Executive Avenue. The Ellipse, which has free weekend parking and shaded bleachers, is located directly to the south.

FLORIDA

1. Castillo de San Marcos National Monument
2. De Soto National Memorial
3. Fort Caroline National Memorial
4. Fort Jefferson National Monument
5. Fort Matanzas National Monument

Castillo de San Marcos National Monument

In 1565, Spanish navigator Pedro Menéndez de Avilés founded Saint Augustine, the oldest settlement in the United States. The wood and earth fort originally built to protect the settlement was replaced by the stone structure of the Castillo de San Marcos, begun in 1672. The stone fortification was built as a result of the threat to Florida posed by the English settlement of Charleston, South Carolina, in 1670.

Today this massive gray structure overlooking the Atlantic Ocean is an impressive reminder of the 235-year Spanish presence in Florida. Constructed of locally quarried coquina, a stone made of shells compressed by geological time and held together by the shells' lime, the Castillo is the first masonry fortification built on the northern border of Spanish controlled lands in North America. It was not completed until 1695 due to labor problems and delays in funding. The present appearance of the Castillo, resulting from the replacement of beam work with arched casemates and other changes, emerged in the mid-18th century.

The square stronghold with bastions at each corner sits on a 20-acre park in downtown Saint Augustine. It has all the features of a storybook fort: sentry boxes at each bastion, battlements, many-angled walls, and a surrounding moat.

From lookout points atop the fort's 32-foot-high walls, which measure ten feet at the base, one gets a splendid view of the nearby barrier island, Anastasia, and the Atlantic Ocean beyond.

A museum displays period artillery and cannon balls, and features exhibits on salient points of the fort's history. On display are three Spanish silver coins, depicting a soldier's daily pay. On weekends, the park's living history program includes people dressed in Spanish colonial garb of 1702–1754 and cannon firings. You will hear the gunners receiving commands just as they were given in the mid-18th century.

Visitors can go on guided tours when offered, or can wander alone through most of the Castillo's 31 rooms. Romantic torchlight tours of the fort are offered about three times a year. Check for times and dates. Twice each year, usually in June and December, the city celebrates the British and Spanish colonial past with Grand Illuminations, candlelit processions of people dressed in period costume. Check for details.

Open: 9 a.m. to 5:15 p.m. daily, extended to 6 p.m. mid-June to Labor Day. Closed Christmas Day.

Fees: $1, ages 17–62.

Mailing Address: Castillo de San Marcos National Monument, 1 Castillo Dr., Saint Augustine, FL 32084.

Telephone: 904-829-6506.

Getting There: Exit I-95 to Fla. 16 and 207 and from U.S. 1 to San Marco Ave., Castillo Drive, and King Street. Fla. A1A runs immediately parallel to the Castillo grounds.

‖ De Soto National Memorial

The De Soto National Memorial near Bradenton, Florida, marks the site where the Spanish conquistador Hernando De Soto landed in the New World in 1539 to begin his search for riches.

From Camp Ucita, an Indian village on the western coast of Florida, De Soto and his men embarked on a four-year odyssey through the South and the Southwest, the first exploration by Europeans of this uncharted territory. De Soto's unsuccessful search for an overland route to Mexico took him to North Carolina, Arkansas, and Texas. The explorer never did find the riches he was after, but his discovery of the Mississippi River and his observations of the Indians laid the foundation for future European claims.

North America presented De Soto with many hardships—fierce Indians, harsh weather, alligators, and insects. But De Soto's heavy-handed treatment of the Indians certainly did not endear him to the Native American population. His path was a bloody one, marked by battles, Indian enslavement, and brutal slayings. The expedition got as far as Texas before De Soto's plans to march to Mexico were abandoned. Instead, the group took a water route to Mexico via the Mississippi River. When the expedition ended four years after it began, only 322 men from the original group of 500 remained. De Soto had died along the way.

From December through mid-April, the park at the De Soto Memorial has daily demonstrations of life among the 16th-century Spanish explorers, including cooking, building, and weaponry.

The park also has a half-mile nature trail though the red mangrove swamps. Plaques along the way describe Florida plants and wildlife. Pelicans, herons, and the majestic anhinga are among the birds that frequent the area. Watch out for snakes, poison ivy, sharp cacti, and barnacles. The park runs two nature walks daily from December to April, at 11 a.m. and 1 p.m.

The museum in the visitor's center shows a 22-minute movie on the conquistador. Displayed artifacts from the expedition include a complete suit of fluted armor dating from 1540, a shirt of mail, and original weapons. There is also a replica of De Soto's small boat, the *Caravelle*.

Each year near Easter Sunday, the town celebrates De Soto's arrival in the area with parades and a re-enactment of the landing. Check the local chamber of commerce for details.

Open: 8 a.m. to 5:30 p.m. daily. Closed Christmas Day.

Fees: $1 per person, ages 17–62.

Mailing Address: De Soto National Memorial, P.O. Box 14871, Bradenton, FL 34280.

Telephone: 813-792-0458.

Getting There: From St. Petersburg and Tampa, take I-75 south to Bradenton. Turn off at state route 64 west. Follow Rt. 64 until you reach 75th Street N.W.

‖ Fort Caroline National Memorial

On June 25, 1564, three small ships carrying 300 French Huguenots led by René de Laudonnière anchored in the river known today as the Saint Johns. Shortly thereafter, Fort Caroline, triangular in shape and built of earth, wood and sod, was constructed. For the next 15 months this settlement—named in honor of Charles IX, boy king of France—was home for this hardy group of French Protestants. The spot they chose was only ten miles east of present-day Jacksonville.

Like many other groups of colonists who journeyed to the New World from Europe, these men hoped to discover riches and begin new lives free of Old World problems.

For the French, this Florida experience was one of discovery and disappointment, joy and frustration, excitement and despair. Adapting to their new environment required extraordinary sacrifice and effort. Strong religious and national motivations inspired the French in their attempt to establish an outpost of culture and power in North America.

Fort Caroline, however, existed but a short time. It quickly became the catalyst prompting Spain to defend her New World possessions by eliminating the French presence. The capture of the French fort and slaughter of most of its inhabitants by Spanish forces in September, 1565, marked the first major conflict between European powers for control of New World territory. This struggle would continue for another 200 years.

Fort Caroline National Memorial was established in January 1953 to preserve, protect, and interpret the historic French settlement. Although the site was washed away after a river channel was deepened in 1880, a replica of the fort stands near the river bank today.

Insight into the park's historical significance is provided through an interpretive program for visitors. Exhibits in the visitor center and museum illustrate the interaction between European and Indian cultures. The site preserves the history of the early French presence in an area more noted for its Hispanic past.

There are nature trails, a picnic area (no fires allowed), and observation areas at Spanish Point, Saint John's Bluff, and the river. Bring mosquito repellent and a camera to photograph wildlife, which includes armadillos, opossums, and raccoons.

Open: 9 a.m. to 5 p.m. daily.

Fees: None.

Mailing Address: Fort Caroline National Memorial, 12713 Fort Caroline Rd., Jacksonville, FL 32225.

Telephone: 904-641-7111.

Getting There: From I-95 south of the Jacksonville airport, take Rt. 9A south over the bridge at Dames Point. Turn left onto Merrill Rd., which leads into Fort Caroline Rd. From downtown Jacksonville, 13 miles away, take Atlantic Blvd. (Rt 10) east past Regency Square Mall to Monument Rd. Follow Monument Rd. northeast until it runs into Fort Carolina Rd., where you turn right.

‖ Fort Jefferson National Monument

The stark coral reefs of the Dry Tortugas, 70 miles west of Key West, make up Fort Jefferson National Monument. Built on Garden Key by the U.S. government in 1846, Fort Jefferson was part of a string of coastal defense fortifications. In a prison here, Dr. Samuel Mudd served time for unwittingly setting the broken leg of President Lincoln's assassin, John Wilkes Booth. Mudd was pardoned in 1869 for helping to combat an outbreak of yellow fever. Today, you can visit his cell.

Visitors to Fort Jefferson can browse in the small museum, watch a slide program, and take a self-guided tour of the fort's red brick ramparts. Though still unfinished, Fort Jefferson, which measures one-half mile in perimeter, is touted as the largest fortification in the Western Hemisphere. It covers nearly all of Garden Key.

These islands were discovered in 1513 by Ponce de Leon, the Spanish explorer who came to the New World in search of the Fountain of Youth. He named the islands the Dry Tortugas because they lacked fresh water and because of the many turtles (*"los tortugas,"* in Spanish) that lived on the deserted beaches.

For years Garden Key was a haven for pirates until the U.S. assumed control in 1821. The army began building Fort Jefferson on Garden Key in 1846 to protect the Gulf of Mexico.

Despite its strategic location, Fort Jefferson never did defend shipping activities in the Gulf. Instead, the fort was converted into a prison where death row convicts could earn their liberty by serving seven years of hard labor. There were no successful escapes. In 1874, after a hurricane and an outbreak of yellow fever decimated the island's population, the Army abandoned Fort Jefferson.

If the area has been a difficult one for humans, the animals have found the Dry Tortugas a haven. The pristine coral reefs in the 47,000-acre-park teem with yellowtail, grouper, and snapper as well as sharks and barracuda.

Snorkeling and scuba diving here are excellent. The park service has a map indicating the best spots. Spear fishing, however, is prohibited. The Dry Tortugas are also one of the best bird-watching spots in the country. Bring binoculars so you can watch rare birds such as peregrine falcon and sooty tern.

Fort Jefferson, in the Dry Tortugas off the southern tip of Florida, can be reached only by boat or airplane.—*M. Woodbridge Williams, NPS photograph*

On Garden Key, there is a small beach and a primitive camping area with grills and picnic tables. Bring all the food and drink you will need for your stay. There is no fresh water, and no telephones on the island. Only about 20,000 people venture to Fort Jefferson a year, so it is unlikely to be crowded.

Use of the public docking facilities is limited to two hours per boat during daylight hours. Boats staying overnight must anchor in the protected waters within a mile of the island.

Coral, shells, turtles, lobsters, and other living marine life are considered natural resources and should not be disturbed, but visitors may gather uninhabited shells from the shore.

Open: 8 a.m. to sunset daily. Bush Key is reserved for birds during the nesting season of March through September. All keys, except Garden Key and Loggerhead Key, are closed during turtle season, May through Sept. 30.

Fees: None.

Mailing Address: Fort Jefferson National Monument, c/o Everglades National Park, P.O. Box 279, Homestead, FL 33030.

Telephone: 305-247-6211 (Everglades National Park).

Getting There: Fort Jefferson is accessible only by boat or seaplane. Private charters are available from Key West or Marathon. Seaplane service operates out of Key West for about $100 per person. For reservations call Air Taxi Charter Limited at 305-294-0999, Key West Seaplane Service at 305-249-6978, and Air Sea Key West at 305-296-5511.

For more information, contact the Greater Marathon Chamber of Commerce, 3300 Overseas Highway, Marathon, FL 33050.

‖ Fort Matanzas National Monument

Beginning in 1569, the Spanish in Saint Augustine erected successive wooden watchtowers to guard the Matanzas inlet area, 14 miles south of the Saint Augustine settlement. The watchtower sighted vessels approaching from the south and gave warning so that Saint Augustine could prepare for its defense.

The unsuccessful British attempt to seize Saint Augustine in 1740 reaffirmed the strategic importance of Matanzas inlet. Despite the British blockade, the inlet enabled the Spanish to communicate and bring in needed food.

Fort Matanzas was built in 1740–1742 to guard the inlet permanently. The stone structure consisted of a six-gun platform and a two-story tower with a sentry shelter on top. Besides serving as a lookout post for vessels, the fort could now actively delay an enemy attempt to enter the inlet. Fort Matanzas was the vital auxiliary unit of Saint Augustine's defense. For this reason, it was designated a national monument.

Before the advent of the first wooden tower, the Matanzas inlet area had been the stage for the final defeat of the French, who had settled Fort Caroline near Jacksonville in 1564. The French settlement challenged the Spanish title to Florida and threatened Spanish shipping along the east coast of Florida.

No sooner had the Spanish established Saint Augustine in 1565 than French ships sailed to attack it. But a storm blew the ships southward and wrecked them. The Spanish then captured Fort Caroline and confronted French survivors at the southern tip of Anastasia Island near the Matanzas inlet. Less then half of the 500 French soldiers surrendered unconditionally; the others escaped southward. The Spanish slaughtered the prisoners, sparing only 31. The name Matanzas, which means "slaughters" in Spanish, comes from this bloody event.

The park is located on both the southern tip of Anastasia and the northern half of Rattlesnake Island. Anastasia is fringed with delightful sandy beaches and dunes. Sun-bathing is excellent but swimming in the dangerous waters of the inlet is not advised. There is a visitor center with exhibits on Anastasia. To reach the fort, a free ferry is available from Anastasia to Rattlesnake Island most days between 9 a.m. and 4:30 p.m., weather permitting.

Open: 8:30 a.m. to 5:30 p.m. daily, except Christmas Day.

Fees: None.

Mailing Address: Fort Matanzas National Monument, 1 Castillo Drive, St. Augustine, FL 32084.

Telephone: 904-471-0116.

Getting There: From St. Augustine, take Fla. A1A south 14 miles to the park entrance sign.

GEORGIA

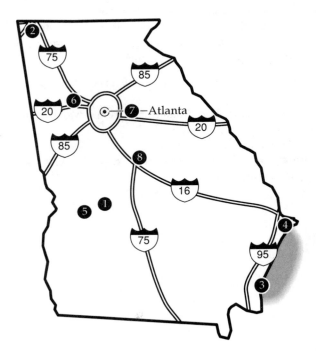

1. Andersonville National Historic Site
2. Chickamauga and Chattanooga National
   Military Park
3. Fort Frederica National Monument
4. Fort Pulaski National Monument
5. Jimmy Carter National Historic Site
6. Kennesaw Mountain National Battlefield Park
7. Martin Luther King, Jr., National Historic Site
8. Ocmulgee National Monument

|| Andersonville National Historic Site

From the time it opened in February 1864 to its closing 14 months later, 12,912 Civil War prisoners died at Camp Sumter in Andersonville. They died of exposure, starvation, and disease in this infamous Confederate prison-of-war camp. Andersonville National Historic Site and National Cemetery is dedicated to these men, and to American prisoners of all wars.

More than 45,000 non-commissioned Union soldiers—as well as a few dozen officers—passed through this 26.5-acre patch of hell. Rations were scanty: coarse cornmeal—cobs and all—cornbread, and whatever vegetables the prisoners could occasionally buy or barter from the camp sutler.

Since absolutely no shelter was provided, the prisoners had to improvise. The fortunate men had tents. Others made wooden lean-tos or burrowed themselves into the Georgia clay. Many had nothing at all. ". . . As we entered, I saw men without a thread of clothing upon their dirty skeletons, some panting under old rags or blankets raised above them. One was trying to raise himself; getting upon his hands and feet, his joints gave way; he pitched like a lifeless thing in a heap. . . . Such things are frequent," wrote John Worrell Northrop, a member of the 76th New York Infantry. Today, a 200-foot corner section of Andersonville's 15-foot-high log stockade has been rebuilt and more construction is planned.

In the tragic story of the Andersonville prison, two men in particular stand out: camp commandant Captain Henry Wirz and Dorence Atwater, a paroled prisoner who recorded the names of the dead. (During the Civil War, it was common for captured soldiers to give their word, or "parole," that they would not escape if allowed to leave the prison on work details.) Wirz, who was deemed responsible for the wretched conditions of the camp, was hanged after the war. Yet history now views him as the scapegoat of a nation bent on venting anger at the atrocities of war.

Ironically, Atwater, who smuggled a copy of the camp's death register to Washington, D.C., ended up in prison a second time for his efforts to publicize the names. Impatient with the government for not releasing the names after purchasing the list from Atwater for $300, Atwater and Red Cross founder Clara Barton arranged to have the names printed in the New York Tribune. Atwater kept the $300, which made him, in the eyes of the government, a criminal. But there is a happy ending to the tale. Pardoned by Andrew Johnson in 1868, Atwater was eventually named U.S. Counsel to the Seychelles, a republic of islands in the Indian Ocean. Later, he was transferred to Tahiti where he married an island princess.

Today, thanks to the efforts of Atwater and Clara Barton, engraved marble headstones mark the graves of all the Andersonville prisoners buried in the cemetery there. These headstones, in their neat and seemingly endless rows, are small white monuments to the suffering these men endured. The cemetery, still an active burial ground for American veterans, is divided into quadrants and 17 sections, lettered A through R. Andersonville prisoners are buried in sections E, F, H, J and K. Park personnel will help you locate specific names.

In a rectangular plot near section J are graves of the "Andersonville Raiders." This gang of thugs terrorized the camp for four months, stealing food and clothing, and brutalizing the weaker prisoners. They were executed on July 11, 1864.

The visitor center has a museum about Civil War prisoners, with artifacts from Andersonville, including letters, diaries, weapons, and the pipe bowls, rings, and wood carvings made by prisoners to pass the time. A card catalog contains the names of 90 percent of the 45,000 prisoners sent to Andersonville. Near the prison site is the Prisoner of War Museum, dedicated to the history of captive American soldiers.

Guided 30-minute walking tours of the National Cemetery begin each morning at 10 a.m. A ranger-conducted prison talk starts at 2 p.m. daily. A free 30-minute taped tour is also available.

Though not part of the site, the town of Andersonville is a quaint southern village with a 19th-century train depot and a free museum, open daily (except Christmas) from 9 a.m. to 5 p.m. The town's log church, Pennington Saint James, was designed by Chramm and Ferguson, the architects who designed the Cathedral of St. John the Divine in New York City. The Andersonville Historic Fair held during the first week in October each year has flea markets, parades, dancing, crafts, and re-enactments of Civil War battles. For more information, contact the Andersonville Guild in Andersonville, Georgia 31711. Telephone: 912-924-2558.

Open: Visitor Center: 8:30 a.m. to 5 p.m. daily.

Fees: None.

Mailing Address: Andersonville National Historic Site, Andersonville, GA 31711.

Telephone: 912-924-0343.

Getting There: The site is located in southwest Georgia along Route 49, ten miles northeast of Americus.

‖ Chickamauga and Chattanooga National Military Park

The battles for Chickamauga, Georgia, and Chattanooga, Tennessee, in the summer and fall of 1863 were two of the Civil War's most complex and costly campaigns. After a three-month struggle for control of this strategic rail junction, the Union army pushed Confederate General Braxton Bragg's forces into retreat. Union forces had already split the South vertically with the successful siege of Vicksburg on the Mississippi River. With Chattanooga firmly in Union hands, the stage was set for General William Sherman's campaign across Georgia from Atlanta, the famous "march to the sea" that split the midsection of the Confederacy. But the price of the confrontation over Chattanooga was tremendous: 34,000 men died in the battle for Chickamauga and 12,000 died in the fighting over Chattanooga.

Chickamauga and Chattanooga National Military Park, established in 1890 in northwestern Georgia and southeastern Tennessee, is the country's first national military park. The park's major units are the Chickamauga Battlefield, Orchard Knob, Lookout Mountain, Missionary Ridge, and Signal Point. In all, there are over 8,000 acres of historic battlefields.

This is one of the nation's best monumented military parks. More than 1,400 monuments, markers, and plaques indicate troop movements through the thickly forested landscape of the Chickamauga Battlefield and throughout the city of Chattanooga.

Bragg lost an early chance to rout Union General William S. Rosecrans' troops from their encampment along the Chickamauga Creek and by September 19, 1863, Federal forces were concentrated along a six-mile line in the dense woods by the creek, with rebel forces facing them. Confederates gained the battlefield when Union commanders,

View of the Tennessee River from Chickamauga and Chattanooga National Military Park, the nation's oldest and largest national military park.—*Jack E. Boucher, NPS photograph*

confused by the heavy forests, moved their troops creating a gap in their line. Rebel soldiers streamed through, forcing half of the Federal troops to flee towards Chattanooga. Only Union General George H. Thomas, who held Snodgrass Hill, remained on the field, fighting wave after wave of Confederate assaults and retreating after dark. Thomas's performance earned him the sobriquet the "Rock of Chickamauga."

From the visitor center at Chickamauga battlefield, which features a slide program about the battle and displays 355 weapons from the period, a tour road leads by the spot where fighting began on the second day of the battle. This site near the creek is where Union commanders made their fatal error allowing Confederate forces to break through the Union line. The last stop on the tour is Snodgrass Hill, where the "Rock of Chickamauga" held firm.

On September 9, 1863, the Federal troops occupied Chattanooga.

Confederate forces besieged the city from Missionary Ridge and Lookout Mountain. Upon taking command from Rosecrans, General George H. Thomas declared: "We will hold this town until we starve." That almost happened. The men, cut off from supplies, were on half-rations and the bodies of starved horses and pack animals littered the streets.

"It looked, indeed, as if but two courses were open: the one to starve, the other to surrender or be captured," so wrote Union General Ulysses S. Grant upon his arrival in Chattanooga, shortly after taking command of all Federal forces between the Appalachian Mountains and the Mississippi River. Grant quickly set to work opening up a supply line and bolstered his troops with food and reinforcements.

On November 23, Grant stunned the Confederates on Missionary Ridge with what appeared to be a full-dress military parade of 20,000 troops that unexpectedly opened fire and took Orchard Knob. The next day, Union General Joseph Hooker's forces climbed Lookout Mountain under cover of a dense fog and fought a battle popularly known as the "Battle Above the Clouds." By November 25, Union soldiers had planted the Stars and Stripes at the mountain's summit. The fight for Missionary Ridge, which took place later in the day, resulted in one of the most spectacular Union victories of the war. Shouting the battle cry "Chickamauga!" Union soldiers drove Rebel riflemen from their pits so quickly that both armies seemed to advance up the hill simultaneously. Carried away by their success, Union soldiers continued up the crest.

Several trails in the park, including the Bluff Trail taken by Hooker's men, wind up Lookout Mountain to the site of the Confederate fortifications above the Tennessee River. (Of course, Hooker's men did not have the luxury of taking a trail.) Two public roads also lead to the crest and to the city of Lookout Mountain.

Today two rifled Parrott cannon and two 12-pound Napoleons are on display at the summit of Lookout Mountain. The Ochs Museum and Overlook, named in honor of Adolph S. Ochs, former publisher-owner of *The New York Times* and resident of Chattanooga, tells the story of the battle for Chattanooga.

With its mountains and ridges, thick forests and fields, the park gives visitors a unique opportunity to view the ground of some of the most remarkable and brilliant fighting of the American Civil War. While the park's emphasis is on history, there are opportunities for hiking and picnicking. The landscape is at its peak in spring, when wildflowers bloom, and during the fall foliage season.

In the summer, a living history program illustrates the life of soldiers during the campaign for Chattanooga. Check for activities and times.

Open: Visitor Center: 8 a.m. to 4:45 p.m. daily; the park is open until dark. Closed Christmas Day.

Fees: None.

Mailing Address: Chickamauga and Chattanooga National Military Park, P.O. Box 2128, Fort Oglethorpe, GA 30742.

Telephone: 404-866-9241.

Getting There: From Chattanooga, take Route 27 south. The Chickamauga Battlefield Visitor Center is located just south of Fort Oglethorpe.

‖ Fort Frederica National Monument

The walls are crumbling now and the settlement long gone, but when it was built in the 18th century, Fort Frederica on Saint Simons Island, Georgia, was the most expensive and elaborate stronghold in the New World. From 1736–48 it was a major base from which England challenged Spanish colonization in Florida.

Protected on one side by the fort and on the other by an earthwork wall and moat, Fort Frederica was once a thriving military community. Its avenues were laid out in a grid: Broad Street, which led from the town gate to the fort, intersected with Barracks Street, where 200 soldiers commanded by founder James Oglethorpe were quartered. Wayside exhibits indicate the sites where houses and shops once stood. Today, one wall of the barracks, many house foundations, and the Kings Magazine near the river are all that remain of the settlement.

In summer, park staff in colonial costume give tours of the site and demonstrate early colonial cooking and military activities typical of British garrison life in the 18th century. The month of August marks the annual lime burning festival, when park staff build a kiln and burn oyster shells to make the construction material known as "tabby," from which the fort was built.

Like many of the early outposts in the New World, Fort Frederica had a relatively brief lifespan. It played a central role in the war between England and Spain for control of North America, serving as the base for Oglethorpe's 1739 attack on the Spanish settlement at the Castle of Saint Augustine, Florida (now known as the Castillo de San Marcos).

Fighting came closer to Fort Frederica in 1742, when Spanish soldiers attacked nearby Saint Simons. This battle, known as the Battle of Bloody Marsh, ended forever the threat of Spanish invasion into British territory in North America. In 1748, with the threat of warfare gone, Oglethorpe's troops were removed. Fort Frederica lost its economic base and withered. By 1763 few people were left and the settlement, which had been ravaged by fire a few years earlier, lay in ruins.

The visitor center has a film about the fort's history and a museum displaying artifacts from the original colony. There are no camping or picnicking facilities at the park, but these are available nearby. The Bloody Marsh Battle Site, open daily, is located six miles south of Fort Frederica. Pine, live oak, palmetto trees, and Spanish moss grow in the park and about 200 species of birds inhabit the area.

Open: The park is open 8 a.m. to 5 p.m., with extended hours in summer. Visitor Center: 9 a.m. to 5 p.m. daily. Closed Christmas Day.

Fees: $3 per car, $1 for bicyclists.

Mailing Address: Fort Frederica National Monument, Route 9, Box 286-C, Saint Simons Island, GA 31522.

Telephone: 912-638-3639.

Getting There: The fort is on Saint Simons Island in the Atlantic Ocean off the coast of southern Georgia, 12 miles north of Brunswick. Take the Brunswick-Saint Simons toll causeway which connects with Route 17 at Brunswick.

Fort Pulaski National Monument

Projectiles from the Civil War are still embedded in Fort Pulaski's weathered bricks, the walls are pock-marked and riddled with holes. Once, this island bastion in the mouth of the Savannah River was considered to be "as strong as the Rocky Mountains." But even the strongest brick masonry fort in the world was no match for the newly developed rifled cannon, and Fort Pulaski crumbled during the opening shots of the Civil War. When the Confederates surrendered Fort Pulaski to Union troops on April 11, 1862, the defeat was of military significance: It heralded the age of rifled heavy artillery and closed the era of masonry forts, used for the past thousand years, as effective installations.

Today, Fort Pulaski, holes and all, commemorates the first use of rifled artillery. Rifling—the spiral grooves in the barrel of a cannon—puts a spin on projectiles making them so accurate and deadly that they can rip through brick walls. Two of the fort's five walls show the damage inflicted by this technological advance. Bright red brick, added when the wall was repaired (by the Union forces), indicates the spot where the rifled missiles destroyed the wall and threatened to blow up the fort's gunpowder magazine, prompting the Confederate surrender.

Weekends throughout the year and daily in summer, rangers in Civil War costume tell the story of American coastal fortifications and discuss the development of rifled artillery. Visitors can explore this extraordinarily well-preserved, five-sided fort with drawbridges, moats, arched casements, and ample parade grounds.

Fort Pulaski was part of a string of coastal fortifications proposed by President James Madison after the War of 1812. The fort was named for Casimir Pulaski, the Polish count who fought with the patriots during the Revolutionary War and who died in the Battle of Savannah. Designed by General Simon Bernard, who had been a military engineer under Napoleon I, Fort Pulaski was built on Cockspur Island at the Georgia-South Carolina border between 1829 and 1847. It cost $1 million and consumed 25 million bricks. Early in his military career, Confederate Civil War General Robert E. Lee spent two years at Fort Pulaski building the dikes and drainage system.

A small monument to John Wesley, the founder of Methodism who landed on Cockspur Island in 1736 on his way to Savannah, is accessible by paved trail near the fort.

On an oyster island nearby stands a 50-foot-high brick lighthouse. From it you can see the surrounding salt marshes and the top of the fort. The island site is open but there is no transporation.

The reclaimed salt marsh of Cockspur Island has two miles of walking trails with Spanish-moss-draped palmetto and red cedar trees. The island's abundant coastal wildlife includes herons, egrets, and pelicans along with rabbits, raccoons, opossums, and other small mammals. Beware of alligators; they occasionally slip into the fort's moat. And look out for rattlesnakes.

On the weekend nearest April 10, the site celebrates the shelling of Fort Pulaski during the Civil War. Pulaski Day, with programs to commemorate the fort's namesake, is October 11. Check for details.

Open: 8:30 a.m. to 5 p.m. daily; extended to 7 p.m. in summer. Closed Christmas and New Year's Day.

Fees: $1 a person; $3 a carload from April 1 to Oct. 31; free during other seasons.

Mailing Address: Fort Pulaski National Monument, P.O. Box 30757, Savannah, GA 31410.

Telephone: 912-786-5787.

Getting There: The park is located on the coast, near the border between Georgia and South Carolina. It can be reached via Rt. 80 east from Savannah.

Jimmy Carter National Historic Site

This new addition to the National Park Service is dedicated to former President Jimmy Carter and the rural southern culture of his hometown of Plains, Georgia. Carter, who served from 1976 to 1980, is known for his efforts to bring peace to the Middle East and for focusing worldwide attention on human rights.

More than any other town in the country, Plains, Georgia, population 650, is associated with an American president. For it was here, on October 1, 1924, that Jimmy Carter was born, attended school, and lived with his young family before he entered national politics. And it was here that Jimmy Carter returned after serving as the 39th President of the United States. Today he still lives in the three-bedroom ranch-style house with green trim that he built in 1961—the only house the Carters ever owned. (Their home and the surrounding area is under Secret Service protection, so don't try to visit.)

The Jimmy Carter National Historic Site preserves the buildings associated with the president's life. Headquarters are located in the old Plains Railroad Depot, a wooden frame building built in 1888, which served as Carter's campaign headquarters during the 1976 presidential campaign.

The depot has a wide selection of books on Carter and an exhibition of photographs of Carter. A free self-guided tour through Plains is available at the depot and a taped tour, with comments by Jimmy and Rosalynn Carter, is available for rent at $2. Across the street, buried under a marble headstone, is Jay Who, the friendly stray dog who wandered into the depot one day and became the presidential campaign's mascot.

The Carter Boyhood Home is a small, turn-of-the-century farmhouse about two miles west of Plains, where Carter lived from age four to just before his 18th birthday. Plains High School, a combined elementary and secondary school that Carter attended for 11 years, has been donated to the Park Service by the city of Plains.

The hospital where Jimmy Carter was born is also in Plains. (Carter was the first American president born in a hospital.) Other sites include brother Billy Carter's gas station, still operating, the Big Smiling Peanut, a 7-foot-high sculpture of a peanut given to the Carters by an admirer during the presidential campaign, and the church where Carter now teaches Sunday school.

Open: 9 a.m. to 5 p.m. daily. Closed Christmas Day.

Fees: None.

Mailing Address: Jimmy Carter National Historic Site, P.O. Box 392, Plains, GA 31780.

Telephone: 912-824-3413.

Getting There: Plains is located 10 miles west of Americus on Rt. 280.

‖ Kennesaw Mountain National Battlefield Park

At the Kennesaw Mountain battlegrounds near Marietta, Georgia, Confederate General Joseph E. Johnston briefly held off Union General William T. Sherman on his inexorable march to Atlanta. But while Sherman suffered defeats at Kennesaw Mountain in late June and early July of 1864, these were only temporary setbacks. In the end, he managed to bypass the mountain with its entrenched southern troops, and lay siege to Atlanta.

At 9 a.m. on June 27, Sherman attacked Confederate troops that were firmly entrenched on the high ground. His men made three attempts to assault rebel positions; each time, Confederate artillery and gunfire mowed down the Union soldiers as quickly as they appeared. "At all points the enemy met us with determined courage and great force. By 11:30 the assault was over, and had failed," Sherman wrote in his memoirs. Sherman lost 2,000 of his 16,225 men; Johnston lost about 350 of his 17,733 men.

Kennesaw Mountain Battlefield Park preserves more than 11 miles of original Civil War trench lines and the sites of two major battles—the Battle of Kolb Farm, fought on June 22, and the Battle of Kennesaw Mountain, fought on June 27. The Kolb farmhouse, where Union General Joseph Hooker had his headquarters, is the only remaining Civil War structure in the park. It is not open to visitors.

More than 15 miles of hiking trails snake through the park past the Kolb farmhouse, Cheatham Hill, and the Big and Little Kennesaw mountains. A mountainside trail up Big Kennesaw, 1,808 feet high, gives a panoramic view of Marietta and, on clear days, the Atlanta skyline. The visitor center has a ten-minute slide presentation about the battle, shown on request. Picnic facilities are available; camping is not allowed.

Open: Visitor Center: 8:30 a.m. to 5 p.m. daily, extended to 6 p.m. summer weekends. Closed Christmas and New Year's Day. Parking is available evenings for an hour after the visitor center is closed. During weekends, there is a free shuttle to the top of Kennesaw Mountain.

Fees: None.

Mailing Address: Kennesaw Mountain National Battlefield Park, P.O. Box 1167, Marietta, GA 30061.

Telephone: 404-427-4686.

Getting There: The park is located two miles north of Marietta off Route 41. From Atlanta take I-75 north about 20 miles to exit 116 (Barrett Parkway), turning left (west). At the second traffic light, turn right (north) onto Route 41 north (Cobb Parkway) and at the first traffic light, turn left (west) onto "Old 41 Highway." The park's Visitor Center is about 2½ miles further on the right.

⏐ Martin Luther King, Jr., National Historic Site

Sweet Auburn is the name of this prosperous black section of Atlanta, although it could also be called "Bittersweet." Here, Martin Luther King, Jr., the Nobel Prize-winning preacher who fought for black equality and civil rights, was born on January 15, 1929. Here he was buried after his assassination on April 4, 1968.

The Martin Luther King, Jr., National Historic Site is dedicated to the man who gave his life to the civil rights movement. It includes the house at 501 Auburn Avenue where Dr. King was born, the Ebenezer Baptist Church at 413 Auburn Avenue where several members of the King family preached, and The Martin Luther King, Jr., Center for Non-Violent Social Change, Incorporated.

Start your tour at the Park Service Information Kiosk across the street from The King Center, which has maps and brochures on the Auburn community's influence on Dr. King.

The Birth House, where Dr. King lived from 1929 until he was 12 years old, is open from 10 a.m. to 4 p.m. daily. Free tours of the two-story, Queen Anne-style structure are given daily on a first come, first served basis. The house, which is currently undergoing restoration, has 12 rooms furnished with period pieces from the 1930s. There is even an old-fashioned ice box in the kitchen.

The Martin Luther King, Jr., Center for Non-Violent Social Change contains Dr. King's crypt and an extensive exhibit about Dr. King's life as a family man, a civil rights leader, and a minister. Here you will see the original leather workboots and the bluejeans Dr. King wore in 1965 during the famous civil rights march from Selma to Montgomery, Alabama. Exhibits include his minister's robe and Bible, the suit he wore the day he was stabbed in New York in 1958, and the key to the hotel room in which he was assassinated. Copies of his Nobel Prize, his Congressional Medal of Honor, and other awards are on display. Dr. King's crypt is made of Georgia white marble and sits on a circular concrete base in the reflecting pool of the plaza outside The King Center. The staff offers workshops and lectures to community groups on civil rights and the King legacy.

The Ebenezer Baptist Church nearby, where Dr. King's father, Reverend Martin Luther King, Sr., and his brother, Reverend Alfred Daniel Williams King, were preachers, is open to the public from 10 a.m. to 4 p.m. daily. Sunday services, held from 11 a.m. to 1 p.m., are packed.

Other buildings in the community include the neo-classical Herndon Building, built by black entrepreneur Alonzo F. Herndon, a barber who founded the Atlanta Life Insurance Company, and the Odd Fellows Building, built in 1914 by Georgia's largest black fraternity. This six-story building, festooned with terra cotta figures symbolizing black success, was the cultural, political, and economic center of Atlanta's black community in the early 20th century. The offices of the Southern Christian Leadership Conference are in the Prince Hall Masonic Lodge. Walking tours of the neighborhood are given upon request. Contact the Information Kiosk for details.

On January 15 each year, The King Center commemorates Dr. King's birthday with special activities. Check for details.

Open: The Information Kiosk is open 9 a.m. to 5 p.m. daily. Closed Thanksgiving, Christmas, and New Year's Day. Visitors are free to walk about the Auburn community at all times.

Fees: None.

Mailing Address: Martin Luther King, Jr. National Historic Site, 522 Auburn Ave. N.E., Atlanta, GA 30312.

Telephone: 404-331-3919.

Getting There: The site is located in Atlanta along Auburn Ave., 1½ miles from downtown. Visitors traveling to the park on southbound I-75/85 should exit at Butler Street; northbound vehicles will take the Edgewood/Auburn Avenue exit. The route from there to the park is marked by signs.

‖ Ocmulgee National Monument

In the countryside southeast of Macon, where the Southern Railroad tracks lie close to the Ocmulgee River, an Indian town once flourished. From 900 to 1100, the Mississippian Indians who lived in the area hunted, fished, tended crops, and built the earthen mounds that rise from the grassy fields today. These flat-topped, pyramidal earthworks, which range in height from two to 48 feet, were used for ceremonial purposes; some supported buildings while others are burial mounds.

Ocmulgee National Monument preserves seven of these mounds and an earth lodge that may well be the oldest public structure in the United States. The floor and first 18 inches of wall of the lodge's grassy structure are over 1,000 years old. The rest of the 48-by-48 structure is reconstructed. Archeologists believe that high chiefs sat in the three-seat Bird Platform near the lodge's central fire pit, while lesser members sat in the 47 seats that line the walls. There is a self-guided, audio-visual presentation inside the mound for visitors.

The largest of the park's earthworks is the squared, flat-topped hillock known as Great Temple Mound, which was probably topped by a thatched shelter with wood and clay walls. Lesser Temple Mound nearby was damaged when the rail line through the area was built. A funeral mound stands near the parking lot. Also visible are trenches in an arc that could indicate the outer edge of the village. In addition, the park is the site of an English trading post built by the British in 1690 along the Lower Creek Trading Path. James Moore, a colonist from South Carolina, recruited the area's Creek Indians to fight against the Spanish settlement in Saint Augustine, Florida. The Creeks dominated Georgia and Alabama until they were relocated to the West by President Andrew Jackson in the first half of the 19th century.

The visitor center, a white, round art deco structure, is as interesting as the mounds themselves. It has a two-story rotunda topped with glass blocks and murals of photographs made during excavations in the 1930s. The museum has a video about pottery-making and flint-knapping, an award-winning film about life in the region from the ice age to the present, and displays of Indian pottery, shell beads, stonework, and copper "sun discs." Dioramas illustrate the earth lodge use, the Creek Green Corn ceremony, and the trading post era. Various special programs and craft demonstrations are scheduled throughout the year. Check for details.

Open: Visitor Center: 9 a.m. to 5 p.m. daily. Closed Christmas and New Year's Day.

Fees: $1 ages 17–62.

Mailing Address: Ocmulgee National Monument, 1207 Emery Highway, Macon, GA 31201.

Telephone: 912-752-8257.

Getting There: The monument is on the east edge of Macon, GA, on Rt. 80 and Alt 129. Take I-75 to I-16 east. Take either the first or second exit from I-16 and follow the signs one mile to the park entrance.

GUAM/SAIPAN

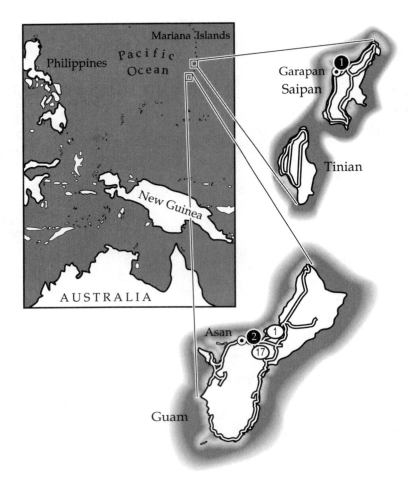

1. American Memorial Park
2. War in the Pacific National Historical Park

|| American Memorial Park

A stone memorial obelisk and a 133-acre recreational park in Tanapag Harbor, Saipan, commemorates the Americans who died in the Mariana Islands Campaign of World War II. The successful capture of Saipan, a Japanese colony since 1920 and the site of a major military installation, gave the Allied forces a base from which to bomb Japan. (Japan captured the Northern Marianas, then known as the German Marianas, from the Germans in World War I. But the islands were not truly a colony of Japan until the League of Nations gave them to Japan by mandate in 1920.)

After the area was secured on July 9, 1944, nearly 3,000 B-29 bombers took off each day from Saipan. The nearby island of Tinian, secured August 1, is known as the base for the atomic bomb carrier the Enola Gay. The bomber made its historic flight nearly a year later, on August 6, 1945.

Under heavy fire from the Japanese, the first wave of marines landed on Saipan's southern beaches at 8:40 a.m. on June 15, 1944. By nightfall, 20,000 troops were on the island, but they could advance no farther than the beachheads because Japanese forces occupied the high ground. While U.S. marines were desperately struggling to establish a beachhead on Saipan, an extraordinary air-sea battle, known as "The Great Marianas Turkey Shoot," raged in the surrounding waters as the Allies picked off more then 300 Japanese airplanes, devastating the enemy navy.

Japanese supplies and manpower on Saipan remained virtually unchanged from mid-April until the capture by U.S. forces in July 1944. On June 19, the U.S. forces won the Battle of the Philippine Sea, clearing the way for Allied operations in the Philippines. But it took almost three weeks of fighting Japanese suicide attacks to advance across the island.

By July 6, the U.S. advance so threatened Japanese positions that the two remaining Japanese admirals on the island committed suicide rather than surrender. Following their example, thousands of Japanese troops and many Japanese civilians on the island hurled themselves from high cliffs on the northern end of the island into shark-infested waters. Military personnel leapt from the 600-foot-high Suicide Cliffs to their watery death; civilians jumped from the 75-foot high Banzai

Cliffs. Because of these suicides, the Japanese lost 37,000 men; American casualties amounted to 3,500 dead and 13,000 wounded.

The park's facilities, administered by the National Park Service in conjunction with the Northern Marianas government, are still under development. They include portions of Micro beach, one of the island's most beautiful waterfront areas, a marina, several picnic areas, and a monument. The park grounds have World War II bunkers, a fuel storage tank, ruined barracks, and a Japanese garden area. Future developments include two marinas, sports fields, a nature center, and a major Saipan Cultural Center.

Saipan is a small island, 14.5 miles long and 5.5 miles at the widest point. It is located 130 miles north of Guam and about 2½ hours by air from Tokyo. Vegetation is typically tropical, with coconut palm, tangan-tangan, iron wood, and breadfruit trees.

Snorkeling and scuba diving in the pristine waters of the lagoon are excellent. There are wrecked ships, aircraft, and underwater grottoes to explore. Watch out for sharks and unexploded mines. Deep-sea fishing for tuna, marlin, and skipjack is another popular activity. For further information about activities and accommodations on the island, contact the Marianas Visitors Bureau, P.O. Box 861, Saipan, MP 96950.

Open: The park is always open.

Fees: None.

Mailing Address: P.O. Box 198, CHRB, Saipan, MP 96950.

Telephone: 670-234-7207.

Getting There: The site is located in Garapan, Saipan. Continental, Northwest, Guam Marianas, and Japan Air Lines serve the island, and All Nippon Airlines run charters from Tokyo.

‖ War in the Pacific National Historical Park

The concrete bunkers, hideout caves, and war artillery in this historical park are grim reminders of the fighting in the Pacific Theater of World War II. This historical park in Guam commemorates the bravery and sacrifices of all people, from all nations, who were involved in the Pacific Theater. Divided into seven separate units, the

The 1944 Battle for Guam, interpreted in War in the Pacific National Historical Park, marked a turning point in the Pacific Theater of World War II.
—*NPS photograph*

park preserves the remains of over 70 sites associated with the recapture of Guam from the Japanese. The sites are located both on land and underwater.

Guam, a U.S. possession since 1898, is located 1,500 miles southeast of Tokyo and is the largest and southern-most of the 15 islands that make up the Mariana Islands. These islands formed a strategic line of defense along Japan's southeastern Pacific flank.

Guam was bombed by the Japanese on December 8, 1941, and invaded and captured by Japanese forces two days later. For two-and-a-half long years, Guamanians were forced to live under a brutal Japanese occupation.

The campaign for this region, known as Operation Forager, began on July 21, 1944, when 535 U.S. ships loaded with airplanes and 55,000 troops moved towards the Phillipine Sea. As the Americans advanced, the Guamanians were pressed into forced labor. Many were tortured and ultimately executed for their American sympathies. The island was declared secured on August 10, 1944. Japanese stragglers remained hidden on Guam for months. The last known holdout was found in 1972.

Of the park's seven units, the Asan Beach Unit and the Agat Unit were two of the major invasion beaches. The Piti Guns Unit was the site of three Japanese coastal guns. The Asan Inland Unit and the Mount Alifan Unit were both battlefield sites. The Mount Tenjo-Mount Chachao Unit was a high ridge system overlooking the Philippine Sea and the Fonte Unit held part of the Japanese command center.

The T. Stell Newman Visitor Information Center, located on the beach side of Marine Drive in Asan, has a museum with displays on the events of the Pacific Theater. Audiovisual programs about the Marianas during the war years and Guam's history and culture are available upon request. Contact the site for information about the research library, with over 700 volumes and 200 photographs, and about other sites around the islands and Micronesia.

Among the interesting war-related spots on Guam is the War Dog Cemetery containing the remains of 23 German shepherds and Doberman pinschers. The dogs were used to relay messages and locate Japanese forces hidden in the foliage. The graves of this brave K-9 Corps are marked by white picket-shaped memorials with a black dog profile.

Also on the island is Tweed's Cave in Pagua Point, one of the hiding spots used by George R. Tweed, a U.S. Navy radio man who refused to report for internment at a Japanese prisoner-of-war camp. Tweed lived underground for 21 months until he was rescued by a U.S. warship. He became a cause célèbre among the Guamanians, a symbol of defiance to Japanese rule, and he was supported by the islanders throughout the occupation. Father Jesus Duenas, an ardent American sympathizer known for using the American flag as his altar cloth, was beheaded by the Japanese for aiding Tweed.

Guam is 32 miles long and four-to-eight miles wide. Its moderate climate makes it an ideal place for outdoor activities. The year-round average temperature is 80 degrees; the ocean temperature averages 81 degrees.

May to November is the rainy season and you can expect hot, wet, and humid days. Temperatures cool down from November through April, the dry season, and tropical trade winds are common. Typhoons can occur in any month but are more common during the rainy season. Popular activities include water recreational sports, such as scuba diving, snorkeling, sailboarding, water skiing, deep sea fishing, and sunset cruises.

The landscape is widely varied, with sandy beaches, saw grass savannahs, lush jungles, spectacular waterfalls, and 1,000-foot-high mountains. Natural life on the island includes the Guam rail, a flightless bird, and orchids growing wild in the tropical foliage.

Open: Visitor Center: 7:30 a.m. to 3:30 p.m. Monday–Friday; 8:30 a.m. to 2 p.m. on weekends and federal holidays. Closed Thanksgiving, Christmas, and New Year's Day.

Fees: None.

Mailing Address: War in the Pacific National Historical Park, P.O. Box FA, Marine Drive, Asan, Agana, Guam 96910.

Telephone: 671-477-9362 or 472-7240. Guam is 15 hours ahead of Eastern Standard Time.

Getting There: Continental Airlines, Air Micronesia, and Hawaiian Airlines provide direct service from the U.S. mainland via Honolulu, Hawaii. Northwest Orient Airlines, All Nippon Airways, and Japan Airlines provide service to Guam from the U.S. via Tokyo, Japan. Continental/Air Micronesia provides air service to and from Guam to Saipan and other destinations in the area.

HAWAII

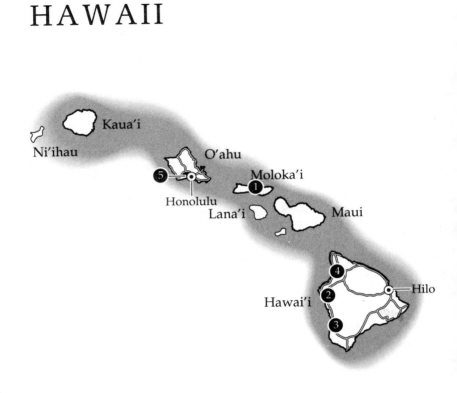

‖ Kalaupapa National Historical Park

Hawaiian patients of Hansen's Disease, also called leprosy, were once banished to this peninsula on the north coast of Molokai Island, an isolated tract of land bordered by a forbidding 3,000-foot-high cliff. The settlement here became one of the best-known patient colonies in the world. In the late 19th century, the Belgian priest Father Damien, soon to be canonized by the Catholic Church, lived and worked here. More recently, this community was popularized by James A. Michener's epic novel *Hawaii*. The area is reserved for the people who have lived here since childhood.

Some 100 former patients and another 50 or more attendants live on Kalaupapa in a settlement that remains extremely isolated. Islanders receive provisions by air and from a barge that visits the peninsula only twice each summer. Tourists need permits from the Department of Health before they can visit and children under 16 are not allowed in the settlement, a restriction upheld more for traditional rather than medical reasons. Thanks to medication, all former patients are non-contagious.

Visits to this unusual community, available by guided tour only, are worth making. Kalaupapa's small houses, tidy gardens, and coconut groves convey a unique, old-fashioned style of living that recalls the quiet grace of Hawaii before it was modernized. The peninsula contains the ruins of more than 300 historic Hawaiian structures. Of special note is the stone church built by Father Damien, the priest who arrived at the leper colony on Molokai in 1873. This church, which stands in a coconut grove across from the old settlement, has a large bell tower and an old graveyard where priests are buried. Father Damien eventually died of the disease, and his body was removed from Kalaupapa to Antwerp in 1936.

Damien Tours offers day-long guided tours of Kalaupapa. Charges include transportation, lunch, and tour. For the adventurous, there is a trip by mule train over the 2½-mile switchback trail that snakes down the cliff into Kalaupapa. The views upon descending into the peninsula are spectacular.

Open: Access to Kalaupapa is by guided tour only.

Fees: Fees vary with type of tour, but generally run between $55 and $100 for the day. If you fly, the total will be about $100 a person, including transportation, lunch, and tour. The mule ride is about $55 a person.

Mailing Address: Kalaupapa National Historical Park, Kalaupapa, HI 96748.

Telephone: 808-567-9093.

Getting There: Contact Damien Tours, c/o Kalaupapa Settlement, Kalaupapa, HI 97642.

‖ Kaloko-Honokohau National Historical Park

Kaloko-Honokohau National Historical Park, site of one of the most densely populated areas in prehistoric Hawaii, is currently closed to visitors. The area contains the ruins of three major Hawaiian settlements established before the arrival of Europeans, including temples, or heiau (pronounced hay-yow), and large fishponds. This is the reputed burial place of King Kamehameha the Great, who ruled all the Hawaiian islands in the early 19th century. A park interpreting traditional Hawaiian culture is planned. The privately owned beaches are excellent but permission is needed to swim. The site is ten miles north of Kailua-Kona on the island of Hawaii.

For further information, contact the superintendent at Kaloko-Honokohau National Historical Park, 73-4786 Kanalani Street, #14, Kailua-Kona, HI 96740.

Telephone: 808-546-7584.

‖ Pu'uhonua o Honaunau National Historical Park

With its stone walls, palm-thatched temples, and grimacing wooden gargoyles, this historical park on the island of Hawaii interprets an ancient Hawaiian sanctuary and royal residence. Defeated warriors and islanders who broke the "kapu," or taboos, sought sanctuary among

These effigies, reconstructed by Native artisans, stand outside the temple at Place of Refuge in Kona, Hawaii.—*NPS photograph*

the leaning palms and sandy beaches here; chiefs who made the kapu lived with their attendants in the adjacent royal compound.

Built in the 16th century on a spectacular lava promontory near present-day Kona, Pu'uhonua o Honaunau was used until King Kamehameha II abandoned traditional religious beliefs in the early 19th century. It was one of many sanctuaries where vanquished warriors and islanders who broke taboos, which forbade everything from eating with the opposite sex to walking in the footsteps of a chief, could escape the death penalty. After a few hours or days at the refuge, sinners could return to their normal lives. The problem was getting here. Since land access to the sanctuary was blocked by the royal compound, villagers had to take a boat or swim across the bay to safety before they were caught. Today there are few practitioners of traditional Hawaiian religion and the sanctuary is a cultural relic, but occasional anonymous offerings are left on the altars at the pu'uhonua.

A 1,000-foot-long lava stone wall built jigsaw-puzzle style and without mortar in 1550 separates the two sections of the park—the pu'uhonua, or refuge, and the palace grounds. Of the three temples, called heiau (pronounced hay-yow), that once stood in the sanctuary, only the Hale o Keawe Heiau, which housed the holy bones of 23 chiefs, has been reconstructed. The 'A-le'ale'a Heiau and Old Heiau are ruined stone platforms. The royal side of the site features reconstructions of a chief's residence and typical commoners' quarters, traditional Hawaiian canoes built of koa wood and coconut fibers, the royal canoe landing, and the fishponds where fish caught for the high chief were stored.

The park also has several historic rocks, including the Ka'ahumanu Stone where, according to legend, Queen Ka'ahumanu, a favorite wife of Kamehameha I, hid after a lovers' quarrel. The queen's pet dog barked until the queen was found, and the reunited royal couple lived happily ever after. It may take some imagination to picture the scene because Queen Ka'ahumanu, in accordance with the Hawaiian esthetic, was a very large woman weighing over 200 pounds.

The story of the nearby Keoua Stone, a 20-foot-long monolith, also stretches the imagination. Legend has it that King Keoua was so tall that if he lay with his arms outstretched, he would fit the stone perfectly.

The park's extensive living history program illustrates Hawaiian life in the late 1700s. Islanders in native costume weave mats, carve wooden objects, gather crabs and sea urchins, and fish with handmade nets—a practice known as hukilau, which is no longer legal because it depletes marine life on the reef.

On special flat stones, visitors can play konane, an ancient board game similiar to checkers that is played with black and white pebbles. There is an original board game in the refuge and another on the royal grounds. Copies of the rules are available at the visitor center, which features an exhibition describing life at the site. Fifteen-minute orientation talks are given six times daily in an outdoor amphitheater.

Pack a lunch (no food is available at the site) and plan to spend the whole day. The park is as rich in nature as it is in history. After your tour, you can explore the cliffs and tidal pools, picnic on the white beaches, and swim and snorkel in the royal canoe landing and the reef beyond, which contains brightly colored tang and butterfly fish. Beware of black sea urchins, which have stinging spines. Indigenous plants include palm trees, mulberry, hibiscus, ti used for preserving food, and candlenut, the state tree. Most of the palms here are shaved, but several have been left in their natural state. Look out for falling coconuts and palm fronds. A Hawaiian cultural festival, which opens and closes with a re-creation of a royal court procession, is held on the last weekend in June. Craft demonstrations include the making of fish nets and hooks, mats, cloth from tapa bark, sandals, and leis. During the festival, visitors can sample such traditional foods as poi, a native starch, dried fish and fruit, and roast pig.

Open: Visitor Center: 7:30 a.m. to 5:30 p.m. daily, all year; the park is open until midnight.

Fees: $1, ages 16–61

Mailing Address: Pu'uhonua o Honaunau National Historical Park, P.O. Box 129, Honaunau, Kona, HI 96726.

Telephone: 808-328-2326.

Getting There: The park is on the island of Hawaii. From Hilo, take Route 11 south to Route 160 (milepost 103) and turn left onto Route 160 about four miles to the park. From Kaliua-Kona, take route 11 south for 18 miles and turn right onto route 160 to the park.

‖ Puukohola Heiau National Historic Site

The Puukohola Heiau (pronounced hay-yow), a temple on the island of Hawaii above Kawaihae Bay, is one of the last major religious structures built King Kamehameha I in 1791. A symbol of the power of the great warrior-king Kamehameha I, who conquered the Hawaiian islands in the early 19th century, the temple was dedicated to the family war god, Ku-ka'ili-moku, and used from 1791 to 1819. The heiau, meaning "temple," consisted of a three-sided stone platform that fronted the sea, an altar, a prayer tower, thatched houses for the chief and priests, and many carved religious images. Today all that remains is the temple's stone foundation, which was made without mortar. Puukohola Heiau along with the ruins of two other temples and of the house of Kamehameha's trusted advisor, John Young, are preserved in this unusual historical park.

According to Hawaiian legend, Kamehameha built the temple because a priest told him that if he did so, he would become king of Hawaii. He dedicated the temple with the blood of his cousin and archrival, Keoua Ku'ahu'ula, who was killed when he arrived by canoe to pay tribute to the newly constructed temple. By 1810, the prophesy was fulfilled. Kamehameha's reign marked the peak of traditional Hawaiian civilization. But even during Kamehameha's reign, western culture was beginning to take root, heralding a change in the old ways. In fact, Kamahameha's chief advisor, John Young, was a British sailor who had been stranded in Hawaii in 1790. After Kamehameha died in 1819 his son Liholiho, known as Kamehameha II, abandoned the traditional religion and destroyed the temples and wooden images.

After 150 years of earthquakes and neglect, the temple's foundation is crumbling and visitors are prohibited from climbing onto it. But a trail leads close enough for visitors to see the extraordinary 224-foot-by-100-foot stone platform. The trail also winds by the ruins of the smaller Mailekini Heiau, a temple once crowded with idols and used by Kamehameha's ancestors, and the Stone Leaning Post from which the chief priest watched sharks devour offerings placed in a now-submerged temple. Archeologists believe the remains of this submerged temple, Hale-O-Ka-Puni, stand just off the shore. The park also contains Pelekane, the site of the royal residence, where both Kamehameha I and his son lived while in Kawaihae Bay. The site of John Young's house is across the street. Historians believe the house was probably built of stone and mortar reflecting both European and Hawaiian architectural styles.

The park is on an open, grassy patch of land on a rise above the sea. A rare fern, the pololei, grows on the site, but otherwise vegetation is sparse and uninteresting. Some coconut trees and other native species grow near the coast. Except for a few owls and the small rodents they feed on, little wildlife lives on the site.

Tours of the park are self-guided, but special ranger-led walks are available on request for groups of more than ten. The trail from the information center to the sites in the park is long, hot, and rugged. The park service suggests visitors wear good walking shoes. Swimming is not recommended at Puukohola, which is near a deep water harbor, but nearby Spencer Beach Park has a good beach and picnic facilities. In August, the park celebrates the establishment of the park with the festival of Kekulana Noeau O Kawa Kahiko, a two-day event of Hawaiian culture.

Open: 7:30 a.m. to 4:00 p.m. daily.
Fees: None.
Mailing Address: Puukohola Heiau National Historic Site, P.O. Box 44340, Kawaihae, HI 96743.
Telephone: 808-882-7218.
Getting There: The site is on the island of Hawaii along Route 270 near Hapuna Beach. Taxis and car rentals are available at airports in Hilo and Waimea-Kohala.

‖ USS *Arizona* Memorial

On December 7, 1941, the Japanese bombed Pearl Harbor, sinking the USS *Arizona* and killing 1,177 of her crew. The attack thrust the United States into World War II. The hull of the *Arizona* still lies where the ship sank, in 38 feet of water. Built on pilings over the ship, the USS *Arizona* Memorial commemorates this fateful attack. Inside is a white marble shrine engraved with the names of the sailors who perished in the *Arizona*.

The off-shore monument together with the exhibitions in the visitor center on shore interpret the attack on Pearl Harbor and America's involvement in the Pacific during World War II. The visitor center has a free 30-minute film about the history of the *Arizona*, what led to the attack, and actual film footage of the event. The museum has a rotating display of photographs, model ships, uniforms of the men in the *Arizona*, dishes, and other items that have been salvaged from the waters of Pearl Harbor.

Throughout the war, Hawaii served as a center for Allied operations in the Pacific and as a fueling station for ships. The *Arizona*, a 608-foot-long battleship built in 1915, was one of the biggest ships stationed at Pearl Harbor on the morning of the attack.

Free Park Service tour-boat rides, which leave from the visitor center about every 15 minutes, take visitors to the memorial in the harbor. The trip lasts about six minutes, and visitors can stay as long as they like until the memorial closes. Only the *Arizona*'s #3 gun turret foundation extends above the surface, but the waters of Pearl Harbor are so clear that parts of the ship's deck are also visible. Tickets are available on a first-come, first-served basis. Pick them up early. Visitation is limited to 4,350 people a day and tickets are often distributed by noon. A two-hour wait is not uncommon.

Special ceremonies for invited guests are held at the monument on December 7, the anniversary of the attack. Services and speeches are also conducted on Memorial Day, May 27.

The USS *Bowfin*, a World War II submarine, and the Submarine Museum is located just across the visitor center's parking lot. Tours through the ship and museum are self-paced and could take as long as 1½ hours. The cost is $6 a person.

Open: Visitor Center: 7:30 a.m. to 5 p.m. Tours from 8 a.m. to 3 p.m., seven days a week. Tours are not offered on Thanksgiving, Christmas, and New Year's Day.

Fees: None for the memorial.

Mailing Address: USS *Arizona* Memorial, National Park Service, 1 Arizona Memorial Place, Honolulu, HI 96818.

Telephone: 808-422-2771.

Getting There: The visitor center is at 1 Arizona Drive in Pearl Harbor. For information about bus service from Waikiki, nine miles from Pearl Harbor, call 808-926-4747. For information about commercial tours and accommodations, contact the Chamber of Commerce at 735 Bishop Street, Honolulu, HI 96813, 808-531-4111 or the Hawaii Visitor's Bureau, 2270 Kalakaua Ave. Suite 804, Honolulu, HI 96815. Telephone: 808-923-1811.

IDAHO

1. Craters of the Moon National Monument
2. Hagerman Fossil Beds National Monument
3. Nez Perce National Historical Park

|| Craters of the Moon National Monument

Extending like an endless lunar landscape in the sagebrush plains of southern Idaho is the garden of rock known as Craters of the Moon. The park was formed by molten rock that forced its way through the earth's surface at various times during the last 15,000 years. This area was visited by astronauts in preparation for later visits to the moon.

The desolate 53,000-acre monument is a vast playground of volcanic formations. They include aa (pronounced ah-ah) lava, so rough that it shreds shoes, and the more negotiable, rope-like pahoehoe (pronounced pa-hoy-hoy) lava. Tree molds, which are hollow, upright tubes formed when lava flowed around trees, still stand, and lava bombs, formed when airborne molten rock fell to earth, litter the fields.

A seven-mile loop road leads visitors past most of the park's major geologic attractions, including Big Cinder Butte, the largest cinder cone in the world. Most visitors take two to three hours to complete this route.

At first glance, this barren, rocky environment may seem devoid of all living creatures, but the area is actually home to many different plants and animals. Brilliantly colored wildflowers carpet the park from June through August, providing a dazzling contrast to the black and red rocks. Cinder cones host crowds of magenta-colored monkey flowers; sagebrush and mock orange defy the unyielding lava flows. In all, more than 200 species of plants are native to this seemingly inhospitable landscape.

Bobcats, great-horned owls, and falcons hunt the smaller animals that inhabit the park, while reptiles and insects—some 2,000 species of them—scurry from fissure to crack.

The region was first explored in 1921 by Robert Limbert and W.L. Cole, two hardy adventurers who had to carry their dog over the sharp lava beds.

A film shown in the visitor center explains the area's unique geology and dioramas depict local animals and plants. Rangers conduct tours of the park during the summer, including walks through Indian tunnels and some of the smaller caves.

A flow of pahoehoe lava, distinguished by its "ropy" texture, at Craters of the Moon National Monument.—*NPS photograph*

There is a 51-site campground at the monument with running water and restrooms, but no electrical hook-ups or dump stations. Fees are $5.00 per campsite nightly. Backcountry camping and hiking are allowed, but you must register with the ranger first. Permits are free. No open fires are allowed in the park. Cross-country skiing on the loop road in the park is excellent from January to March. The nearby town of Arco, the first city in the world to be powered by atomic energy, holds a festival near the Idaho International Engineering Labs each year around July 4th. Check with the local city hall for details.

Open: Visitor Center: 8 a.m. to 4:30 p.m. daily, with hours extended to 6 p.m. from mid-June to Labor Day. Closed Thanksgiving, Christmas, New Year's Day, George Washington's Birthday, and Martin Luther King's Birthday.

Fees: $3 per car, or $1 per person per bus.

Mailing Address: Craters of the Moon National Monument, P.O. Box 29, Arco, ID 83213.

Telephone: 208-527-3257.

Getting There: There is no public transportation to the park. The nearest airports are located in Idaho Falls, Twin Falls, and Hailey, ID. From Idaho Falls in the southeastern part of the state, take Rt. 20 West to Arco. Turn left at the blinking red stoplight and continue down Rt. 20 towards Boise for about 18 miles until you reach Craters of the Moon, on the left side of the road.

▌Hagerman Fossil Beds National Monument

This recent addition to the Park system boasts one of the world's best collections of Pliocene fossils, ranging from 2.5 to 3.5 million years old. Among the many fossils preserved at the site are mega-fossils such as the Hagerman Horse, a proto-horse that resembles a zebra.

In the scientific community, Hagerman is prized for its well-preserved collection of small rodents, birds, amphibians, reptiles, and fish. Since small animals have short reproductive cycles, the monument provides a window into the evolution of these animal types.

The 4,200-acre monument is located on the west bank of the Snake River near Hagerman, Idaho. There are no developed facilities, no drinking water, and no restrooms.

Open: The park is always open.

Fees: None.

Mailing Address: Hagerman Fossil Beds National Monument, 2647 Kimberly Road East, Twin Falls, ID 83301.

Telephone: 208-733-8398.

Getting There: Take U.S. 30 off I-84 to Hagerman. The Monument is directly west across the Snake River.

▌Nez Perce National Historical Park

This park system, scattered in 24 sites throughout north central Idaho, is dedicated to the Nez Perce Indians, a powerful tribe of skilled horsemen who once ruled the river-veined countryside of Idaho.

To visit the majority of the park sites would require a 400-mile drive, from the sacred grounds at East Kamiah where, according to Indian legend, life began, to the Lolo Trail high in the Bitterroot Mountains, which early explorers Lewis and Clark followed on their trek to the Pacific in 1805.

The Nez Perce (meaning "pierced nose" in French, although as a tribe the Indians probably did not pierce their noses) lived peacefully with the trappers and traders who traveled their lands until the discovery of gold in 1860 brought miners and settlers into the region. The Indians were forced onto ever-smaller reservations. The first treaty in 1855 gave the Indians essentially all of their traditional homeland. The Treaty of 1863, however, greatly reduced this area to the current reservation boundaries.

In 1877, tensions between the Nez Perce and white settlers led to the battle at White Bird Canyon, where the Nez Perce emerged victorious over U.S. Army troops and civilian volunteers. Hoping to find peace in Canada, a group of Indians led by Chiefs White Bird, Looking Glass, and Joseph fled the federal troops.

After battles at the Clearwater site in Idaho and Big Hole in Montana, the exodus ended in the Bear Paw Mountains of Montana, 42 miles from the Canadian border. Demoralized and depleted, the Nez Perce surrendered in early October. Most were sent to reservations in Kansas, later to Oklahoma. Eventually, many of them returned to Idaho while others were exiled to the Colville Reservation in Washington. Today, about 2,000 Nez Perce live on or near the reservation in Idaho.

Although the park itself does not have campgrounds, there are almost unlimited opportunities for camping and hiking in state and national forests nearby. The Clearwater, Nez Perce, and Wallowa-Whitman forests have numerous trails and campgrounds. The nearby Snake and Salmon rivers are excellent for white water rafting and kayaking. The Clearwater River is famous for its steelhead salmon. Fishing requires a state license.

Wilderness areas near the park include the Selway-Bitterroot Wilderness south of the Lochsa River, the River of No Return Wilderness, and the Gospel Hump Wilderness.

One of the most interesting historical hikes is along the ancient Lolo Trail, followed by Lewis and Clark on their famous transcontinental trek, and used for centuries before them by Native Americans. This trail starts in Wieppe, Idaho, and travels over the crests and ridges of the Bitterroot Mountains for 100 miles. The views are rugged and spectacular, and you can camp at any of the Lewis and Clark campsites along the route. Plan on at least four to five days of vigorous hiking to complete the route. There is also a very primitive four-wheel-drive road that parallels the trail. The road, constructed in the 1930s, is not maintained. At the park visitor center, you can purchase a book about the Lolo trail that indicates key natural features and historic sites.

Shorter self-guided trails are found at Spalding and the East Kamiah sites. The visitor center in Spalding is near the site of a traditional Nez Perce camping ground and not far from the first Christian mission among the Nez Perce. The center has exhibits on Native American culture, with tools, elaborately beaded clothing, fishing gear, and ceremonial items. Once a thriving frontier town, Spalding withered in the early 1900s after the Indian Agency located there moved away three miles south to Lapwai, Idaho. Beautiful Nez Perce crafts are on sale in the visitor center.

Nearby are Coyote's Fishnet and Ant and Yellowjacket, two unique land formations tied to Nez Perce legends. There is also Donald MacKenzie's post, a fur-trading depot built in 1812 for John Jacob Astor's American Fur Company that is thought to have been near Lewiston. A sign commemorates this bit of history.

Eastward along the Clearwater River is the Lenore archeological site and Canoe Camp, both of which bear evidence of 10,000 years of human habitation. A nearby sign tells of Indian houses during this period. Canoe Camp, near Orfino, Idaho, is where Lewis and Clark stopped to build canoes for the final leg of their historic trek across North America to the Pacific Ocean.

The park holds a Nez Perce Cultural Day at the Spalding site each summer, with traditional arts and crafts, dancing, singing, and storytelling. Check with the park for details. Throughout the summer, the Native American groups hold numerous pow-wows in the area.

Visitors seeking hotel and motel rooms can find them in Lewiston, Idaho, and Clarkston, Washington, twin cities located about 12 miles west of the Spalding site. Motels are also available in Kamiah, Grangeville, Orfino, and other small towns in Idaho.

Open: Visitor Center and park headquarters in Spalding is open 8 a.m. to 4:30 p.m. from mid-October to mid-April, with evening hours from spring to early fall. Check for specific hours. Closed Thanksgiving, Christmas, and New Year's Day.

Fees: None.

Mailing Address: Nez Perce National Historical Park, P.O. Box 93, Spalding, ID 83551.

Telephone: 208-843-2261.

Getting There: Three airlines, Empire Airways, Horizon Air and United Express, provide daily service to Lewiston. Greyhound Bus Lines also operate in the region. The nearest rail passenger connections are at Spokane, Washington, Pendleton, Oregon and Boise, Idaho. Route 12 is the principal east-west road in Idaho and Rt. 95 goes north-south.

ILLINOIS

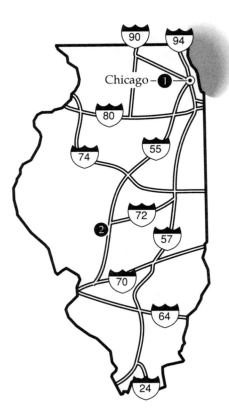

Chicago Portage National Historic Site

A small park near the intersection of Harlem Avenue and 46th Street in Cook County, Illinois, marks the spot of the famous Chicago Portage, a 1.5-mile stretch of dry land between the Des Plaines and Chicago rivers. The portage, discovered in 1673 by the French explorers Louis Jolliet and Jacques Marquette, linked the Great Lakes with the Mississippi River, and was responsible for the establishment of Chicago as a major trade center. French traders used this route until it fell under the control of hostile Indians about 1700. By 1795 this vital commerce route had been secured for the United States under the Treaty of Greenville.

Near the memorial is the Laughton Trading Post, the site of a historic trading post. This area, still under development, will be made into a dramatic historical park in the next few years.

The site, which is owned and administered by the Cook County Forest Preserve, is part of the Chicago Portage Canoe Trail, a 14.4-mile water trail on the Des Plaines River between Stony Ford and Lemont. The trail follows the same historic route Marquette and Jolliet took 300 years ago. The Chicago Sanitary and Ship Canal and the I & M Canal parallel the route. Although the river winds through a mostly urban area, the city is screened from view by the bordering woods. Visitors can bring their own canoes, or contact the Forest Preserve for information about local concessions.

Open: The historic site and Chicago Portage Canoe Trail are open during daylight hours.

Fees: None.

Mailing Address: Chicago Portage National Historic Site, c/o Cook County Forest Preserve, 536 N. Harlem Avene, Cummings Square, River Forest, IL 60305.

Telephone: 312-771-1130.

Getting There: The site is located near the intersection of Harlem Avenue and 46th Street in Cook County, just southwest of Chicago.

|| Lincoln Home National Historic Site

Abraham Lincoln, the 16th president of the United States, raised his family in this Greek Revival house in Springfield, Illinois. This was the only house the Lincolns ever owned, and they lived here until they moved to the White House in Washington, D.C., on February 11, 1861.

Located at the corner of Eighth and Jackson streets, the Lincoln home in downtown Springfield is a reminder of the man before he became a legend, when he was just an ordinary member of the community who chopped wood, indulged his children, and lived and worked like his neighbors.

Abraham and Mary Lincoln purchased the house for $1,500 ($1,200 in cash and a $300 lot in downtown Springfield) in 1844 and lived there for 17 years. As the family grew, the house was expanded to accommodate the Lincoln children—Robert Todd, Edward Baker, William Wallace, and Tad. In 1850, Lincoln added a brick wall and picket fence along the front yard. In 1855 and 1856, workmen raised the roof of the building, creating a second floor with five bedrooms and a trunk room.

The building is at the heart of Springfield's historic district, a 4-block area with 15 historic buildings. Many of these homes are under restoration, but none—except the Lincoln home itself—are open to visitors. Walking tours of the historic district are available through the Lincoln Home Visitor Center on Seventh Street. Check for times.

The visitor center presents a movie about Springfield during Lincoln's time and a detailed video tour of the Home itself. In addition, the visitor center schedules many special programs relating to the Lincoln Home and the National Park Service. There are also Lincoln theme exhibits and a bookstore selling Lincoln-related books.

The Lincoln House, furnished with a mixture of original and period pieces, is open year-round for self-guided tours. Visitation is especially heavy in the summer, when people from all over the world pay tribute to America's most famous president. For those who like to linger, non-tourist season offers a less crowded atmosphere for exploring the site.

Springfield features about a dozen Lincoln-related attractions, including the Lincoln Wax Museum (where Abraham, Mary, and three of their four sons are buried), the Lincoln-Herndon law office, the Old State Capitol, the family's church pew, and even Lincoln's bank ledger. The Illinois State Historical Library, in the basement of the restored Old Capitol, operates a free Lincoln Museum as well as maintaining the largest collection of Lincoln-associated historical documents and artifacts in the world. For further information, contact the Springfield Convention and Visitor's Bureau at 624 East Adams. Telephone: 217-789-2360.

Every Fourth of July weekend, Springfield hosts a Lincoln Fest, a 15-block-long street festival that features people in period costume, a Civil War encampment, old-style debating, the Grand Levee (an old-time ball), crafts, and big-name entertainment.

Open: 8:30 a.m. to 5 p.m. daily. Closed Thanksgiving, Christmas, and New Year's Day.

Fees: None, but free tickets are required to tour the Home. They are available only at the Lincoln Home Visitor Center, 426 South Seventh Street.

Mailing Address: Lincoln Home National Historic Site, 526 South 7th Street, Springfield, IL 62703.

Telephone: 217-492-4150.

Getting There: Take I-55 to 6th St. The site is located between Edwards and Capitol streets. The Springfield area is well-covered with signs directing visitors to the site.

INDIANA

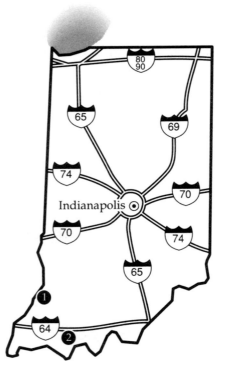

1. George Rogers Clark National Historical Park
2. Lincoln Boyhood National Memorial

|| George Rogers Clark National Historical Park

The George Rogers Clark Memorial in Vincennes, Indiana, commemorates the general whose efforts won the Northwest for the United States during the Revolutionary War. George Rogers Clark was the brother of William Clark who, with Meriwether Lewis, explored the American Northwest to the Pacific Ocean. Between them, these two men helped to double the size of the country.

Clark's string of Revolutionary War victories against British and Indian strongholds from Ohio to Illinois influenced England to eventually cede territory that extended as far west as present-day Wisconsin. Clark's victory at Vincennes was a great coup. Exhausted from crossing the icy, flooded Illinois plains in mid-February, Clark's 175 men made the British think they were outnumbered by shooting extra rounds and making a lot of noise. The ruse worked.

The memorial is part of a 26-acre park on the site of old Fort Sackville in western Indiana. Clark took the fort from Henry Hamilton, the British commander at Detroit, after a battle in freezing weather on February 25, 1779.

Built of marble, granite, and limestone, the circular, columned memorial houses a bronze statue of Clark and seven murals depicting events from Clark's campaign. Formally landscaped gardens surround the memorial.

The visitor's center has a 23-minute movie shown every half-hour about Clark and the capture of Fort Sackville. Tours of the park are self-guided, but interpreters are on duty. In summer, there are exhibitions of period firearms through the park's living history program. During the weekends, patriots in frontier garb and uniformed British soldiers re-create camp life with military drills and firearm demonstrations. On Memorial Day weekend, the park hosts a "rendezvous" recalling the days when trapper and trader met to exchange wares.

Vincennes, the oldest city in the state, hosts a variety of other historic sites. The St. Francis Xavier Church, built on the site of the first log church in the region, recalls the French influence in the area. Other sites include the old Territorial Capitol, the Governor's House, and the Printing Office, where newspapers were printed as early as 1804.

Open: 9 a.m. to 5 p.m. daily. Closed Thanksgiving, Christmas, and New Year's Day.

Fees: Clark Memorial: $1 ages 17–61, April through November.

Mailing Address: George Rogers Clark National Historical Park, 401 S. Second Street, Vincennes, IN 47591.

Telephone: 812-882-1776.

Getting There: The park is located on the banks of the Wabash River along I-50. Follow Rt. 50, which intersects Rt. 41 in Vincennes. The park can be reached from the Sixth St. or Willow St. exits. Entrance is on Second St., south of Rt. 50.

‖ Lincoln Boyhood National Memorial

From the ages of seven to 21, Abraham Lincoln, the 16th president of the United States, lived in a crude log cabin on this site in southern Indiana. The 200-acre Lincoln Boyhood Memorial has a reconstructed log cabin and farm and the grave of Lincoln's mother, Nancy Hanks Lincoln.

It was in this cabin, according to legend, that young Abe mastered his lessons by the light of candle and fireplace, using chalk on a shovel to do his figuring. Corn, flax, oats, and potatoes—the same crops the Lincoln family raised—are grown in the park's fields. During the summer, people in period costume carry out farm chores, illustrating life on a 19th-century farm.

The memorial's visitor center contains exhibits telling the story of Lincoln's life in Indiana. There is furniture made by Lincoln's father, Thomas Lincoln, as well as farm machinery and a 24-minute film, "Here I Grew Up," shown every hour.

Outside the memorial building, an allee designed by the renowned landscape architect Frederick Law Olmsted leads by the giant flagpole to the gravesite of Nancy Hanks Lincoln. On national holidays, the park staff raises a flag that measures 20 feet by 38 feet and weighs 45 pounds.

The rest of the Lincoln story is illustrated at the Abraham Lincoln Birthplace National Historic Site in Kentucky, and the Lincoln Home National Historic Site, where he lived as a young lawyer, in Springfield, Illinois.

Located in wooded countryside, the Lincoln Boyhood Memorial cannot be reached by public transporation. The park provides picnic tables but no food concessions. Wildlife in the region includes deer, squirrels, woodchucks, and other small animals.

Open: Visitor's Center: 8 a.m. to 5 p.m. daily. Closed Thanksgiving, Christmas, and New Year's Day.

Fees: $1 per person ages 16–62, or $3 per family.

Mailing Address: Lincoln Boyhood National Memorial, Lincoln City, IN 47552.

Telephone: 812-937-4757.

Getting There: The site is located on Indiana Highway 162, four miles south of Dale, Indiana. Take exit 57 off I-64, travel south on U.S. Highway 231, and follow the signs to "Lincoln Parks."

IOWA

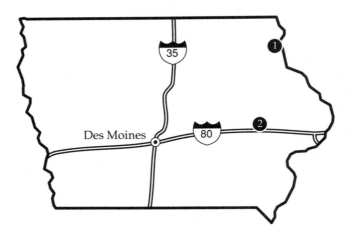

1. Effigy Mounds National Monument
2. Herbert Hoover National Historic Site

Effigy Mounds National Monument

Effigy Mounds, a unique prehistoric Indian site in the upper Mississippi River valley, features earthen mounds from the Woodland Culture that lived here from 500 B.C. to A.D. 1300. The early mounds are conical circles while later mounds are constructed in the likeness of bears and birds with outstretched wings. The monument preserves 191 known mounds in nearly 1,500 acres located among the bluffs of northeast Iowa.

Twenty-six of the mounds are effigies of animals. Perhaps the most impressive is the Great Bear Mound measuring 137 feet long, 70 feet wide, and 3.5 feet high. The Marching Bear Group consists of ten bears along with several bird mounds high atop the bluffs of the Mississippi River.

The Woodland Culture Indians were hunters and gatherers who lived in small groups along the river in summer and in rock shelters

Effigy Mounds National Monument contains outstanding examples of prehistoric Indian mounds, some in the shapes of birds and bears.—*NPS photograph*

during the winter. The mounds they constructed contain burials as well as copper artifacts, stone and shell ornaments, and spear points, all of which indicate an extensive trade network throughout North America.

An hour-long, self-guided tour takes visitors by major mound groups and past scenic overlooks of the Mississippi River. Rangers give four guided walks daily from Memorial Day to Labor Day. The visitor center has exhibits and artifacts found in the area and a short film that introduces visitors to the mound builders and the monument.

The monument's lush forest and prairies have many wildflowers and offer some of the best bird-watching in the region.

Open: 8 a.m. to 5 p.m. daily, extended to 7 p.m. in summer. Closed Christmas Day.

Fees: $1 per person ages 17–61, or $3 per car.

Mailing Address: Effigy Mounds National Monument, Rural Route 1, Box 25A, Harpers Ferry, IA 52146.

Telephone: 319-873-3491.

Getting There: The monument is in the northeastern corner of Iowa, 3 miles north of Marquette on Highway 76. From Dubuque, take Rt. 52 north to Highway 18 east, turn off at Marquette to Highway 76 north.

‖ Herbert Hoover National Historic Site

The modest cottage where Herbert Hoover, the 31st President of the United States, was born on August 10, 1874, the grave where he was buried in 1964, and the Hoover Library are preserved in this historic park in West Branch, Iowa. A stroll through the 186-acre site, with its green lawns, shade trees, white picket fences, and colorful flowerbeds, is like stepping back into a late 19th-century Iowa farm community.

Guides often wear clothing from the 1870s. Some dress in the traditional, unadorned Quaker garb to remind visitors of the Hoovers, a devout Quaker family. In the tiny two-room house where Hoover grew up, some of the original furniture, including Hoover's childhood cradle, are on display.

The park also has the one-room school where Hoover's brother Theodore learned his lessons, the Quaker meetinghouse where his family worshipped, and a reconstruction of a blacksmith shop much like the one in which his father labored. Herbert was six when his father died; his mother died three years later. He then went to live with an uncle in Oregon.

The visitor center has a slide show about Herbert Hoover and displays models of the Hoover birthplace cottage and the stone blacksmith shop. Outside, the site maintains 76 acres of restored Iowa prairie in memory of the six- to eight-foot-high grasses that once covered much of the state.

Hoover's library museum, a reconstruction of his presidential office in the White House, has Hoover's original desk and nearly 20,000 books. The library also contains 5 million documents that Hoover generated while president, letters exchanged by Hoover and the late president Harry Truman, and many souvenirs from Hoover's worldwide travels, including First Lady Lou Hoover's collection of Chinese porcelain.

As a young man, Hoover traveled the world working for mining companies and became a millionaire by the time he was 40. His work with European refugees during World War I earned him a reputation as a great humanitarian. After a seven-year stint as Secretary of Commerce, Hoover was elected president by a landslide victory in 1928.

But Hoover soon lost the popular support that swept him into office. On October 29, 1929, the stock market plunged, triggering the Great Depression that devastated the American economy. He was denounced by those who thought he was not doing enough to help the country's impoverished population and lost his office in 1932 to Franklin D. Roosevelt.

West Branch is a quaint midwestern town outside Iowa City, full of turn-of-the-century homes, antique shops, and quiet cafes. Each year, on the Sunday nearest Hoover's birthday on August 10, there is a celebration and a graveside ceremony.

Open: Visitor Center: 8 a.m. to 5 p.m., extended to 6 p.m. during summer. Closed Thanksgiving, Christmas, and New Year's Day. The site is always open.

Fees: $1 for the site; $1 for the Presidential Library.

Mailing Address: Herbert Hoover National Historic Site, P.O. Box 607, West Branch, IA 52358.

Telephone: 319-643-2541.

Getting There: From Iowa City, take I-80 east to West Branch. The Visitor Center is on Parkside Drive and Main Street, ½ mile from exit 254 off I-80 in West Branch.

KANSAS

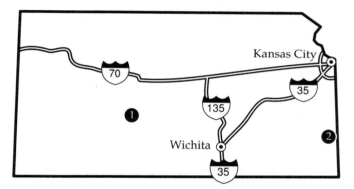

1. Fort Larned National Historic Site
2. Fort Scott National Historic Site

‖ Fort Larned National Historic Site

Established in 1860 to defend the settlers and traders who traveled the Santa Fe Trail, Fort Larned played an important role in the taming of the American West. Troops stationed here provided armed escorts for mail stages and wagon trains, distributed government food and supplies to the Plains Indians, and defended construction of the railroad line that eventually ended the post's usefulness.

Fort Larned was a center for operations against hostile Indians, and hosted such famous Indian fighters as Kit Carson, "Buffalo Bill" Cody, and General George Armstrong Custer. Ironically, the fort also served as the local Indian Agency, whose function was to distribute free food and supplies to Native Americans.

The fort was all but abandoned in 1878, by which time most of the region's Indians had been removed to the Indian Territory (now Oklahoma). But during its brief, colorful lifetime, the fort spawned the bustling pioneer town that owed its name and peaceful settlement to the valiant soldiers of Fort Larned.

Today, nine original stone buildings outline the five-acre parade ground with its majestic 100-foot flag staff. A tenth building, the six-sided defensive blockhouse, was reconstructed by the National Park Service in 1988. The windswept prairie grasses covering much of the 718-acre historical site at Fort Larned recall the harsh and lonely life on the frontier.

The visitor center in one of the barracks has a ten-minute audio-visual presentation and a museum with Indian artifacts, including a shield with a human scalp and a buffalo-tooth necklace embellished with a coin of President James Monroe.

In summer, hour-long guided tours of the fort are scheduled at regular intervals throughout the day; the tours are available on request during the rest of the year. Eight of the buildings around the fort's central quadrangle are open to the public. These include the enlisted men's barracks, the hospital, bakery, carpenter and blacksmith shops, the commissary, the school room, blockhouse, the quartermaster storehouse, and the officers' quarters.

Nearby, a portion of the old Santa Fe Trail, deeply rutted by the wheels of countless wagons on their way westward, has been pre-

The blacksmith's shop at Fort Larned, Kansas. The Fort was established in 1859 midway along the Santa Fe Trail to protect mail stages and travelers. —*William S. Keller, NPS photograph*

served. Fort Larned also has a splendidly restored prairie, with a variety of mixed native grasses, colorful wildflowers, colonies of prairie dogs, coyotes, larks, owls, hawks, and even eagles.

The park features a living history program every weekend in the summer, which provides glimpses into past life at this frontier outpost. Park rangers and volunteers dressed as soldiers and frontier settlers demonstrate everything from cooking to riflery, from blacksmithing and medicine to cannon firings.

Open: 8 a.m. to 5 p.m., Labor Day to Memorial Day, with hours extended to 6 p.m. in summer. Closed Thanksgiving, Christmas, and New Year's Day.

Fees: $1 age 17 and above.

Mailing Address: Fort Larned National Historic Site, Route 3, Larned, KS 67550.

Telephone: 316-285-3571.

Getting There: The site is located in south-central Kansas, six miles west of Larned, KS, on Rt. 156.

| Fort Scott National Historic Site

Established along the permanent Indian territory in 1842, Fort Scott was home to the colorful dragoons, the mounted soldiers who roamed the West keeping peace among the Indians and escorting settlers through the wilderness. The fort was named for General Winfield Scott, the military hero of the Mexican War (1846–48).

Fort Scott's 18 buildings, most constructed in the Greek-Revival style, were built by the infantry itself. The original bakery, hospital, officers' quarters, and quartermaster's storehouse have been restored to look as they did in the 1840s, while the enlisted men's barracks, stables, post headquarters, and guardhouse have been historically re-created.

An army base at different periods until the 1870s, Fort Scott played an important role in the development of the American West. Troops were stationed here from the days of the Indian frontier and the Mexican War through the Bleeding Kansas and Civil War eras and the building of the railroad from Texas to Kansas.

Visitors can wander through the grounds on their own. In summer, park personnel lead hour-long tours of the 16-acre site on weekends at 11 a.m. and 2:30 p.m. The fort has a living history program that features people in period attire re-creating life on the frontier and special weekend programs on topics including military garrison life, the Mexican and Civil wars, and Native Americans. Check for details.

Fort Scott features a five-acre section of specially cultivated tall-grass prairie surrounding the historic site, a reminder of the almost extinct vegetation that once covered much of the Midwest.

Open: 8 a.m. to 5 p.m. daily, extended to 6 p.m. from Memorial Day to Labor Day.

Fees: $1 ages 17–61.

Mailing Address: Fort Scott National Historic Site, Old Fort Boulevard, Fort Scott, KS 66701.

Telephone: 316-223-0310.

Getting There: The fort is located in southeastern Kansas near the Missouri border, within the community of Fort Scott, three blocks west of the intersection of Rt. 68 and Rt. 54.

KENTUCKY

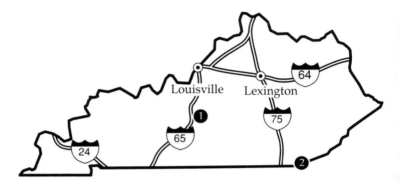

1. Abraham Lincoln Birthplace National Historic Site
2. Cumberland Gap National Historical Park

‖ Abraham Lincoln Birthplace National Historic Site

In an earthen floor log cabin on this site in central Kentucky, Abraham Lincoln was born on February 12, 1809. The Lincoln farm was called Sinking Spring Farm for the cool water that bubbled from the ground on the property.

The farm itself was divided up shortly after the Lincolns moved away in 1811. But the spring—and a log cabin dating from the era —still exists. Lincoln may not have actually lived in the cabin now enshrined in a large granite memorial building near the spring, but it stands as a reminder of our 16th president's humble roots.

The 116-acre park on the site of the Sinking Spring Farm has a museum about Lincoln, including a copy of the family Bible, a diorama of the farm, and an 18-minute film. The one-room cabin, which measures only 12 feet by 17 feet, is a short walk from the visitor center. Nearby is the small forest where young Abraham played until the family moved ten miles north to Knob Creek in 1811. The park has picnic facilities, grassy fields, and several hiking trails.

In the late 1890s the cabin was dismantled and re-erected in many cities around the country until a group of prominent citizens, including author Mark Twain, labor leader Samuel Gompers, politician William Jennings Bryan, and publisher Robert Collier bought the farm and the cabin and turned the site into a permanent memorial.

This act is celebrated each year on Founder's Day on the second weekend in July, when the park hosts demonstrations of quilting, crafts, rail-splitting, and basket making from the early 19th century. On February 12 each year, a more solemn ceremony commemorates Lincoln's birthday.

Open: 8 a.m. to 4:45 p.m., extended to 5:45 p.m. in spring and fall and 6:45 p.m. in summer. Check for exact dates. Closed Christmas Day.

Fees: None.

Mailing Address: Abraham Lincoln Birthplace National Historic Site, 2995 Lincoln Farm Road, Hodgenville, KY 42748.

Telephone: 502-358-3874.

This 19th-century log cabin is similar to the one in which Abraham Lincoln was born.—NPS *photograph*

Getting There: Located in central Kentucky, south of Louisville. From Louisville, take I-65 south to Elizabethtown, then take Ky. 61 south 13 miles to the park.

|| Cumberland Gap National Historical Park

It was through the Cumberland Gap, the only natural break in the Appalachian mountains between Georgia and Maine, that Daniel Boone and the frontiersmen who followed him crossed into the Midwest. The park at Cumberland Gap commemorates this historic passageway that made it possible to settle the Midwest.

For a breathtaking overview of the gap and the green ripples of the Blue Ridge Mountains beyond, visit Pinnacle Overlook. The site is reached by a scenic road that snakes up the 2,440-foot-high Pinnacle Mountain. From this vantage point, it's easy to imagine the pioneers plodding westward through the gap, trailing carts and cattle. It is a four-mile drive from the visitor center to the Pinnacle Overlook. Nearby are two Civil War earthwork forts, Fort Lyon and Fort McCook.

Most of the 20,000-acre park is accessible only by foot trail. One segment tracing the path of the historic Wilderness Trail leads to the ruins of the Iron Furnace. Another trail follows the mountain ridge for 16 miles, with smaller segments leading to such isolated sites as Sand Cave, Skylight Cave, and White Rocks.

Perhaps the most interesting part of the park is the Hensley Settlement, a self-sufficient farming community that operated from 1904 to the 1950s. Tours via shuttle bus may be offered to visitors. Check for details. You can also reach the Hensley site by four-wheel drive vehicle or on foot. There are overnight backpacking sites in the nearby woods. It takes a day to hike into the park. From Caylor, Virginia, follow the Chadwell Gap Trail. Turn up Rt. 690 in Caylor and follow to the trail head at the end. Be prepared for a rugged trip. The 3.5-mile trek into Hensley is one of the steepest and most challenging trails in the park.

Slide presentations and articles exhibited at the visitor center in Middlesboro, Kentucky, tell the story of the early pioneers who traveled through the Cumberland Gap, and of the Indian traders and warriors that used the path before them. In summer, guides in pioneer costume lead walks along the Wilderness Trail and take visitors to the Pinnacle Overlook. Check for times.

A 160-unit campground has no electrical or water hookups. Warm showers are available. Visitors must register with the ranger to use any of the four primitive campgrounds located on the ridge trail. Fires may be restricted in the backcountry, so bring plenty of fuel. Middlesboro has numerous motels and restaurants.

On the weekend nearest July 4, the park hosts a Civil War encampment; and on the last Sunday in July, there is a quilt show and contest.

Open: Visitor Center: 8 a.m. to 5 p.m., extended to 7 p.m. from June through Aug. Closed Christmas. The park is open year-round.

Fees: None.

Mailing Address: Cumberland Gap National Historical Park, P.O. Box 1848, Middlesboro, KY 40965.

Telephone: 606-248-2817.

Getting There: The park, located in the southeastern-most corner of Kentucky and western Virginia, can be reached by taking Rt. 25E from Kentucky and Tennessee or Rt. 58 from Virginia.

LOUISIANA

1. Jean Lafitte National Historical Park and
   Preserve
2. Poverty Point National Monument

‖ Jean Lafitte National Historical Park and Preserve

The elegance of old New Orleans, the romance of its diverse cultures, and the mystery of the Louisana bayous are preserved in this historical park named for the privateer and rogue Jean Lafitte.

The park has four sections: The main visitor center in the French Quarter; the Chalmette Battlefield, where American troops under Andrew Jackson beat the British in a battle that ended the War of 1812; the Barataria Unit, which preserves the wildlife and ecology of the bayous; and the Isleno Center, dedicated to the culture of the Canary Islanders who settled the region in the 1700s.

In the late 18th and early 19th centuries, Lafitte and his Baratarians ran a privateering and smuggling operation from their hideout in the bayous, confounding French, Spanish, British, and American authorities for decades. It is said that when American Governor Claibourne posted signs offering a $500 reward for information leading to Lafitte's arrest, Lafitte responded by offering $5,000 for information leading to Claibourne's arrest. Today the legend of Lafitte is remembered as almost a symbol of the city: independent, a bit reckless, and ever exciting.

Start at the visitor center in the Customs House of the old French Quarter, where excellent free movies and an ongoing folklife program introduce the city of New Orleans and its unique blend of French, Spanish, Cajun, and American culture. There, you can sample New Orleans-style food while listening to back-porch musicians singing and strumming. Free tours of the city leave from the visitor center several times daily.

The most popoular tours are the Faubourg Promenade Walk through a neighborhood of lavish mansions in the Garden District, and the "City of the Dead" tour of St. Louis Cemetery #1. Burial space was at a premium in New Orleans' cemeteries, where people were entombed above ground to keep the decaying bodies from contaminating the water, and deceased relatives were cycled through the crypts at 18-month intervals. Only 25 people at a time can go on this tour, so make reservations at least one day in advance. Telephone: 504-589-2326.

Open: 9 a.m. to 5 p.m. daily, with extended hours in summer. Check for details. Closed Christmas, New Year's Day, and Mardi Gras.

Fees: None.

Mailing Address: Jean Lafitte National Historical Park and Preserve, 916 Peters Street, New Orleans, LA 70130.

Telephone: 504-589-2636.

Getting There: From Canal St., go down Decatur St. until you reach the 900 block. Behind the front row of French Market buildings is a second set of buildings; walk through the passageway and you will see the Visitor Center.

Chalmette Battlefield

Down along the Mississippi River, southeast of the city, is the Chalmette Battlefield. Here, in the sugar cane fields of a plantation, General Andrew Jackson and a band of American patriots, including Lafitte's Baratarians, defeated 10,000 troops under Major General Sir Edward Michael Pakenham on Jan. 8, 1815. This skirmish, known as the Battle of New Orleans, was the greatest American land victory in the War of 1812, even though it was fought two weeks after the peace treaty ending the war had been signed.

A 1.5-mile tour road takes visitors through the battlefield with its re-created earthworks and original artillery. The Beauregard House, a beautiful Greek-Revival mansion typical of French Louisiana plantations of the period, devotes the entire first floor to interpretive displays on the local history. Walk down to the levee for a spectacular view of the Mississippi River and the striking New Orleans skyline.

The park commemorates the Chalmette battle each year near January 8 with the re-creation of a 19th-century bootcamp. The Chalmette National Cemetery, established in 1864 for Union soldiers who died in Louisana during the Civil War, was originally dedicated by Andrew Jackson in 1840, on the battle's 25th anniversary.

Open: 8 a.m. to 5 p.m. daily, extended to 6 p.m. from Memorial Day to Labor Day. Closed Christmas, New Year's Day, and Mardi Gras.

Fees: None.

Mailing Address: Jean Lafitte National Historical Park, Chalmette Unit, 8686 St. Bernard Highway, Chalmette, LA 70043.

Telephone: 504-589-44280.

Getting There: The park is located six miles from downtown New Orleans. From Canal St., follow the main thoroughfare that begins at North Rampart St. and merges into St. Claude Ave., then into St. Bernard Highway (Rt. 46), which passes directly in front of the park. There is no public transportation to the battlefield.

Barataria Unit

Down the road from Chalmette is Barataria, a unique natural world of marsh wetlands veined with bayous that dominate the west bank of the Mississippi River. (The French used the word bayou, meaning "sleeping waters," because the bayous lack visible movement.) It was among these sluggish creeks and moss-draped cypress trees that Jean Lafitte conducted his business. The 9,000-acre unit in Barataria preserves one of the most productive habitats on earth. Depending on the season, you can see nutria, mink, otter, alligators, turtles, and snakes.

At 11:15 a.m. and 3:15 p.m., rangers lead free walks through the site on raised boardwalks. On Sunday mornings at 8:30 a.m., you can paddle your own canoe—or a rented one—into the wilds of Barataria. Twice a month, you can enjoy a moonlit evening canoe trip.

Both tours are ranger-guided and reservations are required. Canoe rentals are available from local concessionaires and a list of boat rental services is available form the park. A 25-minute film, "Jambalaya: a Delta Almanac," provides a good introduction to the Barataria area. The film is shown every half-hour.

Open: 8 a.m. to sunset. Closed Christmas and New Year's Day.
Fees: None.
Mailing Address: The Barataria Unit, 7400 Highway 45, Marrero, LA 70072.
Telephone: 504-698-2002.
Getting There: The Barataria Unit is located about 20 miles from New Orleans. Cross the Crescent City Connection (Bridge) and follow Rt. 90 West, The Westbank Expressway, to Barataria Blvd., also known as Rt. 45. Turn left onto Rt. 45 and continue until you arrive at the park.

Isleno Center

Also on the river's west bank is the Isleno Center. In an effort to establish a colonial presence in the strategic Mississippi River Delta,

Spain recruited Canary Islanders to the region in the 1700s. To this day, the Islenos, as they are called, have maintained their culture. They still speak a unique Spanish dialect dating from the 17th century. Another cultural remnant of the language still heard is the 16th-century *decima*, a ten-line stanza (poem) that is sung.

A small cottage houses the Isleno Center where displays interpret the lifestyle and history of the community. Traditional crafts are demonstrated at the center and performances of the *decimas* are also given. Today the Islenos, who earn their living as shrimpers and oyster farmers, live mostly in Saint Bernard Parish. Check for information about local festivals.

Open: 9 a.m. to 5 p.m. daily. Closed Christmas and New Year's Day.

Fees: None.

Telephone: 504-589-0862.

Mailing Address: The Isleno Center, 1357 Bayou Road, St. Bernard, LA 70085.

Getting There: Go east on Rampart St., which becomes St. Claude Ave. (also known as Rt. 46 and St. Bernard Highway). Follow this road to the sign announcing the park, about eight miles east of Chalmette.

Note: The administrative offices of the Headquarters of Jean Lafitte National Historical Park and Preserve are located in the U.S. Custom House, 423 Canal Street, Room 210, New Orleans, LA 70130. Telephone: 504-589-3882.

|| Poverty Point National Monument

This 400-acre park in northeastern Louisiana, with its unique earthwork mounds, is the site of one of the most intriguing and mysterious prehistoric Indian cities in North America.

The earthworks at Poverty Point consist of six concentric horseshoe-shaped terraces and a large bird-effigy mound measuring 70 feet high and 700 to 800 feet at the base.

Archeologists have determined that the settlement, which flourished at Poverty Point from 1800 to 500 B.C., supported an estimated 4,000 to 5,000 people at one time, making it a major prehistoric city. Although many artifacts have been unearthed at the site, the exact purpose of the earthwork configuration remains a mystery.

Equally mysterious is the question of how these pre-agricultural Indians supported themselves. While the Macon Ridge on which Poverty Point is located is totally without minerals, the site shows evidence of minerals that were imported from great distances. Recovered objects from the site include spear points, knives, and other flint-knapped material from as far away as Arkansas, Mississippi, Oklahoma, and Missouri. Copper artifacts from Michigan were found also.

Yet for all the evidence of imported items, indicating that the site may have been a trade center, little seems to have been taken out of the prehistoric settlement at Poverty Point. One theory suggests that the area may have been a religious and ceremonial center, exchanging spiritual services for materials needed for survival.

Unique artifacts found at the site include several thousand "artificial cooking stones," sun-dried mud stones that were used for cooking. It is believed that ten to 12 million of these stones were manufactured at Poverty Point. Also, imprints of split-cane baskets and animal skins used to move the earth—50 pounds at a time—have been uncovered.

The museum has more than 1,000 artifacts on display and a 25-minute video presentation about the site and the culture of the early Indian inhabitants. There are two self-guided hiking trails and a 45-minute interpretive vehicle trail.

In late September, Poverty Point has a special Louisiana Archeology Week, with activities such as earth-oven cooking, flint-knapping demonstrations, and "atl-atl" (spear) throwing.

Wildlife in the park includes deer, raccoon, rabbit, beaver, nutria, and the many birds that migrate through the area.

Open: 9 a.m. to 5 p.m. from October 1 to March 31, extended to 7 p.m. from April 1 to September 30. Closed Thanksgiving, Christmas, and New Year's Day.

Fee: $2 ages 13–61.

Mailing Address: Poverty Point National Monument, HC 60, Box 208A, Epps, LA 71237.

Telephone: 318-926-5492

Getting There: From Monroe, travel east on I-20 for 35–40 miles to the town of Delhi; go north on Highway 17 to the town of Epps. At Epps, turn right on Highway 134 for five miles and turn left on 577. The park is one mile from that point.

MAINE

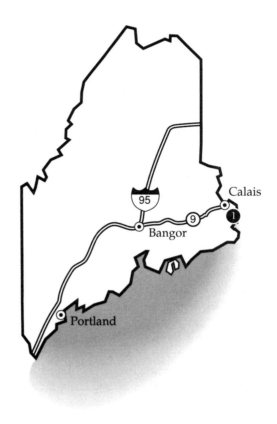

1. Saint Croix Island International Historic Site

Saint Croix Island International Historic Site

Saint Croix Island, located in the Saint Croix River between Maine and Canada, is as desolate, raw, and undeveloped as the most adventurous traveler could ask for. The hardy tourist who ventures to Saint Croix Island will find it little changed from the time French explorers landed here in 1604—except, of course, that the Indians are long gone.

Alternately windswept and enshrouded in fog, snowbound in winter and rainy in summer, the island is ravaged by 18-foot tides that leave only six-and-a-half acres of dry land at high tide.

A good time to visit the island, especially for avid bird watchers, is during the spring and fall migrations when swallows, warblers, cormorants, and gulls, among other birds, make their seasonal visits to this lonely island.

Although Saint Croix is uninhabited today, it was the site of a French settlement attempted in 1604 by colonist Pierre du Gua, Sieur de Monts. The encampment here predates the Pilgrims landing at Plymouth Rock by 16 years.

De Monts thought Saint Croix would provide a good vantage for protecting the fur trade he hoped to establish in North America. He was mistaken. The Saint Croix River froze in winter, leaving 79 men ill-prepared for the harsh weather. Almost half of them died. The rest abandoned the island and moved to the more hospitable environment at Port Royal.

Since then, the island has been used only sporadically by mariners. A lighthouse, built in 1856 and remodeled in 1901, stood until it was destroyed by fire in 1976.

There are no campgrounds, no shelters, no toilets, no water sources, no electric or power lines, and no facilities whatsoever for visitors on the island. The park is a day-use area only. Campfires and hunting are prohibited.

The only interpretive exhibits are a plaque affixed to a boulder during the 1904 tricentenary celebration and a wayside sign on the mainland overlook that summarizes the island's history.

Eastern Maine offers some of the best hunting and fishing in the country, with abundant deer, moose, and bear and excellent fresh- and salt-water fishing. There are accommodations in nearby Calais and camping in Moosehorn National Wildlife Refuge about 14 miles to the west.

Open: Day use only.

Fees: None.

Mailing Address: Saint Croix Island International Historic Site, c/o Acadia National Park, Box 177, Bar Harbor, ME 04609.

Telephone: 207-288-3338.

Getting There: The entrance to the park is eight miles south of Calais, ME, on U.S. 1.

MARYLAND

1. Antietam National Battlefield
2. Chesapeake and Ohio Canal National Historical Park
3. Clara Barton National Historic Site
4. Fort McHenry National Monument and Historic Shrine
5. Fort Washington Park
6. Hampton National Historic Site
7. Monocacy National Battlefield
8. Thomas Stone National Historic Site

‖ Antietam National Battlefield

One of the bloodiest—and most important—battles of the Civil War took place in the rolling green countryside along Antietam Creek near Sharpsburg on September 17, 1862. Antietam marked Confederate General Robert E. Lee's first incursion into Northern territory, a bold move that, if successful, could have earned him sorely needed foreign aid and recognition. But the battle ended in a draw and Lee retreated to Virginia, giving President Abraham Lincoln the political opening he needed to issue his Emancipation Proclamation.

At dawn on the day of battle, the Union, having fortuitously intercepted Lee's battle plans, took the initiative. Union General Joseph Hooker opened fire on Farmer Miller's cornfield, just north of the present-day visitor center. The field changed hands 15 times before the battle was over. "Every stalk of corn . . . was cut as closely as could have been done with a knife, and the slain lay in rows precisely as they had stood in their ranks a few moments before," Hooker wrote.

The nearby Dunker Church, which has been reconstructed, and the East Woods were sites of heavy action that morning. But the greatest carnage of the battle took place in the West Woods just north of the Dunker Church, where Union General John Sedgwick lost more than 2,200 men in 20 minutes when he attempted to charge Confederate troops.

By midday, the action had moved south to Sunken Road, where four hours of intense fighting in the narrow roadway left 4,000 casualties. The spot was renamed Bloody Lane. For an excellent overview of the battlegrounds, climb the observation tower at the corner of Bloody Lane.

Across Route 34 is Burnside Bridge. You can stand on the high ground above the bridge where Confederate sharpshooters picked off Union soldiers as easily as if they were ducks at a shooting gallery. It took Union General Ambrose Burnside almost four hours to cross the bridge.

By the time the battle ended at dusk, 23,000 men were wounded or killed. Antietam National Cemetery has the remains of 4,776 Federal soldiers who fell here. Confederates were buried in nearby Frederick and Hagerstown, Maryland, and in Shepherdstown, West Virginia.

Although Lee retreated to Virginia, Union General George B.

McClellan failed to press his advantage. It has been said that this stalemate, with no clearcut victory for either side, prolonged the war for another two-and-a-half bloody years.

The visitor center has an excellent movie presentation on the battle, with displays of uniforms, swords, and medical equipment that have been found on the battlefield. Four large oil paintings of the conflict painted by Captain James Hope dramatize the battle.

A self-guided car tour leads through 8.5 miles of roadside exhibits. In summer, weekend volunteers in both Union and Confederate Army garb re-create Civil War camp life with firing drills and authentically reproduced field equipment.

Sharpsburg is a quiet rural community of about 900 residents. Wildlife includes racoons, white-tailed deer, small rodents, and numerous birds. Fishing requires a Maryland license. There is no camping in the park, but nearby Hagerstown, Maryland, and Martinsburg, West Virginia, have accommodations and restaurants. Antietam is an easy day's outing from Washington, D.C.

Open: 8:30 a.m. to 5:00 p.m. daily, Sept. to May. Tour road closes at dark. Hours extended from 8 a.m. to 6 p.m. in summer. Closed Thanksgiving, Christmas, and New Year's Day.

Fees: $1 ages 17–61.

Mailing Address: Antietam National Battlefield, Box 158, Sharpsburg, MD 21782.

Telephone: 301-432-5124.

Getting There: The battlefield is located in northwestern Maryland, near the West Virginia border, at the intersection of Rt. 34 and Rt. 65. From Washington DC, take I-270 north to Frederick, turning onto Rt. 70 west at Frederick. At Hagerstown, take exit 29 and turn south on Route 65. The park is about ten miles from that point.

‖ Chesapeake and Ohio Canal National Historical Park

Mules strain against taut ropes while a boatman with a banjo sings to passengers on a 19th-century canal boat tour down the Chesapeake and Ohio Canal. This once bustling waterway, now a quiet park paralleling the Potomac River from Cumberland, Maryland, to Washington, D.C., is a 184-mile tribute to the colorful days of canal commerce.

From April through October, two canal boats staffed by crews in period costume bring the canal's bygone era to life again. The Canal Clipper, which operates Friday through Sunday, leaves from the Great Falls Tavern. The second boat, the Georgetown, departs from Georgetown in D.C. For more information about fares and departure times, call 301-299-2026 (Great Falls, Virginia) or 202-472-4376 (Georgetown).

Even in winter, when the canal boats are dry-docked, the canal is a favorite for locals and tourists. With its graceful trees, picturesque locks, arching aqueducts, and easy access to a gravelly, 12-foot-wide towpath, the canal is excellent for jogging, leisurely day strolls, overnight hiking, bicycling, canoeing, and horseback riding.

George Washington laid the groundwork for the canal in the late 1700s, when his Potowmack Company tried to make the Potomac River navigable for commerce. In 1828, the federal government funded an ambitious proposal to build a canal between Georgetown in Washington, D.C. and Pittsburgh on the Ohio River.

But the project was plagued with difficulties, and construction stopped in Cumberland, Maryland, less than halfway to Pittsburgh. By the time the last mile of canal was built in 1850, trains had gained prominence as the country's major form of transportation and had begun supplanting the mule-pulled barges. The Chesapeake and Ohio Canal was in operation from 1850 to 1924, and while it never made money, it provided a good livelihood and profit for the people who used it.

Biking is excellent on three sections of the canal: Georgetown to Great Falls, Virginia, Fifteen Mile Creek to Paw Paw Tunnel, and dam 4 to lock 33. There are 32 "hiker-biker" campgrounds along the canal, located at six-mile intervals. Water is generally available from late April to late November. Drive-in campgrounds, open in summer until Labor Day, are located at Spring Gap (mile 173.6), Fifteen Mile Creek (mile 140.8), and McCoys Ferry (mile 110.5).

Several parts of the canal have been re-watered, and are good for canoeing. The stretch from Georgetown to Violettes Lock at mile 22 is a popular canoeing segment. The protected waters of the canal are fine for beginners but only experienced canoeists should attempt the Potomac River, which has swift currents, strong winds, and many outcroppings of rocks. There are 25 boat ramps along the canal. Contact the park for a full listing of equipment rental services.

The park is divided into three districts, each with its own visitor center. The main headquarters is near Sharpsburg, Maryland. Anglers will find bass, catfish, and other fish in the Potomac. Rabid animals have been found within park borders, so beware of them. Walking along the towpath at night, especially unaccompanied, is not recommended.

Open: The park is always open. Visitor areas and boat launching ramps are open daylight hours.

Fees: None for the park. Use of the picnic facilities at Carderock cost $90 on weekdays and $160 on weekends. Check on fees for barge ride.

Mailing Address: Chesapeake and Ohio Canal National Historical Park, Box 4, Sharpsburg, MD 21782.

Telephone: Piedmont District (park headquarters, mile 31-106) 301-739-4200.

Getting There: The park parallels the Potomac River from Georgetown in Washington, DC, to Cumberland in western Maryland. There are 45 access points to the 185-mile canal park.

‖ Clara Barton National Historic Site

Clara Barton, founder of the American Red Cross, lived in this 3½-story house overlooking the Potomac River valley at Glen Echo near Washington, D.C. for the last 15 years of her life. Of the house's 32 rooms, 13 have been meticulously restored to look as they did when Barton herself lived here, and one-third of the Victorian furnishings are original.

Visitors can tour the unusual yellow house, which has an open gallery to the second floor and a suspended third floor with no vertical supporting beams. Originally constructed as a warehouse for Red Cross supplies, the house has numerous closets for storage. It served as national headquarters for the American Red Cross in 1904, and home to Barton until she died in 1912 at the age of 90.

Barton, a famous humanitarian, tended the wounded at bloody Civil War battlefields such as Antietam, Manassas, and Fredericksburg. After the war, she worked to identify missing and dead soldiers and lobbied the U.S. government to adopt the Treaty of Geneva establishing the International Red Cross. Upon retiring to Glen Echo after many long years of social service, she tended garden and cared for her horses and domestic animals.

The Park Service holds monthly programs at the Barton House; they range in topic from living history demonstrations with guides dressed in period costume performing Red Cross work to re-enactments of 19th-century field relief efforts. Check for details, schedules, and information about tours.

Open: 10 a.m. to 5 p.m. daily. Closed most federal holidays.
Fees: None.
Mailing Address: Clara Barton National Historic Site, 5801 Oxford Road, Glen Echo, MD 20812.
Telephone: 301-492-6245.
Getting There: The site is located just north of Washington, DC. From Washington, take McArthur Blvd. to Oxford Road, which is located just beyond the intersection of McArthur and Goldsboro Rd. Turn left on Oxford. The Barton house is located on the left soon after the Oxford turnoff. From Maryland, take I-495 to exit 41, the Glen Echo exit. Follow the George Washington Memorial Parkway toward Washington, DC and Glen Echo, taking the left lane to Glen Echo and MacArthur Blvd. From Virginia, take I-495 north across the American Legion Bridge to exit 41, and follow the directions given above.

‖ Fort McHenry National Monument and Historic Shrine

Fort McHenry earned its place in American history during the War of 1812, when the flag that flew over its ramparts during a 25-hour British bombardment inspired Francis Scott Key to pen the poem that became the American national anthem.

This war marked the last time that the British challenged American independence and it established the United States as a formidable

Francis Scott Key wrote "The Star-Spangled Banner" to commemorate the successful defense of Fort McHenry during the War of 1812.—*Richard Frear, NPS photograph*

military force. Fort McHenry was an important proving ground in this test of national strength.

Key, a 35-year-old lawyer from Washington, D.C., who was being held by the British, watched from a ship in Baltimore Harbor on September 13 and 14, 1814, while Fort McHenry endured 1,800 British bombs. When the smoke cleared, Key was so overjoyed to see the American flag still flying that he wrote "The Star-Spangled Banner." Set to music, this popular song triumphed over such favorites as "Yankee Doodle" and "America the Beautiful" to become the country's anthem in 1931.

The flag that symbolized American determination to be free of British domination was made by Baltimore resident Mary Pickersgill. The original, measuring 30 by 42 feet, with 15 stars and 15 stripes, now hangs in the Smithsonian's Museum of American History in Washington, D.C.; a replica flies at Fort McHenry, weather permitting.

Exhibits of historic and military memorabilia bring back the fort's role in the War of 1812, the Civil War, and World War I. The visitor center, which is located outside the fort walls, has a 16-minute film on the Battle of Baltimore and a museum displaying a British cannonball and rocket.

On weekends in the summer, a group of volunteers in period uniform known as the Fort McHenry Guard re-creates the life of the early American soldier, demonstrating chores, drills, and flag ceremonies. An annual Defenders' Day celebration held on the second Sunday in September features fireworks and the Fort McHenry Guard. There is also a special program with fireworks on Flag Day.

Open: 9 a.m. to 5 p.m. daily, hours may be extended from Memorial Day to Labor Day. Closed Christmas and New Year's Day.

Fees: $1 ages 17–61.

Mailing Address: Fort McHenry National Monument and Historic Shrine, East Fort Avenue, Baltimore, MD 21230-5393.

Telephone: 301-962-4299.

Getting There: From Interstate 95 northbound or southbound, take Exit 55 (Key Highway/Fort McHenry National Monument) and follow the blue and green signs on Key Highway to Lawrence St. Turn left on Lawrence St. and left on Fort Ave. Proceed to Fort McHenry National Monument. From the Inner Harbor take Light St. south to Key Highway. Turn left and follow the blue and green signs to Lawrence St. Turn right on Lawrence St. and left on Fort Ave. to the Monument.

‖ Fort Washington Park

Fort Washington, overlooking the Potomac River and directly across from George Washington's Mount Vernon home, is an excellent example of early 19th-century coastal defense. The massive stone and brick structure, which has a dry moat, a drawbridge and seven-foot thick walls, was built after the British destroyed an earlier structure during the War of 1812. French engineer Pierre Charles L'Enfant, who also designed Washington, D.C., was the architect.

Construction began in 1814 and was finished ten years, 200,000 bricks, and $426,000 later. From its high walls, black cannon kept watch over the scenic Potomac. Union soldiers were stationed there during the Civil War. The fort was abandoned in 1872.

Fort Washington has an extensive living history program with firing demonstrations. On Sundays, people in costume conduct tours of the site. Monthly torchlight tours during the summer convey the feel of life at the fort during the 1800s. The visitor center has a slide program with general information about the site.

There are picnic grounds and spots that can be reserved for groups. Call the park to make reservations.

Open: The Visitor Center is open 8:30 a.m. to 5 p.m. weekdays, extended to 7 p.m. on weekends and longer in summer. The park is open daily from 7:30 a.m. until dark. Closed Christmas Day.

Fees: None.

Mailing Address: Fort Washington Park, National Capital Parks, East, 1900 Anacostia Drive, S.E., Washington, DC 20020.

Telephone: 301-292-2112.

Getting There: The fort is located on the Maryland side of the Potomac River, south of Washington, DC. From Washington, cross the South Capitol Street Bridge and drive south on I-295 and east on I-495. Turn right onto Indian Head Highway, Rt. 210, and right again on Fort Washington Road.

‖ Hampton National Historic Site

Lavish Georgian architecture and exquisite landscaping make the stately Hampton house in Towson, Maryland, one of the country's most interesting and beautiful historic mansions. The monumental house, built between 1783 and 1790 by Maryland iron magnate Charles Ridgely, is topped with an ornate cupola. Unlike so many early estates, the mansion was occupied by the Ridgely family for 158 years, until it was sold in 1948. Many of the original furnishings, including a large collection of painted furniture, are in the mansion's 33 rooms.

Throughout this period, the influential Ridgely family entertained many distinguished guests at their lavish mansion, including Lafayette and Theodore Roosevelt.

Rivaling the house in elegance are the expansive grounds, believed to be designed by renowned landscape architect Andrew Jackson

Downing in the first half of the 19th century. The 60-acre estate has formal gardens and elaborate flower beds known as parterres, natural English parks, broad grassy greens, an herb garden, exotic evergreens, and prize-winning trees from around the world.

In all, there are 200 different species of trees at Hampton, including a tulip tree, a purple European beech, a cedar of Lebanon, and several catalpa. The grounds also have greenhouses, stables, slave quarters, and a delightful reconstructed orangery. Victorian cast iron benches provide elegant resting places.

Guided tours of Hampton house last 30 to 40 minutes and are given on the hour. For an elegant finale to an elegant outing, have lunch in the mansion's Tea Room.

Open: Grounds are open 9 a.m. to 5 p.m. daily; the house is open 9 a.m. to 4 p.m. daily. Last tour begins at 4 p.m. Closed Thanksgiving, Christmas, and New Year's Day.

Fees: None.

Mailing Address: Hampton National Historic Site, 535 Hampton Lane, Towson, MD 21204.

Telephone: 301-962-0688.

Getting There: The site is located north of Baltimore. From I-695 (the Beltway) take exit 27B. Take Dulaney Valley Rd. (Rt. 146) north and turn right onto Hampton Lane, which leads to the park. The Hampton turn is at a dangerous intersection. Be careful not to enter the Beltway ramps located adjacent to Hampton Lane.

‖ Monocacy National Battlefield

Still under development, the Civil War battlefield at Monocacy commemorates the successful first line of defense of Washington, D.C., by Union General Lew Wallace, who repelled Confederate troops led by General Jubal Early on July 11, 1864.

The Park Service is currently planning to construct facilities on the 1,600 acres of land south of Frederick, Maryland, which will eventually become Monocacy National Battlefield. The project could take several years to complete.

When finished, Monocacy promises to be a delightful park with a combination of historical and recreational activities within easy reach from Washington. The Monocacy Creek, which runs through the center of the battlefield's rolling farmland, is good for canoeing and fishing.

Although several monuments have been placed on the battlefield by veterans of the battle—one of the hardest fought of the entire war—the land is currently in private ownership. Anyone wishing to explore the grounds should seek permission from local landowners.

For more information, contact Antietam National Battlefield, Box 158, Sharpsburg, MD 21782.

Telephone: 301-432-5124.

Getting There: The battlefield, which is located one mile south of Frederick, Maryland, can be reached by Rt. 355.

‖ Thomas Stone National Historic Site

The plantation of Thomas Stone, Maryland patriot and signer of the Declaration of Independence, is not fully restored and therefore closed to the public.

Located between Port Tobacco and La Plata, Maryland, the house, known as Habre-de-Ventre, is a fine example of colonial Maryland architecture. It combines a Georgian brick front with wood- and brick-frame structures on the sides. The main section of the house was destroyed by fire in 1977.

Stone was a member of the Continental Congress and a Maryland state senator. He died on his estate in 1787 at the age of 44, and he is buried alongside his wife in the adjacent family cemetery.

Open: The site is undergoing renovations and is not open on a regular basis.

Mailing Address: For visiting information, contact George Washington Birthplace National Monument, Rural Route 1, Box 717, Washington's Birthplace, VA 22443.

Telephone: 804-224-1732.

Getting There: The site is located in southern Maryland. From Rt. 301, take Rt. 6 West, turn right onto Rose Hill Road. The house is on the left between Rt. 6 and Rt. 225.

MASSACHUSETTS

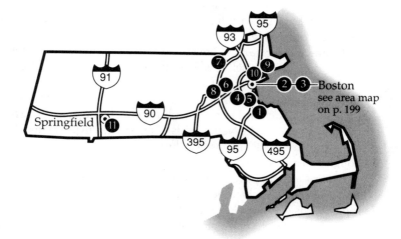

Boston
see area map
on p. 199

1. Adams National Historic Site
2. Boston African American National Historic Site
3. Boston National Historical Park
4. Frederick Law Olmsted National Historic Site
5. John Fitzgerald Kennedy National Historic Site
6. Longfellow National Historic Site
7. Lowell National Historical Park
8. Minute Man National Historical Park
9. Salem Maritime National Historic Site
10. Saugus Iron Works National Historic Site
11. Springfield Armory National Historic Site

| Adams National Historic Site

With four generations of continuous habitation by one of America's most prominent families, the Adams house in Quincy, Massachusetts, is one of the richest in original artifacts and best maintained historical houses in the country. John Adams, the second president of the United States, bought the Adams mansion at 135 Adams Street in 1787 when he was in England with his wife Abigail. It was inhabited by family members until 1927.

Unlike most historical houses, where the owner's possessions are either painstakingly collected over the years or represented by period pieces, all the furniture in the Adams house is original and in excellent condition. Downstairs features the formal Louis XV furniture that Adams purchased in 1780 with his own money for the first U.S. embassy abroad in the Netherlands. (Determined to prove that Americans were civilized, Adams bought the best. But ever frugal, he also bought used furniture at auction.)

Adams' walking stick, his dishes, and his silverware are on display, as is the chair in which he died in July 1826. Ironically, he died the same day as did his political rival and close friend Thomas Jefferson.

Over the years, the Adams family expanded the structure. One of the first additions was the East Wing, which includes the Long Hall, the Long Room on the first floor, and the Long Hall and Study on the second floor.

The Stone Library, which housed a copious collection of books, is a separate structure built in 1870. John Quincy Adams, sixth president of the United States, read seven languages including Russian. (He was minister to Russia in 1809.) His library includes Greek and Latin classics, moral writings, books about astronomy, and law texts.

The 20-room, $3\frac{1}{2}$-story house is open to the public by guided tour only. One of the most interesting rooms is the study, which has John Adams' desk and a unique collection of wooden globes. During the period following John Quincy's occupation of the Old House, John Quincy's wife, Abigail, and son Charles Francis changed the landscape surrounding the house from that of a working farm to that of a country estate, with an English boxwood hedge planted in 1731 and a rosebush planted in 1781, which still blooms.

The library at the Adams National Historic Site. The site was home to presidents John Adams and John Quincy Adams, to U.S. Minister to Great Britain Charles Francis Adams, and to writers and historians Henry Adams and Brooks Adams.—*NPS photograph*

The small wooden house where John Adams was born is located at 133 Franklin Street. His son John Quincy was born in a similar house at 141 Franklin. Both birthplaces are located about 1½ miles from the Adams National Site. See the ranger for directions.

Other area sites relating to Adams Family history include the

Quincy Homestead, at 1010 Hancock Street, the Josiah Quincy Homestead at 20 Muirhead Street, and the Adams Academy at 8 Adams
Street.

Open: The Adams Mansion at 135 Adams St. is open from 9 a.m.
to 5 p.m. daily, from April 19 to November 10. Closed all other
times. The John Adams and John Quincy Adams birthplaces, at 133
and 141 Franklin Street, are open 9 a.m. to 5 p.m. from April 19 to
November 10. Closed all other times.

Fees: Admission to the Adams Mansion is $.50, ages 16 to 62;
admission to the birthplace site is free.

Mailing Address: Adams National Historic Site, 135 Adams Sreet,
P.O. Box 531, Quincy, MA 02269.

Telephone: 617-773-1177.

Getting There: The site is located eight miles south of Boston in
Quincy, MA. Take exit 24, Furnace Brook Parkway of the Southeast
Expressway or Hancock St. to Newport Ave. By public transportation,
take the Red Line from Boston to Quincy Center.

❙ Boston African American National Historic Site

The brick meetinghouse with high arched windows at 8 Smith
Court in downtown Boston, the oldest black church in the country,
marks the beginning of Boston's Black Heritage Trail. This 1.6-mile
walking tour through Boston's Beacon Hill district, once the center
of the city's free black community in the 19th century, highlights the
homes and businesses of influential blacks.

Massachusetts has had a long history of the black struggle for racial
equality: The first federal census in 1790 revealed the state to be the
first in the Union without slaves.

The trail begins with the Robert Gould Shaw and 54th Regiment
Memorial, a bas-relief by the great sculptor Augustus Saint-Gaudens
commemorating the first black Civil War regiment recruited in the
North. The 54th Regiment distinguished itself at Fort Wagner, South
Carolina, in July 1863 when William Carney of New Bedford, Mas-
sachusetts, wrapped the Union flag around his body to protect it from

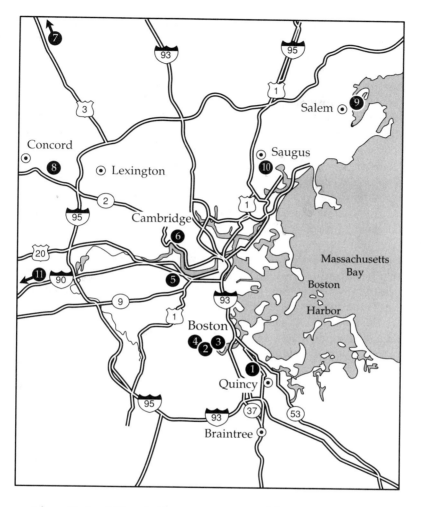

1. Adams National Historic Site
2. Boston African American National Historic Site
3. Boston National Historical Park
4. Frederick Law Olmsted National Historic Site
5. J. F. Kennedy National Historic Site
6. Longfellow National Historic Site
7. Lowell National Historical Park
8. Minute Man National Historical Park
9. Salem Maritime National Historic Site
10. Saugus Iron Works National Historic Site
11. Springfield Armory National Historic Site

from capture. In protest over salaries that were lower than their white counterparts, the entire regiment refused to accept pay for two years until Congress retroactively granted an increase.

Other stops along the trail include the Abiel Smith School, a city grammar and primary school for black children; the home of George Middleton, colonel of the "Bucks of America," an all-black company that fought in the Revolutionary War; the Phillips School, Boston's first racially integrated school; the house of abolitionist John J. Smith, and the Lewis and Harriet Hayden House, a stop on the Underground Railway. The Coburns Gaming House, where, in the mid-1800s, the "upper ten (members of the community) who had acquired a taste for gambling" would meet, is the last site on the trail.

The African Meeting House, constructed almost entirely with black labor and dedicated in 1806, served as a house of worship, a school, and a political center until it was sold in the late 19th century to a Jewish congregation that turned the structure into a synagogue. The building has been restored to its 1855 appearance and is used as a community meeting place and interpretive structure. The other 14 sites along the trail are privately owned and not open to the public.

Public facilities can be found in the Smith School and Meeting House. All other sites are privately owned and can be viewed from the street any time. Call to arrange free private tours. In summer, a ranger stationed at the Robert Gould Shaw and 54th Regiment Memorial will answer questions. Inquire about special activities that may be offered in Black History Month (February).

Open: 9 a.m. to 5 p.m. daily. Closed all federal holidays. Tours are by reservation only in fall, winter, and spring.

Fees: None.

Mailing Address: Boston African American National Historic Site, 46 Joy Street, Boston, MA 02114.

Telephone: 617-742-5415.

Getting There: The trail is in Boston's Beacon Hill neighborhood, near the Boston Common. Take the subway to the Park Street Station, come upstairs and look for the golden dome of the Statehouse, walk up the hill toward the dome. The Shaw Memorial is located at Park and Beacon streets, directly in front of the Statehouse.

Boston National Historical Park

From the Old South Meeting House, where irate colonists participated in the Boston Tea Party, and the 17th-century wooden house
of Paul Revere, to the granite obelisk commemorating the Battle of
Bunker Hill, the city of Boston is a virtual museum of early American
history. More than a dozen of these sites, joined by the three-mile
long Freedom Trail, make up the Boston National Historical Park.

Sites in the park are owned by both public and private groups, so
check with the visitor centers by calling 617-242-5642 (downtown) or
617-242-5601 (Charlestown Navy Yard) about charges, schedules, and
special activities. The Freedom Trail starts near the kiosk in the Boston Common; it leads through the historic downtown area and across
the Charles River to the Navy Yard. The Common was purchased
in 1634 as a "trayning field" for the militia, and for the "feeding of
Cattell." Schedule about a day to take in all the buildings, longer if
you like to linger.

The first stop on the tour is Boston's golden-domed "new" State
House. This structure, with its classical columns and arched windows, was built in 1795 by Charles Bulfinch, creator of Federalist-style
architecture.

From there the trail leads by the Granary Burying Ground, where
John Hancock, Samuel Adams, and the victims of the Boston Massacre are buried. Nearby Kings Chapel, originally an Anglican church
built in 1754, has the graves of Governor John Winthrop and William
Dawes. The church is now Unitarian. The Old Corner Book Store, built
in 1712, is located at the corner of School and Washington streets.
Once, noted authors such as Ralph Waldo Emerson, Nathaniel Hawthorne, and Oliver Wendell Holmes gathered here. The building, a
functioning bookstore, is owned by *The Boston Globe*.

From the bookstore, a short walk down Washington Street leads to
the Old State House built in 1713. Some of the earliest revolutionary activity took place in this building, once the seat of the royal
government in colonial Boston. Here the people of Boston first heard
the Declaration of Independence, which established the new nation.
The building is topped by an elaborate gabled roof flanked by sculptures of a lion and a unicorn. A circle of cobblestones in the street
nearby marks the site of the Boston Massacre on March 5, 1770,

when British soldiers opened fire on a crowd, killing five people and foreshadowing the Revolutionary War.

Faneuil Hall, the city's first centralized market, is located a few blocks away. Peter Faneuil, a local merchant, built this structure, later enlarged by Charles Bulfinch, and donated it to the city in 1742. As in colonial days, Faneuil Hall still combines the commercial and the civic, with shops and restaurants downstairs and a community meeting room upstairs. Behind Faneuil Hall is Quincy Market, a 500-foot-long Greek Revival building with additional shops and eateries.

Further along the Freedom Trail is the wooden house in which Paul Revere, silversmith and patriot, lived between 1770 and 1800. The house, circa 1676, is the oldest surviving house in Boston. Visitors can tour the house for a small fee. For more information, call 617-523-1676.

Revere did not live far from Old North Church where, on the night of April 18, 1775, two lanterns in the steeple warned that the British would be heading "by sea" across the harbor to Charlestown. Armed with that information, Revere made his famous midnight ride, warning the Minutemen that the British were coming. Clergy are generally on hand to answer questions.

Two park sites lie across Charlestown Bridge—the Navy Yard, home of the USS *Constitution*, and The Bunker Hill Monument, which is actually on Breed's Hill. Since opening in 1800, the Navy Yard has become the major dry dock for the U.S. Navy. The *Constitution*, called affectionately "Old Ironsides," is one of the best known warships in American Naval history and is the oldest commissioned warship afloat in the world. This three-masted frigate fought in the War of 1812 and has sailed around the world. The Navy conducts free tours of Old Ironsides, which last about 30 minutes. On July 4 each year, the *Constitution* is towed into the harbor for its annual "Turn Around," a maintenance procedure necessary to keep the boat in good operating condition. Visitors can also tour the World War II destroyer USS *Cassin Young*.

Two museums interpret the Navy Yard, the *Constitution*, which is dedicated to the history of the USS *Constitution*, and the Boston Marine Society. A fee is charged for admission to the *Constitution* museum; the Boston Marine Society museum is free. Check at the visitor center in Building 5 for more information about fees and activities.

The Freedom Trail ends at the Bunker Hill Monument, commemorating the battle of June 17, 1776. Here, according to legend, patriot Colonel Prescott gave the famous command: "Don't shoot until you see the whites of their eyes." Rangers are on duty at the site to answer questions and talk about the battle on request. From the top of the obelisk, a vigorous 294-step climb, you get a great view of the Boston skyline and the Atlantic Ocean beyond. The Bunker Hill Pavilion in the Navy Yard has dioramas depicting the battle.

Open: Most sites are located on city streets and exteriors can be viewed at any time. For information about access to interiors, contact the Park Service. Visitor Centers are open 9 a.m. to 5 p.m. daily.

Fees: Vary from site to site, although most sites are free.

Mailing Address: Boston National Historical Park, Charlestown Navy Yard, Boston, MA 02129.

Telephone: 617-242-5642 (downtown); 242-5601 (Navy Yard).

Getting There: The main visitor center is located on Court St., near the Government Center subway stop. Directions are available to other sites from there.

❙ Frederick Law Olmsted National Historic Site

On a quiet street in this Boston suburb, away from the strains of urban life, lived Frederick Law Olmsted, creator of the modern city park. He is known as the father of American landscape architecture, the man who designed Manhattan's Central Park, Boston's "Emerald Necklace" of parks, and hundreds of other parks and properties throughout the nation.

An avid conservationist who was active in the movement to preserve America's natural areas in national parklands, Olmsted came to landscape architecture in the late 18th century, when he was 35. His first landscaping job was as superintendent of Central Park in New York. Plans submitted by Olmsted and Calvert Vaux won the park's design competition, and Olmsted was hired as the chief landscape architect.

After managing Central Park, Olmsted set up business with his two sons in 1883 in this house in Brookline, Massachusetts, and worked here until his retirement in 1895. The firm continued operating until

1979. During that time, the company generated more than 60,000 photographs and an estimated 130,000 to 150,000 landscape architecture plans, drawings, blueprints, and the like.

The offices inside the modest red clapboard house have a turn-of-the-century atmosphere, with antique drafting desks, a Wagonhurst blueprinter circa 1900, and primitive solar light tables. Lithographs of Olmsted creations, including one of the Biltmore Estate in Asheville, North Carolina, which has marginalia in Olmsted's handwriting, decorate the walls.

The backyard, though small, is as lush and lovely as any Olmsted creation. In fact, Olmsted used his garden as a living laboratory, a place to test his ideas. In less than two acres, there is a hollow, a woods, a rock garden, and lawns, all with Olmsted's trademark use of perspective, vistas, and obscuring backgrounds.

Park personnel introduce these formations in guided tours of the yard, and they discuss the two styles of landscaping used by Olmsted to create his trademark naturalistic effect: the Pastoral, which used greenery to soothe the spirit, and the Picturesque, which made dramatic use of shadow and light. Olmsted used pastoral elements in most of his city parks to counteract what he believed was the artificial stress of urban life.

The house, which was bought by the National Park Service in 1979, has been restored to its circa 1930 appearance. Much of the archived material is fragile and a storage system is being devised. Access is by appointment only.

Open: 10 a.m. to 4:30 p.m., Friday, Saturday, and Sunday. Closed all federal holidays. Other times by reservation for groups of 10 or larger.

Fees: None.

Mailing Address: Frederick Law Olmsted National Historic Site, 99 Warren Street, Brookline, MA 02146.

Telephone: 617-566-1689.

Getting There: Via public transportation: The park is a 15-minute walk south of the Brookline Hills subway station. Follow signs for the First Parish Church of Brookline, and when you get to the church, go left (south) on Warren Street to the site. Via car: From Boston, follow Rt. 9, Boyleston Street, west to third stoplight past Brookline Village. Turn left (south) on Warren Street to intersection of Dudley Street, where the Visitor Center parking lot is located.

‖ John Fitzgerald Kennedy National Historic Site

Every mother can influence her son to a great extent . . . And what you do with him and for him has influence, not for a day, or for a year, but for time and eternity.—Rose Kennedy

This three-story house at 83 Beals Street in Brookline, a dwelling as ordinary as any in a Norman Rockwell painting, was the birthplace of one of America's best-loved presidents, John Fitzgerald Kennedy. Young Jack, who later went on to become the 35th president, lived here from his birth on May 29, 1917, until the family moved to a residence on Naples Road in 1921.

Joseph P. and Rose Kennedy moved into the Beals Street house after their honeymoon, and immediately set about starting their family. Four of the nine Kennedy kids were born while the family lived here: Joseph (at the family summer residence in Hull), John Fitzgerald, Rosemary, and Kathleen.

John Kennedy, who served as a U.S. representative and senator, was elected president in 1960. He was a young and stylish president, popular both at home and abroad, who stood firm against Soviet threats of nuclear warfare during the Cuban missile crisis. His assassination in 1963 shocked the world. John Kennedy's younger brother Robert, who served as U.S. Attorney General in the Kennedy administration and as a senator from New York, was assassinated in 1968. Edward Kennedy, still active in politics, has been a senator from Massachusetts since 1962.

The Beals Street house was repurchased by the Kennedy family in 1966, and restored and refurnished with both period and original furniture to its 1917 appearance. The house features the master bedroom, arranged as it was on the day John F. was born; the nursery, with the bassinet in which the Kennedy children, including the president-to-be, took their rest; and a favorite book of stories. Downstairs are the napkin rings, forks, and spoons that the young Kennedys used. A Mother's Day poem, given to Rose Kennedy by her children, hangs on the wall above the study.

Ranger-guided tours of the eight-room house are presented approximately every half hour with taped anecdotes from Rose Kennedy about the family's early years.

Other Kennedy-related sites in the area include the Naples Road residence (now a private residence), at the corner of Abbotsford and Naples Road in Brookline, where John Kennedy lived until he was ten; the Saint Aidan's Catholic Church, where young John was baptized and served as altar boy; and the Dexter School site and Edward Devotion School attended by the Kennedy boys. A map of these sites is available at Beals Sreet.

The Park Service offers neighborhood walking tours in spring and fall. Call for details. Special school programs are also available, free of charge, by reservation only.

Open: 10 a.m. to 4:30 p.m. daily. Closed Thanksgiving, Christmas, and New Year's Day.

Fees: $1 ages 17–61.

Mailing Address: John F. Kennedy National Historic Site, 83 Beals Street, Brookline, MA 02146.

Telephone: 617-566-7937.

Getting There: Take exit #18 from Mass Turnpike Extension, proceed toward Allston along Cambridge St., turn left (south) onto Harvard St. then turn left (east) from Harvard St. onto Beals St. The site is three-quarters of the way down the block on the right.

‖ Longfellow National Historic Site

In 1837, a young poet and language professor at Harvard University named Henry Wadsworth Longfellow took a room in this spacious mansion at 105 Brattle Street in Cambridge, Massachusetts. He lived here as a lodger until he was given the house by the father of his bride, Fanny Appleton. He continued living here with his children until his death in 1882.

Longfellow, unlike many great writers, was an enormously popular poet in his day, accepted by an elite circle of New England intellectuals, and loved by the public for such classic narrative poems as *Evangeline* (1847), *The Song of Hiawatha* (1855), and *The Courtship of Miles Standish* (1858). Walt Whitman described him as the "poet of the mellow twilight of the past," and the "poet of all sympathetic gentleness— and universal poet of women and young people." Among the many well-known people who visited Longfellow at 105 Brattle Street were

Ralph Waldo Emerson, Charles Sumner, Harvard president Cornelius Felton, and former Bowdoin College classmate Nathaniel Hawthorne.

A fine example of Georgian architecture, the Longfellow House is a symmetrical, 2½-story mansion with 16 large rooms. It was built in 1759 for a wealthy Tory and once served as headquarters for General George Washington during the siege of Boston in 1776. The house is furnished as it was when Longfellow lived here, full of original furniture and artwork. In the study, the poet's oval sitting desk, with inkwell, quill pens and paper, and the standing desk where he did most of his writing are preserved. When he was at work, Longfellow often refreshed himself with the spectacular view of the Charles River from the window above his standing desk. The house still has the chair given Longfellow by the Cambridge school children on his 72nd birthday. The chair is made from the wood of "the spreading chestnut tree," which Longfellow immortalized in his poem *The Village Blacksmith*. Several rooms still have the original wallpaper, complete with water stains from a once-leaky roof. The house is open to visitors by guided tour, which takes 30 to 45 minutes.

Longfellow's house is on a two-acre lot with a beautiful formal garden in the rear. Concerts are held in the garden on alternate Sunday afternoons in summer. The site also sponsors a Christmas open house in December and a celebration in late February in honor of Longfellow's birthday, as well as periodic outdoor poetry readings. Check for details.

Open: 10 a.m. to 4:30 p.m. daily. Closed Thanksgiving, Christmas, and New Year's Day.

Fees: $2 ages 16–62.

Mailing Address: Longfellow National Historic Site, 105 Brattle Street, Cambridge, MA 02138.

Telephone: 617-876-4491.

Getting There: The site in Cambridge, Massachusetts, is half a mile from the Harvard Square subway stop. Follow Brattle Street west six blocks to the site.

‖ Lowell National Historical Park

If any spot in the country can be considered the cradle of the Industrial Revolution in America, it would be Lowell. This 19th-century mill town, built on the banks of the Merrimack River north of Boston, was one of the nation's earliest—and most successful—experiments in mass manufacturing. Today, Lowell National Historical Park helps preserve and interpret the city's canal system, seven of the ten original mills, some early boarding houses, the trolley system, and the immigrant neighborhoods.

Originally named East Chelmsford, the town of Lowell was established in 1826 with one purpose: to be a mill town. Even its name, after Francis Cabot Lowell, underscores its connection to manufacturing. Francis Cabot Lowell was a pioneer in the Industrial Revolution, the man who helped build the first "integrated" mill in the country (in Waltham, Massachusetts), which turned raw material into finished product in one building. By combining technology with a paternalistic social system for workers, Lowell quickly attracted international attention.

During its first two decades, the mills of Lowell were run primarily on woman power. The daughters of farmers from around the region flocked to Lowell for jobs. These "mill girls," as they were called, lived closely monitored lives; they slept in boarding houses, worked more than 70 hours a week, and spent what leisure time they had at classes and lectures. For their labors, they received $2.25 to $4.00 a week. Between 1840 and 1845, the factory girls of Lowell published "The Lowell Offering," one of the first women's literary publications.

By the middle of the 19th century, competition caused the mill owners to pay less and demand more from workers, creating labor-management disputes that often ended in strikes. Then came the immigrants, waves of Irish, French Canadians, Poles, Greeks, and Jews. These newcomers, hungry for work, flocked to Lowell's factories and created the cultural diversity that remains today. Lowell flourished for nearly a century, until the textile industry modernized once again, and moved to the southern states.

Lowell National Historical Park is a tribute to the city's origins, from the days of the "mill girls" to the immigrants and labor problems of the 20th century. The park visitor center, where visitors can make reservations for several excellent tours of the city, is located in the restored mill complex called Market Mills. Don't miss the slide show "Lowell: The Industrial Revolution," and the exhibits about labor, technology, capital, and industry that explain the city's background.

Every day there are guided tours. One of the most popular is the Mill and Canal Tour, a 2½-hour trip on canal boat, by trolley, and on foot. The tour is offered regularly each day from Memorial Day through Labor Day. A restored boarding house, the Morgan Cultural Center, features the "Working People Exhibit." Free, guided walking tours are offered year-round. Exhibit hours and tour availability vary. Call for details.

Three times a week in summer, the park presents "Tunes and Tales," a live performance of music, anecdotes, and songs about the mill era. Suffolk Mill has a working turn-of-the-century power loom operated by hydro-turbine, viewable on guided tours only.

Throughout the summer, Lowell hosts ethnic festivals with food, dance, and song, a celebration of the many immigrant ethnic groups that sought work in the mills. Dates and themes vary; check for details. The rangers provide access to many of the privately owned historic structures in downtown Lowell through interpretive programs and literature. Information is available in print, Braille, large-print, and on cassette.

Open: Visitor Center: 8:30 a.m. to 5 p.m. daily. Closed Thanksgiving, Christmas, and New Year's Day.

Fees: None for Park Service facilities. For boat and trolley tours: $1 and $2, children 16 and under admitted free.

Mailing Address: Lowell National Historical Park, 169 Merrimack Street, Lowell, MA 01852.

Telephone: 508-459-1000.

Getting There: The park is located 36 miles north of Boston; the Visitor Center is at 246 Market. Take the Lowell Connector from either I-495 or Rt. 3, and exit on Thorndike St. north. Go about one-half mile to Dutton St. Take a right on Dutton to the parking lot. Trains leave from Boston North Station to Lowell.

‖ Minute Man National Historical Park

This six-mile stretch of road between Lexington and Concord, Massachusetts, is perhaps the country's most historical highway. Here, on April 19, 1775, the "shot heard round the world," was fired when British soldiers clashed with colonial minutemen in the opening conflict of the Revolutionary War.

In anticipation of armed resistance to British rule, the colonists of Massachusetts had been stockpiling arms and ammunition in the towns outside of Boston. Bent on seizing them, British soldiers, led by Lieutenant Colonel Francis Smith, marched into the countryside. But the colonists had been forewarned. Just a few hours earlier, Paul Revere had galloped through to arouse the countryside with his famous message: "The British are coming." Some farmers gathered at Lexington, where the first volleys were exchanged.

The bridge at Concord, Massachusetts, where colonial minutemen clashed with British troops in the opening volleys of the Revolutionary War. —*Richard Frear, NPS photograph*

After the confrontation at Lexington, British troops marched on to Concord where they burned the military stores found there. The smoke attracted other minutemen and another skirmish occurred. Sniping at the British continued throughout the day, until the redcoats finally retreated to the safety of Boston. They sustained 273 casualties; the patriots had only 95.

Minute Man National Historical Park preserves this historic stretch of road where the Revolutionary War began. It includes the battlefields at Lexington and Concord, the site of Paul Revere's capture by the British, and several houses dating from the colonial era. The North Bridge Visitor Center in Concord displays artifacts from the battle, including muskets and parts of soldiers' equipment. In good weather, a ranger stationed at the bridge gives historical talks about the fighting in Concord. The Battle Road visitor center in Lexington, which is closed in winter, has a 24-minute film about the events leading up to the battle and an electric map program depicting the fighting.

The Wayside house just down the road, home of authors Nathaniel Hawthorne, Louisa May Alcott, and Margaret Sidney, is open for tours. The house is a Victorianized, yellow wood colonial structure with 20 rooms. It contains mostly furniture from the 1920s along with Hawthorne's stand-up desk. The Hartwell Tavern, a restored 18th-century inn where minutemen gathered, is open during summer, staff permitting.

Each year on April 19, commemorative ceremonies are held to recognize the anniversary of the battle on April 19, 1775.

Open: The North Bridge Visitor Center: 8:30 a.m. to 5 p.m. daily. Closed Christmas and New Year's Day. The Lexington Battle Road Visitor Center: 9 a.m. to 5 p.m. daily. Closed December to March. The Wayside: 9:30 a.m. to 5:30 p.m. daily.

Fees: None for the Visitor Centers. $1 for ages 16–62 to tour The Wayside house.

Mailing Address: Minute Man National Historical Park, P.O. Box 160, Concord, MA 01742.

Telephone: 508-369-6993.

Getting There: From Boston, take Route 2 into Concord Center. The Visitor Center is off Liberty Street in Concord. The Battle Road Visitor Center is off Route 21 in Lexington.

| Salem Maritime National Historic Site

The romance of New England's early seafaring days, when Salem was a bustling port with 50 wharves, with ships unloading exotic cargo, with bulging warehouses and chowder houses filled with rich sea captains and businessmen, is recalled in this historic waterfront park. Salem was one of the pre-eminent colonial commercial cities. Ships returning with goods from India, Africa, and the Far East docked here after many months at sea along with privateers who came to cash in their booty. The taxes levied on cargo and harbor services generated some 20 percent of the nation's income, making Salem one of the dominant 18th century commercial cities.

The two-story brick Custom House where duties were collected was immortalized in the introduction to Nathaniel Hawthorne's classic novel, *The Scarlet Letter*. Today, the Custom House preserves the offices of Customs Service employees of the late 19th century. Hawthorne's office, where he worked from 1846 to 1849, is also preserved.

Only two of the original wharves remain. Central Wharf now houses the orientation center and Derby Wharf features a lighthouse dating from 1871. Derby Wharf, at one time owned by millionaire merchant Elias Hasket Denby, was the largest of Salem's docking facilities.

The Bonded Warehouse contains original barrels of rum, chests of tea, and hoisting equipment; the Scale House has antique weighing and measuring devices; and the restored Denby House, home of the rich trader Elias Denby, is furnished with some interesting original pieces, including an ivory fan from the Orient and the pewter tankard from which old Denby quaffed his ale. The 13-room, brick Georgian house dates from 1762. The West India Goods Store, which once ran a brisk trade in imported items, has also been restored. This store still sells china, candles, pewter, coffee, teas, and spices just as it did two centuries ago.

A good time to visit the city is during the Salem Heritage Days held the third week in August. Near Halloween in October, Salem offers Haunted Happenings, with programs on pirates, sea monsters, and witches.

Open: Visitor Center: 8:30 a.m. to 5 p.m. daily, extended to 6 p.m.

from July 1 to Labor Day. Closed Thanksgiving, Christmas, and New Year's Day.

Fees: None.

Mailing Address: Salem Maritime National Historic Site, Derby Street, Salem, MA 01970.

Telephone: 617-744-4323.

Getting There: The site is on Denby Street in Salem, 20 minutes north of Boston on Route 1A.

‖ Saugus Iron Works National Historic Site

The water wheel turns, the bellows pump, and the blacksmith's hammer sings as it pounds metal into shape in this picturesque 17th-century iron mill town, reconstructed by the American Iron and Steel Institute as a memorial to the country's early iron industry.

With its furnace and forge, its rolling and slitting mill, and its ready supply of energy and resources, the settlement here, known as Hammersmith, was one of the most advanced iron mills of its time, one of only a dozen mills in the world capable of making the iron rods used for manufacturing nails. Hammersmith was also the first "integrated" ironworks in North America, where raw materials were converted into finished products in a single place.

Although it eventually foundered for lack of funds, Hammersmith was the seed of the domestic iron industry. The sons of the men who worked here spread their craft throughout New England, starting new mills and managing existing ones, and supplying the country with a steady supply of raw and finished iron products.

Visitors can tour the blast furnace, where ore was heated to extract the iron, the reconstructed forge, where bars of cast iron were turned into wrought iron and the rolling and slitting mill, where iron bars were flattened and cut into rods for making nails. Fires no longer burn in the furnace, but you can see a replica of a water wheel power an enormous bellows and watch a blacksmith at work.

The museum has fish sinkers, clay pipes, and pottery used by the factory's early inhabitants as well as a 500-pound iron hammer and a segment of the original water wheel. During the tour season, a 17th-century post-Iron works house, with period rooms and exhibits, is open to the public.

This quiet, quaint park with its old-fashioned, weathered-wood buildings is a delight to visit. The park also has a nature trail. Special summer activities include arts and crafts classes for children and Wednesday evening concerts.

Open: 9 a.m. to 4 p.m. daily, extended to 5 p.m. from April through October. Closed Thanksgiving, Christmas, and New Year's Day.

Fees: None.

Mailing Address: Saugus Iron Works National Historic Site, 244 Central Street, Saugus, MA 01906.

Telephone: 617-233-0050.

Getting There: From Boston, take Route 1 north over the Mystic River Bridge and make a right at the Main Street/Saugus exit, three-fourths mile to the town center. From the circle, follow Central Street to the parking lot. The site is about 20 minutes from Boston.

‖ Springfield Armory National Historic Site

With more than 10,000 guns in its collection, the Springfield Armory Museum has the largest array of military small arms in the world—everything from the sleek, long-barreled muskets of 1795, the famous Springfield Rifle, to the M-1 rifle used in World War II and the M-16 in use today. The armory, established in 1794, also houses a collection of firearms donated by Presidents Kennedy, Eisenhower, Roosevelt, and Wilson.

From 1777, when General George Washington designated Springfield as the nation's arms facility, until its closing 174 years later, Springfield Armory has been one of the most important facilities in the world for the design and production of military small arms. The site was also the scene of a rebellion in early 1787 that, more than any single incident in the history of the United States, led to the adoption of the U.S. Constitution.

The 1787 insurrection, known as Shays Rebellion, was mounted to stop the harsh treatment of debtors at a time when local economies were foundering. A group of 1,100 men led by Daniel Shays, a poor farmer who had been unable to raise $12 to pay a debt, tried to capture Springfield's court in 1786 and, a year later, he attempted to seize the arsenal.

Since Congress was powerless to respond to Massachusetts' pleas for help, the local militia handled the insurrection. The attack was quickly countered, but it convinced Americans that a stronger federal government would be needed to handle future rebellions. Soon after, a new constitution was drafted, one of the country's most enduring documents.

Springfield Armory made scientific as well as political history in 1819, when inventor Thomas Blanchard fashioned a lathe that made identical rifle stocks. This early experiment in mass production revolutionized gun-making. (For his contribution, Blanchard made a royalty of 9 cents on every musket produced at the Springfield Armory and at Harpers Ferry, West Virginia.)

Springfield continued to stand at the forefront of arms manufacturing throughout its lifetime. The 1861 rifle musket, a percussion firearm that saw duty in the Civil War and on the frontier, was manufactured here, as was the semi-automatic M-1 rifle. This gun, adopted in 1936, was considered one of the most reliable modern shoulder weapons. Another well-known firearm produced here was the Springfield rifle, a .30 caliber, bolt-operated rifle adopted by the U.S. Army in 1903.

Armory Square has more than a dozen buildings, but only the Main Arsenal, a forbidding brick fortress-like structure that houses the Springfield Museum, is open to the public. The Commanding Officer's lavish residence built in the 1840s can be viewed from the outside.

Open: 8:30 a.m. to 4:30 p.m. daily. Closed Thanksgiving, Christmas, and New Year's Day.

Fees: None.

Mailing Address: Springfield Armory National Historic Site, One Armory Square, Springfield, MA 01105.

Telephone: 413-734-6477.

Getting There: The site is within the city of Springfield, Massachusetts. Take I-291 from either direction (I-91 or I-90, the Massachusetts

Turnpike) to the Armory Street exit (#3) and follow to Federal Street. The park entrance is on Federal Street, near the intersection with State Street. Drive through the grounds of Springfield Technical Community College to the main arsenal. City buses operate on State Street and connect with the railroad station and the bus terminal.

MICHIGAN

1. Father Marquette National Memorial

‖ Father Marquette National Memorial

A museum and outdoor pavilion near the Straits of Mackinac in Saint Ignace, Michigan, commemorates Father Jacques Marquette, the French Jesuit missionary who explored North America in the 17th century. Marquette's journeys into the continental interior led him to discover the northern Mississippi River. The Jesuit missions he established, among them Saint Ignace in 1671, helped to settle present-day Canada and the United States. He died on the Lake Michigan shore of Michigan's Lower Peninsula on May 18, 1675, at the age of 37.

The memorial, in the Marquette Unit of Straits State Park, has exhibits about Marquette's canoe journey from Michigan to Illinois along with a 16-minute film, "The Mind of the Man," which portrays key scenes from Marquette's life, and a copy of Marquette's journal in the original French with English translation. The park has a spectacular view of the Straits of Mackinac, through which Father Marquette once paddled, and Mackinac Bridge, a 5-mile-long suspension bridge (the longest suspension bridge in the world) between Lake Huron and Lake Michigan. The site is administered in cooperation with the Michigan Department of Natural Resources. Straits State Park, which is located nearby, has 322 camping sites, some trails, and a summer swimming beach. Wildlife in the park includes deer, skunks, and racoons.

Open: Museum: 10 a.m. to 6:30 p.m. daily, June 1 to September 30. Closed in winter.

Fees: None for the museum; entry to the park is $2 per car.

Mailing Address: Father Marquette National Memorial, 720 Church Street, Saint Ignace, MI 49781.

Telephone: 906-643-8620 or 906-643-9394.

Getting There: The monument is in Straits State Park, in Saint Ignace. Going north from the Mackinac Bridge, take Route 2 west, the second exit, and follow the signs into the park.

MINNESOTA

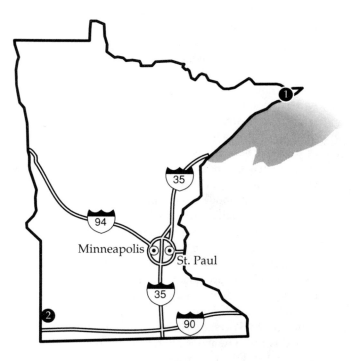

1. Grand Portage National Monument
2. Pipestone National Monument

| Grand Portage National Monument

Grand Portage on the western shore of Lake Superior was the main headquarters and meeting place for fur traders and trappers during the height of the North American fur trade era. Each summer, voyageurs ladened with pelts and trade goods would gather at the wooden stockade to sell their wares. At Grand Portage National Monument, this depot has been reconstructed, with a stockade, warehouse, a kitchen, and the Great Hall (which measures 95 feet by 30 feet), where entrepreneurs would drink and conduct their business.

The collection of wood buildings at Grand Portage marked the halfway point between civilization and the wilderness, where grizzled voyageurs feasted and caroused with friends and associates before returning once again to the forest. On the flat lakeshore lands nearby, as many as 800 to 1,000 voyageurs would make camp each summer, some in tents, others sleeping beneath their 36-foot-long birchbark canoes. Close by is the reconstructed dock where canoes ladened with manufactured goods from Montreal in Canada landed. In summer, a boat leaves daily from the dock for Isle Royale National Park in Michigan, located 22 miles from the site.

For hikers, an 8.5-mile trail leads from the monument to the place that marks the site of Fort Charlotte. It was here, where the waters of the Pigeon River are no longer navigable, that trappers from the north had to portage their canoes and furs overland to the port on Lake Superior. "Portage" comes from the French word for "carry"; hence the name Grand Portage. The typical voyageur could carry 180 pounds over this route in about 2½ hours. By the lakeshore, the landscape is low and flat, but the terrain is rougher along the Grand Portage trail, with its ridges and valleys. Pine, spruce, fir, and deciduous trees such as the white birch, maple, aspen, ash, and sumac trees shade the area.

Another excellent hike is the Mount Rose Trail, a 300-foot climb that takes about an hour to complete. The summit gives a panoramic view of the northeastern tip of Minnesota and Lake Superior.

The stockade at Grand Portage was built in 1778 by the North West Company, a group of independent fur traders in skin-to-skin competition with the successful British Hudson's Bay Company. This business, formed by Montreal traders Benjamin and Joseph Frobisher, Simon McTavish, and James and John McGill, became fabulously successful.

Fur traders, Indians, explorers, and missionaries stopped at this portage on one of the main 18th-century routes to the Northwest.—*Jack E. Boucher, NPS photograph*

At its peak in 1792, some 200,000 beaver skins passed through Grand Portage, earning McTavish $70,000 in profit during an era when a pound of beef cost only 5 cents. The site was abandoned in 1803, when the company moved its trading center north to avoid American taxation.

To commemorate the rousing rendezvous of fur trade times, the park holds a special Rendezvous Day on the second weekend in August. This event, open to the public, features dancing by Ojibwa Indians, craft sales, canoe races on Lake Superior, fiddling and tobacco spitting contests, and a turkey shoot.

Open: 8 a.m. to 5 p.m. daily from mid-May to mid-October.

Fees: $1 per person, ages 17–62.

Mailing Address: Grand Portage National Monument, P.O. Box 666, Grand Marais, MN 55604.

Telephone: 218-387-2788.

Getting There: The monument is located in the northeastern-most corner of Minnesota on the shore of Lake Superior, along Rt. 61, 36 miles northeast of Grand Marais, MN.

▌Pipestone National Monument

Hundreds of years ago, Indians from all over North America would quarry stone for their ceremonial pipes in these sacred grounds in the southwestern corner of Minnesota. According to Indian legend, the soft, red stone and the Indians themselves were made of the same substance. Smoking from a ceremonial pipe, then, was a way of communicating with the spiritual world.

Pipestone National Monument, which protects this pipestone quarry, was once the clay of a prehistoric sea bed. Today, only Native Americans are allowed to remove the precious stone from the earth. If you happen to be in the park when Indians are digging for pipestone, usually in fall, you can witness this ancient tradition. The visitor center, which houses the Upper Midwest Indian Cultural Center, displays and sells the pipes, quillwork and beadwork, pottery, and other handicrafts.

A three-fourths-mile scenic trail runs through the tall grasses of the virgin prairie in the 283-acre site. The trail leads by the exposed red rubble of the quarries and along the Pipestone Creek to Winnewissa Falls. The spot was a favorite gathering center during the 19th century, when great numbers of Plains Indians met at the site. George Catlin, whose paintings documented the costumes and lifestyles of Native Americans, traveled here in 1836. Pipestone is called "catlinite" in his honor.

Pipestone pipes have been found in archeological sites thousands of miles from the region, attesting to the importance of the area. Ancestors of the Oto and Iowa Indians, who lived in the region about 400 years ago, were probably the first to use the quarries. Indians smoked tobacco in their red clay pipes to seal agreements, conclude treaties, and solidify alliances. Because of this tradition, the pipes were commonly known as peace pipes.

Native Americans clung to their sacred pipestone quarries long after the white man had taken over much of their lands in Minnesota. It was not until 1893, when the government seized the land after building a Federal Indian school there, that the Indians lost control of the region. It became a park in 1937.

Overnight camping facilities are available at Split Rock Creek State Park, located on Route 23 south of Pipestone, and at Blue Mounds State Park, on Route 75 south of the monument.

Open: Visitor Center: 8 a.m. to 5 p.m.; in summer, from 8 a.m. to 6 p.m. Mon.–Thurs., and from 8 a.m. to 8 p.m. Fri.–Sun. Closed Christmas and New Year's Day.

Fees: $1, ages 17–61. Native Americans, educational groups, and handicapped admitted free.

Mailing Address: Pipestone National Monument, P.O. Box 727, Pipestone, MN 56164.

Telephone: 507-825-5464.

Getting There: Located in the southwestern corner of Minnesota, the park is adjacent to the city of Pipestone. From Sioux Falls, SD, take I-90 east to Rt. 23 north and U.S. 75 north of Pipestone to the park turn-off.

MISSISSIPPI

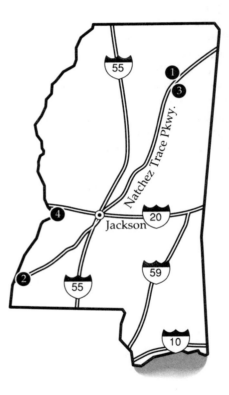

1. Brices Cross Roads National Battlefield Site
2. Natchez National Historical Park
3. Tupelo National Battlefield
4. Vicksburg National Military Park

|| Brices Cross Roads National Battlefield Site

Protected by thick forests and dense underbrush, the Confederate soldiers led by General Nathan Bedford Forrest skillfully overwhelmed Union troops at Brices Cross Roads on June 10, 1864.

In the aftermath of the battle, Union General S.D. Sturgis called a chaotic retreat to the Northern stronghold of Memphis. Forrest and his men doggedly pursued Union troops for 22 miles, harassing the stragglers and sending many of the fleeing soldiers to a watery death in Tishomingo Creek and nearby Hatchie Bottom.

In numerical terms, the victory was spectacular. The Yankees lost over 2,600 men while the outnumbered Rebel forces lost only 492. But perhaps more important than the heavy losses suffered by Union forces, the southern army captured sorely needed stores—250 wagons and ambulances, 18 cannon, and thousands of arms and rounds of ammunition.

The one-acre historical park at the Brices Cross Roads Battlefield has no facilities or interpretive programs. An interpretive marker and map tell the story of the battle. Ten granite markers along the approach and retreat route provide information about what happened on location. The adjacent Bethany Church cemetery contains the graves of 102 Confederates who died while fighting there.

Open: The battlegrounds are always open. The Visitor Center for the Natchez Trace Parkway in Tupelo is open from 8 a.m. to 5 p.m. daily. Closed Christmas Day.

Fees: None.

Mailing Address: Brices Cross Roads National Battlefield Site, c/o Natchez Trace Parkway, Rural Route 1, NT-143, Tupelo, MS 38801.

Telephone: 601-842-1572.

Getting There: The battlefield site is located in northeastern Mississippi about 15 miles north of Tupelo on U.S. Highway 45 North and six miles west of Baldwyn on MS Highway 370.

‖ Natchez National Historical Park

The city of Natchez, once the commercial and cultural center of the South's historic Cotton Belt, has one of the best preserved concentrations of antebellum properties in the United States. Still under development, the Natchez National Historical Park preserves the Melrose plantation in Natchez.

This estate, built in 1845, includes grounds and the main house, a brick structure with big columns, as well as outbuildings like the kitchen and slave quarters. Many of the original furnishings are still in the house.

Also in the park is the site of Fort Rosalie on the bluffs of the Mississippi River, where the French built a fort in 1500. Other historic structures in Natchez may be incorporated into the park in the future.

Park facilitites are still under development. For information about hours, fees, and tours of historic houses including the Melrose House, contact: the Natchez National Historical Foundation, P.O. Box 1403, Natchez, MS 39121, or the Natchez National Historical Park, c/o Natchez Trace Parkway, Rural Route 1, NT 134, Tupelo, MS 38801.

‖ Tupelo National Battlefield

During the hot and dusty days of June 13 and 14, 1864, Union and Confederate soldiers clashed in the cornfields at Harrisburg near Tupelo, Mississippi. Rebel soldiers, commanded by General Nathan Bedford Forrest, were out to cut the rail line that delivered vital supplies to the Federal army in the South. This rail line transported ammunition and food through Nashville and Chattanooga, Tennessee. Federal forces, led by Generals A.J. Smith and Joseph A. Mower, successfully protected the precious rail link.

Technically, the Union won this skirmish. When the dust had settled, the North sustained fewer casualties than the South, and the vital train route remained intact. But with little food and almost no water to sustain them, Union troops had to withdraw. The Confederates, however, were too exhausted to give chase.

Facilities at this one-acre battlefield in the middle of the town of Tupelo include a large granite memorial commemorating both armies and an interpretive marker and map. Handouts with information on Brices Cross Roads/Tupelo are available on site. Hiking trails criss-cross the field where fighting took place. For more information, contact the visitor center at the nearby Natchez Trace Parkway.

Open: Tupelo Battlefield is always open. The Natchez Trace Visitor Center is open 8 a.m. to 5 p.m. daily. Closed Christmas Day.

Fees: None.

Mailing Address: Tupelo National Battlefield, c/o Superintendent, Natchez Trace Parkway, Rural Route 1, NT-143, Tupelo, MS 38801.

Telephone: 601-842-1572.

Getting There: The park is located within the city limits of Tupelo, MS, in the northeastern part of the state. It is on MS Highway 6 about one mile west of the intersection with U.S. Highway 45, or about 1.2 miles east of the Natchez Trace Parkway.

‖ Vicksburg National Military Park

At 10 a.m. on July 4, 1863, Confederate soldiers raised the white cloth of surrender, marched out of their trenches, and laid down their arms. Low on supplies and exhausted from constant bombardment during the 47-day siege, the Rebel forces gave up Vicksburg and with it went control of the Mississippi River and access to the wealthy Confederate states beyond. General Ulysses S. Grant's victory over Confederate General John C. Pemberton was one of the most important Union victories in the war.

This beautifully landscaped park overlooking the former channel of the Mississippi River is one of the most heavily monumented battlefields in all the world—1,300 pieces of monumentation in all. A 16-mile interpretive tour of Confederate earthwork defenses and Northern siege works tells the story of the slowly tightening noose of Union troops around Vicksburg in 1863.

The Union army marched south from camps at Milliken's Bend, Louisiana, which lay across the river from Vicksburg. On April 30, 1863, Grant ferried his troops across the Mississippi to the south and prepared to attack Vicksburg from the east. On his way, he stopped off to capture Jackson, the capital of Mississippi. Then, with supplies and reinforcements for Vicksburg cut off, he marched toward the city.

The siege began May 11, with Union forces constantly shelling the city while they inched ever closer to Confederate trenches. At the Third Louisiana Redan, Union soldiers got so close to Rebel troops that they tunnelled under the earthworks and blew them up. But the attack was repulsed. (At 13 places along the front, northern soldiers dug approaches, in many cases to within a few feet of the Confederate line.)

With supplies to Vicksburg cut off since May 18, Rebel troops were put on reduced rations. The main meal of the day, illustrated by a display in the visitor center, consisted of a small portion of rice, a handful of beans, and two thin strips of meat. Poor food and constant fighting wore down the Confederate forces quickly. By the time of surrender, 5,878 soldiers were in the hospital, many of them suffering from malnutrition and exposure.

The situation was only a little better for some 4,600 people living in Vicksburg. Food was available, but profiteering was rampant. (In those days, armies existed on their own stores of rations and trips into town for food were rare.) It is believed that anger over food prices provoked the bad fire that raged through the city on June 1.

Vicksburg National Cemetery, one of the largest Civil War burial grounds in the country, has the remains of 17,000 Union soldiers who died during the battle. Confederate soldiers are buried in a separate graveyard in the town of Vicksburg. The cemetery also contains the remains of American veterans of every war from the Mexican War (1846–1848) to the Vietnam War.

Vicksburg was not only the site of one of the most grueling campaigns of the Civil War, it was also the site of one of the most interesting maritime operations. Here, on December 12, 1862, the Union ironclad boat *Cairo* (pronounced KAY-row) became the first vessel in history to be sunk by an electronically detonated torpedo. The *Cairo* went to the bottom of the Yazoo River in only 12 minutes. The only casualty was Union pride.

The restored boat, which was raised in 1964, is now on display in Vicksburg National Military Park adjacent to the USS *Cairo* Museum, which houses hundreds of artifacts recovered from the ill-fated ship. The museum is located in the northwestern corner of the crescent-shaped park and can be reached from the tour road or through the city of Vicksburg via Fort Hill Drive and Connecting Avenue.

Vicksburg's visitor center has an 18-minute video on the campaign, shown every half-hour. A six-minute video on the sinking of the *Cairo* is shown at the *Cairo* Museum. In summer a living history program with soldiers in uniform simulates a Confederate battery. There are rifle and cannon firings and first-person interpretation. Check for details. The visitor center has a Union officer's tent with a desk and Union General Pemberton's sword. There are also life-sized dioramas of a trench, a field hospital, and the caves in which residents hid during the fighting.

Visitors can wander through the 1,800-acre park on their own or sign up at the park headquarters for a licensed tour guide. If you want a guided tour, make reservations and check on fees well in advance of your visit. (Spring is the busiest season.)

Picnic tables are scattered throughout the park. Fires and camping are not allowed. A commercial campground is located one-half mile from the main entrance.

Open: Visitor Center: 8 a.m. to 5 p.m. daily; extended in the summer. The *Cairo* Museum is open from 9 a.m. to 5 p.m. daily, extended in summer. Check dates. Closed Christmas Day. The park closes at sundown.

Fees: $3 per vehicle or $1 per person on bus. Persons over 62, free. Scout troops and school groups, free.

Mailing Address: Vicksburg National Military Park, 3201 Clay Street, Vicksburg, MS 39180.

Telephone: 601-636-0583.

Getting There: The park is located in the northeastern section of Vicksburg; the entrance and Visitor Center are on Clay St. (Rt. 80), within one-fourth mile of I-20. From downtown Vicksburg, proceed east on Clay St. (Rt. 80 Historic). The park is located at 3201 Clay St., diagonally across from the Holiday Inn. From I-20, exit at 4-B and go west on Clay St. to the park.

MISSOURI

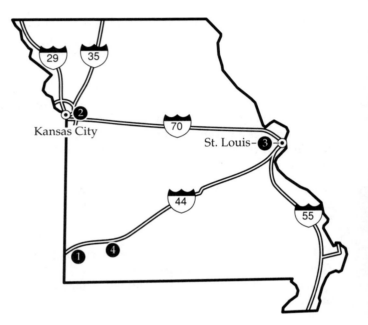

1. George Washington Carver National Monument
2. Harry S Truman National Historic Site
3. Jefferson National Expansion Memorial
4. Wilson's Creek National Battlefield

George Washington Carver National Monument

George Washington Carver, who started life as a black slave and became one of the country's foremost scientists, spent his youth on this small farm in southwestern Missouri. The park preserves the farm of Moses and Susan Carver, the white couple who raised the orphaned George as their own son. It was among these hills and trees that Carver developed his relationship with nature, one that would fascinate and sustain him throughout his life. In fact, he became so knowledgeable about plants that as a child he was locally known as the "plant doctor."

Carver was born here shortly before the end of the Civil War, and remained until age 12, when he left to pursue an education. The Carver farm inspired in George a self-confidence and acute awareness of his relationship with nature. This awareness and his abilities eventually lead to a successful career as an educator, botanist, and agronomist.

The time George spent at the Carver farm also allowed him to develop his artistic talent. As a child, Carver chewed on branches until the fibers made a brush for painting. He made his own pigments from berries and clay. Throughout his life he painted using the same unique tools and media he had devised in his youth. And he never lost the belief that all things in nature have a use and a purpose.

Carver did most of his work and research at Tuskegee Institute in Alabama, a school started by black educator Booker T. Washington. While at Tuskegee, Carver discovered over 300 uses for peanuts and more than 100 uses for sweet potatoes, two crops that helped southern farmers make the transition from growing predominantly cotton to raising a range of crops.

The visitor center has two short films on Carver's boyhood and one on his adult life, and a museum that commemorates his boyhood life as well as his many great achievements. A self-guided nature trail winds through the forests where young George played (be careful of the abundant poison ivy). Visitors may walk through the 1881 Moses Carver house, built after a storm destroyed the log cabin in which young George was born and lived. Although George never lived in the 1881 house, he did visit the Carvers there. There is a reconstructed log outline marking the probable location of the original birthplace cabin.

The woods where George spent so much of his time observing plants and wildlife are as beautiful today as they were in the 19th century. As you walk through, you will find quotes from Carver and information about his youth in Missouri.

On the second Sunday in July, the park celebrates Carver's birthday with speeches and a memorial ceremony. Call ahead for exact dates.

Open: 8:30 a.m. to 5:00 p.m. daily, extended to 7 p.m. from Memorial Day to Labor Day. Closed Christmas Day.

Fees: $1, ages 17–62.

Mailing Address: George Washington Carver National Monument, P.O. Box 38, Diamond, MO 64840.

Telephone: 417-325-4151.

Getting There: From Joplin, take I-44 east, exit south on Alt. 71 to Diamond. Go west (right) on Highway V and follow the signs to the Visitor Center, approximately 2½ miles.

‖ Harry S Truman National Historic Site

While Harry S Truman served as the country's 33rd president, the United States exploded the first atomic bombs in Japan during World War II, sent soldiers to fight in Korea, and pursued a policy of aiding anti-communist governments around the world. The Trumans' white clapboard house in Independence, Missouri, with its porches and Victorian windows, was known as the Summer White House.

Harry and Bess Truman lived in this house on North Delaware Street from their marriage in 1919 until Truman entered the White House in 1945. They returned to the home when Truman retired from public service in 1953, and continued to live there until their deaths. Harry died at age 88 on December 26, 1972, and Bess at age 97 on October 18, 1982. Both are buried in the courtyard of the Truman Library.

With its homey furniture, book-lined study, and cozy arrangements, the house looks as it did when the Trumans lived here. One of the most popular sights is Margaret Truman's baby grand piano, which almost fell through the White House floor. Six of the house's 14 rooms are open to visitors.

Guided tours of the Truman Home are offered for a small fee. Tours are popular and limited—only eight people at a time can enter the house—so pick up your ticket early in the day. Tickets are distributed on a first-come, first-served basis and visitors must pick up their tickets in person. For more information, telephone: 816-254-7199.

The ticket center, which shows a free 12-minute slide program about the Truman Home, is a good place to start a tour of the Truman site in Independence.

Open: 8:30 a.m. to 5 p.m. daily, Memorial Day to Labor Day. Closed Mondays throughout the rest of the year. Closed Thanksgiving, Christmas, and New Year's Day.

Fees: $1 ages 17–61, others free. Tickets, available from the information center at the corner of Truman Road and Main Street in Independence Square, are required.

Mailing Address: Harry S Truman National Historic Site, 223 N. Main Street, Independence, MO 64050-2894.

Telephone: 816-254-2720.

Getting There: The presidential home is located in Independence, in western Missouri near Kansas City. From I-70, follow the tourist signs into Independence which lead you to the site. The Ticket and Information Center is located at the corner of Truman Road and Main Street.

Jefferson National Expansion Memorial

Rising 630 feet above the Mississippi riverfront is the famed Gateway Arch, a soaring symbol of St. Louis' role in opening up the American frontier between 1800 and 1900. The 91-acre Jefferson National Expansion Memorial is dedicated to President Thomas Jefferson, whose purchase of the Louisiana Territory opened up the country to westward expansion in 1803. It encompasses St. Louis' old commercial district, where pioneers outfitted themselves for the journey across the prairies, mountains, and deserts of the West.

A four-minute ride on a vertical tram takes visitors to the top of the arch, where, on a clear day, you can see barges pushing loads of corn and coal down the brown waters of the Mississippi, or look out

This 630-foot stainless steel arch along the Mississippi river-front in St. Louis, Missouri, commemorates the American pioneering spirit.—*NPS photograph*

across 30 miles of Illinois and Missouri farmland. This architectural wonder was designed in 1948 by Eero Saarinen, an architect of Finnish extraction. It is made of 42,878 tons of steel and concrete, and is 75 feet higher than the Washington Monument in Washington, D.C. The trip up the arch's sloping legs is a gentle ascent in a small, barrel-like capsule that rights itself every few feet.

In the underground complex below the arch, several interesting movies and presentations chronicle the pioneering days of the 19th century. Two movies, "Time of the West" and "Monument to the Dream," tell the story of the country's westward expansion and the arch itself. There are also interpretive programs and publications for sale.

The Old Courthouse, between Fourth Street and Broadway, has an astonishing 164-foot-high iron dome. In this courthouse, the slave Dred Scott sued for his freedom in 1847. Scott lost his case, but won in a second trial held in 1850. When this decision was appealed, Scott lost again but was freed by his owner after the decision. The case sparked a debate over slavery that was ultimately decided by the Civil War. The courthouse contains portraits of Scott and presents a film about the early history of the region.

Sites near the park, but not part of it, include the Old Cathedral, Greek Revival structure that is the first cathedral west of the Mississippi; Eads Bridge, built in 1874 as the world's first steel truss bridge; two riverboats, the *Admiral* and the *Goldenrod*; the Sports Hall of Fame; the National Bowling Hall of Fame and Museum; and several old warehouses of architectural interest. The waterfront area, with the Gateway Arch and visitor center, has been restored with brick sidewalks, little ships, and eateries in renovated buildings.

The story of America's expansion from coast to coast is the tale of the many men and women who endured great hardships to make their homes in the vast, unsettled West. St. Louis, a river port and link with the manufacturing centers of the East, played a central role as the country pushed its borders ever westward. In every sense of the word, St. Louis was the Gateway to the West.

Open: Visitor Center: 8:00 a.m. to 10:00 p.m. in summer, check for exact dates, and 9 a.m. to 6 p.m. in winter. The Old Courthouse is open 8:00 a.m. to 4:30 p.m. daily, year-round. Closed Thanksgiving, Christmas, and New Year's Day.

Tickets for the Gateway Arch are on sale from 9:30 a.m. to 5:15 p.m. daily, with trips every ten minutes in winter and every five minutes in summer. Get there early as tickets sell out quickly. Closed Christmas, Thanksgiving, and New Year's Day.

Fees: $1 per person, ages 17–61, or $3 per family. Tram ride is $2.50 for adults, $.50 for children. Movies are $.75 for adults.

Mailing Address: Jefferson National Expansion Memorial National Historic Site, 11 North Fourth Street, St. Louis, MO 63102.

Telephone: 314-425-4465.

Getting There: The historic district is located between Walnut Street and Delmar Blvd., and stretches from 18th St. to the Levee on the Mississippi River. Trailways and Greyhound bus stations are conveniently located, and the Amtrak rail station is nearby. Lambert

St. Louis International Airport is located 14 miles out of town. Local buses serve the entire downtown region. For more information, call 231-2345. For literature on St. Louis, contact the Convention and Visitors Bureau at 421-1023.

‖ Wilson's Creek National Battlefield

The second major battle of the Civil War, a bloody struggle for control of the strategically important state of Missouri and the Federal arsenal in St. Louis, was fought among the sinkholes and fields of Wilson's Creek.

Here, Union forces commanded by Brigadier General Nathaniel Lyon and Confederate troops led by Benjamin McCulloch clashed on Bloody Hill on August 10, 1861. When the smoke had cleared, losses totaled 2,353 including Lyon, who was the first Union general to die in the Civil War. The 1,750-acre park at Wilson's Creek commemorates this battle, which, though won technically by the South, left control of Missouri and the St. Louis arsenal in Federal hands.

The five-mile road through the park leads by Bloody Hill, a portion of which was once littered with dead and wounded soldiers. One Confederate soldier said the carnage was so great that you could walk from body to body without ever touching the ground. Three-quarters of a mile away is the Ray House, which, by accident of location, became part of this historic event.

While his family huddled in the cellar of their three room farmhouse, John Ray watched the fighting from his porch. The Confederates took over the house during the battle. Now restored to its 1861 appearance, the Ray House is open to visitors. Check for times.

The rolling hills, fields, and woodlands of the battleground at Wilson's Creek are virtually unchanged from Civil War days, and the park has excellent interpretive exhibits and a living history program that brings the era to life. There is a walking tour through the battlefield and an auto route around the entire park.

The visitor center, which is built into the side of a hill, boasts a fiber-optic display system that explains the battle. There is also an exhibit of uniforms illustrating the differences in some uniforms that created confusion during the battle.

On Sunday afternoons, the living history program features exhibitions of Civil War activities such as cannon and musket firing, infantry drilling, period music, and medical procedures. On special occasions, visitors to the Ray house will be greeted by interpreters who play the role of family members at the time of the historic battle. August 10 is the date of the park's anniversary celebration. This event is marked with cannon firings and a keynote address. In spring and fall, on nights with a full moon, there are moonlight tours of the battlefield. Check with the ranger for exact dates.

Every three to four years thousands of visitors descend on Wilson's Creek to watch a large encampment that recreates the lifestyle of a Civil War soldier. Volunteers pitch tents, pull out cannon, cook, and drill. The next encampment is scheduled for 1991, the 130th anniversary year of the battle. Check with the park for the exact date.

Wildlife in the secluded rural atmosphere of Wilson's Creek includes coyote, fox, deer, and hawk. The park is a delightful spot for an outing. Picnic tables are available but overnight camping is not allowed.

Open: 8 a.m. to 5 p.m., with extended hours in summer. Check for exact summer dates. Closed Christmas and New Year's Day.

Fees: None.

Mailing Address: Wilson's Creek National Battlefield, P.O. Box 403, Republic, MO 65738.

Telephone: 417-732-2662.

Getting There: Located in southwestern Missouri, ten miles south of Springfield and three miles east of Republic. From I-44, take Exit 77 (Mo. 13) south on the Kansas Expressway five miles to US 60. Turn right on US 60 and drive 7 miles to Mo. M, then left for three-fourths of a mile to Mo. ZZ. The park is two miles south on Mo. ZZ. From US 65 at Ozark, drive west 14 miles on Mo. 14 to Mo. ZZ, then turn right. The park is seven miles north on Mo. ZZ.

MONTANA

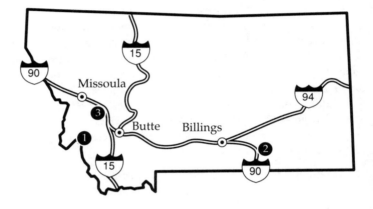

1. Big Hole National Battlefield
2. Custer Battlefield National Monument
3. Grant-Kohrs Ranch National Historic Site

‖ Big Hole National Battlefield

This tract of grassland and pine forest in the western Montana highlands commemorates the bloody battle between U.S. troops and the Nez Perce Indians in August 1877.

Hoping to escape confinement on a reservation in Idaho, a band of 800 Nez Perce Indians, a semi-nomadic tribe, were on their way to join the Crow Indians in Montana. But Colonel John Gibbon, commander of the Seventh Infantry, followed the band through the Bitterroot Valley and onto Big Hole, attacking the sleeping Indian encampment near the North Fork of the Big Hole River shortly before dawn on August 9.

The Nez Perce won the early morning clash, killing 29 soldiers and volunteers and wounding 41. But the losses suffered by the Indians were even greater. Sixty to 90 of their members, more than half of them women, children, and the elderly, lost their lives. Their ranks depleted, the Indians surrendered to Federal troops 57 days later at the Bear Paw Mountains in north central Montana.

The 655-acre battlefield has a small museum that exhibits army equipment and Indian artifacts from the battle, including a coat owned by the brave Nez Perce leader Chief Joseph. Foot trails lead through the battlefield, the camp where the Indians slept, and the woods where the Indian warriors besieged the infantry for 24 hours.

Wildlife in the park, which is at an elevation of 6,200 feet, includes coyote, mule deer, moose, elk, beaver, and muskrat. Hunting is prohibited. Game fishing for brook trout and whitefish requires a license.

Open: 8 a.m. to 5 p.m. daily, with hours extended to 8 p.m. from Memorial Day to Labor Day. The Battle Area Road is closed with the first snow.

Fees: None.

Mailing Address: Big Hole National Battlefield, P.O. Box 237, Wisdom, MT 59761.

Telephone: 406-689-3155.

Getting There: The site is located ten miles west of Wisdom, MT, on Rt. 43. From Butte, take I-15 southwest to Divide, then to Wisdom on Rt. 43.

‖ Custer Battlefield National Monument

White marble tombstones set into the side of a grassy knoll mark the site of the best-known battle in the history of the American West —the Battle of the Little Bighorn. On June 25–26, 1876, Sioux and Cheyenne Indians annihilated five companies of the Seventh Cavalry commanded by George Armstrong Custer.

The Custer Battlefield, located along the banks of the Little Bighorn River, commemorates Custer's famous Last Stand. The park is on two tracts of land, one near the site where Custer died and one five miles away at the Reno-Benteen Battlefield.

Ironically, the Battle of the Little Bighorn was also the last stand for the Indians who fought here. For in 1881, Sioux Chief Sitting Bull and the last of the Indian holdouts to white domination surrendered, marking the end of Native American presence on the Plains.

To this day, the true story of what happened at Little Bighorn remains a mystery. Because everyone directly associated with Custer's skirmish died, no one knows why the flamboyant leader split his troops, sending some men to fight several miles away, at what is now the Reno-Benteen Battlefield. Neither does anyone know the exact route Custer and his detachment took. Most of the soldiers who died here are buried in a common grave on Last Stand Hill. The Indians who fell were removed by their families.

The results of this bloody encounter are documented throughout the park. Rangers give daily talks about the battle, the life of the frontier soldier, and the culture of the Plains Indians. The interpretive programs run throughout the day from June through Labor Day.

The visitor center has exhibits on the battle and on Plains Indian culture, and an excellent 28-minute documentary movie about the battle entitled "Red Sunday." There is also a display of historical photographs of the men who fought in the battle. Other items include Indian weapons and Custer's buckskin suit.

Trails in the park lead through the battlefield and down the ravines. Allow at least two hours to walk both the Reno-Benteen Entrenchment Trail and the Deep Ravine Trail. Beware of snakes. Camping and picnicking are not permitted on the monument grounds.

Guided bus tours of the entire site are conducted by the Custer Battlefield Historical and Museum Association. There is a small fee

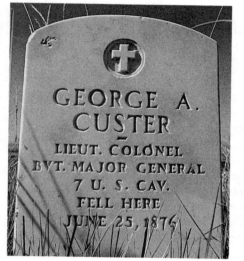

Custer Battlefield National Monument commemorates the Battle of the Little Bighorn and the famous Last Stand of flamboyant Lt. Col. George A. Custer. —*NPS photograph*

for the bus tour, which lasts about one hour. A two-hour van tour is also available. Tours leave from the visitor center twice daily during the summer season. Also during summer, rangers lead talks about the battle, the Plains Indians, and the soldiers of the time.

The Custer Battlefield is situated within the Crow Indian Reservation. In late August each year, the reservation hosts a fair, with a rodeo, Indian dancing, crafts, and other festivities.

Open: 8 a.m. to 4:30 p.m., October through May, extended to 6 p.m. from Labor Day weekend to October and to 7 p.m. from Memorial Day weekend to Labor Day. Closed Thanksgiving, Christmas, and New Year's Day.

Fees: $3 per car, $1 per person in bus groups.

Mailing Address: Custer Battlefield National Monument, P.O. Box 39, Crow Agency, MT 59022.

Telephone: 406-638-2622.

Getting There: From Billings, take I-90 to the Battlefield exit, past Crow Agency. There is no public transportation to the park. Car rentals are available in Billings, MT, 65 miles northwest of the site.

‖ Grant-Kohrs Ranch National Historic Site

The Grant-Kohrs Ranch, once one of the largest cattle ranching operations in the country, brings the open range era back to life.

The 1,500-acre park is virtually unchanged from the days when Conrad Kohrs, the German immigrant who bought the property in 1866, lived and worked the ranch with his family. Today, park staff carry on the daily activities, caring for livestock, branding new calves in summer, and mending and preserving the old buildings and fences.

Visitors can wander through more than 30 buildings, including the bunkhouse where cowboys once lived, the barns for cattle and horses, the blacksmith shop with demonstrations of traditional metalworking, and the buggy barn with its collection of horse-drawn vehicles. The park keeps about 25 head of cattle and half a dozen horses to maintain the flavor of an operating ranch.

Tours of the main floor of the 23-room ranch house, with its sumptuous Victorian furnishings, are free. Get tickets at the visitor center, for tours are limited to 12 people at a time on a first-come, first-served basis. In this house, Conrad Kohrs' beautiful wife Augusta brought a touch of charm and culture to the harsh Montana frontier.

Ranch livestock are representative of the breeds commonly raised by the Kohrs family, including Shorthorn and Longhorn cattle, draft horses, and poultry.

Conrad Kohrs, a butcher by trade, bought the ranch from a Canadian trader named Johnny Grant for $19,200 in 1866. Kohrs then added to the herds, improved the breeds, and acquired additional land. At its height, the ranch stretched over 25,000 acres, with over ten million acres of grazing lands in the four surrounding states and one Canadian province. Kohrs brought 8,000 to 10,000 head of cattle to market each year.

The park hosts a celebration in mid-July with branding, children's programs, chuck-wagon cooking that visitors can sample, quilting demonstrations, and other activities from the cowboy era. Check for details.

Wildlife in the area includes coyote, fox, skunk, deer, heron, and sparrow hawk. Fishing requires a state license. Camping and picnicking are not allowed at the park but food and lodging are available in nearby Deer Lodge, Montana.

Other attractions in the area include the Old Montana Prison, the Towe Ford Museum, Yesterday's Playthings, and the Powell County Museum.

Montana may have changed greatly since the cowboy days, but the harsh climate remains. Be prepared for extreme temperatures that can range from 40 degrees below zero in the winter to 100 degrees in the summer.

Open: 9 a.m. to 4:30 p.m. daily, with hours extended to 7:30 p.m. in summer. Check for exact dates. Closed Thanksgiving, Christmas, and New Year's Day.

Fees: None, but may be charged in the future.

Mailing Address: Grant-Kohrs Ranch National Historic Site, P.O. Box 790, Deer Lodge, MT 59722.

Telephone: 406-846-2070.

Getting There: Greyhound Bus Lines serves Deer Lodge, MT. Airline terminals are located in Butte, Helena, and Missoula, MT. The ranch is located midway between Yellowstone and Glacier National Park. From Butte, go west on I-90 (in a northern direction) about 405 miles to Deer Lodge. The ranch, marked by a brown Park Service sign, is at the north end of Deer Lodge across from the fairgrounds.

NEBRASKA

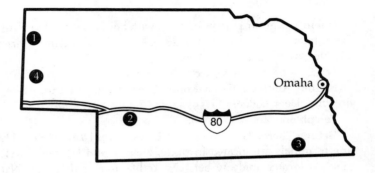

1. Agate Fossil Beds National Monument
2. Chimney Rock National Historic Site
3. Homestead National Monument of America
4. Scotts Bluff National Monument

|| Agate Fossil Beds National Monument

One of the finest fossil beds in the country is hidden in the grassy hills of this western Nebraska park, a "bare bones" record of the animals that roamed the region 19 million years ago. Here extraordinary beasts of the Miocene Epoch—including Menoceras, a two-horned rhino; Dinohyus, known as the "terrible pig"; and Moropus, a curious clawed mammal resembling a cross between a horse, giraffe, tapir, and bear—hunted and grazed on the savannah.

Their fossilized bones, sometimes whole skeletons, have been preserved in two sandstone hills that rise out of the endless prairie like gentle swells on a sea of green. The hills are named Carnegie and University for Carnegie Museum in Pittsburgh and the University of Nebraska at Lincoln, institutions that conducted many of the excavations. Over half the fossils on the site have yet to be uncovered.

A two-mile round-trip trail from the visitor center takes visitors to the fossil beds in these hills. The trail shows fossils exposed in the rock. Tours of the area are self-guided, but rangers will take groups on walks with prior arrangements. Fossil collecting is prohibited.

The visitor center/museum has a good collection of representative fossils which were found in the region, including burrows of a prehistoric beaver. The corkscrew-shaped fossil stands three to four feet tall. There is also an exhibit of Sioux Indian artifacts collected at the site by Captain James H. Cook, who settled in the area in 1887. Cook, an amateur paleontologist, is best known for his autobiography *Fifty Years on the Old Frontier* and his friendship with the Oglala Sioux Chief Red Cloud.

Like other prairie areas, Agate Fossil Beds has abundant wildlife. Deer, coyote, fox, and badger are best viewed in the early morning hours. Bring your binoculars for glimpses of the many birds that are attracted to the nearby Niobrara River. The river is stocked with trout; a Nebraska state license is required to fish within the monument. Other animals in the park include raccoon and porcupine. Watch out for rattlesnakes.

The park, which is located about 45 miles from the nearest major city, is very isolated. There are no camping facilities, stores, or gas stations nearby, so stop in Harrison or Mitchell before driving to the park.

The closest food and accommodations are in Scotts Bluff on Route 26, 45 miles away, and in Harrison, 25 miles north of the monument.

Open: The park is open year round. Visitor center is generally open 8:30 a.m. to 5:30 p.m. daily, May 1 through September 30 and 8:00 a.m. to 5:00 p.m. weekends only during the rest of the year. Call ahead for current information.

Fees: None.

Mailing Address: Agate Fossil Beds National Monument, c/o Scotts Bluff National Monument, P.O. Box 427, Gering, NE 69341.

Telephone: 308-668-2211.

Getting There: The monument is located in northwestern Nebraska, north of Scotts Bluff. It is 23 miles south of Rt. 20 at Harrison, via Rt. 29, or 34 miles north of Rt. 26 at Mitchell, via Rt. 29. Rental cars are available at Scotts Bluff.

‖ Chimney Rock National Historic Site

Chimney Rock was one of the major landmarks for pioneers traveling the Oregon Trail in the 19th century. A welcome break in the endless monotony of the prairies, it was known as a good camping spot just south of the North Platte River, which provided a dependable water supply. When the pioneers saw this sandstone spire, which towers above the North Platte River like a 500-foot birthday candle, they knew the Rocky Mountains were near and their arduous journey across the prairie would soon be over.

The column has eroded considerably since it was first sighted in 1813 by Robert Stuart and a band of traders on the way back from the Oregon country, but Chimney Rock continues to be impressive. Its composition of clay, volcanic ash, and hard sandstone has kept it from eroding completely like parts of the original bluff; it will undoubtedly stand for centuries to come.

Chimney Rock National Historic Site, which is jointly administered by the town of Bayard, Nebraska, the Nebraska State Historical Society, and the National Park Service, is visible from Route 92 in western Nebraska. A gravel turnoff just south of the intersection of routes 26 and 92 leads to a picnic area within a half mile of the site. From there, the route to the site is a foot trail over rough terrain,

Pioneers traveling westward on the Oregon Trail camped near Chimney Rock, which stands 500 feet above the North Platte River.—*NPS photograph*

where the loose rocks, rattlesnakes, and yucca plants make good boots and proper hiking clothes a must. Wildlife in the area includes deer, antelope, golden eagle, and hawk. From Memorial Day through Labor Day, the Nebraska State Historical Society maintains a mobile trailer with exhibits about the history and geology of the site. The Scotts Bluff National Monument in Gering, 23 miles away, has additional exhibits. (See entry for Scotts Bluff National Monument, Nebraska.)

Open: 9 a.m. to 6 p.m.

Fees: None.

Mailing Address: Chimney Rock National Historic Site, c/o Scotts Bluff National Monument, P.O. Box 427, Gering, NB 69341.

Telephone: 812-937-4757.

Getting There: The site is in western Nebraska, near the intersection of Route 92 and Route 26.

‖ Homestead National Monument of America

Homestead National Monument, which marks the site of one of the first claims staked out under the great land giveaway of 1862, commemorates the pioneers who settled the American frontier.

It was here, in this grassy corner of southeastern Nebraska, that Daniel Freeman and his wife Agnes claimed their free 160 acres under the Homestead Act. They busted the sod, cultivated the land, and built the brick school house that still stands today. For communities throughout the prairies, these one-room school houses served as a social and civic center. The Freeman school was so used until 1967.

The 160-acre site includes the Palmer-Epard cabin, a typical log home. This small structure was built on a nearby homestead in 1867. In places where no wood was available, the pioneers cut blocks of the densely packed sod out of the ground and built structures known as "soddies."

Photographs of these sod homes, displays of the tools used to make them, and chronicles of the stalwart people who plowed the prairies are on exhibit in the park's visitor center. From there, a 2.5-mile, self-guided trail takes you by the Palmer-Epard cabin, into the forest surrounding Cub Creek, through the restored prairie, and by the Freeman gravesite.

During a Homestead Days celebration in the last week of June, there are demonstrations of pioneer crafts. Check for details. Prairie Appreciation Week, with nature walks and films, is held during the third week in September.

Open: 8 a.m. to 5 p.m. daily, Labor Day to Memorial Day, extended in summer. Closed Christmas Day.

Fees: None.

Mailing Address: Homestead National Monument of America, Route 3, Box 47, Beatrice, NE 68310.

Telephone: 402-223-3514.

Getting There: The monument is located in southeastern Nebraska about 4.5 miles west of Beatrice and about 40 miles south of Lincoln. Take Rt. 4 west from Beatrice to the park. Coming via U.A.-77 from Lincoln, go into Beatrice, turn onto Rt. 136W, Rt. 4W, or Court Street, go three miles west of town, turn right and go northwest on Rt. 4.

|| Scotts Bluff National Monument

Rising 800 feet above the wrinkled rocks of Nebraska's North Platte Valley is Scotts Bluff, a landmark for the pioneers who traveled westward along the Oregon/California Mormon trails.

The craggy bluff, which Indians called Me-a-pa-te, meaning "the hill that is hard to go around," was a tonic to the tired eyes of the pioneers who traveled the unrelentingly flat prairies. Before the settlers, fur trappers passed through on their way to trading posts, and Sioux, Cheyenne, and Arapaho Indians hunted buffalo here.

Robert Stuart, a traveler en route to a fur-trading post in Oregon in 1812–13, was supposedly the first white man to see the bluff. Many years later, in 1843, Brigham Young led a group of Mormon pioneers through the area on their way west.

When the West became more settled, the Pony Express, Overland Mail, Pacific Telegraph, and Overland Stage built stations nearby. Only when the Union Pacific railroad was completed in 1869 did the route by Scotts Bluff lose its importance.

The 2,998-acre park etched in the sandstone and silt of the plain preserves a short segment of the old Oregon Trail. A 1.6-mile section of trail leads to the summit of the bluff, which gives a view of the North Platte River and Mitchell Pass.

Exhibits in the visitor center, including a 12-minute slide presentation and an exhibition of paintings by pioneer artist and photographer William Henry Jackson, tell the story of westward migration. One of the most unique items on display is a replica pioneer odometer, a complicated contraption that was attached to wagons with cogs.

In summer, a weekend living history program re-creates pioneer life along the Oregon Trail, with volunteers in period costume demonstrating wagon cooking. Visitors can sample the hard tack and vinegar pie. The park has two wagons, a Conestoga Wagon, which was used for freight, and the smaller Murphy Wagon, used for a family's personal possessions.

A scenic, 1.6-mile paved road leads from the visitor center to the summit of Scotts Bluff. In spring and summer, the wildflowers bloom, carpeting the area with the blossoms of yucca plants, spiderworts, and loco weeds. Deer, coyote, mice, rabbit, falcon, and eagle frequent this semi-arid prairie habitat. Beware of rattlesnakes and crumbling rock when hiking in the park.

Open: Visitor Center: 8 a.m. to 5 p.m. Closed Christmas and off-season federal holidays.

Fees: $3 per car.

Mailing Address: Scotts Bluff National Monument, P.O. Box 427, Gering, NB 69341.

Telephone: 308-436-4340.

Getting There: The monument is located in western Nebraska, near the Wyoming border and not far from the city of Scottsbluff. The monument is five miles southwest of Scottsbluff via Rt. 26, which connects with Rt. 71 north of the river. From I-80, it is 42 miles north to the monument via Rt. 71.

NEW HAMPSHIRE

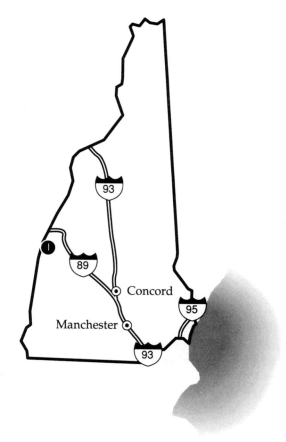

1. Saint-Gaudens National Historic Site

|| Saint-Gaudens National Historic Site

Nestled in the gentle green countryside of Cornish, New Hampshire, is the estate of Augustus Saint-Gaudens, one of America's greatest sculptors. The 150-acre site overlooks Mount Ascutney and the Green Mountains. It includes the artist's home, Aspet, the studios where he worked from 1885 until his death in 1907, his carefully crafted gardens, an extensive collection of his artwork, and the unspoiled beauty of the surrounding Blow-Me-Down woodlands area.

Once an old country inn, the house is striking for its eccentric architecture. To what was originally a stark New England Federal structure, Saint-Gaudens added a classical columned porch and trellis. The result has been described by an acquaintance of the artist as "a recalcitrant New England old maid struggling in the arms of a Greek fawn." The building has three historically furnished rooms, including the kitchen, and contains 17th-century Flemish tapestries, 18th-century American furniture, as well as paintings by the artist's wife, Augusta Homer Saint-Gaudens.

A building for special exhibits, the Ravine Studio, which houses a sculptor-demonstrator, and a small Greek temple with the remains of the artist and his family are also on the property.

Saint-Gaudens landscaped the grounds with picturesque pools, fountains, and evergreen hedges. Ravine Trail, a quarter-mile walk along an old cart path, leads through fern gardens, 100-foot-tall pines, and a hardwood forest with maple, birch, oak, ash and beech trees. Born in Dublin in 1848, the year of the Potato Famine, Saint-Gaudens emigrated with his family to New York when he was an infant. At age 13, he was introduced to sculpture as an apprentice cameo cutter. He studied several years in Paris and Rome, returning to America at age 27.

Throughout his lifetime, the artist completed nearly 150 pieces of sculpture, as well as many relief portraits, medallions, and plaques. The artist's masterful works are on display throughout the country. His celebrated sculpture of Admiral Farragut, recognized as a landmark in modern sculpture, is in Madison Square in New York City. The Adams Memorial in Rock Creek Church Cemetery in Washington, D.C., where a sculpture of a seated woman wrapped in a cloak marks the grave of Henry Adams and his wife, is considered one of

Aspet was the home of Augustus Saint-Gaudens, one of the foremost sculptors of the United States in the late 19th and early 20th centuries.—*NPS photograph*

America's highest artistic achievements. Saint-Gaudens also designed a $20 gold piece, prized by collectors, at the request of President Theodore Roosevelt in 1907.

In the early 1900s, the town of Cornish became the focal point for an artist's colony, attracting such luminaries as artist Maxfield Parrish, the poet Percy MacKaye, and the young actress Ethel Barrymore.

On Sunday afternoons from mid-June to mid-August, the Saint-Gaudens Memorial Trustees produce a chamber concert series. Check for details.

Open: Buildings: 8:30 a.m. to 4:30 p.m. daily, from the last weekend in May to Oct. 31. Grounds: 8:00 a.m. till dark.

Fees: $1, ages 17 and older.

Mailing Address: Saint-Gaudens National Historic Site, Rural Route #2, Box 73, Cornish, NH 03745.

Telephone: 603-675-2175.

Getting There: From Concord, take I-89 north to Lebanon, exit south onto Rt. 12A. The site is located just off NH Route 12A in Cornish.

NEW JERSEY

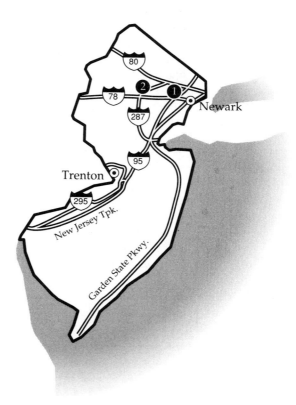

Edison National Historic Site

This collection of red brick buildings in West Orange, New Jersey, was Thomas A. Edison's "invention factory." Here the inventor of the electric light and the phonograph developed the first motion picture camera and produced motion pictures, improved his phonograph, and improved the electronic storage battery.

Even the building complex itself, which Edison devoted to the "rapid and cheap development of inventions," is an invention in its own right–the first private research and development laboratory. Edison had moved his headquarters from Menlo Park, New Jersey, to the West Orange labs in 1887.

At West Orange, 60 crack technicians added perspiration to Edison's inspiration for 44 years, until the hard driving, eccentric genius died in 1931 at age 84, a millionaire with 1,093 patents to his credit. More than half of them were developed in the West Orange labs. The others date from his Menlo Park days and before, when he created the incandescent bulb and the phonograph, among other inventions.

The West Orange Labs were not only an invention factory, they were also a place for Edison to manufacture his inventions. Several manufacturing buildings burned in a spectacular fire in 1914. "Get your mother!" Edison reportedly told his son Charles while the blaze raged on. "She'll never see another fire like this!"

Each year almost half a million visitors explore the West Orange grounds, the library, laboratories, machine shops, and stock rooms that appear untouched by time. A few blocks away is Glenmont, the 23-room mansion into which the inventor moved in 1886 with his 19-year-old bride Mina Miller.

The visitor center in the old lab powerhouse has introductory exhibits, a video theater, and a kinetoscope parlor. The laboratory tour takes about one hour and includes stops in the phonograph room, where original equipment is on display, the chemistry lab, with original beakers and apparatus still in place, and the Black Maria, a replica of the first movie studio. The tour also covers the experimental machine shop, where prototypes were made, and the stockroom of supplies and materials. On the tour you will see the time clock that Edison punched along with his time cards. He regularly logged 80 to 100 hours a week.

Thomas Alva Edison called his laboratory complex in West Orange, New Jersey, his "idea factory."—*Richard Frear, NPS photograph*

Don't miss Edison's magnificent two-story library, a handsome reading room with 10,000 volumes. Near the inventor's paper-stuffed desk is the "Genius of Electricity" statue Edison bought at the 1889 Paris exhibition, a cherub lofting a single electric bulb.

Glenmont, Edison's 15-acre estate in exclusive Llewellyn Park, has been restored. Check for hours of operation. Tickets go quickly, so arrive early. The Queen-Anne-style mansion was designed by Henry Hudson Holly and constructed in 1881 of stone, brick, and timber, with a slate roof.

Open: Visitor Center: 9 a.m. to 5 p.m. daily. Tours given from 9:30 a.m. to 3:30 p.m. daily. Closed Thanksgiving, Christmas, and New Year's Day.

Fees: $2, ages 17–61, others free.

Mailing Address: Edison National Historic Site, Main Street and Lakeside Avenue, West Orange, NJ, 07052.

Telephone: 201-736-0550.

Getting There: Take Garden State Parkway to exit 145 and follow signs for I-280 West toward The Oranges. Take exit 10 off I-280. Turn right on Northfield Ave., and left on Main St., about one-half mile. From Newark International Airport, take Transport of New Jersey bus #24 or #21. From Port Authority in New York, take bus #66.

‖ Morristown National Historical Park

For a glimpse into a soldier's life during the Revolutionary War, visit Morristown National Historical Park. Morristown was headquarters for the Continental Army during the winters of 1777 and 1779–80. The "hard winter" of 1779–80 was one of the most difficult periods endured by the American patriots during the war.

The park's nearly 1,700 acres commemorating the patriot encampment includes: Jockey Hollow, where some 10,000 troops lived in crude log huts; the Georgian-style Ford Mansion, temporary home to George Washington and his wife and staff; and the site of the low earthwork redoubt of Fort Nonsense.

Morristown's fields and woods are serene today, but two centuries ago they were the site of great hardships. Deprivation and disease dogged the army throughout the winters. Smallpox struck in 1777, blizzards blanketed the area with snow in 1780, and scarce supplies left the soldiers with little food and almost no clothing.

But if Morristown saw much suffering, it also marked a turning point in the war for independence from English domination. In May 1780, the Marquis de Lafayette arrived in Morristown to tell General Washington that the French allies would be sending an army to help the patriot cause.

The Ford Mansion, located on the park northeast of Morristown Green, was Washington's headquarters during the encampment. (The Fords themselves crowded into two rooms on the first floor of the building). Nearby is a museum with a short orientation movie about life in the Continental Army. Guided tours of the headquarters leave hourly from the museum.

Six miles to the south is Jockey Hollow, with reconstructed huts occupied by the soldiers during the miserable winters, and the historic Wick farmhouse, a six-room, Cape Cod-style building also used by Major General Arthur St. Clair as a headquarters. The visitor's center offers a brief audio-visual presentation.

Between Jockey Hollow and Wick farmhouse is Fort Nonsense, so called because it was supposedly created to keep the soldiers busy as they waited out the winters. The fort is long gone, but the hill on which it was built offers a good view of Morristown.

Morristown itself has claim to more of American history than just the Continental Army encampment. The infamous Benedict Arnold was court-martialed here, and Samuel Morse developed the telegraph in this area.

Periodically, the city hosts special events, from Continental Army encampments, where soldiers in uniform drill and demonstrate camp life, to programs of colonial lifestyle.

Open: 9 a.m. to 5 p.m. daily. Closed Thanksgiving, Christmas, and New Year's Day. Jockey Hollow buildings are open Wednesday through Sunday.

Fees: $1, ages 17–62, for entry to the museum and Washington's Headquarters.

Mailing Address: Morristown National Historical Park, Washington Place, Morristown, NJ 07960.

Telephone: 201-539-2085.

Getting There: From New York, take the Lincoln Tunnel to Rt. 3 West until it becomes Rt. 46 near Montclair. Shortly after Rt. 46 begins, take the exit for I-80 west, and follow it to exit 287 south, the Morristown exit. Take the first Morristown exit, which is marked for Washington's Headquarters with a brown National Park Service sign. Take the left fork of the exit road, and turn left at the first traffic light, Ridgedale Ave. At the stop sign, go left onto Morris Ave. Follow signs to come full circle to the park headquarters.

NEW MEXICO

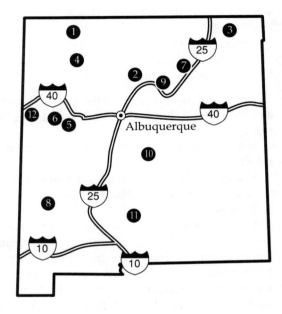

1. Aztec Ruins National Monument
2. Bandelier National Monument
3. Capulin Volcano National Monument
4. Chaco Culture National Historical Park
5. El Malpais National Monument
6. El Morro National Monument
7. Fort Union National Monument
8. Gila Cliff Dwellings National Monument
9. Pecos National Monument
10. Salinas Pueblo Missions National Monument
11. White Sands National Monument
12. Zuni-Cibola National Historical Park

|| Aztec Ruins National Monument

The pioneers who settled the Animas Valley of northwestern New Mexico in the 1870s thought this assemblage of ruined pueblos and ceremonial "kivas" was built by the Aztecs of Mexico. They were wrong: The architects were the Anasazi Indians, a prehistoric race of farmers and skilled masons. The name stuck, however, and today the crumbling walls of this 800-year-old site are known as Aztec Ruins. The buildings were occupied between 1100 and 1300, then abandoned completely after a prolonged drought in the 13th century caused the Indians to move toward the Rio Grande and other sources of water.

One of the most striking features of the monument is the extraordinary 500-room "apartment building" located near the visitor center. This dwelling, constructed of sandstone in the early 1100s, measures 360 feet by 275 feet and housed as many as 450 people. The walls are built of stones that were hauled from several miles away, shaped by hand, and set with mud to heights of three and four stories. Roofs were made of adobe placed atop the uppermost layers of wooden roofing material. Six wooden ladders found at the site were used by inhabitants to move from floor to floor.

The main ruin is interesting not only for its size but also for its elegance and unity of design—an indication of careful planning and attention to aesthetic matters. The dwelling was built in an E-shape around a central plaza that housed the community's kiva, a circular subterranean building used for ceremonial purposes. Indian religious ceremonies were related to the seasons, with special sprouting ceremonies in the spring, rain rites in summer, and harvest ceremonies in fall. Kivas were also used as dormitories for initiation rites and as community weaving rooms. Several other kivas survive in the park but only this one, known as the Great Kiva, has been reconstructed on the original walls and is open to visitors. Kivas are still in use among the descendants of the Anasazi Indians.

A self-guided, one-fourth-mile trail leads by the west pueblo and kiva, and the excavated ruins of a roughly circular tri-walled structure known as the Hubbard Ruin. Two other ruins on the site have not yet been excavated. Vegetation here is sparse, but there is a picnic area shaded by cottonwood trees.

Archeological evidence from the site shows its inhabitants grew corn on unirrigated land and decorated their baskets and pottery with designs showing the influence of both the Mesa Verde region to the north and Chaco Canyon to the south. The visitor center has exhibits describing this prehistoric community and the small tools, baskets, pottery, and other items excavated from the ruins.

Camping is not allowed in the monument, but accommodations are available in nearby Farmington, 12 miles west of the ruins. A private campground is located near Bloomfield, 12 miles from the site, along Route 64.

Open: 8 a.m. to 5 p.m. daily, extended in summer. Closed Christmas and New Year's Day.

Fees: $3 per car, or $1 per person. People under 17 and over 62 admitted free.

Mailing Address: Aztec Ruins National Monument, P.O. Box 640, Aztec, NM 87410.

Telephone: 505-334-6174.

Getting There: The site is in northwest New Mexico near the four-state area. In Aztec, take Ruins Road north off Highway 550 for one-half mile to the ruins.

▌Bandelier National Monument

Hundreds of ruined Indian pueblos, built centuries ago in the erosion-pocked cliffs and canyons of the Jemez Mountains, are surrounded by spectacular gorges, forested mesas, and tumbling waterfalls at Bandelier National Monument. This scenic park south of Los Alamos has more than 65 miles of hiking trails, some of them along ancient Indian footpaths that are deeply rutted from use.

The rich diversity of ruins here, which range from adapted caves to free-standing masonry pueblos with hundreds of rooms, has attracted archeologists since the 19th century. Adolph F. A. Bandelier, the Swiss-American scholar for whom the park is named, is one of the most famous. He studied the region in the 1880s and set his novel about prehistoric Indian life, *The Delight Makers*, in Frijoles Canyon. The Anasazi Indians who lived here between 1200 and 1550 cultivated corn, beans, and squash in the fertile canyon bottoms and wore yucca-

Bandelier National Monument has a rich cache of 13th-century Pueblo Indian cliff dwellings.—*NPS photograph*

fiber sandals and cotton clothing woven on simple looms. They stood about 5 feet 4 inches tall.

Frijoles Canyon was the most heavily populated area in the park and has several well-preserved ruins. Frijoles means "beans" in Spanish and is most likely derived from that essential crop raised by the Indians. A self-guided trail leads from the visitor center along the cliff to a large kiva, a circular underground structure used by the Indians for ceremonial purposes.

Traditionally, kivas have a firepit, a ventilator shaft for fresh air intake, and a hole in the floor known as a "sipapu," through which the Indians believed their ancestors entered the world. The trail also leads by the Tyuonyi (pronounced chew-OHN-yee) settlement. The ruins of this large circular pueblo, which once stood three stories high and had 400 rooms, have been excavated and stabilized with the addition of fresh mortar to the original stone-and-mud walls. Only the original foundation remains.

Ladders along the cliff trail allow visitors to enter several cave dwellings. The Indians gouged these shelters out of the soft volcanic ash of the canyon. Some of the houses were made of talus, rocks that had fallen into the canyon, while others were made of shaped stones. Long House, a pueblo built against a sheer cliff wall, was probably the largest settlement in the area. Holes were bored into the cliff to hold the "vigas," or wooden beams that supported the roof. Just above the holes, petroglyphs, simple figures carved into the rock, are still visible. Other interesting ruins in the park's backcountry include the Stone Lions Shrine and the pueblos at San Miguel and Yapashi.

Bandelier offers a wide choice of hikes. The trail to the main ruins can be completed in 45 minutes while the routes to Painted Cave and Rio Grande take two days. One of the best side-trips is to Tsankawi, a large, unexcavated ruin atop a high mesa located 11 miles north of the monument on Route 4. The two-mile, self-guided tour through Tsankawi offers spectacular views of the Rio Grande Valley, the magnificent snow-capped Sangre de Cristo Mountains to the east, and, of course, the Jemez Mountains.

The geology and natural life of the region, which was formed by volcanic activity thousands of years ago, is extremely varied. Creeks carved waterfalls and deep gorges into the soft volcanic "tuff" as they raced to the Rio Grande, leaving the high mesas and cliffs that give this monument its characteristic craggy look. The high forests are dense and quiet. Spiky green yucca plants, fragrant sage, piñon, gnarled juniper, and 150-foot-tall ponderosa pines grow here. In spring, scarlet, white, and lavender wildflowers bloom in abundance. Wildlife includes lizards, snakes, deer, elks, bears, and birds of prey.

Visitors are free to hike the main trails and explore the entire park, ninety percent of which is backcountry, but should register at the visitor center if they plan to spend time in the wilderness area. Fishing is permitted with a state license. In summer, rangers conduct guided walks and evening campfire programs. Make special reservations for the weekly night walk. The visitor center has a free, ten-minute introductory slide show, a half-hour film on pottery-making, and dioramas of the pueblos, stone tools, and pottery found in the ruins. There are also weekend demonstrations of Pueblo Indian pottery-making, weaving, and artwork.

The park has a curio shop, a snack bar, and two campgrounds. Juniper Campground has tent and trailer sites (no electrical hookups) with a 14-day limit on use. Ponderosa Group Campground is open April 15 to November 1. Other accommodations are available in nearby Los Alamos and White Rock. Contact the Los Alamos Chamber of Commerce by calling 505-662-5595.

Open: Visitor Center: 8 a.m. to 4:30 p.m. daily, extended to 6 p.m. from Memorial Day to Labor Day. Closed Christmas Day.

Fees: $5 a car, or $2 a person for commercial groups. Juniper campground costs $6 per night; Ponderosa Group Campground costs $1 per person with a $10 minimum, by reservation only.

Mailing Address: Bandelier National Monument, Los Alamos, NM 87544.

Telephone: 505-672-3861.

Getting There: The park is 46 miles west of Santa Fe, New Mexico. From Santa Fe, take Route 285 north to Pojoaque, turn west on Route 502, then take Route 4 to the park entrance.

Ⅱ Capulin Volcano National Monument

Capulin Volcano is one of the few extinct volcanoes in the world that you can actually walk through. A short, paved trail descends into the crater of this 1,000-foot-high volcanic mountain, where trees and grasses now grow among the black volcanic rocks. A plaque marks the vent from which molten lava and gases escaped from the earth 5,000 to 10,000 years ago. The view from inside, circumscribed by the volcano's rim, is eerie; the view from above is a breathtaking panorama of New Mexico's mesa country and the distant, snow-capped peaks of the Sangre de Cristo Mountains.

The volcano represents the final stage in a period of volcanic activity that began in the area two million years earlier. Its characteristic smooth, round dome was formed when the volcano erupted, spewing cinders, ash, and rock into a high cone. Lava leaked out a vent in the side of the volcano and flowed for many miles north and south of the one-square-mile park.

A paved, two-mile-road spirals up the mountain, offering a close look at the many plants that grow in the nutrient-rich soil. One of the most prominent plants is the chokecherry, called capulin in Spanish, for which the mountain is named. Its small, tart, red berries are good for jellies and jams. Lupine, golden pea, paintbrush, penstemon, and sunflowers bloom in the grasslands; trees include gambel oak, squawbush, and tall ponderosa pines. Wildlife includes mountain lions, bobcats, bears, mule deer, and many songbirds. Beware of rattlesnakes. And loose rocks and cinders off the paved trail can make footing unsure at times.

In the 1920s, a cowboy passing through the region discovered the bones of the famous Folsom Man, who lived here 10,000 to 12,000 years ago. The Folsom site, on private property about ten miles away, is closed to visitors. However exhibits in the visitor center tell the story of this early cave dweller and interpret the volcano and surrounding wildlife. The park has a picnic area at the base of the mountain but camping is not allowed. Accommodations are available in nearby Capulin.

Open: Visitor Center: 8:30 a.m. to 4:30 p.m. daily, extended to 8 a.m. and 6 p.m. from Memorial Day to Labor Day. The crater rim road is open daily until sunset.

Fees: $3.00 per car; $1 per person for busloads.

Mailing Address: Capulin Volcano National Park, Capulin, NM 88414.

Telephone: 505-278-2201.

Getting There: The site is in the northeastern corner of New Mexico. From Las Vegas, New Mexico, take I-25 north and turn right (east) on Route 64-87, just south of Raton. Follow the road to the town of Capulin and turn left (north) on Route 325. An access road on the right leads to the park.

‖ Chaco Culture National Historical Park

From the tenth to the 12th century, this broad, shallow sandstone canyon in northwestern New Mexico was the cultural, economic, and political hub of a vast pre-Columbian Indian civilization, the Chacoan Anasazi. More than 300 miles of roads linked some 400 settlements to this central point. Today 13 major ruins stand along the arroyo of the now-dry river that cuts through Chaco Canyon. At one time, some of these pueblos had 800 rooms and beautifully finished stone walls rising four and five stories high.

Many of the structures have survived the centuries remarkably intact, with original timbers still in place; others are little more than collapsed piles of unexcavated masonry. Here and there, partially fallen walls offer an unusually close look at the masonry techniques used by the early Indians.

The Chacoan Anasazi traded widely and had a highly developed, specialized culture. The bones of parrots from Central America have been found in the ruins, along with pottery made in nearby settlements that specialized in pottery-making. The Chacoans were particulary skilled jewelers who made ornaments of turquoise that came from far quarries. But their greatest talent was as architects and masons. Their techniques improved over the centuries, but when building was at its peak, the walls of Chaco's villages were made of an inner core of rubble veneered with finely shaped sandstone blocks covered with stucco.

The ruins have Spanish names like Pueblo Bonito, the "Beautiful Village," and exotic Indian names, like Kin Ya'a, from the Navajo for "House Rising Up High," and Kin Bineola, "House Where the Wind Whirls." The name Chaco may have come from the Navajo word "Tsaco," a broad, shallow canyon. Pueblo Bonito, occupied from the 900s to about 1200, is the largest and most striking ruin. Built of hard, dense sandstone quarried from the cliff immediately behind the pueblo, Bonito covered three acres and housed a community of about 1,000 people. Its four-story walls contained 800 rooms, many of them filled with trash—an archeologist's delight—and 37 round kivas, underground rooms used for ceremonial purposes.

Other major ruins in the monument include: Chetro Ketl, which had 500 rooms, 16 kivas, and an enclosed plaza; Pueblo del Arroyo, with about 284 rooms and 17 kivas; Kin Kletso, which has 55 rooms on the ground floor and may have risen three stories; and Casa Riconada, the largest kiva in the park.

There are five self-guided trails through four major ruins in the park (Pueblo Bonito, Casa Riconada, Chetro Ketl, and Pueblo del Arroyo and Una Vida) and three backcountry trails to the more isolated ruins of Pueblo Alto, Penasco Blanco, and Wijiji.

Trails that lead to backcountry sites have a visitor register to be signed before going into the backcountry and after departing. Camping in the backcountry is not allowed.

A new museum in the visitor center has artifacts excavated from the site, including pottery painted with characteristic black and white geometric designs, cooking and eating utensils, sandals, spearheads, turquoise jewelry, and copper bells from Mexico.

Chaco Canyon is a place of wild and stark beauty where vegetation is sparse and shade almost non-existent. In summer the yellow sandstone and scrubby flatlands bake in the unrelenting heat; in winter the ruins are dusted with snow. Come prepared for extreme temperatures and bring plenty of water. Watch out for rattlesnakes, scorpions, and stinging harvester ants.

The park operates a free 46-unit campground with minimal facilities, no drinking water, and no utility connections. Stays are limited to 14 days. The nearest town is 60 miles away; a trading post on Route 44 sells staple items. Guided tours are offered daily and campground talks are offered in the evenings during the summer.

Open: Visitor Center: 8 a.m. to 5 p.m. daily, extended to 6 p.m. from May to late August. The ruins are closed at sundown.

Fees: $3 per vehicle.

Mailing Address: Chaco Culture National Historic Park, Star Route 4, P.O. Box 6500, Bloomfield, NM 87413.

Telephone: 505-786-5384.

Getting There: The park is in northwestern New Mexico. From Albuquerque, take I-25 north to exit 242B for Rt. 44 west toward Farmington, Cuba, and Aztec. Follow highway 44 for more than 100 miles. At the Nageezi trading post, there will be a small sign on the right side of the road indicating the site. Turn left onto an unpaved road, take the right fork after a few hundred feet, follow for 11 miles to a T-intersection, turn left and follow to the Visitor Center. Travel on the dirt roads is treacherous during rain and snow. Call for information about road conditions.

‖ El Malpais National Monument

In Spanish, El Malpais means "badlands." This valley of lava flows was created during 3 million years of volcanic eruptions. El Malpais National Monument preserves 115,000 acres of striking landscapes and rock formations. Five major flows are still visible on the surface, the most recent only 700–1,000 years old. El Malpais also contains prehistoric Indian pueblos and roads built by the Indians.

The site features the largest and longest lava tube system in North America, a system measuring more than 16 miles long with some tubes as large as 100 feet in diameter. Lava tubes are formed when flowing lava cools to form an outer crust while the hotter lava inside continues to flow. Some tubes now contain ice and others are home to Mexican free-tailed bats, which leave their lava caves in a spectacular spiral of flight.

The Indian ruins on the site are considered part of the outlying structures of the great Chacoan culture. Evidence indicates that roads were also of Chacoan origin. At Las Vantanas, there are ruins of two religious structures called kivas. Tower Kiva was probably three stories high and the Great Kiva was a low round structure.

Other attractions in the monument include the Zuni-Acoma Trail, a Pueblo trade route across the lava fields that connected the pueblos of Zuni and Acoma, the striking Sandstone Bluffs Overlook, and forested areas. Wildlife includes black bear, elk, deer, mountain lion, bobcat, antelope, eagle, hawk, and owl.

The monument is a recent addition to the Park Service and facilities are not yet fully developed. The monument offers guided walks in summer, jeep tours, and a campfire program. Check for details. Wilderness camping is available.

Open: Visitor Center: 8 a.m. to 5 p.m. Memorial Day to Columbus Day, closing at 4:30 p.m. during the rest of the year. Closed Thanksgiving, Christmas, and New Year's Day.

Fees: None.

Mailing Address: El Malpais National Monument, P.O. Box 939, Grants, NM 87020.

Telephone: 505-285-5406.

Getting There: The monument is located 16 miles south of I-40 on NM 53 or eight miles south of NM Rt. 117. The information center is located in the town of Grants at 620 E. Santa Fe Avenue.

|| El Morro National Monument

When the Spaniards refreshed themselves at the cool waters at the base of this striking sandstone bluff, they could not resist the temptation to leave their mark by carving messages into the soft rock. Thus began Inscription Rock, a chronicle of the people who passed through the region over the last thousand years.

Even before the arrival of the Spanish, the prehistoric Anasazi Indians who lived on top of the bluff chiseled petroglyphs of mountain sheep, bear paws, and other animals. Then, between 1605 and 1900, more than 2,000 inscriptions were carved by Europeans into the 200-foot-high mesa.

The earliest mark made by a European was that of Don Juan de Oñate, who was the first to colonize what is now New Mexico. His inscription reads (in translation): "Passed by here the Governor Don Juan de Oñate, from the discovery of the Sea of the South on the 16th of April, 1605." Almost a century later, another one of New Mexico's governors carved the following modest message: "Here was the General Don Diego de Vargas, who conquered for our Holy Faith, and for the Royal Crown, all of New Mexico at his own expense, year of 1692."

Braggadocio was not uncommon in the inscriptions. In 1620, Governor Eulate described himself as "a most Christian-like [gentleman] extraordinary and gallant soldier of enduring and praised memory." (The word "gentleman" was scratched out by some unknown passerby.)

After the United States gained Spain's North American territory in 1846, numerous soldiers, immigrants, and traders left their names. Lieutenant J.H. Simpson and the artist R.H. Kern "visited and copied these inscriptions" as their inscription reads, on September 17th and 18th, 1849, and in 1868 surveyors for the Union Pacific Railroad carved "U.P.R." after their names. (The railroad line was never built.) When the site became a National Monument in 1906, the practice was made illegal, and today, rangers patrol the site carefully.

Two self-guided trails are available: a half-mile trail, which leads from the visitor center to Inscription Rock, and a two-mile trail, which leads to two unexcavated Anasazi ruins at the top of the mesa. Occupied in the 13th and 14th centuries, the largest site, called Atsinna (a Zuni word meaning "writing on the rock"), stood three stories high and housed about 1,500 people. Sixteen rooms and two structures called kivas, which were used for religious rites, have been excavated. The site is noteworthy for having both round and square kivas, as most of these special subterranean buildings are round.

The sheltered water hole at El Morro created a lush oasis of green in the arid New Mexico landscape. Piñon and ponderosa pines grow in the forest. The rainy season lasts from July through August, creating a wonderful array of wildflowers in the fall, when the asters, groundsel, and sunflowers bloom. Bird watching is excellent; red tail hawks, two species of hummingbirds, swallows, and woodpeckers have been sighted. During the summer, watch out for rattlesnakes and gopher snakes.

In summer, rangers hold weekend campfire programs on the history, archeology, and wildlife of the monument, which has a picnic area and a nine-unit campground that is filled to capacity most weekends. Food and overnight accommodations are available in nearby Grants or Gallup. The upper trail may be closed during the winter months.

Open: 8 a.m. to 5 p.m. daily, extended to 7 p.m. from Memorial Day to Labor Day. Closed Christmas.

Fees: $3 per car or $1 per person per busload.

Mailing Address: El Morro National Historic Site, Route 2, Box 43, Ramah, NM 87321-9603.

Telephone: 505-783-4226.

Getting There: From Gallup, take NM State Road 602 south 30 miles and turn east on NM State Road 53 for 26 miles to the entrance. From Grants, take NM State Road 53 southwest for 42 miles to the entrance.

‖ Fort Union National Monument

Weathered adobe ruins and a few chimneys are all that remain of Fort Union, once the largest frontier fort west of the Mississippi River. At its peak in the 1870s, Fort Union was a sprawling military post and quartermaster supply depot with more than 50 buildings arranged in tidy rows. The dragoons and infantry stationed here protected travelers and traders from Indian raids along the Cimarron branch of the Santa Fe Trail.

The civilians who lived here worked at the supply depot, shipping food, clothing, arms, ammunition, and building materials to all the military installations in the state. Throughout its history, Fort Union was synonymous with Indian fighting: The troops stationed here fought against hostile Apaches, Navajos, Utes, Kiowas, Cheyennes, Arapahoes, and Comanches until the Indian raids on white travelers and settlements ended.

The earliest Fort Union, a timber structure built in 1851 to anchor United States' claims to territory newly acquired from Mexico, is located a mile from the monument and is not open to visitors. The second fort is an eight-pointed earthwork constructed by Colonel Edward R.S. Canby under threat of a Confederate invasion during the Civil War, and the third Fort Union, a large adobe fortification erected between 1863 and 1869, is in ruins.

A self-guided, 1¼-mile trail leads through the grassy field and around the foundations and walls of structures that once stood here. The fort was divided into two sections: the post and the quartermaster depot. The post includes the commander's home, officers' quarters, company barracks, corrals, prison, and parade ground. The quartermaster depot had the depot, the quartermaster's house, commissary, storehouses, workshops, and corrals. One of the best-equipped hospitals in the West was here, a 36-bed complex that civilians could use for $.50 a day.

A ghost story concerns an event at Fort Union during a cholera epidemic in the 1870s. A soldier stricken with cholera awoke from a coma at midnight to find himself locked in the morgue. In his struggle to get out, the weakened man fell on a pile of lime, which made him look as white as a ghost. His calls for assistance were greeted by the guard with a startled: "Quiet, you're dead!"

The Old Santa Fe Trail, one of the most important routes west, passes by Fort Union. Originating at the Missouri River, this trail led through Fort Larned, Kansas (also a national monument). An alternate mountain route, which passed through Bent's Old Fort in Colorado (another national monument) on the way to Fort Union, took longer but was safer. The shorter but more dangerous southern trail, known as the Cimarron Cutoff, met the Mountain Branch near Fort Union. The ruts the wagons made as they rolled westward are still visible.

Soldiering on the Santa Fe Trail is celebrated on the last weekend of July with a frontier military encampment of the 1850s. A variety of demonstrations depicting military life of the period occur on this weekend.

The visitor center museum has exhibits about life in the fort, with a cavalry dress jacket and yellow horsehair plume and helmet. Other items on display include equipment such as animal brands, stencils used to mark shipping boxes, and keys. Local wildlife includes bald eagles, the brilliant mountain bluebirds, Says Phoebes, a kind of songbird, antelopes, and rattlesnakes.

There are picnic tables near the visitor center. Accommodations are available at Las Vegas, New Mexico, and Raton, New Mexico, on I-25. Nearby campgrounds include a private park at Romeroville, four miles south of Las Vegas on I-25, and Storrie Lake State Park, six miles north of Las Vegas on Route 3.

Open: 8 a.m. to 5 p.m. daily, extended to 6 p.m. in summer. Closed Christmas and New Year's Day.

Fees: $3 per car or $1 per person, Memorial Day to Labor Day.

Mailing Address: Fort Union National Monument, Watrous, NM 87753.

Telephone: 505-425-8025.

Getting There: The site is about 28 miles from Las Vegas, New Mexico. Take I-25 north to Watrous, and turn west (left) on Route 161 into the park, about eight miles.

‖ Gila Cliff Dwellings National Monument

These unusual stone masonry dwellings, built in the rippled cliffs of the Gila River (pronounced HEE-la) Valley of southwestern New Mexico in the late 12th and early 13th centuries, are well preserved. They represent one of the few sites in the National Park Service dedicated to the Mogollon (pronounced muggy-OWN) Indians, also known as ancient Pueblo Indians. This ancient mountain people existed in

New Mexico at the same time that the early Anasazi and Hohokam Indians lived in Arizona and Colorado. The Anasazi were outstanding masons, the Hohokam were known for irrigating their crops, and the Mogollon made beautiful Mimbres pottery, decorated with stylized black drawings of animals and fish. Today this pottery is highly prized by collectors. The Mogollon had an abundance of water, game, and plants in their mountain environment. Their ceremonial rooms, called kivas, were above ground rather than subterranean like most kivas of other prehistoric Indians.

A self-guided, mile-long trail leads to the dwellings, a total of 35 rooms built in caves. The adobe houses range in size from single family homes to multi-dwelling complexes that held an estimated 40 to 50 people.

Located in the wild and rugged lands of the Gila National Forest and Gila Wilderness area, the monument has mountains, high deserts—an elevation of 5,700 feet at the site of the cliff dwellings—deep canyons, and pinelands. There are 24 miles of hiking and horseback trails and an 80-acre, man-made lake stocked with trout. Wildlife includes deer, elk, wild turkeys, bears, mountain lions, foxes, hawks, eagles, and rattlesnakes. Avoid contact with wild or wounded animals. Twenty tent sites are available free of charge at the Scorpion Camp Ground in the national forest. The visitor center has a brief slide presentation of the region's historic and natural life.

Open: Visitor Center: 8 a.m. to 4 p.m. daily. Closed Christmas and New Year's Day. Cave dwellings: 9 a.m. to 4 p.m. in winter; extended from 8 a.m. to 6 p.m. from Memorial Day to Labor Day.

Fees: None.

Mailing Address: Gila Cliff Dwellings National Monument, Route 11, Box 100, Silver City, NM 88061.

Telephone: 505-536-9461.

Getting There: The park is located in the Gila National Forest in southwestern New Mexico. From Albuquerque, take I-25 south past Truth or Consequences to Route 90 west and go 75 miles to Silver City. Take Route 15 north about 45 miles to the park.

|| Pecos National Monument

When the Spanish conquistador Francisco Vasquez de Coronado came through the area in the spring of 1541, he found a massive pueblo that stood four to five stories high and housed two thousand people. The Indian village of Cicuye, as it was called then, was one of the largest in what is today New Mexico. Today, the ruins of the village along with a Spanish church and mission established in the 17th century are preserved in Pecos National Monument near Santa Fe.

The Indians of Pecos farmed the Pecos River Valley, trading for buffalo skins with the Plains Indians to the north and for cotton with the pueblo tribes to the south. They lived in a huge pueblo of more than 600 rooms and used ladders to climb through hatchways.

Several Spanish explorers visited the prosperous village at Pecos, but it was not until the early 1600s that Franciscans, hoping to convert the Indians and introduce them to European customs, so they could become citizens of New Spain, founded a mission. The mission consisted of a large church and "convento" with classrooms, workshops, living quarters, corrals, and grazing lands.

When the Indians revolted in 1680, driving the Spanish from their lands and burning the church and convento, the Indians of Pecos built a kiva, an underground structure used for religious ceremonies, right in the middle of the mission courtyard.

The circular kiva is now restored. Kivas varied from settlement to settlement, but they were all built of rock, covered with plaster, and contained roof entries, a central firepit, and a "sipapu" or spirit hole through which the Indians believed their ancestors entered the world. Some had elaborate murals on the walls, others were plain. Present-day descendants of the Pueblo Indians still use kivas for religious and community activities.

After the Spanish re-conquered New Mexico 12 years later in 1612, the mission was re-established and a smaller church was built on the foundations of the larger one. The existence of the original church was confirmed when archeologists excavated the site in 1967.

A 1¼-mile trail from the visitor center takes visitors by the monument's major points: the defensive wall that once surrounded the Indian settlement; the pile of rubble that was once a 660-room pueblo; the partially excavated ruins of a smaller pueblo; two kivas, both restored; and the foundations of the mission. The visitor center has dioramas of the site, and a display of pottery, arrowheads, clay effigies, and jewelry made from shell and bone found in the area.

On the first Sunday in August, the park commemorates the Spanish influence with a traditional mass, held in the ruins of the mission church. The mass commemorates the feast day of Our Lady of the Angels—Pecos' patron saint. When the last Pecos Indians left in 1838, they asked the village of Pecos to care for the saint's painting and to return it to the church ruins once a year for a mass in her honor.

Open: 8 a.m. to 5 p.m. daily, extended to 6 p.m. from Memorial Day to Labor Day. Closed Christmas and New Year's Day.

Fees: $1 per person or $3 per carload.

Mailing Address: Pecos National Monument, P.O. Drawer 418, Pecos, NM 87552-0418.

Telephone: 505-757-6414.

Getting There: The park is in north central New Mexico, 25 miles southeast of Santa Fe. From Santa Fe, take I-25 north in a southeasterly direction toward Las Vegas. Exit at the Pecos-Glorieta Interchange, about 25 miles from Santa Fe, travel six miles to the town of Pecos and turn right two miles on State Route 63 to the monument.

‖ Salinas Pueblo Missions National Monument

Three ruined Pueblo villages—Gran Quivira, Abó, and Quarai—and the Spanish colonial missions that attached themselves to the settlements are preserved in the high desert of central New Mexico at Salinas National Monument. The Mogollon (pronounced Muggy-OWN) Indians who lived here traded the salt they gathered from nearby lakes (Salinas means "salt" in Spanish) for buffalo meat and hides from the Indians of the East, for shells from the California coast, birds from Central America, and flint and obsidian tools.

The area attracted the Spanish in the late 16th century when Juan de Oñate brought the first European expedition to the Salinas Valley. By 1629, the small San Isidro church had been constructed at the largest settlement, now called Gran Quivira. Other missions were built at Abó and Quarai. The Spanish enlarged the San Isidro church, which evolved into the massive San Buenaventura Church that lies in ruins today. The Indians left the area in the 1670s, probably because of severe drought and Apache raids.

A self-guided, 30-minute walking trail leads through two ruined missions and the partially excavated pueblo at Gran Quivira, located 26 miles south of the town of Mountainair on highway 55. Guided tours are available by reservation only. Unexcavated ruins at the site are covered with centuries of rubble. The visitor center has a ten-minute slide presentation on the site, a 45-minute film, shown on request, and displays of tools and pottery recovered from the ruins.

From the ruins of the old church, courtyards, and Campo Santo, the mission burial ground, the trail leads through the excavated pueblo at Gran Quivira and five kivas, the circular underground chambers used for religious purposes.

The ruined Spanish mission Abó is ten miles west of Mountainair on Route 60. And Quarai, which has a fairly complete mission, picnic tables, and a mountain spring, is ten miles north of Mountainair on Route 55. Indigenous plants and animals include cactuses, rabbits, lizards, rattlesnakes, and hawks. Camping is prohibited at all three sites.

Open: 9 a.m. to 5 p.m. daily. Closed Christmas and New Year's Day.

Fees: None.

Mailing Address: Salinas Pueblo Missions National Monument, P.O. Box 496, Mountainair, NM 80736.

Telephone: 505-847-2585.

Getting There: The monument is located near Mountainair, New Mexico. See individual mileages and road numbers in text, above.

‖ White Sands National Monument

In the evening, when the shadows lengthen and the sun settles into the crown of the San Andres Mountains, the gypsum grains of White Sands National Monument sparkle like diamonds. This is the world's largest gypsum dune field, a 230-square-mile expanse of glistening, shifting, snow-white sand in southern New Mexico's Tularosa Basin. Some of the dunes rise 45 feet and have wind-blown edges that appear razor-sharp; others are long and rounded, like the backs of whales. In the distance, the dunes, blinding white and striped by shadows, assume abstract shapes.

It took centuries of rain and wind to leach this gypsum from the mountains and funnel it into Lake Lucero. Evaporation causes the formation of large yellow gypsum crystals on the lakeshore, which are split and scoured by the dry winds into clear, sand-sized bits. The process continues today, with new dunes forming while the southwest winds move the older dunes as much as 20 feet a year.

A 16-mile loop drive with turn-offs leads to a picnic area in the heart of the dunes, with the last 6.5 miles of road made of pure, packed gypsum. Posts along the route explain the natural life. The deep root systems anchor the saltbush, iodine, yucca, soaptree, and cottonwood plants in the slower sands and form "gypsum pedestals" when the tightly bound sand in the roots is exposed by the wind.

Despite the harsh environment, bird watching can be excellent here and at least 190 species have been sighted. While few birds inhabit the gypsum sand dune, many occur in the surrounding desert plains. Other animals include the oryx, a transplanted African antelope, kit foxes, coyotes, badgers, kangaroo rats, and white mice.

The stark white dunes, dark shadows, blue sky, and the distant hazy mountains—the San Andres to the west, the Sacramento range to the east—make for dramatic photographs. But photographing can be tricky, especially at midday, when the white sands reflect the high sun. Set cameras one f-stop lower than would normally be used on a sunny day; underexpose and overdevelop black-and-white film; and take light meter readings off the subject of the photograph, not the background.

Three rooms of exhibits in the visitor center explain the unique geology and biology of the area. Rangers also conduct patio talks and evening strolls. On nights with a full moon in June, July, and August, there are special slide lectures by noted archeololgists, astronomers, biologists, and historians. For specifics about tours, tune into 1610 AM on the radio or call 505-479-6124.

Car caravans to Lake Lucero, where the gypsum crystals form, are offered on the last Saturday of every other month, starting in January. This lake is not accessible at any other time because it is within the

White Sands Missile Range. The trip starts from the visitor center and lasts about three hours along a paved road with the last half mile on foot. Participation is limited to 30 cars, so make reservations early.

There is a primitive backcountry camping site—no facilities, not even a toilet—one mile off the dunes tour road for backpackers. Register at the visitor station, which is also the only place where drinking water is available. Other camping facilities are in Lincoln National Forest, 35 miles east, and at Aguirre springs, 30 miles west.

The summer days are hot and the sun strong, so wear sun screens and protective clothing and carry plenty of water. In the evenings, the temperature can drop to fifty degrees. Visitors should pay attention to their whereabouts; it is easy to become disoriented in the shifting dunes.

The monument is entirely surrounded by the White Sands Missile Range and Holloman Air Force Base, and is occasionally closed to visitors while weapons and military equipment are being tested. Sometimes you can hear explosions and see missile vapor trails. Emergency evacuations, which are extremely rare, are announced on the park's public address system.

The White Sands Missile Range, where the first atomic bomb was exploded, provides an interesting side trip. The blast from this test, conducted on July 16, 1945, was so intense that the sand melted into glass-like "trinitite" and people saw the strange mushroom cloud for hundreds of miles. A lava obelisk now marks the spot.

The radioactive material has been cleared away, and the area is now considered radiologically clean. Adjacent to the site is the MacDonald Ranch, the adobe building where the bomb was assembled. The empty rooms of the house have been refurbished to look as they did during the Manhattan Project.

Tours of the Trinity Site are conducted on the first Saturday in April and October. Entrance to the site is by car caravan from Alamogordo or through Stallion Gate northwest of the site. For further information, contact the post public affairs office by calling 505-678-1700. The base also has a visitor center and an outdoor museum displaying missiles that have been tested. Grounds are open 9 a.m. to 5 p.m. daily; the visitor center is open 8 a.m. to 4 p.m. on weekdays.

Open: 8 a.m. to 4:30 p.m. daily; extended to 8 a.m. and 7 p.m. from Memorial Day to Labor Day; extended to midnight on full moon program nights in June, July, and August. Car trips to Lake Lucero leave at 9 a.m. on the last Saturday of alternating months. Reservations are required for this trip. Closed Christmas Day.

Fees: $3 per car; $1 per person for busloads.

Mailing Address: White Sands National Monument, P.O. Box 458, Alamagordo, NM 88310.

Telephone: 505-479-6134.

Getting There: The park is in south central New Mexico. From Alamogordo, take Route 70-82 south 14 miles to the park.

‖ Zuni-Cibola National Historical Park

This proposed 400-acre park consists of four sites with major Pueblo villages and ruins that date from 1200 to the 1670s. The sites are: Village of the Great Kivas, Yellow House, Hawikuh, and Kechipbowa. The park is located near Gallup on Zuni tribal lands, so the sites are closed to visitors at this time.

For more information, contact Zuni Project Coordinator, P.O. Box 728, Santa Fe, NM 87504-0728.

NEW YORK

1. Castle Clinton National Monument
2. Eleanor Roosevelt National Historic Site
3. Federal Hall National Memorial
4. Fort Stanwix National Monument
5. General Grant National Memorial
6. Hamilton Grange National Memorial
7. Home of Franklin D. Roosevelt National Historic Site
8. Martin Van Buren National Historic Site
9. Sagamore Hill National Historic Site
10. Saint Paul's Church National Historic Site
11. Saratoga National Historical Park
12. Statue of Liberty National Monument
13. Theodore Roosevelt Birthplace National Historic Site
14. Theodore Roosevelt Inaugural National Historic Site
15. Vanderbilt Mansion National Historic Site
16. Women's Rights National Historical Park

281

|| Castle Clinton National Monument

At the southernmost tip of Manhattan in Battery Park sits a squat, circular fortress known as Castle Clinton. Although rich in history, Castle Clinton is not very well known; most visitors find it quite by accident. But a special trip to this hidden gem, which has been a fort, a concert hall, an immigration center, and an aquarium, is worth the effort.

Constructed from 1807 to 1811 as part of a series of U.S. coastal fortifications, Castle Clinton was originally called the South-west Battery. Its sandstone walls stood in 35 feet of water and the fort was connected to land by a wooden bridge. It was later named Castle Clinton after DeWitt Clinton, a former governor of New York. In 1824 the site had been renamed Castle Garden and turned into a fashionable theater, the Madison Square Garden of its day. Here Jenny Lind, the "Swedish Nightingale," made her American debut.

Located at the edge of the harbor, Castle Clinton was a natural point of entry for immigrants who came to this country between 1855 and 1889. During that time period, more than eight million immigrants, two out of every three, entered the country through Castle Clinton until Ellis Island became the headquarters for immigration. The castle's last incarnation was as the enormously popular New York City Aquarium, which operated until 1941, when plans to construct a Brooklyn-Battery tunnel threatened the structure's existence. After languishing unused for 34 years, Castle Clinton was re-opened by the Park Service in 1979.

A museum, with three panoramic displays of the downtown Manhattan area in the years 1812, 1866, and 1941, explain the evolution of the monument and its environs. There is a traditional flag-raising ceremony by the Veterans Corp of Artillery on Independence Day every year. The Veterans Corp is the oldest military unit in New York and dates back to the War of Independence. The unit that appears at the park is dressed in War of 1812 regalia.

The view of New York Harbor, with its boats and barges, is excellent from Battery Park. On a clear day, you can see beyond the Statue of Liberty and Ellis Island to Staten Island and to Governor's Island. The panorama of the northern New Jersey industrial skyline is also visible. Ferries for the Statue of Liberty leave from Battery Park on the hour and half-hour. You can purchase tickets at the monument. The Staten Island Ferry is located just east of Battery Park. A ten-minute walk up Water Street takes you to the museums, shops, and restaurants of the South Street Seaport.

Open: 9 a.m. to 5 p.m. daily. Check for changes.

Fees: None.

Mailing Address: Castle Clinton National Monument, c/o Manhattan Sites, 26 Wall Street, New York, NY 10005.

Telephone: 212-344-7220.

Getting There: The site is located in Battery Park at the tip of Manhattan. From New York Port Authority, take city buses M1, M6, M15, or M25 to Battery Park. The subway IRT line stops at Battery Park.

‖ Eleanor Roosevelt National Historic Site

This picturesque plot of land on the banks of Val-Kill Creek in Hyde Park, New York, was the retreat where Eleanor Roosevelt, wife of president Franklin D. Roosevelt, escaped the glare of public life. It has since become a shrine to one of the most influential women of the 20th century, a place where world leaders including Nikita Khrushchev and John F. Kennedy came to pay homage to Eleanor Roosevelt, the "First Lady of the World."

Built in 1925 on land that was part of the Roosevelt estate in Hyde Park, Val-Kill started out as little more than a fieldstone cottage sanctuary for Eleanor and her close friends, Nancy Cook and Marion Dickerman. Later, it became the site of Val-Kill Industries, an experiment in rural self-sufficiency that produced replicas of Early American crafts. When President Roosevelt died in 1945, Eleanor returned to Val-Kill's cozy simplicity where she lived until her death in 1962.

Eleanor Roosevelt was an influential member of the Democratic Party, a supporter of women's rights, and one of the leading humanitarians of her time. As the First Lady, she traveled around the nation, bringing first-hand information about the country's poor to the White House and influencing FDR's New Deal policies of social welfare. Her work helped maintain the popularity of the only American president elected four times.

Eleanor Roosevelt's role did not end with her husband's death. In 1946 she served as a delegate to the United Nations General Assembly, where she was chairperson of the Human Rights Commission. She traveled widely, taught at Brandeis University, worked with human rights groups, and hosted a television talk show. Yet for all this activity and the impact she made, Eleanor Roosevelt modestly maintained that she was "without any particular gifts."

Today, the two buildings at Val-Kill, the Dutch-colonial fieldstone house known as Stone Cottage and the headquarters for Val-Kill Industries, known as Val-Kill Cottage, memorialize this tireless crusader for human rights and dignity. Visitors can watch a 20-minute film biography of Eleanor Roosevelt and tour the two cottages where she lived and worked. Note the furniture; many pieces were produced by Val-Kill Industries. A swimming pool, tennis court, rose garden, playhouse, and paths to the pond are open to visitors.

Open: 9 a.m. to 5 p.m. daily, from May through October. Closed Thanksgiving Day through the end of February. For winter hours, call 914-229-9115.

Fees: Entry to the site is free.

Mailing Address: Eleanor Roosevelt National Historic Site, Roosevelt-Vanderbilt National Historic Sites, 249 Albany Post Road, Hyde Park, NY 12538.

Telephone: 914-229-9115.

Getting There: From New York City, take the Henry Hudson Parkway (Route 9A) to Saw Mill River Parkway to the Taconic State Parkway, north. Exit at Route 55 West (Poughkeepsie). Follow this road to Route 9 north to the stop light at St. Andrews Rd. Turn right on St. Andrews Road and left at the next stop light. The entrance sign is a very short distance on the right. From the New York State Thruway, get off at Exit 18, New Paltz, follow signs to the Mid-Hudson Bridge. Cross the bridge and follow Route 9 north to the stop light at St. Andrews Pond.

‖ Federal Hall National Memorial

Federal Hall, site of the country's first capitol building, is located at the intersection of Wall and Nassau (Broad) streets in lower Man-

Federal Hall National Memorial, which stands in the midst of Manhattan's financial district, marks the site of President George Washington's inauguration.—*Richard Frear, NPS photograph*

hattan, the very heart of the financial district. On March 4, 1789, the government of the newly-proclaimed United States began to operate here, and eight weeks later George Washington was inaugurated as the nation's first president on the building's front steps. Here, too, the Bill of Rights, one of the most important documents in U.S. history, was written, and the principle of freedom of the press was established during the 1735 trial of publisher John Peter Zenger.

The old Federal Hall, with its House and Senate chambers and central cupola, was destroyed in 1812 when New York City moved its municipal offices to the present site in City Hall Park. A wood-frame Customs House was erected on the spot and later was replaced by the Greek Revival Customs House that stands today. It served until 1920 as a sub-treasury and repository for 70 percent of the nation's money supply.

A statue of George Washington stands on the steps of Federal Hall. Exhibits inside tell the story of the young republic. One of the most interesting early artifacts is the Yankee-made suit that George Washington wore on his inauguration. There are also some bronze buttons that spectators wore, the first presidential souvenirs. Visitors can view the vaults used when the buiding was a sub-treasury; there are also exhibits from the customs house era.

Park rangers give guided tours and show free films about Federal Hall and the nation's early years. Free classical concerts also are offered. Check for schedules.

Open: 9 a.m. to 5 p.m. weekdays, throughout the year. Closed weekends and federal holidays, except George Washington's Birthday and July 4.

Fees: None.

Mailing Address: Federal Hall National Memorial, c/o Manhattan Sites, 26 Wall Street, New York, NY 10005.

Telephone: 212-264-8711.

Getting There: Federal Hall is located at the corner of Wall Street and Nassau Street (the continuation of Broad Street), just off Broadway. It is within walking distance of South Ferry, from which ferries depart for Staten Island, Governors' Island, and the Statue of Liberty. By subway, take: the Lexington Ave. IRT express to Wall Street; the RR BMT to Rector Street, the K/J BMT to Broad Street, the 7th Avenue IRT express to Wall Street, the 8th Avenue A/E IND to Fulton Street. By bus, take the 2nd Avenue bus to Wall Street, or the M15 or M6 South Ferry bus to Broadway and Wall Street.

▌ Fort Stanwix National Monument

Some battles are won by strategy, others by luck. The story of the attempted British siege of Fort Stanwix is one of the latter. It is also a story of determination. Were it not for the superstitious nature of the British Indian allies, a lucky capture by the patriots of a man believed by the Indians to have supernatural powers, and the staunch determination of Colonel Peter Gansevoort and his garrison, the British siege of Fort Stanwix in August 1777 might have been successful.

The British operation against Fort Stanwix and the Mohawk Valley was part of a plan to occupy New York and break into the major supply and communications route between New England and the Middle Colonies. (Since the British navy already controlled most of the sea routes, land transportation within the colonies took on added importance in the early years of the American Revolution.) The land route cut through the area of present-day West Point on the Hudson River in New York.

To accomplish this goal, British General John Burgoyne was to advance on Albany and link up with a smaller group commanded by General Barry St. Leger, who would be advancing down the Mohawk Valley. Once in Albany, Burgoyne would join Sir William Howe to fight the colonists in the Lower Hudson Valley.

But St. Leger was stopped at Fort Stanwix and General Howe went on to Pennsylvania, leaving Burgoyne to falter near Albany at Saratoga without reinforcements.

The ruse that won Fort Stanwix for the patriots is known as "Arnold's Bluff" because it was designed by Benedict Arnold, still a patriot at that time. Since Arnold did not have enough men to capture the fort from its British and Indian occupiers, he sent Hon Yost Schuyler, a loyalist and unusual fellow captured by the patriots, to tell the Indians that a patriot force numbering as many as "the leaves on the trees" was approaching. (Schuyler's family was held hostage to assure his cooperation.) The Indians, who thought Schuyler had supernatural powers, believed him and deserted Fort Stanwix, leaving the British commander St. Leger with insufficient troops to continue the siege.

St. Leger retreated to Canada, leaving Colonel Peter Gansevoort in command of Fort Stanwix until he was relieved by Arnold, who arrived with his troops on August 23, 1777. According to local legend, the Stars and Stripes first flew in battle at Fort Stanwix, but recent research indicates that the flag was most probably a homemade Grand Union.

After the war, the Treaty of Fort Stanwix of 1784 between the Americans and the Iroquois Nation was signed at Fort Stanwix. The treaty offered harsh terms for the Indians who collaborated with the British and forced the Iroquois to cede a large portion of their lands east of the Ohio River to the United States. This land, which was later distributed to soldiers and sold to pay off war debts, became a stepping stone in the western settlement of the nation.

Fort Stanwix was built by the British during the summer of 1758 to protect a strategic portage in the waterway between Lake Ontario

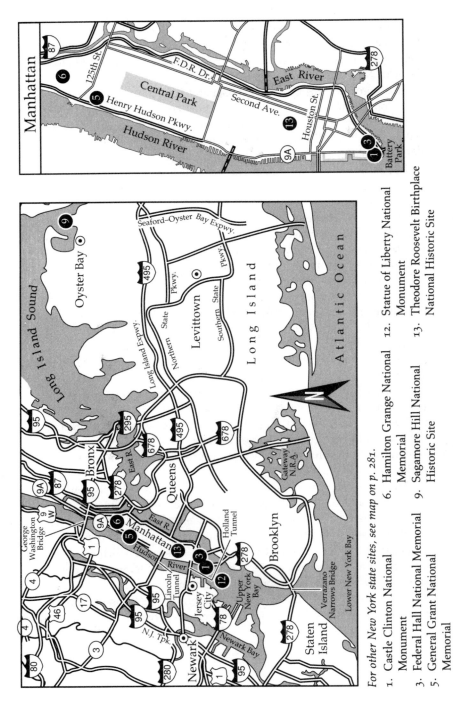

Manhattan

For other New York state sites, see map on p. 281.

1. Castle Clinton National Monument
3. Federal Hall National Memorial
5. General Grant National Memorial
6. Hamilton Grange National Memorial
9. Sagamore Hill National Historic Site
12. Statue of Liberty National Monument
13. Theodore Roosevelt Birthplace National Historic Site

and the Hudson River during the Seven Year's War. It was named for Brigadier General John Stanwix, who was in charge of the construction.

Although it was badly damaged by fire in 1781, the four-sided log and earth fort with its four diamond-shaped bastions was reconstructed in the mid-1970s on its original site in the city of Rome, New York. The fort has earthworks, wooden palisades, barracks, officers' quarters, and a museum with artifacts from the Revolutionary War period. In the summer, interpreters in Continental Army garb interpret the story of the fort.

Open: 9 a.m. to 5 p.m. daily. Closed Thanksgiving and Christmas Day, and from Jan. 1 to March 31.

Fees: $1, ages 16–62.

Mailing Address: Fort Stanwix National Monument, 112 E. Park Street, Rome, NY 13440.

Telephone: 315-336-2090.

Getting There: The fort is located in Rome, New York, and can be reached by car, bus, train, or plane. Routes 26, 48, 49, 69, and 365 pass within sight of the fort. A city parking garage on North James St. is available for visitor parking and is within one-half block of the park entrance.

‖ General Grant National Memorial

Ulysses S. Grant, the military genius of the Civil War and 18th U.S. president, is interred in this extraordinary mausoleum at 122nd Street in New York City. The shrine, which overlooks the Hudson River, was designed by New York architect John Duncan to reflect the grandest elements of the world's most impressive monuments. It has a 150-foot high dome and combines elements of the tomb of King Mausolus at Halicarnassus in present-day Turkey, and the tomb of the Roman emperor Hadrian. Inside, Grant and his wife Julia Dent are entombed in identical, 8.5-ton red granite sarcophagi.

Allegorical reliefs on the monument's walls represent Grant's life and the crypt's bronze busts sculpted in 1938 portray Grant's favorite generals, including Civil War Generals William T. Sherman, Philip Sheridan, and George Thomas. The memorial was erected between

1891 and 1897 and took 8,000 tons of granite, hundreds of workers, and more than $600,000 donated by 90,000 people.

Grant was born Hiram Ulysses Grant in 1822 in Ohio, but he changed his name at age 17 when he discovered that he was mistakenly registered at West Point as Ulysses Simpson. His early military career was undistinguished and he resigned from the army in 1854 after being reprimanded for drunkenness. Grant was a failure in almost every trade he tried, until he joined the Union Army after the Confederates fired on Fort Sumter in 1861.

The first hint of Grant's abilities as a military leader was his 1862 victory at Fort Donelson in northern Tennessee, where he demanded "complete and unconditional surrender." Impressed by this performance, President Lincoln promoted him to Major General. Grant's tenaciousness, his sense of timing, and his ability to move men quickly over vast distances made him almost invincible. After winning the Battle of Chattanooga, Grant became General-in-Chief of the Union Army and began the three-pronged assault on the South that eventually ended the war. Grant's strategy: Union General George Gordon Meade would move against Confederate General Robert E. Lee; General Benjamin Franklin Butler would go after Lee's support troops; and General William Tecumseh Sherman would fight General Joseph Johnston in Atlanta, Georgia. Grant ended the war at Appomattox Court House, Virginia, after the ten-month siege of Petersburg, Virginia.

In 1868, the popular Civil War hero was elected president. The two terms Grant served were marked by his humanitarian attitude towards the South and marred by the financial scandals of his appointed cronies. The scandal over Crédit Mobilier, a shell corporation designed to skim profits from the Union Pacific Railroad, rocked the administration and discredited many prominent Republican politicians. In 1875, Treasury Secretary Benjamin Helm Bristow and other high government officials were implicated in a whiskey ring to defraud the government of revenue.

After leaving the White House in 1877, Grant made a goodwill tour of the world. He then settled in New York City, where he lost his fortune in a Wall Street banking business. But if Grant was a failure as a businessman, he showed a literary talent few suspected. Grant's memoirs, written to keep himself out of debt, were a bestseller, praised even by Mark Twain. Ironically, the man who reached the pinnacle of public service died penniless on July 25, 1885, of throat cancer. Grant, ever the hero, was mourned by northerners and southerners alike; Confederate Generals Simon Buckner and Joseph Johnston served as pallbearers at his funeral.

The Park Service runs hourly tours at the memorial, lasting about 45 minutes. Monthly activities include music and lectures. Contact the park for details. There is a wreath-laying ceremony on April 27 in commemoration of Grant's birthday in 1822.

Open: 9 a.m. to 5 p.m., Wednesday through Sunday. Closed Monday and Tuesday, and all federal holidays.

Fees: None.

Mailing Address: General Grant National Memorial, 122nd Street and Riverside Drive, New York, NY 10027.

Telephone: 212-666-1640.

Getting There: The monument is located at 122nd St. and Riverside Drive, in Manhattan's Morningside Heights neighborhood. It is near Columbia University and adjacent to Riverside Church. Take the IRT subway 7th Avenue local (#1) to 116th Street. By bus, take the M4 or M104 to Broadway and 122nd streets. Walk west two blocks to the site.

Ⅱ Hamilton Grange National Memorial

In the early 19th century, when New York City was little more than a narrow band of land at the southern tip of Manhattan Island, Alexander Hamilton built a country estate in the wilds of upper Manhattan. He called it Hamilton Grange, after the family homestead in Scotland. Here the feisty politician, who died in a duel with his lifelong enemy Aaron Burr, retreated from the vicissitudes of his tumultuous public life.

New York has changed considerably since Hamilton's time, but Hamilton Grange, with its shuttered windows and carefully trimmed hedges, still stands, a monument to the man who helped design the structure of early American government.

Hamilton was born in the West Indies in 1755, the brilliant but illegitimate son of a Scottish lord. He started his lifelong career in politics as a student at Kings College, now Columbia University, in

New York. Later, he served as George Washington's aide-de-camp during the Revolutionary War. After American independence, Hamilton worked on the Constitution and was one of the authors of the influential Federalist Papers, which argued for a strong central government. When George Washington became president, he appointed Hamilton as the first Secretary of the Treasury.

Hamilton helped to outlaw dueling in New York, yet he himself fell victim to the practice. He died after exchanging shots with his nemesis Aaron Burr in Weehawken, New Jersey, on July 11, 1804. The two-story, Federal-style wooden house at Hamilton Grange was designed by New York City Hall architect John McComb, and built in 1802. Its outstanding features are the octagonal dining room and the parlor on the second floor. Since the eight-room house is still under renovation, visitors are limited to the second floor only. Most of the family's possessions are in the Museum of New York City, but several items, including a piano and one of Mrs. Hamilton's dresses, are on display in the house.

The site celebrates Hamilton's birthday on January 11 each year with tree-trimming, refreshments, singing, and speeches by local politicians. February is Black History month at the Grange, with cultural and educational programs and community activities. Check for details.

Open: 9 a.m. to 4:45 p.m. daily. Closed Monday and Tuesday, and all federal holidays, including the following Wednesday if a holiday falls on Monday or Tuesday.

Fees: None.

Mailing Address: Hamilton Grange National Memorial, 287 Convent Avenue, New York, NY 10031.

Telephone: 212-283-5154.

Getting There: The site is located at Convent Avenue and West 141st Street, just north of the City College Campus. Take the 8th Avenue IND express subway to West 145th Street; or take the 7th Avenue IRT local to 137th Street, or the M3 Convent Avenue bus to 142nd Street.

Home of Franklin D. Roosevelt National Historic Site

In this rambling stone and stucco mansion Franklin Delano Roosevelt (FDR), the 32nd U.S. president, was born and spent his childhood. Here, Roosevelt and British Prime Minister Winston Churchill signed the agreement sanctioning the development of the first nuclear bomb. And here Roosevelt was buried in 1945. The Roosevelt home in Hyde Park, New York, commemorates the famous statesman, the man whose "New Deal" program of public assistance brought the country through the Depression and established the country's social welfare system.

A cousin of President Theodore Roosevelt, FDR belonged to a prominent New York family. He grew up in this 35-room mansion in the Hudson River Valley countryside and returned here to marry and raise his own family.

From the outside, the Roosevelt house seems an odd but comfortable mixture of architectural styles. Originally a clapboard-frame house built in the early 19th century, the house was later covered with stucco, fronted with a small, columned portico, and flanked with stone wings. Visitors can take a self-guided tour of the house and grounds. Inside are the family heirlooms, including an 18th-century grandfather clock, a Dresden porcelain chandelier, ancestral portraits, and Roosevelt's collection of mounted birds.

The nearby Franklin D. Roosevelt Library displays model boats and naval prints, photographs of the Roosevelts, gifts from visiting dignitaries, 40,000 books, and more than 15 million pages of historic documents, which are available to scholars and writers. Of particular note are Roosevelt's declaration of war against Japan on Dec. 8, 1941, and a letter from Einstein about the development of the atomic bomb. The newly opened Eleanor Roosevelt Wing is dedicated to the career of FDR's wife, a world-famous humanitarian.

FDR was born on Jan. 30, 1882. He studied at Harvard and, like his cousin Theodore Roosevelt, he had a love of nature and a talent for politics. After serving as Assistant Secretary of the Navy under Woodrow Wilson, FDR made an unsuccessful bid for the vice presidency. In 1921, he fell victim to polio.

The disease restricted FDR's physical activities, but it did not stop his political aspirations. With the help of his wife Eleanor, who was FDR's distant cousin, he re-entered public life. He was twice elected governor of New York, before becoming president of the United States in 1932. An enormously popular president, Roosevelt's policies brought the nation through the Depression and through World War II. He was president from 1932 until 1945, the only man elected to serve four terms in the White House.

FDR and Eleanor are buried in the rose garden near the house. Roses were a favorite flower of the Roosevelts; the family name means "field of roses" in Dutch. In accordance with FDR's instructions, the grave is simple, with no mention that he was president. The estate's ice house, carriage house, and stables are open to visitors. From the terrace at the southern end of the house, tourists can see the view of the Hudson River that Roosevelt so often admired. Two miles to the east is Val-Kill, Eleanor Roosevelt's cottage and home after her husband's death.

Open: 9 a.m. to 5 p.m. daily. Closed Thanksgiving, Christmas, and New Year's Day. Also closed Tuesday and Wednesday from December through February.

Fees: $3.50, ages 16 to 62. The fee is good for both the Roosevelt home and the Franklin D. Roosevelt Library.

Mailing Address: Home of Franklin D. Roosevelt National Historic Site, 249 Albany Post Road, Hyde Park, NY 12538.

Telephone: 914-229-9115.

Getting There: The site is located on Rt. 9 in Hyde Park, Dutchess County, NY. From New York City, take the Henry Hudson Parkway (Rt. 9A) north to Saw Mill River Parkway north to Taconic State Parkway north. Exit at Rt. 55 West (Poughkeepsie). Follow this road to Rt. 9 north. The house is located approximately five miles north on Route 9.

From the New York State Thruway, get off at Exit 18, New Paltz, and follow the signs to Mid-Hudson Bridge. Cross the bridge and follow Rt. 9 north. The site is located approximately five miles from the bridge.

❙ Martin Van Buren National Historic Site

This 36-room house in Kinderhook, New York, was the home of Martin Van Buren, the eighth president of the United States.

Van Buren was born in Kinderhook in 1782, practiced law in New York City, and held public office for 33 years. He was a sharp political operator, a behind-the-scenes man, whose acumen and cunning earned him the moniker "Red Fox." As president, Van Buren is known for establishing the national treasury system and for reducing the federal work day from 16 to ten hours. He bought the property, known as Lindenwald, in 1839 at the height of his presidential career.

The two-and-a-half story brick house is eclectic in design. Initially a Federal-style building, Italianate and Victorian Gothic features were added when the president's son Smith Thompson Van Buren moved in with his family. Smith added a 42-foot Palladian-style ballroom, a four-story Italianate brick tower, a front porch, two dormers, a Victorian Gothic central gable, and Renaissance-looking bay windows.

The house has recently been restored and is now open to visitors. The site, a relatively new addition to the Park Service, features 22 acres of land from Van Buren's original holdings as well as the mansion.

Open: 9 a.m. to 5 p.m. daily, from the last week of April to October 31. Closes for the season on December 5. Call for details.

Fees: None.

Mailing Address: Martin Van Buren National Historic Site, P.O. Box 545, Kinderhook, NY 12106.

Telephone: 518-758-9689.

Getting There: The site is in upstate New York along the Hudson River below Albany, just southeast of Kinderhook. From Albany, take I-90 east to Route 9 south, and on to the first traffic light where Route 9 and Route 9H intersect. Continue straight on Route 9H. The house is two miles south of Kinderhook on the right.

‖ Sagamore Hill National Historic Site

With its elephant tusks and riding crops, bric-a-brac and books, the clutter of Sagamore Hill is a fitting monument to the "strenuous life" of the man who lived here. Theodore Roosevelt, the 26th President of the United States, built this rambling Queen Anne style house on Long Island's Oyster Bay in 1884, after the near-simultaneous deaths of his mother and wife. He moved in with his infant daughter Alice and his sister Anna the following year. Roosevelt lived at Sagamore Hill with his second wife Edith until he died on January 6, 1919.

As the home of the popular Spanish-American war hero, politician, and big-game hunter, Sagamore Hill was one of the most closely watched and talked about houses in the country. Here, Roosevelt was notified of his nomination as Governor of New York in 1898, as the vice president in 1900, and as the president of the United States in 1904. Here, too, in 1905, Roosevelt met with envoys from Russia and Japan to hash out an agreement between the warring nations, which resulted in the Treaty of Portsmouth and a Nobel Peace Prize for Roosevelt—the first ever for an American. Throughout Roosevelt's tenure as president, Sagamore Hill was known as the Summer White House.

The twenty-three-room Victorian house is little changed from the days when Teddy and Edith Roosevelt and their six children lived here. About 80 percent of the furniture is original, and many of Roosevelt's hunting trophies have been preserved. The first floor contains the president's famous library, where the historic agreement between Russia and Japan was struck, the drawing room, with a polar bear rug given to Roosevelt by Admiral Perry, the family dining room, and the elegant North Room, full of family memorabilia.

Upstairs are the bedrooms, guest rooms, and the children's quarters. The Gun Room on the third floor has a display of Roosevelt's extensive collection of firearms, and offers a sweeping view of the surrounding woods and fields, the bay, and the Connecticut coastline.

The site includes the Old Orchard Museum. Once the home of Theodore Roosevelt Jr., this house is now a museum to Roosevelt's political career, family life at Sagamore Hill, and the lives of the six Roosevelt children. Theodore Roosevelt Jr. served as governor of Puerto Rico in 1929 and of the Philippines in 1932. He distinguished

President Theodore Roosevelt's estate, Sagamore Hill, contains original furnishings of the man who relished the "rough life."—*Richard Frear, NPS photograph*

himself for bravery in both world wars and was posthumously decorated with the Congressional Medal of Honor. His decorations and military uniforms are on permanent display in the house. Old Orchard Museum also contains a collection of recent television documentaries on President Theodore Roosevelt, and several silent films produced in the 1920s by the Theodore Roosevelt Association.

Open: 9:30 a.m. to 5 p.m. daily. Closed Thanksgiving, Christmas, and New Year's Day.

Fees: $1, ages 16–62.

Mailing Address: Sagamore Hill National Historic Site, 20 Sagamore Hill Road, Oyster Bay, NY 11771.

Telephone: 516-922-4447.

Getting There: Take either Exit 41 North of the Long Island Expressway or Exit 35 North of the Northern State Parkway to Route

106 Northbound. Follow Route 106 to the Village of Oyster Bay. Turn right at the third traffic light in Oyster Bay to East Main Street. Follow green and white signs to Sagamore Hill. By Long Island Railroad from New York City (Penn Station, Jamaica, and Brooklyn), take either the Oyster Bay branch or the Huntington/Port Jefferson line. Change at Jamaica for Oyster Bay, in most cases, or for Syosset. The Oyster Bay station is three miles from the historic site; Syosset is five miles. Taxis are available at both stations. Call the Long Island Railroad for schedule: 212-739-4200 or 516-435-0500.

‖ Saint Paul's Church National Historic Site

Saint Paul's Church in Mount Vernon, New York, is linked historically to events that led to the famous John Peter Zenger trial in 1735, which established the legal precedent for freedom of the press. Zenger was tried for libel for a series of articles he had published denouncing an election held in front of the church in October, 1733.

Apart from its connection with the Zenger trial, Saint Paul's has had a long and varied history. In 1642 Anne Hutchinson, the religious renegade from the Massachusetts Bay Colony, settled in the area. In 1702 the Presbyterian parishioners resisted for four years a decree stating that all church members in New York must belong to the Church of England. In October 1776 the church was used as a hospital for wounded Hessian soldiers and many Hessians were buried in a mass grave in the churchyard. Colonial politician Aaron Burr practiced law in the church, which functioned during the week as one of Westchester County's early courthouses.

The Zenger case stemmed from a controversial election for Westchester County assemblyman. The British governor supported a loyalist candidate, the colonists backed a popular choice. The British authorities then attempted to influence the election's outcome: Landowning Quakers were denied the right to vote for refusing to swear on the Bible that they owned property, a practice their faith did not permit; in addition, the time of the voting was posted only shortly before the election so that people would not know it was taking place. Despite these and other improprieties, the popular candidate won.

Zenger published an account of the circumstances surrounding the election in the first edition of his "New York Weekly Journal." This article, along with others that lambasted corrupt officials, sparked the famous lawsuit. Zenger's lawyer, the well-known Philadelphian Andrew Hamilton, persuaded the jury that his client was innocent of libel because he had, in fact, printed the truth. Zenger was acquitted. When the Bill of Rights was adopted in 1791, the Zenger decision was cited as evidence of the need to include freedom of the press in the First Amendment.

The Georgian-Revival church that stands on this historic site today was built from 1763 to 1787 of local fieldstone, brick, and timber. The mortar was made with seashells from Eastchester Creek, lime from Long Island, and sand from the churchyard. The bell, cast by Lester and Pack at the Whitechapel Foundry in London, is the "sister" of the Liberty Bell in Philadelphia. The organ, built by Henry Erben in 1830, is one of the oldest working organs built in the country.

The newly established Bill of Rights Museum, which has permanent exhibits about the formulation of the First Amendment, the history of the church, Westchester history and dioramas of the Zenger trial, is housed in a restored carriage shed adjacent to the church. The museum also has a replica of an 18th-century printing press, and artifacts from the colonial and Revolutionary War days. The grounds include the historic Village Green and six acres of historic cemetery. Tours of the site are available.

Open: 9 a.m. to 5 p.m., Tuesday through Friday, and 12 p.m. to 4 p.m. Saturday. Tours held on Saturday at 12:30 p.m., 1:30 p.m., and 2:30 p.m., and on weekdays by appointment.

Fees: None.

Mailing Address: Saint Paul's Church National Historic Site, 897 South Columbus Avenue, Mount Vernon, NY 10550.

Telephone: 914-667-4116.

Getting There: From the Hutchinson River Parkway, take exit 8 from the north to Sanford Boulevard west, or exit 9 from the south. The park is on south Columbus Ave., just beyond south Fulton Ave. on the left. By train from Grand Central Station in New York City, take the Metro-North New Haven Line to Mount Vernon and call Reliable Cab (664-1234). Or take the Dyre Avenue Subway to the last stop and board Bus #55 going north. The bus passes by the church. Buses leave on both the hour and the half-hour. For further information, call Westchester Transit at 914-682-2020.

‖ Saratoga National Historical Park

To quash the American rebellion, the British planned to divide and conquer New York. Three armies would converge on Albany, the headquarters of the patriot military. General Barry St. Leger would arrive from the West, General Sir William Howe from New York City, and General John Burgoyne from Canada. But St. Leger was stopped at Fort Stanwix and Howe went to Philadelphia, leaving Burgoyne to fight alone at Saratoga. The British surrender here on Oct. 17, 1777, marked the first time in history that British troops had given up on the field. This defeat cost England 5,700 men and control of New York. The patriots gained the French as allies. The Battle of Saratoga was a turning point in the Revolutionary War.

Although the encounter that took place here is formally known as the Battle of Saratoga, the actual fighting took place in Stillwater and the surrender in Old Saratoga, now Schuylerville.

It took two battles fought over a three-week period to end the confrontation at Saratoga. In the first battle, British troops on their way to Albany tried to fight their way through patriot forces entrenched near Freeman Farm. Unable to get to Albany, the British set up camp in the area and waited for reinforcements that would never come. When General Burgoyne tried to fight his way out of Saratoga to return to Canada, his army suffered heavy losses. Patriot troops stormed the British earthworks, leaving Burgoyne with little choice but to surrender.

The park at Saratoga features reconstructed earthwork defenses and one historic house, the Neilson House, which was occupied by a few American officers. The one-room house at the Neilson Farm, depicted as a general's headquarters, is open daily in summer. A ranger in period dress is on duty to answer questions.

A nine-mile auto tour through the battlefield has ten interpretive stops. The visitor center has a twenty-one-minute movie, "Checkmate on the Hudson," about the battle. On Wednesday evenings in summer, rangers lead either a night walk using lanterns or a lecture program in the visitor center.

Visitors can tour the Schuyler House, the country residence of Philip Schuyler, a statesman and commander in the Revolutionary War. The Saratoga (or Surrender) Monument, a 155-foot-high obelisk, has been closed for several years due to structural problems.

Also in the park is The Boot Monument, dedicated in 1887 to Benedict Arnold, who rallied American troops to victory in a key encounter. Arnold broke his leg during the battle, hence the name, Boot Monument. Later, Arnold turned traitor.

Although closed, the Surrender Monument is an unusual structure with statues of American officers Horatio Gates, Philip Schuyler, and Daniel Morgan in three of its four sides. The empty niche was meant for Benedict Arnold.

The 3,400-acre park overlooking the Hudson is as rich in natural beauty as it is in history. The visitor center at the top of the hill features a spectacular view of three mountain ranges—the Taconic Range, the Green Mountains, and the Berkshires—and three states. Autumn, when the foliage is in full flame, is a particularly good time to visit the monument.

Open: Visitor Center: 9 a.m. to 5 p.m. daily, extended to 6 p.m. in summer. Closed Thanksgiving, Christmas, and New Year's Day. The battlefield tour road is closed from early December to mid-April, depending on snow conditions.

Fees: $3 per vehicle for a seven-day pass, $1 for hikers and bikers for a seven-day pass.

Mailing Address: Saratoga National Historical Park, RD 2, Box 33, Stillwater, NY 12170.

Telephone: 518-664-9821.

Getting There: The park entrance is 30 miles north of Albany, NY, on Route 4 and Route 32.

▌Statue of Liberty National Monument

The Lady of the Harbor stands 111 feet and one inch high from head to heel. The torch she has lofted for the past century has been a symbol of freedom and opportunity to millions. The "Lady" is the Statue of Liberty, the 225-ton copper colossus of the New World. For countless boatloads of immigrants, she has been the first, unforgettable glimpse of America.

She was created by French sculptor Frédéric Auguste Bartholdi, with the supporting structure designed by engineer Alexandre-Gustave Eiffel (who later built the Eiffel Tower), and was given to the U.S. by France on July 4, 1884, to commemorate the alliance between the two countries during the American Revolution. Since its dedication amid great hoopla on October 28, 1886, the statue has been host to more than 50 million visitors.

The "Lady with the Lamp," as Emma Lazarus called it in her celebrated poem, is one of the country's best known and most visited monuments, an icon of the American immigrant experience. Tourists can reach the monument by taking an invigorating 15-minute ferry ride that leaves every hour (every half hour in summer) from the docks in Battery Park in Manhattan. A ferry also leaves from Liberty State Park in New Jersey, except during the winter months. With the water sparkling and the wind blowing in your face, it's easy to imagine yourself an immigrant as the boat nears the majestic statue.

The statue, built on a pedestal designed by architect Richard Morris Hunt, stands within the star-shaped walls of old Fort Wood. Inside are two exhibits, the Statue of Liberty Exhibit and the Immigration Exhibit.

An elevator takes visitors to the observation deck only. To get to the crown, which offers a spectacular view of the New York City Harbor and Manhattan skyline beyond, you'll have to take the spiral staircase. There are 354 steps in all, equivalent to a 22-story building. The climb through the statue's innards is strenuous, and should not be attempted by people with physical difficulties. The torch, which can be reached by a 42-foot ladder, has been closed to the public since 1916.

Nearby is Ellis Island, the most famous processing point for immigrants who entered this country through New York. Between 1892 and 1954, when it was closed as an immigration depot, 12 million people passed through Ellis Island, and as many as 2,000 a day during its peak years at the turn of the century. Starting in 1924 immigrants were processed at U.S. consulates in their host countries, and only people with medical or legal problems used Ellis Island as a point of entry. The island is closed during restoration, and is scheduled to reopen in 1990. Check for details.

Open: 9 a.m. to 5 p.m. daily, with extended hours in summer. Closed Christmas Day.

Fees: None, but donations are welcome.

Mailing Address: Statue of Liberty National Monument, Liberty Island, New York, NY 10004.

Telephone: 212-363-3200.

Getting There: Ferry service to Liberty Island is provided by the Circle Line, which leaves from Battery Park at the southern tip of Manhattan. Boats leave Manhattan every hour on the hour, and return every hour on the half-hour. The trip takes 15 minutes. In summer, and on spring weekends, trips run every half hour. For information about tickets and schedules, contact the Circle Line-Statue of Liberty Ferry, Inc. at 212-269-5755. Ferries also leave from Liberty State Park, New Jersey, except during the winter months.

‖ Theodore Roosevelt Birthplace National Historic Site

A stuffed lion stands proudly on a pedestal and mounted big game heads stare down from the walls. These trophies, bagged by Theodore Roosevelt, are on display in the 26th president's birthplace home at 28 East 20th Street in Manhattan.

In the handsomely appointed chambers of this four story brownstone, the president, explorer, and winner of the 1906 Nobel Peace Prize spent the first 14 years of his life. The house, which was razed in 1916, has been painstakingly reconstructed and furnished with original and period pieces with advice from members of the Roosevelt family.

Rooms open to the public include the master bedroom, library, rococo Revival parlor, formal dining room, nursery, the "Lion's Room," and "Lower Museum" exhibit rooms.

Roosevelt was born on October 27, 1858, a sickly child who grew into a robust outdoorsman. He was a cowboy and rancher in the Dakota Territory, a colonel in the Rough Riders during the Spanish American War, and he was New York State governor before becoming president upon William McKinley's death in 1901. As president, Roosevelt was known for his aggressive trust-busting policies and his concern for conservation. After serving for two terms, Roosevelt hunted big game in Africa, and explored the Brazilian wilderness. He died at his home on Sagamore Hill in Oyster Bay, Long Island, on January 6, 1919.

Several short films about Roosevelt and his life are shown free of charge in the museum. Free concerts are presented on Saturdays from mid-September to mid-June. On Sundays there are occasional plays and lectures.

Open: 9 a.m. to 5 p.m., Wednesday to Sunday. Closed all government holidays, and on following Wednesdays when the holiday falls on Monday or Tuesday.

Fees: $1 ages 17–62, free for children and seniors.

Mailing Address: Theodore Roosevelt Birthplace National Historic Site, 28 E. 20th Street, New York, NY 10003.

Telephone: 212-260-1616.

Getting There: The house can be reached via IRT and BMT subway stops at 23rd and 14th streets. An American flag marks the site.

‖ Theodore Roosevelt Inaugural National Historic Site

In this handsome Greek Revival home in Buffalo's historic district, Theodore Roosevelt was inaugurated as the 26th president of the United States on September 14, 1901. Roosevelt was sworn in after William McKinley, the 25th U.S. president, died from an assassin's bullet in a house down the street. The inaugural house was owned by Ainsley Wilcox, a prominent Buffalo attorney.

A tour of the site, with its restored turn-of-the-century rooms furnished with original and period pieces, takes about an hour. The backyard herb garden is a special attraction. Visitors can buy herbs and herb jellies, vinegars, and potpourri made by park volunteers. Check for details on lectures and special programs held throughout the year.

The Roosevelt Inaugural Site contains one of the most extensive collections of period costumes in the country, with more than 10,000 pieces dating from 1840. The collection is regularly used for historical research and textile design. Visitors interested in using the costume resource center should make an appointment in advance. Fashion show fundraisers featuring pieces from the collection are held each December and bi-annually in a downtown hotel. Check for specific dates and make reservations early.

During the first week of December each year, the house holds a Victorian Christmas celebration, with house decorating, luncheons, speakers, and music. In August there is a Teddy Bear Picnic for children. Lunch is served and teddy bear stories are told. Bring your own bear. The date varies.

Open: 9 a.m. to 5 p.m. weekdays, 12 p.m. to 5 p.m. weekends. Closed Saturdays from January through March. Closed Thanksgiving, Christmas Day, New Year's Day, Fourth of July, Memorial Day, and Labor Day.

Fees: $2 for adults, 12 years and over, $1 for children, $5.50 for families.

Mailing Address: Theodore Roosevelt Inaugural National Historic Site, 641 Delaware Avenue, Buffalo, NY 14202.

Telephone: 716-884-0095.

Getting There: From downtown Buffalo, take Franklin Street (one way, going north) to Allen Street. The entrance to the parking lot is one block from this intersection on the left.

Vanderbilt Mansion National Historic Site

In the picturesque countryside along the Hudson River, the turn-of-the-century "New York nobility" built lavish estates and million-dollar mansions where they entertained in storybook splendor. The most magnificent of these, without doubt, is the mansion of Frederick W. Vanderbilt in Hyde Park, a baroque style palace filled with centuries-old antiques and 19th century reproductions.

Vanderbilt, a businessman, financier and philanthropist, hired the famed architects McKim, Mead, and White to build this extraordinary vacation home in 1898. No expense was spared. Workmen cut and carved limestone from Indiana, marble from Italy, and walnut from Russia. Not including the furnishings, the house cost $660,000—a small fortune at the time. The family spent spring and fall here, and lived in the Pavilion on the grounds during winter weekends.

A portico with corinthian columns that are two stories high dominates the entrance. Columned porches flank the sides and a sweeping balustrade caps the structure, adding an airy touch to the mansion's heavy classical symmetry.

The inside of the Vanderbilt Mansion is every bit as palatial as the outside. Renaissance tapestries hang on the walls, and priceless antiques and artwork decorate the lavish hallways, drawing room, and reception areas. The Gold Room, where the Vanderbilts' guests were treated to sherry before dinner, is decorated in gold. A painted-over ceiling fresco by Edward E. Simmons and dated from 1897 was discovered when the ceiling was being cleaned.

Upstairs are the master bedrooms: Louise Vanderbilt's sumptuous Louis XV bedroom, which recreates a room in the Hôtel Soubise in Paris, and Frederick Vanderbilt's eclectic bedroom, with bed and dressers built into Russian walnut woodwork and original tapestries on the walls. Visitors can tour the first and second floors on their own. Guided walks are available upon request.

The estate is landscaped with recently restored gardens that are open to the public.

Open: 9 a.m. to 5 p.m. Thursday through Monday, November through March, daily during the rest of the year. Closed Thanksgiving, Christmas, and New Year's Day.

Fees: $2 ages 16 to 62.

Mailing Address: Vanderbilt Mansion National Historic Site, 249 Albany Post Road, Hyde Park, New York, 12538.

Telephone: 914-229-9115.

Getting There: The Vanderbilt Mansion is located in Hyde Park, NY, about a two-hour drive from New York City. Take the New York State Thruway to Exit 18, New Paltz, following signs to Mid-Hudson Bridge. Cross Bridge and follow Route 9 North. The site is about seven miles from the bridge.

From the Taconic State Parkway, going north, exit at Route 55 west (Poughkeepsie), follow to Route 9 North. The site is about seven miles north on Route 9.

|| Women's Rights National Historical Park

Today the fading industrial city of Seneca Falls, New York, hardly seems a hotbed of radicalism. But in the mid-19th century, when manufacturing replaced farming in the area and women began working outside the home, this town was the center of the early women's movement. Here Elizabeth Cady Stanton, Jane Hunt, Mary Ann McClintock, and others organized the first political convention dedicated to women's rights. Women's Rights Historical Park is dedicated to the pioneering woman of Seneca Falls and to the early struggle for equality, which launched the suffragist movement.

Elizabeth Cady Stanton, who moved here with her husband and children in 1847, was the catalyst. She and a coterie of like-minded women drafted a manifesto of women's rights they called the "Declaration of Sentiments" and planned a convention to publicize the plight of the country's disenfranchised female population. The convention was held at the Wesleyan Chapel at the corner of Fall and Mynderse Streets, formerly the Seneca Falls Laundromat. Three hundred men and women attended the convention; 68 women and 32 men signed the controversial Declaration of Sentiments, which declared that "all men and women are created equal," and called for women to be given the vote. It was the start of the Women's Movement.

Women's Rights National Historic Park is one of the newest additions to the Park Service. So far, the only buildings open to the public are the visitor center at 116 Fall Street, and the restored Elizabeth Cady Stanton home at 32 Washington Street, which contains Stanton's original chairs, desk, and books. A foundation is now acquiring the original furniture and china for the house. The Wesleyan Chapel is open for "pre-restoration" tours. Check daily schedule for times at the visitor center.

The home of Mary Ann McClintock at 16 E. Williams Street in Waterloo, where the "Declaration of Sentiments" was written, will be open to the public in the near future. The home of early activist Jane Hunt, at 401 E. Main Street in nearby Waterloo, is privately owned and not open to the public.

The park offers a variety of hour-long walking tours of the Seneca Falls historic district, which include an 1844 mill with workers' houses. Special festivals are held on Elizabeth Cady Stanton's Birthday, November 12, and on "Convention Day," near July 19 and 20, and on "Women's Equality Day," August 26. Check for details. Also in the area is the National Women's Hall of Fame, at 76 Fall Street.

Open: 9 a.m. to 5 p.m. daily. Closed Thanksgiving, Christmas, and New Year's Day. Elizabeth Cady Stanton House: 9 a.m. to 5 p.m.

daily, May 1 to October 31. By appointment only, November 1 to April 30.

Fees: None.

Mailing Address: Women's Rights National Historical Park, P.O. Box 70, Seneca Falls, NY 13148.

Telephone: 315-568-2991.

Getting There: The park is located in Seneca Falls, in upstate New York, 15 minutes off New York State Thruway Exit 41. Turn south on Route 414 to Seneca Falls. Airports within an hour drive include Rochester, Syracuse, and Ithaca. The Visitor Center is at 116 Fall Street (Routes 5 and 20).

NORTH CAROLINA

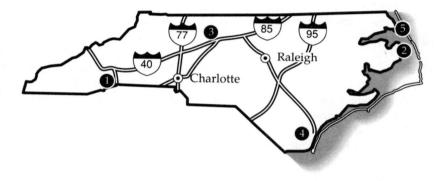

1. Carl Sandburg Home National Historic Site
2. Fort Raleigh National Historic Site
3. Guilford Courthouse National Military Park
4. Moores Creek National Battlefield
5. Wright Brothers National Memorial

|| Carl Sandburg Home National Historic Site

With his green eyeshade waiting by the lamp, his gray sweater slung over a chair, and a bulletin board of cryptic notes ("OK: Houses made with hands 100 ramshackles w stories residents and Her," reads one of these scribblings), it looks as if Carl Sandburg, the 20th-century poet and historian, will soon bend over the waiting typewriter and tap out another page.

Connemara, as this 247-acre estate and goat farm is called, was home to the Sandburgs from 1945 until the acclaimed author died in 1967. In the cluttered study upstairs Sandburg completed the Pulitzer-prize-winning novel *Remembrance Rock*, a hymn to the American experience from the Pilgrims to World War II; *The Complete Poems*, which won him another Pulitzer Prize; and *Always the Young Strangers*, his autobiography. Before his Connemara days, Sandburg was a Chicago journalist and author of a six-volume biography of Abraham Lincoln, which earned him his first Pulitzer. Recently, a sequel to his life story, an uncompleted manuscript entitled *Ever the Winds of Chance*, was discovered in the home's safe.

Visitors will find the 22-room house little changed from the days when the poet lived here. Books still line the bookshelves, cigars and butts (Sandburg smoked his stogies to a stub, and chewed them when he could no longer smoke) fill the ashtrays, and the dining room table is set as if coffee is about to be served.

Goats, tame enough to be petted, bleat in the background, a reminder of the prize-winning herd of Chikaming goats kept by Sandburg's wife Paula. At its peak, the herd numbered about 250. Today, there are about 17 goats at Connemara representing Nubian, Toggenburg, and Sanaan breeds.

Guided tours of the white farmhouse, built in 1838 as the summer home for Christopher Gustavus Memminger of Charleston, South Carolina, the first secretary of the Confederate treasury, last 25 minutes and are limited to 15 people.

Schedule about two hours to explore the grounds and visit the farm's 20 outbuildings, including the goat house, milkhouse, the springhouse where goat cheese was cured, and the Swedish House, where the writer stored his magazines, books, and research material. Sandburg loved to wander the pastures and woodlands, and could be seen walking the pathways late at night, his flashlight bobbing in the darkness. Hiking trails lead to the top of the estate's two small mountains.

A summer performance series brings the artist's work to life each summer as actors and musicians read Sandburg's poems and sing his favorite folksongs. An avid collector of folk music, Sandburg loved to sing and accompany himself on the guitar. Twice weekly, the Flat Rock Playhouse Vagabond Apprentices perform a free dramatization of Sandburg's children's work *Rootabaga Stories*. There are also free afternoon performances of the excerpts from the Broadway play "The World of Carl Sandburg." Check for time and dates.

Open: 9 a.m. to 5 p.m. daily. Closed Christmas Day.

Fees: None. $1 per person, ages 16–62, for house tours. Expect a wait for tours during the peak visitation months of June through August and October.

Mailing Address: Carl Sandburg Home National Historic Site, 1928 Little River Road, Flat Rock, NC 28731.

Telephone: 704-693-4178.

Getting There: The house is located in western North Carolina, 26 miles south of Asheville, near Hendersonville. Going south from Hendersonville, turn off Rt. 25 onto Little River Road at the Flat Rock Playhouse. The Visitor Center is on your left.

❙❙ Fort Raleigh National Historic Site

One of the most intriguing mysteries of American history is the story of the "Lost Colony," the English settlement on Roanoke Island that disappeared without a trace three years after it began in 1587. Gone were the 150 men, women and children who came to live at Fort Raleigh. Gone, too, was Virginia Dare, the first child born to British parents in the New World. The only clue to their whereabouts was the inscription "CRO" possibly referring to "Croatoan"—the name of an Indian tribe and a nearby island—that had been hastily carved on a wood post inside the earthen fort.

Fort Raleigh National Historic Site preserves the story of this ill-fated attempt to establish a colony. A reconstructed earthen fort with a dirt parapet and a moat marks the spot where the "Newe Forte in Verginia" once stood. The visitor center has clay pots and pipes, pottery, an abacus-like English counter, and other artifacts from the settlement. There are also reproductions of watercolors painted by John White, one of the early settlers. If anyone had a sense of life at Raleigh, it was White. He was a member of the first military expedition to the area, governor of the second colony at Raleigh, grandfather of Virginia Dare, and the man who found the mysteriously abandoned settlement. The visitor center also has a free film about the colony, from the fundraising by Sir Walter Raleigh to the fort's untimely demise.

The entire park reflects the Elizabethan culture that spawned the colony. People in period costume cook, tend their gardens, and demonstrate other activities during the summer. The Elizabethan Room in the visitor center has authentic oak panelling and a fireplace taken from a house similiar to the kind lived in by the Roanoke colony investors. A formal Elizabethan Garden, maintained by the Garden Club of North Carolina, conveys aspects of 16th-century English culture.

Each summer the Roanoke Historical Association sponsors a play about the Roanoke settlement entitled "The Lost Colony" by Pulitzer-prize winning dramatist Paul Green. Performances are held in the outdoor Waterside Theater. Check for times, prices, and dates.

There are tours of the site daily in summer. Fort Raleigh celebrates the birthday of Virginia Dare on August 18 with Elizabethan games, dances, and cooking. The Thomas Hariot Nature Trail, studded with quotations from Hariot's "Brief and true report of the new found land of Virginia," winds through the woodlands where it is believed Roanoke's inhabitants built their homes.

Open: 9 a.m. to 5 p.m., Labor Day to June, extended to 8:15 p.m. in summer. Closed Christmas Day.

Fees: None, except for the play and gardens.

Mailing Address: Fort Raleigh National Historic Site, c/o Cape Hatteras National Seashore, Route 1, Box 675, Manteo, NC 27954.

Telephone: 919-473-5772.

Getting There: The site is located on Roanoke Island in North Carolina's Outer Banks on Rt. 64-264, three miles north of Manteo, NC, and 67 miles south of Elizabeth City, NC. From Elizabeth City, take U.S. Rt. 158 east and go through Kitty Hawk. Cross over to Manteo. Or, from Williamstown, follow U.S. Rt. 64 east to Manteo.

‖ Guilford Courthouse National Military Park

On March 15, 1781, British troops under General Charles Earl Cornwallis and Continental troops led by General Nathanael Greene clashed in the cornfields and woodlands near Guilford Courthouse. It was one of the bloodiest battles in the Revolutionary War, a contest between two seasoned commanders that left the British victorious but so depleted that they retreated to the coast. "The Americans fought like demons," Cornwallis said. Almost 30 percent of the British troops died at Guilford Courthouse, while most of Greene's men survived.

The Battle of Guilford Courthouse was a prime example of Greene's southern strategy. About his tactics, Greene said: "We fight, get beat, rise, and fight again." His ability to withdraw from a battle before his army was crushed, regroup, and then try again enabled him to exhaust a vastly superior British Army and undercut their victories with heavy losses. The "victory" at Guilford Courthouse was so devastating to the British that it precipitated the events leading to Cornwallis' eventual surrender at Yorktown. Furthermore, the battle reinforced anti-war feeling in Britain. "Another such victory would ruin the British army," said Member of Parliament James Fox.

The 220-acre battlefield near Greensboro, North Carolina, has 28 monuments commemorating the events at Guilford Courthouse. There is a large equestrian statue of Nathanael Greene, a monument over the grave sites of William Hooper and John Penn, two of North Carolina's signers of the Declaration of Independence, and a monument for Kerenhauppuch Turner, a soldier's mother, who traveled on horseback from Maryland to care for her wounded son.

A self-guided tour begins at the visitor center, which has artifacts from the battle and a film of the war's southern campaign. Seven stops along the 2.5-mile route explain the action.

On March 15 each year the park celebrates the battle with special programs. Check for details.

Revolutionary War soldier Luther W. Clark carried this drum into battle at Guilford Courthouse on March 15, 1781. —*Dan Caldwell, NPS photograph*

Open: 8:30 a.m. to 5 p.m. Closed Christmas and New Year's Day.
Fees: None.
Mailing Address: Guilford Courthouse National Military Park, P.O. Box 9806, Greensboro, NC 27408.
Telephone: 919-288-1776.
Getting There: The park is located in central North Carolina, north of Greensboro on New Garden Road. Take the Holden Rd. exit from I-40 and follow to the junction of Holden Rd. and Benjamin Parkway. Turn left at the light onto Battleground Ave., follow the signs to New Garden Rd, turn right on New Garden to the park entrance.

| Moores Creek National Battlefield

To gain the support of the residents of Moores Creek, the British offered 200 acres and a 20-year tax exemption; the patriots offered independence. But when colonist fought colonist at The Battle of Moores

Creek, on February 27, 1776, independence proved the stronger incentive. In the swamps and thickets of this murky coastal creek, patriot sharpshooters repulsed an army of loyalists bent on regaining North Carolina for the crown.

The Battle of Moores Creek, known as the "Lexington and Concord of the South," was one of the earliest Revolutionary War battles. Colonel Alexander Lillington's victory against British sympathizers showed the strong support for the patriot cause in North Carolina, and encouraged the state to be the first to vote for independence at the Continental Congress in 1776.

The visitor center has a short slide presentation about the battle and original weapons, including a broadsword, a Highland pistol, and a Brown Bess musket. From there, a 30-minute walking trail leads to the earthworks built to block British supporters from reaching Wilmington. Only one patriot was killed in the skirmish, Private John Grady. The cornerstone of a monument to him in the park supposedly contains his remains.

Longleaf pine, used in making turpentine, grow in the park; cypress and sweetgum trees grow in the damp ground near the creek. Spring brings an astonishing array of wildflowers, more than 150 different types. Bass, brim, catfish, and trout live in the black, sluggish waters of Moores Creek.

On the last Sunday in February, the park observes the Battle of Moores Creek with talks by noted speakers and musical flourishes from the local high school marching band. Check for details.

Open: 8 a.m. to 5 p.m. Closed Christmas and New Year's Day.

Fees: None.

Mailing Address: Moores Creek National Battlefield, P.O. Box 69, Currie, NC 28435.

Telephone: 919-283-5591.

Getting There: The battlefield is located in southeastern North Carolina, 20 miles northwest of Wilmington. Take Rt. 421 from Wilmington to the junction with Rt. 210, go west (left) on 210 for five miles to the park.

‖ Wright Brothers National Memorial

On the sandy dunes of Kill Devil Hills in North Carolina's Outer Banks, where gulls careen on sea breezes and the Atlantic Ocean sparkles in the distance, Wilbur and Orville Wright conducted the first successful flight of a heavier-than-air machine on December 17, 1903.

A granite boulder marks the spot where the first crudely constructed airplane left the ground. The plane flew only 12 seconds, traveling a mere 120 feet. But that modest start marked the beginning of a new era in transportation—the age of flight.

Adjacent to the first flight area are reconstructions of the hangar and the combined workshop and living quarters built by the Wright brothers in 1903. These buildings, which were documented in Orville's many photographs, have been appointed as they were when the Wright brothers lived here, down to the labels on the cans of vegetables. Full-size replicas of the 1903 Flyer, which measured 20 feet, and the 1902 Glider, measuring about 15 feet, are on display. In the visitor center, original tools, test and drafting equipment, airfoils, bicycle tools, and an early propellor are on display.

The first airplane had two parallel wings that were slightly bent and a wingspan of more than 40 feet. An engine, built by the Wright brothers especially for flying, was mounted in the center of the lower wing, slightly to the right. The pilot lay prone to the left.

A 60-foot high granite monument commemorating the experiments of the Wright brothers rises from the ever-shifting dunes and offers a beautiful view of the barrier island and surrounding waters. The monument is open periodically in summer; check at the visitor center.

Rangers and interpreters give hourly talks about the Wright brothers and the history of flight. Near the Wright memorial is the First Flight Airstrip, a 3,000-foot paved runway built in 1963 for airborne visitors. Parking for visiting planes is limited to 24 hours, or 48 hours in one month. Kitty Hawk AeroTours, a private concessionaire, offers short flights from the airstrip in late spring, summer and early fall. For more information, call 919-441-4460.

There are kiting programs throughout the summer. Check for details. The First Flight Society holds a special memorial program each year on the morning of December 17, the historic day of the first flight.

Camping is not allowed in the 431-acre park, but the National Park Service operates five campgrounds on the Outer Banks within 18 miles of the area during the summer months.

The Outer Banks, a series of barrier islands along the North Carolina coast, offer a variety of shore activities, from swimming and boating to fishing and bird watching. Anglers catch flounder, bluefish, and sea trout from the surf and piers. Charter and head boats take fishermen out for marlin, dolphin, king mackerel, and other large game fish. In winter, hundreds of Canada geese, mallards, and ducks pass through the area. Bald eagles and peregrine falcon migrate through the area; ospreys and pelicans live there year round.

Open: 9 a.m. to 5 p.m., extended to 7 p.m. during the summer. Check for exact dates. Closed Christmas Day.

Fees: $1 per person or $3 per car.

Mailing Address: Wright Brothers National Memorial, c/o Cape Hatteras Group, Route 1, Box 675, Manteo, NC 27954.

Telephone: 919-441-7430.

Getting There: The park is located in the barrier islands on the northeastern shore of North Carolina, on U.S. Rt. 158 at mile marker 8.

NORTH DAKOTA

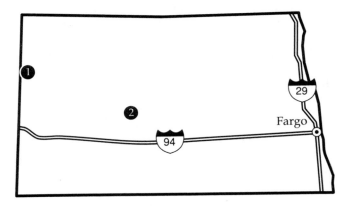

1. Fort Union Trading Post National Historic Site
2. Knife River Indian Villages National Historic
   Site

| Fort Union Trading Post National Historic Site

Fort Union was the site of the principal fur-trading post on the upper Missouri River. It was established in 1829 by Kenneth McKenzie, a fur trader and executive of John Jacob Astor's American Fur Company. Plains Indians, such as the Assiniboin, the Sioux, and the Crows, gathered outside the log walls of the stockade to exchange beaver and buffalo robes for manufactured goods that arrived by steamboat.

The fur trade was at its peak in the 1840s, and Fort Union was a bustling outpost in the midst of Indian country, as civilized as a town on the upper Missouri River frontier could hope to be. Artist George Catlin, famous for his portraits of American Indians, and renowned naturalist and painter John James Audubon are among the prominent people who visited Fort Union.

Throughout its 38-year existence, the fort exchanged hands several times. The St. Louis-based fur trading firm of Pierre Chouteau, Jr. bought it and later sold it to the Northwestern Fur Company. Fort Union was dismantled in 1867.

Some of the fort has been reconstructed to its appearance in 1851. The visitor center contains exhibits of artifacts, bottles, and firearms used at the fort during the 19th century. Rangers, on request, will give a brief tour of the area. A "Rendezvous" in mid-June re-creates the life and times of the fur trade frontier. Contact the rangers for schedules. Depending on your location, you may need a Montana and North Dakota license to fish in the river, where bass, catfish, and walleye are common.

Open: 9 a.m. to 5:30 p.m. daily, with hours extended from 8 a.m. to 8 p.m. from Memorial to Labor Day. Closed Christmas and New Year's Day.

Fees: None.

Mailing Address: Fort Union Trading Post National Historic Site, Buford Route, Williston, ND 58801.

Telephone: 701-572-9083.

Getting There: From Williston, ND, take U.S. 2 west to N.D. 1804. Fort Union is 25 miles southwest of Williston.

❚ Knife River Indian Villages National Historic Site

At the Knife River historic site in central North Dakota, visitors can canoe down the river to the ruins of villages built by the region's Hidatsa and Mandan Indians 200 to 300 years ago. Excavations of the most recently discovered sites are presumed to be 6,000 to 8,000 years old.

The Hidatsa, Mandan, and Arikara were farmers and traders who lived in semi-permanent earth lodges. They cultivated the surrounding land and fished in the Missouri River in bullboats, round boats made of buffalo hides stretched over willow frames. Lewis and Clark visited these colorful people during their western explorations in the 19th century, and artists George Catlin and Carl Bodmer painted them.

The Indians lived in large, dome-shaped wood and earth shelters measuring 30 to 60 feet in diameter and 10 to 15 feet in height. These structures, which were built and owned by women and could last as long as 12 years, accommodated up to 20 people. There is evidence in the area of villages with as many as 120 earth lodges. Depressions on the park grounds indicate their location.

From Memorial Day to Labor Day, park rangers take groups on free, 1½-hour canoe trips down the Knife River to inspect the archeological sites. The trips are given only on Saturdays. Call ahead for reservations. Guided tours of the village sites are available on request.

Flint tools, arrowheads, hide scrapers, bone tools, and elk teeth used in necklaces are on display in the visitors center museum. Archeologists have also found the petrified remains of stored food, such as corn cobs imprinted in dirt, which indicate that these early farmers introduced corn to the area. Aside from these artifacts, the visitor center has a short slide program about the Knife River villages.

Throughout the summer, the park hosts exhibitions of Indian skills, such as flint knapping, bone tool-making, and village cooking. In August each year, a Trade Day commemorates the extensive commercial activities of the Hidatsas, who were intermediaries for the Plains Indians and the white fur traders.

A 3.5-mile nature trail is great for cross-country skiing in winter and hiking in summer. Beware of poison ivy. Local wildlife includes white tailed deer, mule deer, wild turkey, coyote, red fox, bald eagle, hawk, and other birds.

Open: 8:00 a.m. to 4:30 p.m., Mondays through Fridays from Nov. 1 to March 31, with hours extended during the summer. Check for exact times and dates. Closed Thanksgiving, Christmas, New Year's Day, and Presidents' Day.

Fees: None.

Mailing Address: Knife River Indian Villages National Historic Site, Rural Route 1, Stanton, ND 58571.

Telephone: 701-745-3309.

Getting There: From I-94 at Bismarck, go north 40 miles on Rt. 83 to Rt. 200 west. Follow Rt. 200 for about 22 miles to Rt. 31 North, to Stanton, about two miles. The visitor center is three miles north of Stanton.

OHIO

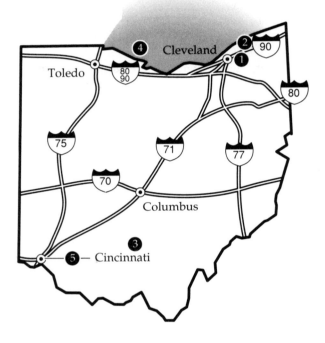

1. David Berger National Memorial
2. James A. Garfield National Historic Site
3. Mound City Group National Monument
4. Perry's Victory and International Peace
   Memorial
5. William Howard Taft National Historic Site

‖ David Berger National Memorial

In front of the Jewish Community Center in Cleveland Heights, Ohio, stands a sculpture to David Berger, the American-born athlete who died with the Israeli Olympic team during the 1972 Munich Games. Berger, a 27-year-old weightlifter, grew up in Shaker Heights and moved to Israel to work with handicapped children after earning a graduate degree in business administration and a law degree from Columbia University in New York City. The 12-foot-high abstract metal sculpture incorporates a broken Olympic symbol of five interlocking rings resting on 11 steel segments, symbolizing the breaking of the Olympic spirit on September 5, 1972, when Black September terrorists of the Palestinian Liberation Organization murdered 11 Israeli athletes. The piece was commissioned by friends of David Berger and sculpted by David E. Davis, a Romanian émigré artist. Congress declared the site a national memorial in 1980.

Open: All times.

Fees: None.

Mailing Address: David Berger National Memorial, c/o Jewish Community Center of Cleveland, 3505 Mayfield Road, Cleveland Heights, OH 44118.

Telephone: National Park Service at the James A. Garfield National Historic Site: 216-526-5256

Getting There: The Jewish Community Center is at 3505 Mayfield Road, Route 322, in Cleveland Heights, Ohio.

‖ James A. Garfield National Historic Site

This victorian mansion in a quiet suburb of Cleveland was the home of James A. Garfield, the 20th president of the United States. Garfield was shot four months after his inauguration in the spring of 1881, and died September 19. His widow Lucretia continued to live in the house after the president's death and established the first presidential memorial library here.

The 30-room mansion, bought by Garfield in 1876, has been restored to look as it did during the period from 1870 to 1890. The house features original furniture throughout and the Garfield library on the second floor. Garfield's Civil War equipment, the clothing belonging to his wife and mother, his walking sticks, and the hat he wore the day he was assassinated are on display.

Garfield was shot at the train station in Washington, D.C., on July 2, 1881, by Charles J. Guiteau, a deranged office-seeker. Garfield had little time to make his mark as president. He is remembered as a Civil War hero and U.S. Congressman, a poor boy who, by dint of intelligence and effort, became president. (He was said to be so bright as a young boy that he could write in Greek and Latin using both hands simultaneously.) Like Abraham Lincoln, Garfield was born in a log cabin and died in the White House.

Western Reserve Historical Society employees give a 15-minute talk about Garfield in the reception area of the house on request. Visitors are free to explore the house on their own. In the first floor bedroom you can see the three Indian clubs Garfield used in fitness exercises. There are also hand grenade fire extinguishers from the 1880s and fireplace tiles that may have been painted by the family.

One of the most interesting parts of the house is the presidential library, elaborately appointed and made of hand-carved white oak. It was funded by donations to Garfield's widow. It contains Garfield's congressional desk, and a rare Wooton mahogany desk that has 122 compartments. There are no presidential documents in the library, but there is an extensive collection of law books, hundreds of biographies, and numerous tomes about the Civil War. Garfield was an insomniac and would read all night in a leather chair specially designed so that he could sling his leg over the left arm. The chair is on display in Garfield's study.

From this house, Garfield conducted the first porch-front presidential campaign. Visitors can tour the building that housed members of the press from the summer through November of 1880. The original telegraph that sent news of Garfield's campaign around the country is still there.

On July 4 each year, the park hosts a Jubilee celebration, with Victorian parlor games, food, home-made ice-cream, and spelling bees.

Open: 10 a.m. to 5 p.m., Tuesday through Saturday, and 12 p.m.

to 5 p.m. Sundays. Closed Mondays, Thanksgiving, Christmas and New Year's Day.

Fees: $3 adults, $1.50 for children 6–12, under 5 free; $2 for seniors over 60.

Mailing Address: James A. Garfield National Historic Site, 8095 Mentor Avenue, Mentor, OH 44060.

Telephone: 216-255-8722.

Getting There: The house is located in Mentor, OH, north of Cleveland near the Lake Erie shore. From Cleveland, take I-90 east to the Mentor/ Kirtland Exit. Follow Rt. 306 to Rt. 20, turn right on Rt. 20 to the home on Mentor. The site is one-half mile east of the Great Lakes Mall.

|| Mound City Group National Monument

Two thousand years ago the Hopewell Indians of Ohio buried their dead in elaborate earthwork mounds. Twenty-three of these extraordinary graves, enclosed by a four-foot high earthwork wall, are preserved at Mound City, the largest earthwork necropolis in the world. These smooth, grassy, conical mounds, which range in height from three to 17 feet, are evidence of the sophisticated culture of the Indians who lived in the Midwest between 200 B.C. and A.D. 500, a civilization with an extensive trading network, beautiful art, and a strong social system.

The mound closest to the visitor center, which has been excavated and glassed in, shows the alternating layers of sand, gravel, topsoil, and river rock that characterize the mound complex. Archeologists believe that the Indians worked here on a seasonal basis, arriving from unknown distances to bury their dead here. Spearheads made from obsidian, a glassy volcanic stone found in the Rocky Mountains, indicate that the Hopewell Indians had a continental trading network. Archeologists have found exquisite copper headdresses, obsidian ornaments, bone buttons, clay pottery, shell beads, and hundreds of stone pipes engraved with bird and animal images at Mound City. Three original pipes are on display in the visitor center, along with two 11-inch copper falcons, rectangular breastplates, and reproductions of other artifacts.

During summer weekends, the park offers hour-long guided tours of the grounds. There is also a self-guided tour that leads by six spots within the earthwork wall enclosing the necropolis.

Ever since the days of the settlers, the origin and purpose of these mounds along the Scioto River have been the subject of much speculation. But after making the first excavations of the 13-acre site in 1848, Ephraim G. Squier, a local newspaper editor, and Edwin H. Davis, a physician, determined they were built by a prehistoric American Indian civilization.

These Indians, known today as the Hopewell, built numerous earthworks throughout the area, some for burial as at Mound City, and others for commerce, social, and political activities. The nearby Seip Mound complex, another prehistoric earthwork site, may have been used for commerce or religious purposes. In all, about 100 Hopewell earthworks have been found in the region.

A short nature trail leads through the woods at the north end of the monument. Bird watching is good from the observation deck at the visitor center. Each year on Memorial Day, the nearby city of Chillicothe celebrates the early pioneer and Indian days with the Feast of Flowering Moon. This occasion features crafts, cooking, and re-enactments of life during the settlement of the Ohio River Valley.

Open: 8 a.m. to 5 p.m., with extended hours in summer. Check for times. Closed Thanksgiving, Christmas, and New Year's Day.

Fees: $1 ages 17–61, maximum $3 per family.

Mailing Address: Mound City Group National Monument, 16062 State Route 104, Chillicothe, OH 45601.

Telephone: 614-774-1125.

Getting There: The site is located in central Ohio, three miles north of Chillicothe, along Rt. 104. From Columbus, take Rt. 23 south to Chillicothe, turning off at the Business 23/Bridge St. exit. Continue south on Bridge St. and turn west (right) on Rt. 35; turn right again on Rt. 104, the first exit past the river. Follow Rt. 104 north for 1.5 miles. Mound City is on the right, immediately beyond the state prison.

‖ Perry's Victory and International Peace Memorial

"We have met the enemy, and they are ours" said Commodore Oliver Hazard Perry when he defeated a British fleet during the Battle of Lake Erie on September 10, 1813. "Two ships, two brigs, one schooner & one sloop. Yours, with great respect and esteem, O.H. Perry." The upstart American navy's hard-won victory broke the British stranglehold on the lake during the War of 1812.

It also cleared the way for General William Henry Harrison's army to invade the Canadian mainland, where a British army was subsequently defeated at the Battle of the Thames on the banks of the Thames River. The dual victories of Lake Erie and Thames enabled the United States to retain control of the Old Northwest territory.

The 25-acre park at Put-in-Bay on Lake Erie's South Bass Island commemorates this important battle, but more significantly, it memorializes the friendship between the two nations with the most massive doric column ever built, a monument to international peace and co-operation.

Constructed of pink Massachusetts granite that appears white, the monument is 352 feet high and 45 feet in diameter at its base. It is topped by a bronze urn that is 23 feet high, 18 feet wide, and weighs 11 tons. Visitors can reach the top of the memorial by elevator. A crypt inside the monument holds the remains of three British and three American officers who died at the Battle of Lake Erie.

Exhibits in the visitor center include a model of Perry's ship and artifacts from the War of 1812 along with explanations of the Battle of Lake Erie and the War of 1812. On the weekend closest to September 10, there are ceremonies commemorating the Battle of Lake Erie. No food is available nor is camping allowed on the grounds, but there are restaurants about five blocks from the park in nearby Put-In-Bay. Camping facilities are available in the state park and at a private campground on South Bass Island.

Open: Visitor Center 10 a.m. to 5 p.m. from late April to late October. Closed from Late October to April.

Fees: $1 adults, free for children under 17 and seniors over 62.

Mailing Address: Perry's Victory and International Peace Memorial, P.O. Box 549, Put-in-Bay, OH 43456.

Telephone: 419-285-2184.

Getting There: The monument is located in Lake Erie, about four miles from the mainland, near Port Clinton. From April through Nov., automobile ferries operate from Catawba Point; passenger ferries leave from Port Clinton. In summer, ferries make frequent round trips from both spots. There is year-round air service from Port Clinton airport. If you are driving from Toldeo, take Rt. 2 east to Port Clinton.

‖ William Howard Taft National Historic Site

William Howard Taft, the only man to serve as both president of the United States and chief justice of the Supreme Court, was born in this two story house on Auburn Avenue in Cincinnati.

During his term as 27th president from 1908 to 1912, Taft introduced the first income tax and federal budget. As Supreme Court Chief Justice from 1921 to his death on March 8, 1930, Taft broke up more monopolies than Theodore Roosevelt.

But if Taft was known as a far-sighted public servant, he was also famous for his foibles. The president would fall asleep during cabinet meetings and was unable to remember the names of reporters in the White House press corps—a weakness that caused him constant embarassment. And he was one of the largest men ever to hold public office. At his heaviest, Taft weighed 327 pounds.

The restoration of the Greek Revival-style house, built in the 1840s, was completed in September 1988. A visit to the birthplace and boyhood home of Taft includes a guided tour of re-created furnished rooms, as well as a self-guided tour of exhibits on his career.

Open: 10 a.m. to 4 p.m. daily. Closed Thanksgiving, Christmas, and New Year's Day.

Fees: None.

Mailing Address: William Howard Taft National Historic Site, 2038 Auburn Avenue, Cincinnati, OH 45219.

Telephone: 513-684-3262.

Getting There: The house is located in downtown Cincinnati. Heading north on I-71 from the Fort Washington Way, exit at Reading Road (exit #2), bear right to Dorchester Street, and turn left at the stop light. Travel West up Dorchester to Auburn Ave., go two stop lights to Southern Ave. and take a left. The parking lot is on the right.

OREGON

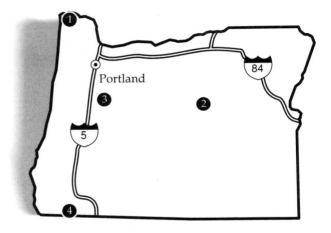

1. Fort Clatsop National Memorial
2. John Day Fossil Beds National Monument
3. McLoughlin House National Historic Site
4. Oregon Caves National Monument

‖ Fort Clatsop National Memorial

In the heavy pine forests and salt marshes of northwestern Oregon, near the mouth of the Columbia River, explorers Meriwether Lewis, William Clark, and 31 other members of the Corps of Discovery, spent the soggy winter of 1805–6. Here Lewis and Clark weathered three months of fierce fleas and constant rain while they prepared for their return trip across North America. "At this place we wintered . . . and have lived as well as we had any right to expect. We can say we were never one day without three meals of some kind . . . not withstanding the repeated fall of rain, which has fallen almost constantly," wrote William Clark on March 23, 1806.

The log encampment at Fort Clatsop was re-created in 1955 according to a floor plan etched on the cover of Clark's field book. It consists of a 50-foot-square stockade with two rows of small cabins separated by a parade ground. Short trails lead to a nearby spring and the canoe landing along the Lewis and Clark River.

Lewis and Clark and the Corps of Discovery began their famous journey in search of a water route to the Pacific in May 1804 at the behest of President Thomas Jefferson. This historic expedition provided the first detailed knowledge of the Northwest. They were joined by Toussaint Charbonneau, a French-Canadian interpreter, his Shoshone wife, Sacagawea, and their infant son.

The visitor center has exhibits about the Lewis and Clark expedition, with pictures, maps, and charts of their route to the Pacific. From June through Labor Day, people in buckskin and Indian dress demonstrate wilderness crafts, canoe making, and frontier survival skills.

At a beach 15 miles southwest of Fort Clatsop, now called Seaside, Oregon, Lewis and Clark set up a small salt-making camp. By tediously boiling seawater, the men who worked this site produced 3½ bushels of salt necessary for preserving food on the long trip back East. Today, a memorial of boulders with five kettles, known as the Salt Works, marks the spot where the salt was produced.

The park has a picnic area. Overnight accommodations are available in nearby towns, with camping at Fort Stevens State Park, five miles away.

Open: 8 a.m. to 5 p.m., extended to 6 p.m. mid-June through Labor Day. Closed Christmas Day.

Fees: $1 per person, from April 1-September 31. Free October-March.

Mailing Address: Fort Clatsop National Memorial, Route 3, Box 604-FC, Astoria, OR 97103.

Telephone: 503-861-2471.

Getting There: The site is located in the northwesternmost corner of Oregon, near the mouth of the Columbia River. From the south, follow Rt. 101 for 12 miles north of Seaside, follow the signs along Rt. 101 to Fort Clatsop. From Astoria, take Rt. 101 south two miles. Follow the signs from Rt. 101 to Fort Clatsop.

‖ John Day Fossil Beds National Monument

The rough and colorful landscape of the John Day Fossil Beds in north central Oregon chronicles over 45 million years of prehistoric plant and animal life. Spread out over three sites—Sheep Rock, Painted Hills, and Clarno—the beds contain an extensive record of four prehistoric epochs.

Short self-guided walking trails (none more than two miles long) lead through the spectacular Blue Basin, the swirling reds and golds of the Painted Hills, and the eroded mud slide Palisades at Clarno. Exhibits along some trails explain the fossils and landscape.

Saber-toothed tigers, early horses, and rhinoceros-like creatures roamed the area. Early oak, laurel, and redwood trees grew in the Painted Hills Region, and the giant beast Notiotitanops and the tapir Helaletes lived in the Clarno region. The wealth of fossil material here attracted many early paleontologists, starting with the Reverend Thomas Condon 125 years ago.

The region was named after John Day, a member of the Astor Fur Company expedition, whose encounter with hostile Indians during the early 1800s left him alive but without any clothes. He was eventually reunited with the expedition and completed the journey to the west coast.

Cant Ranch, which serves as the visitor center at the Sheep Rock section, was the farmhouse for a prosperous sheep and cattle ranch in the region. There are 12 historic buildings on the site, including a barn, bunkhouse, workshop, and storage area. The Cant house has been historically renovated. Exhibits include a vast display of mammal and leaf fossils, rocks, geological time scales, and photographs of turn-of-the-century collecting expeditions.

The 14,030-acre site has a remarkable variety of plant life: Juniper, sagebrush, and bunchgrass cover the landscape at the higher and drier altitudes, cottonwoods and willows grow along the John Day River banks, and fir and pine forests cover the nearby mountains.

Open: The monument is open 24 hours, all year long. Visitor Center: 9 a.m. to 6 p.m. from mid-March to the end of Oct. and 8 a.m. to 5:30 p.m. on weekdays in winter.

Fees: None.

Mailing Address: John Day Fossil Beds National Monument, 420 West Main Street, John Day, OR 97845.

Telephone: 503-575-0721.

Getting There: The park is located in three separate units in north central Oregon. Sheep Rock is nine miles from Dayville west on Rt. 26 and north on Rt. 19. Painted Hills is six miles on a marked country road northwest from Rt. 26 west of Mitchell. Clarno is 20 miles west on Rt. 218 from Fossil, or 30 miles east on Rt. 218 from Shaniko.

‖ McLoughlin House National Historic Site

This two-story colonial house in Oregon City, Oregon, overlooking the Willamette River, was the home of Dr. John McLoughlin, known as the "Father of Oregon." As Chief Factor of Britain's Hudson's Bay Company in the Oregon Territory from 1825 to 1845, McLoughlin played a key role in the settlement and development of an area that was to become the states of Oregon, Washington, Idaho, and parts of Montana, Wyoming, and British Columbia in Canada. He helped to develop the local economy by encouraging agriculture, animal husbandry, and lumber exporting in an area that was considered solely a fur-trapping grounds.

Dr. John McLoughlin, called the "Father of Oregon," lived in this house from 1847 to 1857.—*George Grant, NPS photograph*

But it was McLoughlin's kind and generous treatment of the American settlers who came to the Oregon Territory for which he is remembered today. McLoughlin sheltered starving travelers at his Fort Vancouver headquarters and gave them food, supplies, and credit so they could weather their first difficult years in the Northwest.

McLoughlin built his house near the falls of Willamette in 1845, where he would settle on the land claim he had purchased from the Hudson's Bay Company for $20,000. After a falling out with the Hudson's Bay Governor George Simpson, McLoughlin had resigned from the Company. He lived in Oregon City until his death on September 3, 1857.

The house, administered by the McLoughlin Memorial Association and Oregon City in conjunction with the Park Service, was moved to its present site in McLoughlin Park in 1909. Dr. McLoughlin and his wife are buried next to the house. The house is furnished with original and period pieces to look as it did when the McLoughlins lived here. Furnishings include McLoughlin's desk, his dishes, a chest, a melodeon, and a hand-carved, four-poster bed.

Open: 10 a.m. to 4 p.m. Tuesday to Saturday. Sundays 1 p.m. to 4 p.m. Closed Mondays, holidays, and the month of January.

Fees: $2.50 adults, $2 seniors 62 and over, $1 students age 6–17. Group rates available for 12 or more people.

Mailing Address: McLoughlin House National Historic Site, 713 Center, Oregon City, OR 97045.

Telephone: 503-656-6146.

Getting There: The McLoughlin House is in Oregon City in McLoughlin Park, between Seventh and Eighth streets, less than four blocks east of Route 99. Bus service is available from Portland, 13 miles away.

Oregon Caves National Monument

Rippling marble draperies, striking calcite columns, and petrified mineral flowerlets make Oregon Caves, located in the lush Siskiyou National Forest of southwestern Oregon, an extraordinary underground garden of stone.

Guided tours of the cave's delicate buff and gray dripstone formations are available year-round. Registration for the 75-minute walk through the cavern starts at 9 a.m. Tours fill up quickly, so arrive early.

Although the walk is only .6 mile, it is the equivalent of walking up a 25-story building. It should not be attempted by anyone with heart, respiratory, or walking problems. Plan to wear good walking shoes (no sandals or heels) and clothing warm enough for the 38 to 47 degree temperatures in the cave. A babysitting service is available for children under six.

The Oregon Caves were discovered in 1874 by hunter Elijah Davidson, who followed his dog into an opening in the mountains while chasing a bear. Poet Joaquin Miller popularized the site in 1907, calling it "The Marble Halls of Oregon." Two years later, President Taft named it a national monument.

While awaiting the tour, take time to explore the surrounding countryside. The ¾-mile Cliff Nature Trail at an elevation of 4,000 feet features breathtaking vistas of the forested mountains. The three-mile Big Tree Trail leads past a 1,500-year-old Douglas fir with a

40-foot girth. Other trails wander by mountain streams, mossy cliffs, and fields of wildflowers. Wildlife is varied in the surrounding forests, where everything from black-tailed deer and porcupines to Giant Pacific salamanders make their home.

From mid-June to early September, Oregon Caves Chateau, a lodge in the monument, is open. Rooms are reasonably priced in this delightful mountain hideaway, where you can watch a spectacular sunset over the canyon and dine in a restaurant with a stream flowing through it. For more information, write to the Oregon Caves Chateau at Oregon Caves, Oregon 97523, or call 503-592-3400. Camping is not permitted in the monument, but two campgrounds in nearby Siskiyou National Forest are open from late May to early September and several private campgrounds are also open in the area.

Open: Guided tours offered at 10:30 a.m., 12:30 p.m., 2:00 p.m., and 3:30 p.m. from Oct. 1 through April 30 and from 9 a.m. to 7 p.m. in summer. Closed Christmas Day.

Fees: Adults 12 and over, $6; children 6–11, $3; children under 6 not allowed in caves. $3 for child care during tours.

Mailing Address: Oregon Caves National Monument, 19000 Caves Highway, Cave Junction, OR 97523.

Telephone: 503-592-2100.

Getting There: The monument is located in the southwestern corner of Oregon near the California border, 32 miles southeast of Cave Junction on Rt. 46. From Medford, take I-5 north to Rt. 99 west, and turn on Rt. 199 south to Cave Junction. At Cave Junction, turn left on Rt. 46 to the caves. The last eight miles of Rt. 46 are narrow and winding.

PENNSYLVANIA

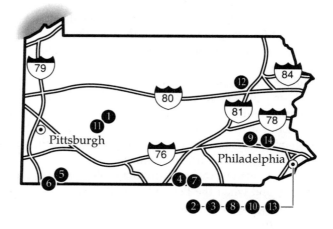

1. Allegheny Portage Railroad National Historic
   Site
2. Benjamin Franklin National Memorial
3. Edgar Allan Poe National Historic Site
4. Eisenhower National Historic Site
5. Fort Necessity National Battlefield
6. Friendship Hill National Historic Site
7. Gettysburg National Military Park
8. Gloria Dei (Old Swedes') Church National
   Historic Site
9. Hopewell Furnace National Historic Site
10. Independence National Historical Park
11. Johnstown Flood National Memorial
12. Steamtown National Historic Site
13. Thaddeus Kosciuszko National Memorial
14. Valley Forge National Historical Park

‖ Allegheny Portage Railroad National Historic Site

The Allegheny Portage Railroad, which opened in 1834, was one of the most extraordinary engineering feats of its time. Using a series of inclined track sections and pulleys to transfer the trains from level to level, the portage hauled canal boats over the 2,400-foot-high Allegheny Mountain and deposited them in the water on the other side. This 36-mile segment of railroad track completed the Pennsylvania Mainline Canal System, the major transportation route between Philadelphia and Pittsburgh.

Using pulleys to hoist railroad cars carrying canal boats over a mountain must have looked strange to the people of the mid-19th century. But it worked. Between 1834 and 1854, canal boats loaded with iron ore, coal, and immigrants going west made the six-hour crossing on the Allegheny Portage Railroad.

Unfortunately, the multi-million-dollar project never did make any money and when the Pennsylvania Railroad was completed in 1854, the portage was abandoned. But while it operated, the Allegheny Portage Railroad brought business to the area and made a very rich man of a local entrepreneur named Samuel Lemon, who ran a tavern from his stone house near the mountain's summit and supplied the railroad with coal.

The first floor of this three-story house serves as a museum and is open to tourists. The museum has a 12-minute slide presentation about the portage. There are original rail spikes, sleepers—the square 500-pound stone ties used on flat stretches of railroad—tools, model trains, and canal boats on display. In a shed nearby sits a full-scale model of a locomotive used at the portage, a Norris locomotive topped by a storybook smokestack.

Visitors can hike along the original rail bed, where sleepers are still embedded in the ground. At Incline Six, you can see the foundation of the engine house, an enormous structure that measured 65 by 90 feet. From the top of Plane Six, you get a good view of the rail route. The Skew Arch Bridge, a bridge twisted at an angle to accommodate a wagon road that ran over the railbed, still stands.

There are 7.5 miles of hiking trails in the park, most of them short, pleasant paths through the surrounding forests. Wildlife in the park includes deer, groundhogs, squirrels, chipmunks, and wild turkeys; the trees are mostly deciduous.

The Johnstown Flood National Memorial is located a short distance from the Allegheny Portage Railroad site. On May 31, 1889, an earthen dam collapsed and flooded the city of Johnstown some 14 miles down the Little Conemaugh River. The flood killed more than 2,000 people and left the once prosperous industrial center completely in ruins.

Open: 8:30 a.m. to 5 p.m. daily, extended to 6 p.m. from mid-June to Labor Day. Closed Thanksgiving, Christmas, and New Year's Day.

Fees: None.

Mailing Address: Allegheny Portage Railroad National Historic Site, P.O. Box 247, Cresson, PA 16630.

Telephone: 814-886-8176.

Getting There: From Altoona, follow Rt. 22 west to Summit exit at the top of the mountain and then follow the National Park Service signs to the visitor center.

| Benjamin Franklin National Memorial

In the octagonal hall of the Franklin Institute, under a rotunda modeled after the Pantheon in Rome, stands a larger-than-life sculpture of Benjamin Franklin—the printer, inventor, and statesman, who was himself larger than life. Sculpted by James Earle Fraser, the figure made of white marble commemorates the man who inspired this delightful hands-on museum of science and technology. The memorial was dedicated in 1972 and contains exhibits on the life and career of Benjamin Franklin.

A printer by trade, Benjamin Franklin moved to Philadelphia from his native Boston as a young man. As a printer, Franklin is remembered for publishing *Poor Richard's Almanac*, but in his day he was known as an enterprising businessman with a string of successful printing and paper-making shops throughout the colonies. In fact, his tombstone reads: Benjamin Franklin, Printer.

Franklin's printing business did so well that he essentially retired at age 40 and he spent most of his time on other projects. He devised the colonial postal system and served as postmaster, he started the University of Pennsylvania and the Pennsylvania Hospital, and, as every American knows, he experimented with electricity. Other Franklin innovations include free lending libraries, municipal fire departments, fire insurance, and street lighting. He was appointed foreign minister during the Revolutionary War and helped to convince the French to support the patriot cause. His home, at Franklin Court, is part of Independence National Historical Park.

The Franklin Institute has been operating since 1824 as an organization to promote education, research, and invention in the mechanical arts. The museum, which opened in 1934, gives visitors a chance to touch, walk through, and manipulate the exhibits. It features a moving 350-ton locomotive that you can board, a giant thumping model of a human heart you can walk through, the world's largest pinball machine, an enormous set of Tinkertoys, and Halloween programs with special effects. The Institute also has the Fels Planetarium, the second oldest planetarium in the country, which has seasonal constellation shows and specials on topics ranging from black holes to UFOs.

Open: 10 a.m. to 5 p.m. daily. Closed Thanksgiving, Christmas, New Year's Day, the Fourth of July, and Labor Day.

Fees: None for the memorial. Museum general admission: $5.50 adults, $4.50 children ages four to 11, $2.50 seniors. Members free. Planetarium shows are $1.50

Mailing Address: Benjamin Franklin National Memorial, The Franklin Institute, 20th Street and Benjamin Franklin Parkway, Philadelphia, PA 19103.

Telephone: 215-448-1200.

Getting There: The memorial is in downtown Philadelphia. From I-76, the Schuylkill Expressway, take the exit marked Benjamin Franklin Bridge/Camden. Turn right on Winter Street at the 23rd Street exit and travel east about 300 yards to the Institute, at 20th and the Parkway. The route is marked with signs.

|| Edgar Allan Poe National Historic Site

Bring your imagination to this site, for there are no cluttered desks, no half-smoked cigars, no sharpened pens to guide you back to the time when Edgar Allan Poe, one of America's greatest writers, lived here. From 1843 to 1844, Poe lived on North Seventh Street in Philadelphia with his wife (and cousin) Virginia, his mother-in-law (and aunt) Maria Clemm, and their cat Catterina.

Since Poe wrote no diary or journal and rarely mentioned his possessions in his letters, little is known about the details of his personal life. In fact, so little is known about him—and the days he spent at 234 North Seventh Street (now number 530)—that the Park Service has intentionally left the house's six rooms absolutely empty. (Today, only two boot hooks, a cane, and a trunk can actually be traced to Poe's ownership, and these are on display at the Edgar Allan Poe Museum in Richmond, Virginia.) During a tour, rangers present possible room uses and point out supporting evidence. Visitors can draw their own conclusions.

But if there is little to see, there is much to hear about Poe and his literary accomplishments. Poe's six years in Philadelphia made up one of the most fertile periods of his life. He wrote such well-known short stories as "The Gold Bug," "The Fall of the House of Usher," "The Tell-Tale Heart," and "The Murders in the Rue Morgue." "The Black Cat," also written while Poe lived in Philadelphia, appears to be set in the cellar of the Seventh Street house.

Rangers discuss Poe's days as literary editor of *Graham's Magazine*, a Philadelphia publication, and Poe's reputation as an alchoholic. Poe had a low tolerance for alcohol and many believe that he may have had some metabolic disorder. Poe was also the victim of a slander campaign by his competitor, the Reverend Rufus Griswold. Griswold, to this day, has affected the public perception of Poe. Ironically, Poe named Griswold his literary executor. Poe died in Baltimore in 1849. "God help my poor soul" were supposedly his last words.

The visitor center has an eight-minute slide presentation about Poe and his works and an original copy of *Graham's Magazine*. One wall has photographs of his family, his mother Elizabeth Arnold Poe, his foster parents John and Frances Allan, his wife, and his mother-in-law. There are also copies of illustrations to Poe's stories. A good selection of Poe's works are for sale. The site honors Poe on his birthday on January 19 with special programs. Past celebrations have included free slide shows and performances of his works. Check for details.

Open: 9 a.m. to 5 p.m. daily. Closed Christmas and New Year's Day.

Fees: None.

Mailing Address: Edgar Allan Poe National Historic Site, 532 North Seventh Street, Philadelphia, PA 19123, or Independence National Historical Park, 313 Walnut Street, Philadelphia, PA 19106.

Telephone: 215-597-8780.

Getting There: The site is located at Seventh and Spring Garden streets in Philadelphia, just a few blocks north of Center City. By public transportation: Take the Market-Frankford subway east to Fifth and Market streets. There, board a #50 bus to Fifth and Spring Garden streets. The park is located two blocks west. By car: Eastbound, via Rt. 76, the Schuylkill Expressway, exit at Spring Garden Street, turn left on Spring Garden. (Caution: Spring Garden St. enters a traffic circle in front of the Philadelphia Art Museum and exits the circle on the other side at the third right.) Follow Spring Garden St. to Seventh St.

‖ Eisenhower National Historic Site

Dwight David Eisenhower, World War II military hero and 34th president of the United States, lived in the White House and at least 37 other residences world-wide. But the only home he ever owned was in Gettysburg, Pennsylvania. That home, a 500-acre country estate at the edge of the Gettysburg battlefield, has been preserved in the Eisenhower National Historic Site.

The Eisenhowers acquired the property in 1951, expanded and landscaped the grounds, and in 1955 built the two-story, modified Georgian house that stands today. It was designed according to the specifications of Eisenhower's wife Mamie by architect Milton Osborne of Pennsylvania State University. In its time, the property was a showplace where the Eisenhowers hosted such dignitaries as Soviet Premier Nikita Khrushchev, French President Charles de Gaulle, and British Prime Minister Winston Churchill.

The house is decorated with a comfortable mixture of the formal and familiar from the 1950s, from the silver serving dishes and expensive crystal in the red dining room to the ordinary Colorado red cedar lamp on the sun porch. A copy of a landscape painted by Eisenhower is displayed on the porch. Seven other originals are on the second floor. Outside is a putting green and sand trap, a gift from the Professional Golfer's Association of America. (Eisenhower was an avid golfer.)

The property was given to the government in 1967, two years before Eisenhower died. Mamie Eisenhower continued to live here until her death on November 1, 1979. The site opened to the public in 1980.

Access to the site is by shuttle bus from the Gettysburg visitor center. Tickets for tours of the house are distributed on a first-come, first-served basis. In summer, rangers give a half-hour outdoor talk about many aspects of Eisenhower's life and the house's role in foreign policy. Groups need to make reservations at least ten days in advance, and may not be able to reserve places during the peak summer season. Contact the park for details.

Open: 9 a.m. to 5 p.m. daily in summer and Wednesday through Sunday from Thanksgiving to April 1. Closed Thanksgiving, Christmas, New Year's Day, and from January 2 to the first week of February.

Fees: $1 for the house, ages 16–62. Shuttle bus fares to site are $1.25, ages 12 and up, and $.70 for children. Under six, free.

Mailing Address: Eisenhower National Historic Site, Gettysburg, PA 17325.

Telephone: 717-334-1124.

Getting There: The Eisenhower visitor center is located in Gettysburg National Military Park visitor center building. The building is located on Taneytown Road in the town of Gettysburg, near the intersection with Steinwehr Avenue (Route 15).

|| Fort Necessity National Battlefield

George Washington's first battle as a military leader was in Jumonville Glen in the mountains of southwestern Pennsylvania on May 24, 1754. Here the 22-year-old Washington commanded colonial troops against the French in what led to the opening sallies of the French and Indian War. Within 15 minutes, the French surrendered to Washington. Fearing retaliation from the French, Washington and his men hastily built the stockades of Fort Necessity.

Retaliation was not long in coming. On July 3, French and Indian troops commanded by Louis Coulon de Villiers engaged in an eight-hour battle, this time forcing Washington to surrender. Colonial troops retreated to Virginia. The French eventually lost the French and Indian War with England for control of North America, and Washington went on to become commander of the Continental Army and first president of the United States.

The 53-foot circular log stockade surrounded by diamond-shaped earthworks that Washington called his "fort of necessity" have been reconstructed. Inside the fort stands a crude log cabin similiar to one which was used by Washington's army. The visitor center has a ten-minute slide program about the battle and artifacts from the era.

The park also has the Mount Washington Tavern, an early 19th-century inn that became a very busy stop on the National Road to Wheeling, West Virginia. George Washington himself once owned the property on which the tavern was built and the Fort Necessity Battlefield area. Although he realized his land would have made a good inn, and even advocated building a public highway along the route, his Pennsylvania investment never made him any money.

After his death the property changed hands several times until, in 1827, Nathaniel Ewing of Uniontown, Pennsylvania, bought it and began constructing the 11-room brick structure that stands today. The tavern is furnished in period pieces and contains a bar room, parlor, and bedrooms. It is open daily in spring, summer, fall, and on weekends in the winter.

The National Road between Baltimore and Vandalia, Illinois, was the nation's first federally funded road. It was one of the main routes for settlers on their way west.

The National Road, a 32-foot bed of three layers of packed gravel, cost the equivalent of $150,000 per mile to build but was fabulously successful. During its heyday, 18,000 people traveled the road in only 4 years, paying six cents for a score of sheep, four cents for a horse and rider, and three cents for a horse. Tolls were collected about every 15 miles. You can see an original toll house on old Route 40 in Addison, Pennsylvania, 15 miles to the east. The National Pike Day celebration is held every year on the third weekend in May.

Open: 10:30 a.m. to 5 p.m. daily, extended in summer. Check for dates. Closed Thanksgiving, Christmas, and New Year's Day.

Fees: $1, ages 17–61.

Mailing Address: Fort Necessity National Battlefield, RD 2, Box 528, Farmington, PA 15437.

Telephone: 412-329-5512.

Getting There: The battlefield is located in southwestern Pennsylvania along Route 40, 11 miles east of Uniontown.

‖ Friendship Hill National Historic Site

This historic house along Route 166 near Point Marion belonged to Albert Gallatin, a Swiss immigrant who was U.S. secretary of treasury under Presidents Jefferson and Madison, and U.S. envoy to Great Britain and France. Gallatin also played a major role in negotiating the truce that ended the War of 1812. His 35-room stone and brick house was built along the Monongahela River in 1789.

Completion of the restoration of Gallatin House is currently scheduled for late 1991. In summer, guides lead tours of the house exterior. A small visitor center has an exhibition on Gallatin's life and contributions. There are five miles of hiking trails through the surrounding countryside. Wildflowers bloom in the meadows in summer; cross-country skiing is excellent in winter.

Open: 9:30 a.m. to 5 p.m. daily, Memorial Day to Labor Day; weekends all other times. Closed Thanksgiving, Christmas, and New Year's Day.

Fees: None.

Mailing Address: Friendship Hill National Historic Site, c/o Fort Necessity National Battlefield, The National Pike, Farmington, PA 15437.

Telephone: 412-329-5512.

Getting There: From Pittsburgh, take I-79 south to Masontown and take Route 21 south to Route 166 south to the site, approximately three miles north of Point Marion, PA, 15 miles north of Morgantown, WV.

‖ Gettysburg National Military Park

The battle for Gettysburg was the biggest and bloodiest encounter of the Civil War, the turning point that marked the peak of Confederate strength and foreshadowed the southern army's eventual decline. Between July 1 and 3, 1863, Federal forces under General George Gordon Meade crushed General Robert E. Lee's second foray into Union territory. But such a spectacular victory did not come without its price: More than 51,000 casualties. Gettysburg was the bloodiest battle ever fought on American soil.

The mass destruction at Gettysburg was as grimly devastating in its time as the dropping of the atom bomb has been in ours. It took five months of bitter controversy to re-bury the 3,512 soldiers in the cemetery at Gettysburg and return the remains of 3,320 Confederates to the South.

Fighting began on July 1, 1863, when Union and Confederate cavalry forces clashed along Chambersburg Road. By the end of the day, Federal troops were entrenched along Cemetery Ridge in a defensive line resembling an inverted fishhook, which ran from Big and Little Round Top hills in the south to Culp's Hill—the "hook" —in the north. Lee's forces lined up along Seminary Ridge to the west. On the second day, fighting started at the Peach Orchard along Emmitsburg Road, as the Confederates maneuvered unsuccessfully to take the two Round Top hills, the highest points on the battlefield. From Devil's Den you can see where southern sharpshooters picked off Union soldiers on the hill. A Confederate charge on Culp's Hill was only marginally successful.

In desperation, Lee ordered an attack on the middle of the Union line on the third day. After bombarding Cemetery Ridge with artillery, 15,000 Confederate troops ran across an open field in a charge known today as Pickett's Charge, although it was actually led by General James Longstreet. Only half the men made it up the hill; most were then captured or killed in fierce hand-to-hand combat. In all, only a third survived the assault. Realizing his invasion of the North was a failure, Lee ordered a retreat on July 4, the same day Confederate troops in Vicksburg laid down their arms.

Only with President Abraham Lincoln's celebrated Gettysburg Address, delivered at the dedication of the Soldier's National Cemetery at Gettysburg on November 19, 1863, did the bitterness begin to abate. The speech was short, only 272 words, and took two minutes to deliver. But the language was so simple and elegant, the intent so poignant, that the Gettysburg Address is considered one of the masterpieces of English rhetoric. A copy of the first or second draft—depending on which day you arrive—is on display in the Cyclorama Center.

Start your tour of the battlefield at the visitor center, which has lectures, Civil War artifacts, and a unique 750-square-foot Electric Map that indicates troop movements with more than 600 colored lights. The Electric Map is shown every half hour and a small fee is charged.

Nearby the Cyclorama, a round mural measuring 356 feet by 26 feet, depicts Pickett's Charge. The painting, by artist Paul Philippoteaux, is combined with a sound and light program explaining the encounter. Cyclorama showings are scheduled every 45 minutes. The Cyclorama Center also contains dioramas depicting key moments in the battle: The Confederate breakthrough of the Union line on the first day, the Union position on Little Round Top on the second day, and the Confederate position after Pickett's Charge.

An auto tour of the battlefield takes two to three hours. (There are also bike paths and hiking routes.) Interpretive signs along the route indicate the sites of major charges and encampments, such as Culp's Hill, the Peach Orchard, Big and Little Round Top, and the High Water Mark, site of the ill-fated Pickett's Charge. Several states have erected memorials in honor of their men who participated in the battle. The Pennsylvania Memorial, with statues of officers and bronze name plates of the nearly 35,000 Pennsylvanians who fought at Gettysburg, is one of the most striking.

Licensed battlefield guides give two-hour private tours of Gettysburg. These informative guides are very much in demand and are booked early, so make advance reservations if you want a private guide. Contact the Park for details and fees.

Adjacent to the 3,862-acre park is the Eisenhower National Historic Site, the farmhouse and farm owned by former President Dwight David Eisenhower and his wife Mamie. The house is open to ticket holders; tickets are available from the visitor center on a first-come, first-served basis. A shuttle bus takes people from the visitor center to the house for a nominal fee.

Open: The park is open from dusk to dawn, year-round. The visitor center is open from 8 a.m. to 5 p.m. weekdays. Closed Christmas and New Year's Day. Hours and days of operation are subject to change.

Fees: None for the battlefield and visitor center. The Electric Map costs $2 for ages 16–62, $1.50 for seniors, and free for children under 16. The Cyclorama costs $1, ages 16–62.

Mailing Address: Gettysburg National Military Park, Gettysburg, PA 17325.

Telephone: 717-334-1124.

Getting There: The battlefield is located in Gettysburg, in south central Pennsylvania, three miles west of U.S. Route 15 near the Maryland border. The visitor center can be reached from Taneytown Rd, Route 134, which intersects with Steinwehr Ave. (Business Route 15).

▌Gloria Dei (Old Swedes') Church National Historic Site

This red brick colonial church is the oldest church in Pennsylvania. The structure, built in 1698 to 1700, is sandwiched between the interstate and the gritty industrial Delaware River waterfront in downtown Philadelphia. It contains many historic items from the original log church built in 1643 by the New Sweden settlement in Tinicum. Items include the baptismal font, paintings, biblical quotations on the wall, and the tongue of the bell.

In front, suspended from the ceiling, are models of the *Fogel Grip* and the *Kalmar Nyckel*—ships that brought Swedish immigrants to this country in 1638. The church also has a replica of a pre-Revolutionary War flag designed by Benjamin Franklin for a group called the Associators, which defended Philadelphia during the French and Indian War. The flag, which has the familiar red, white, and blue colors in a stars-and-stripes motif, may be a precursor of "Old Glory." Coincidently, Betsy Ross, who designed the first American flag, had the second of her three marriages at Old Swedes' Church.

In the church's graveyard stands a memorial to John Hanson, a Swedish-American delegate to the Continental Congress, who was elected chairman of the government after the Articles of Confederation were adopted. Thus Hanson was, arguably, the first president of our country. There is also a memorial to John Morton, who signed the Declaration of Independence, and several other prominent Swedish-Americans.

Through its episcopal services, Gloria Dei continues many Swedish religious traditions. The most popular is the Feast of Saint Lucia, on the weekend near December 13, a pageant of Swedish folk and religious customs involving music, acting, and song. On Christmas Day there is a Swedish service called Julotta. Gloria Dei is a part of the Park Service's roster of historic sites, but it is maintained and administered by the congregation. For more information about Swedes in America, contact: The American Swedish Historical Museum, 1900 Pattison Avenue, Philadelphia, PA 19145. Telephone: 215-389-1776.

Open: Hours vary, call before coming.
Fees: None, donations accepted.
Mailing Address: Gloria Dei (Old Swedes') Church National Historic Site, Delaware Avenue and Christian Street, Philadelphia, PA 19147.
Telephone: 215-389-1513.
Getting There: From I-95 heading north, take "Historic District" exit to a T (Reed Street), turn right to T (Delaware Avenue), left on Delaware Avenue. Church is on the left, one block north. From I-95 heading south, take "Center City" exit to first light, turn left two blocks to T at Delaware Avenue, turn right onto Delaware Avenue. Church is just beyond Penn's Landing, on the right, between Christian Street and Washington Avenue.

‖ Hopewell Furnace National Historic Site

The blast furnace still hisses and the smith's hammer still sings at Hopewell Furnace, a restored 19th-century iron making community in Elverson, Pennsylvania. With its furnace and furnished workers' cottages, its charcoal hearths and ironmaster's house, Hopewell Furnace brings to life the early days of one of the country's most important industries.

It took 24 hours and six tons of raw material—charcoal, iron, ore, and limestone—to produce three tons of molten iron in the furnace at Hopewell Village.
—*Richard Frear, NPS photograph*

Between 1771, when Mark Bird established the furnace at the headwaters of French Creek, and 1883, when the fires finally cooled, Hopewell produced pig iron, iron cookware, and more than 80,000 beautifully crafted cast iron stoves. The site was meticulously restored to its 1820–1840 appearance beginning in 1935 as part of the Works Progress Administration. The National Park Service joined the restoration efforts in 1938. Bethesda Church, a quaint country chapel with the graves of community members dating back to 1807, is still active.

Not only does Hopewell Furnace preserve early iron making technology, it is a monument to an industry that helped spark the American Revolution. With iron making rapidly becoming one of colonial America's most successful industries, Britain tried in 1750 to prohibit America from producing finished iron products. The move prompted general outrage, and encouraged Hopewell's builder Mark Bird to take an active role in the Revolutionary War, supplying arms and provisions for the Continental Army.

The 848-acre site has more than a dozen restored and reconstructed buildings. In summer there is a living history program, with costumed interpreters performing daily tasks that include cooking over an open hearth, charcoal making, molding and casting stove plates, and pounding wrought iron into shape with hammer and anvil. Visitors can wander on their own through the park, and tour the Iron Master's Mansion.

On July 4 each year, the region celebrates Hopewell's role in the Revolutionary War with exhibitions by a Continental Regiment Drill Team. Special events are scheduled for Establishment Day, the first Saturday in August, and in December before Christmas. Check for details.

Open: 9 a.m. to 5 p.m. daily, extended to 6 p.m. from June to Sept. Closed Christmas and New Year's Day.

Fees: $1 per person, ages 17–61.

Mailing Address: Hopewell Furnace National Historic Site, RD. 1, Box 345, Elverson, PA 19520.

Telephone: 215-582-8773.

Getting There: The site is located about five miles south of Bridsboro on Rt. 345. It is ten miles from the Morgantown interchange on the Pennsylvania Turnpike, via Rt. 23 East and 345 North.

‖ Independence National Historical Park

Independence National Historical Park preserves essential American landmarks such as the Liberty Bell, Franklin Court where Benjamin Franklin lived, and Independence Hall, where the Declaration of Independence was adopted and the Constitution drafted. There is as much history packed into this 40-acre park in downtown Philadelphia as anywhere in the country; 40 buildings date from 1727 to 1834, many of them meticulously restored to create the flavor of colonial America at the dawn of the Revolutionary War and during the new nation's first decade.

From 1790 to 1800, Philadelphia served as the nation's capital. Dur-

The Declaration of Independence and the Constitution of the United States were adopted at Independence Hall in Philadelphia. The site is also home to the famed Liberty Bell.—*Richard Frear, NPS photograph*

ing this time, the most creative minds in the country gathered here, men like George Washington, Thomas Jefferson, Alexander Hamilton, and Philadelphia's own irascible inventor and politician, Benjamin Franklin. They wrote the Declaration of Independence, the Articles of Confederation, the Constitution, and the Bill of Rights—all historical documents expressing the principles upon which the country was founded.

Independence Historical Park is one of the most popular historic areas in the country, and with good reason. Philadelphia is so packed with sites that it is impossible to see them in an afternoon, let alone a day. Allow plenty of time to visit everything. Start your tour in the visitor center at Chestnut and Third Street, where the free film "Independence" gives an overview of the park and the events that took place here.

Independence Hall, a red brick Georgian building topped by a white clock and bell tower, is the park's focus. This building, originally the Pennsylvania State House, has been restored to its late 18th-century appearance, down to the very paneling, and furnished with period pieces. Inside this building, the Second Continental Congress met, the Declaration of Independence was adopted, and the U.S. Constitution was drafted. Free tours of the building are offered from 9 a.m. to 4:30 p.m. daily.

Flanking Independence Hall are Old City Hall, second home of the U.S. Supreme Court (until 1800), and the County Courthouse, where Congress met. (The U.S. government was located in New York from 1789 to 1790 and settled permanently in Washington, D.C. after 1800.) Directly across from the Hall, the Liberty Bell, one of America's best-known symbols, stands in its modern glass housing. The bell's famous crack developed over a period of several years. The bell was moved from Independence Hall to its current site in the pavilion on Market Street in 1976.

Franklin Court, the site of Benjamin Franklin's home, is located on Market Street between Third and Fourth streets. The site contains restored townhouses owned by Franklin, and steel "ghost structures" outlining his original house and his 1786 print shop. There is also an underground museum, and a post office—Franklin was the first U.S. postmaster—which imprints letters with the postmark: "B. Free Franklin."

Early American leaders met to discuss business and politics at The City Tavern, considered to be the finest of its time. Today you can re-live that tradition: The tavern has been reconstructed on its original site at Walnut and Second streets and serves meals in an authentic 18th-century atmosphere.

Other interesting buildings include the Second Bank of the United States at 420 Chestnut Street. The bank's portrait gallery has paintings of Alexander Hamilton, John Hancock, Thomas Jefferson, Benjamin Franklin, John Paul Jones, the Marquis de Lafayette, and other Revolutionary War heroes. Also on exhibit is the broadside of the Declaration of Independence read to the people of Philadelphia, and copies of the Articles of Confederation.

The Graff House at Seventh and Market streets, where Jefferson lived for four months while writing the Declaration of Independence, has been reconstructed on its original site and is open from 9 a.m. to 5 p.m. Visitors can view a short movie on Jefferson and see a study re-created to look as it did when Jefferson worked there.

Though slightly out of the way, a visit to the Deshler-Morris house, where the cabinet moved during the 1793 yellow fever epidemic, is worth the side trip. The restored two-story colonial house in Germantown has the bedroom where George and Martha Washington slept. Check to make sure the house is open before making the trip.

Visitation in the park is heavy during the middle part of the day. A good time to see the most popular sites is either early morning or late afternoon. Traffic in the area is heavy, and parking spaces are at a premium. Dress comfortably as Philadelphia can be hot and humid in summer.

July 4th is Freedom Festival Day at Independence Park, with parades, concerts, and ceremonies commemorating the signing of the Declaration of Independence. On July 8, the park commemorates the first public reading of the Declaration of Independence by Colonel John Nixon (no relation to the former president) behind Independence Hall. Check for specific activities if you plan to be in Philadelphia during that time.

Open: 9 a.m. to 5 p.m. daily, with extended hours for Independence Hall and the Liberty Bell until 8 p.m. in summer. The Visitor Center is closed Christmas and New Year's Day, but Independence Hall and the Liberty Bell are always open.

Fees: None for park, $.50 per person at the Deshler-Morris House in Germantown. Some buildings are open to tours only, and tickets are distributed free to visitors on a first-come, first-served basis.

Mailing Address: Independence National Historical Park, 313 Walnut Street, Philadelphia, PA 19106.

Telephone: 215-597-8974.

Getting There: Eastbound via I-76, the Schuylkill Expressway, take the exit at Vine St. and follow to Sixth St. Turn right on Sixth and follow to Chestnut St., three blocks. Turn left on Chestnut and follow to Second St. The visitor center is at the corner of Third and Chestnut. Parking for the visitor center is on Second Street.

Westbound via Benjamin Franklin Bridge, Route 30, follow signs to Sixth St. (south) as you come off the bridge. From there, follow the same directions as outlined above to reach Second St. Southbound via I-95, take the Center City exit to Second St.

Northbound via I-95, take the Tasker St. exit. Continue ahead to Reed St. Turn right on Reed to Delaware Ave. Turn left on Delaware to the Market St. exit and make an immediate left onto Second street.

|| Johnstown Flood National Memorial

On May 31, 1889, 20 million tons of water burst through South Fork Dam and barreled down the valley to Johnstown, Pennsylvania. Within 40 minutes, the raging, 40-foot-high wall of water caused $17 million worth of damage and claimed the lives of 2,209 people. It was the worst flood in American history.

Today, two worn abutments are all that remain of the South Fork Dam built in 1853, once the largest earthwork dam in the world. But the memory of the Johnstown Flood and the South Fork Fishing and Hunting Club where the flood started is preserved in this memorial.

Lake Conemaugh, as the reservoir was called, was originally constructed by the state of Pennsylvania in 1838 as a reservoir on the Main Line Canal System. Abandoned when trains took over 20 years later, the site was purchased in 1879 by a group of wealthy Pittsburgh industrialists who created the exclusive South Fork Fishing and Hunting Club. The club, which enlarged the lake for its members without properly rebuilding the dam, was in part responsible for the tragedy at Johnstown. It took only the heavy rains of late May to push the reservoir past its limits.

Johnstown was flattened by tons of accumulated debris, but the Club, where the disaster started, was scarcely touched. The luxurious 47-room clubhouse with its lattice porch is still standing, as are eight of the Queen Anne style members' "cottages." The clubhouse is a working inn and bar; the cottages are now private homes. A two-mile drive to the North Abutment of the dam leads along the edge of this former lakeside retreat and the new visitor center.

The park offers interpretive programs and film shows at varying times; check for details. During the summer, rangers lead guided walking tours on a wood-chip trail through the old lake bed, and along the park's quiet trails. The dried out lake bed is now a mass of brambles and trees and does not offer good picnicking.

Open: 8:30 a.m. to 6:00 p.m. daily, Memorial Day to Labor Day; 9 a.m. to 5 p.m. during the rest of the year. Closed Thanksgiving, Christmas, and New Year's Day.

Fees: None.

Mailing Address: Johnstown Flood National Memorial, c/o Allegheny Portage National Historic Site, P.O. Box 247, Cresson, PA 16630.

Telephone: 814-495-4643.

Getting There: From Johnstown, take Route 56 east and turn east on Route 219 ten miles to the Sidman exit. Turn left onto the access road.

❙ Steamtown National Historic Site

This 40-acre railroad yard in downtown Scranton, Pennsylvania, with the largest collection of steam era locomotives and cars in the country, preserves and interprets American railroading in the early 20th century.

Steamtown, a recent addition to the Park Service, is a train buff's paradise. Created in the rail yard of the former Delaware, Lackawanna & Western Railroad (DL & W), it features 30 steam locomotives, a round house, and 78 cars, including cabooses, coal hoppers, baggage cars, and passenger coaches. Some are restored and are open to the public. Others are in the process of being restored. Eventually, the park hopes to restore two-thirds of the locomotives to operating condition.

The site offers a free, brief train ride in the yard on one of the operating trains. Check for details about longer rides for which there may be a fee.

Plans call for a visitor center, museum, and theater. Currently, visitors can view videotapes of railroad films in one of the passenger cars. Rangers lead interpretive talks aboard the cars and take visitors to the round house, a pie-shaped maintenance facility where trains were turned and pulled into service bays for minor repairs.

Open: 9 a.m. to 6 p.m. from Memorial Day to October. Check for hours during the rest of the year.

Fees: None.

Mailing Address: Steamtown National Historic Site, P.O. Box 1280, Scranton, PA 18501.

Telephone: 717-961-2033.

Getting There: The site is located in Scranton, PA. on South Washington Ave. From I-81, take Exit 53, the Central Scranton Expressway, and follow signs to the site.

‖ Thaddeus Kosciuszko National Memorial

Thaddeus Kosciuszko (pronounced Ka-SHOE-sko), the Pole who designed the Continental Army's defense works, rented a room on the second floor of this brick boarding house at 301 Pine Street during 1797–98. Exiled from his native country for agitating against Russian domination of Poland, Kosciuszko was greeted with a hero's welcome when he reached Philadelphia on August 18, 1797. He was partially paralyzed from wounds he received fighting the Russians.

A steady stream of distinguished visitors, including his close friend Vice President Thomas Jefferson, came to see Kosciuszko that winter. But his visit to this country did not last long: On May 5, 1798, Kosciuszko left for Europe to be closer to his native country. He died in Switzerland on October 15, 1817.

The modestly furnished chambers where Kosciuszko lived have been re-created with period furniture to look as it might have when the Polish patriot lived here in 1797–98. The divan is readied with a pillow, the table set with paper and quill pen, and a crutch stands in the corner. A short film in English and Polish tells the story of Kosciuszko, and rangers are available to answer questions. The park celebrates Kosciuszko's birthday on February 4 with lectures, tours, refreshments, and candles in the window.

Open: 9 a.m. to 5 p.m. daily. Closed: Christmas and New Year's Day.

Fees: None.

Mailing Address: Thaddeus Kosciuszko National Memorial, Independence National Historical Park, 313 Walnut Street, Philadelphia, PA 19106.

Telephone: 215-597-8974.

Getting There: The site is located in Philadelphia at 301 Pine St.

‖ Valley Forge National Historical Park

An ill-fed, poorly-clothed, disorganized group of American soldiers straggled into Valley Forge on December 19, 1777. Six months later the group left as a skilled and disciplined patriot army, ready to take on the British and win. Since that fateful winter, Valley Forge has become the best known of the Revolutionary War sites.

It was cold. Snow blanketed the ground and a cruel wind whipped through the soldiers' wood huts. With little clothing and hardly any food, 2,000 soldiers died of exposure and disease: "Naked and starving as they are, we cannot enough admire the incomparable patience and fidelity of the soldiery," wrote George Washington of his troops at Valley Forge. Washington chose the high ground along the Schuylkill River for his winter encampment because it was only 18 miles northwest of British-occupied Philadelphia.

Despite the privation, the army survived, indeed flourished. One of the major reasons for the reversal of fortunes was "Baron" Friedrich Von Steuben, the Continental Army's Prussian drillmaster. Von Steuben, once a member of Frederick the Great's elite General Staff, undertook the gargantuan task of standardizing the Continental Army's drill practices to create a unified command. Day after day he barked his commands, drilling the ragtag soldiers into a corps of confident, well-trained regulars.

With its earthworks, soldiers' huts, and the preserved buildings where officers lived, the park at Valley Forge re-creates the scene of the 1777–78 encampment. A film presentation in the visitor center auditorium explains camp life. Artifacts from the encampment, including George Washington's field tent, are on display in the museum.

Visitors can wander through the grounds by car, bicycle (which can be rented in the summer), on horseback (there are ten miles of trails), or on foot. Historic buildings open to the public include Washington's Headquarters and General Varnum's house. Other officers' homes are privately occupied. A National Memorial Arch, dedicated in 1917, commemorates the "patience and fidelity" of the soldiers who wintered here.

From mid-April to October, a bus with a taped narrator takes visitors on a tour of the site. Check for times and fees. There are three picnic areas: Varnum's, Wayne's Woods, and Betzwood. On December 19, the park commemorates Washington's arrival at Valley Forge, and on June 19, there is a re-enactment of Washington's departure.

Open: 8:30 a.m. to 5 p.m. daily. Closed Christmas Day.
Fees: None for park; $1 for Washington's Headquarters per person.

Mailing Address: Valley Forge National Historical Park, P.O. Box 953, Valley Forge, PA 19481.

Telephone: 215-783-1000.

Getting There: The site is located 18 miles northwest of Philadelphia, at the intersection of routes 363 and 23. From Philadelphia, take the Schuylkill Expressway, I-76, to the Valley Forge exit, #24, and follow signs.

PUERTO RICO

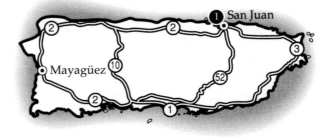

1. San Juan National Historic Site

|| San Juan National Historic Site

In 1508, a century before the Pilgrims landed at Plymouth Rock, the Spanish explorer Juan Ponce de León sailed into a sun-soaked Caribbean harbor known today as San Juan, Puerto Rico, and established a base for trade with the New World. This historic site contains some of the first structures built in the western hemisphere.

By far the most remarkable of these early architectural works is the 350-year-old El Morro Fortress. The walls of this massive stronghold, built in 1540 to guard the entrance to San Juan Harbor, are 20-feet thick and rise 140 feet above the sea.

Following the coastline in both directions from El Morro stand the ancient walls of old San Juan. They were built in the 1630s to pro-

The fortress of San Felipe del Morro in Puerto Rico is the oldest in the territorial limits of the United States. It was begun by Spaniards in the 16th century. —U.S. *Army photograph*

tect Spain's prosperous trading center in the New World from attack. These walls are made of 40-foot-high blocks of solid sandstone.

San Cristobal, located on the Atlantic Ocean side of the old city, is the companion fortress to El Morro. Constructed to protect the city from inland attack, the ingeniously designed fort covers 27 acres and has five separate structures connected by tunnels and dry moats. The park's visitor center, which has weapons, clothes, maps, and drawings of early San Juan, is located here.

A third fort, much smaller, is the El Canuelo battlement on Cabras Island across the harbor. This island, which has sandy beaches, palm trees, and the remains of an old leper colony, is an excellent place for a picnic. During Puerto Rico's colonial days, the huge wooden doors of San Juan Gate on the harbor side of the old city opened for visiting dignitaries.

All of these structures—the forts, the walls, and the gates—are in excellent shape despite their age. Nearby is La Fortaleza, built between 1530 and 1540. This Spanish style mansion, with its wide archways, ironwork balconies, and extensive gardens, is currently the governor's residence.

Old San Juan, with its winding narrow streets, shaggy palms, lush gardens, pastel buildings, and stained stone churches, has a quaint, old-world feel, reminiscent of the days when El Morro kept the city safe from marauding pirates.

Open: Visitor Center: 8 a.m. to 6 p.m. daily, although individual sites may be on a different schedule.

Fees: None.

Mailing Address: San Juan National Historic Site, P.O. Box 712, Old San Juan, PR 00902.

Telephone: 809-724-1974.

Getting There: For information, contact a travel agent, your local airlines ticket office, or the Puerto Rico Federal Affairs Administration, 734 15th St. N.W., Washington, DC 20005. Telephone: 202-383-1300.

RHODE ISLAND

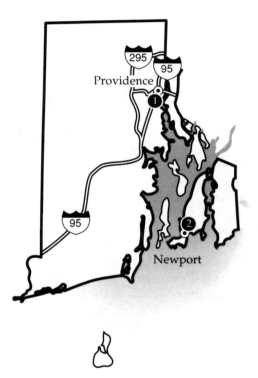

Providence

Newport

‖ Roger Williams National Memorial

The Roger Williams National Memorial in downtown Providence marks the site where free thinker Roger Williams established the colony of Providence in 1636. The memorial is on land given to Williams by local Indians.

Roger Williams was an outspoken libertarian whose belief in religious freedom got him banished from the Massachusetts Bay Colony. He resolved to found a settlement where individuals could pursue whatever religious beliefs they chose. It is Williams' spirit of tolerance and acceptance that is echoed in the First Amendment. His humane treatment of the Indians was well known, and he often mediated disputes between the colonists and various Indian tribes. Williams was given the land for his settlement by Narragansett chieftains. He named it Providence, meaning "foresight of God."

Williams' deeply held doctrine of religious tolerance attracted members of persecuted religious groups. Quakers and Jews came to the area between 1656 and 1658. In 1763, the thriving Jewish community in Newport built the Touro Synagogue, the first synagogue in the New World.

And along with those who sought religious freedom, numerous free spirits and eccentrics also found a haven in Providence. There was, for example, William Blackstone, the recluse who lived alone with his library of 200 books. (Blackstone actually preceded Williams, moving from Boston to the Lonsdale area near Providence in 1635. This area was part of Plymouth until 1746.) On those rare occasions when Blackstone deigned to talk with Roger Williams, he would ride his bull to town.

The 4.5-acre memorial is located within walking distance of the Rhode Island State Capitol and the historic Old State House. The site is also near Benefit Street, Brown University, and the Rhode Island School of Design. It has a small visitor center with a slide show about Roger Williams and displays on early Providence.

Open: 9 a.m. to 5 p.m. daily, April through October, and 8 a.m. to 4:30 p.m. the rest of the year. Closed Thanksgiving, Christmas and New Year's Day.
Fees: None.

Mailing Address: Roger Williams National Memorial, 282 North Main Street, Providence, RI 02903.

Telephone: 401-528-5385.

Getting There: The site is located at the corner of Smith and N. Main Street, at the foot of State House Hill. From Boston, take the Charles Street exit off Route 95 and continue through three traffic lights to the parking lot on the left of Canal St. From New York, take the State Offices exit and bear right. Turn left at end of ramp, and right at the next light. The parking lot is on the left beyond the next light.

‖ Touro Synagogue National Historic Site

Since it was dedicated in 1763, this unassuming but elegant Georgian-style building—the first Jewish synagogue in America—has been a symbol of religious freedom. The spirit of religious acceptance promoted by Rhode Island's founder Roger Williams attracted Sephardic Jews from Spain and Portugal to Newport as early as the mid-17th century. By 1677, Newport's Jewish community had acquired a cemetery plot, but it took another century before enough money could be raised to build a synagogue. Funds were contributed by a Jewish congregation in New York known as Shearith Israel—Remnant of Israel—and by others in Jamaica, Curacao, Surinam, and London. Peter Harrison, who designed King's Chapel in Boston and Christ Church in Cambridge, designed the Touro Synagogue, which is considered his finest work. Reverend Isaac Touro, spiritual leader of the Newport Jewish community called Yeshuat Israel (Salvation of Israel), dedicated the synagogue on December 2, 1763.

According to Harrison's plan, the clean, symmetrical lines of the building's brick exterior contrast with its ornate and airy interior. Twelve Ionic columns, representing the twelve tribes of Israel, support the gallery where, according to the Orthodox custom, the women congregants worship. Twelve Corinthian columns rise from the gallery level to support the domed ceiling, which is richly adorned with five 18th-century brass candelabra. The ark contains a 500-year-old scroll with silver bell tops made by the colonial silversmith Meyer Meyers.

The Touro Synagogue in Newport, Rhode Island, stands as an early symbol to the American tradition of religious tolerance. —*Jack E. Boucher, NPS photograph*

Above the Ark is a painting of the Ten Commandments in Hebrew by Newport artist Benjamin Howland.

In its early days, the synagogue was the finest public building in Newport, used regularly for civic as well as religious activities. Town meetings, the Rhode Island General Assembly, and the state Supreme Court met here. President George Washington visited the synagogue in 1790, and wrote a letter assuring the congregation of his committment to religious tolerance by "the Government of the United States, which gives to bigotry no sanction, to persecution no assistance."

During the 19th century the synagogue was intermittently closed because of financial problems, but it permanently re-opened in 1883 with funds left by Abraham and Judah Touro, sons of Reverend Isaac Touro. Today the local Jewish congregation still worships here, and Jews and religious leaders come from around the world to pay homage to the principle of religious freedom represented by the Touro Synagogue.

Visitors are welcome to attend services, which are held Friday evening and Saturday morning. A 20-minute lecture and tour of the synagogue is available Sundays, weekdays in summer, and on request at other times. The site is administered by the Shearith Israel trustees of New York City, the Newport congregation, and the Park Service.

Open: 10 a.m. to 5 p.m. weekdays and Sunday from late June to Labor Day; 1 p.m. to 3 p.m. Sundays all year; 1 p.m. to 3 p.m. Sunday through Thursday from mid-May to June and in September, and by appointment during the rest of the year. Services are at 6 p.m. Fridays from Labor Day until April, at 7:30 p.m. from April to Labor Day, and at 9 a.m. on Saturday.

Fees: None.

Mailing Address: Touro Synagogue National Historic Site, 85 Touro Street, Newport, RI 02840.

Telephone: 401-847-4794. Call weekdays between 9 a.m. and 5 p.m.

Getting There: From the Newport Bridge, take the exit ramp for Farewell Street (south) and follow to Thames Street, turning left (east) at the traffic light near Washington Square onto Touro Street. The synagogue is on the left, near the intersection of Spring Street.

SOUTH CAROLINA

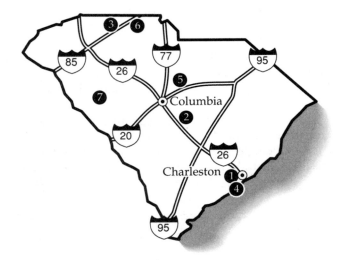

1. Charles Pinckney National Historic Site
2. Congaree Swamp National Monument
3. Cowpens National Battlefield
4. Fort Sumter National Monument
5. Historic Camden
6. Kings Mountain National Military Park
7. Ninety Six National Historic Site

‖ Charles Pinckney National Historic Site

Snee Farm is the estate of Charles Pinckney, who fought in the Revolutionary War and was one of the principal framers of the U.S. Constitution. He was Governor of South Carolina, a member of both the U.S. House of Representatives and Senate, and served as Thomas Jefferson's minister to Spain.

This site, soon to be acquired by the Park Service, is not yet open to the public.

For further information, contact Fort Sumter National Monument, 1214 Middle Street, Sullivans Island, SC 29482.

‖ Congaree Swamp National Monument

Barred owls hoot at noon, snakes slither in the moist and murky wetlands, wild pigs forage in the perpetual twilight for paw-paw and persimmon fruit. This is Congaree Swamp, the last significant old-growth bottomland hardwood forest in the Southeast. The park, located only a half-hour drive from downtown Columbia, has ancient pines and cypress trees more than ten feet in girth and 100 feet high, creating a canopy of leaves so dense it reduces rain to a fine mist.

Congaree has 85 species of trees, including tall, straight loblolly pines, striking elms, tupelo, and stately bald cypress trees, with their wood projections known as "knees," reaching up from the soggy ground. In the drier areas, there are oak, maple, hickory, sweet gum, cottonwood, and willow. This quiet, lush swamp forest supports a variety of wild animals, from fox and deer to opossum and otter. About 130 different types of birds have been seen in the park, and 52 species of fish inhabit the sluggish waters of Congaree's creeks and oxbow lakes.

Flooding occurs infrequently; most of the year the area is dry. However, insects thrive in the damp environment so bring insect repellent and wear long sleeves and long pants year round. Most visitors prefer to come in spring, fall, or winter, when the insect population is lowest.

Although the park, established in 1976, is still under development, 22 miles of trails including a raised boardwalk (accessible to the handicapped) have been completed. A ranger leads free walking tours on Saturdays at 1:30 pm. The two-mile hike lasts about 2½ hours. Watch for poison ivy and snakes—several water moccasins, rattlers, and copperheads have been found. There are no campgrounds in the monument, but primitive camping is allowed with a permit. For visitors with canoes, there is a 20-mile canoe trail along Cedar Creek.

Open: 8 a.m. to 5 p.m. daily. Closed Christmas and New Year's Day.

Fees: None.

Mailing Address: Congaree Swamp National Monument, 200 Caroline Sims Road, Hopkins, SC 29061.

Telephone: 803-776-4396.

Getting There: The swamp is located 20 miles southeast of Columbia, SC. Travel south, past the University of South Carolina stadium on Bluff Road, Rt. 48, for 11 miles. There is a sign for the site on the right side of the road. Just past the sign there is a fork in the road. Take the right fork onto Old Bluff Road. Continue traveling down this road for 4.5 miles. There will be a wooden sign for Congaree Swamp on the right. Take a right at the sign and travel down the dirt road to the entrance gate and ranger station.

‖ Cowpens National Battlefield

One of the most brilliant victories by the Continental Army over the British in the American Revolution took place in the open woods at the Cowpens. On January 17, 1781, General Daniel Morgan, considered one of the best field tacticians in the Continental Army, successfully fought the advances of the British Colonel Banastre Tarleton.

Adopting unorthodox tactics, Morgan placed his troops with their backs to the river so they could not retreat. (General Morgan told his troops they would drown in the Broad River if they tried to run from the battle; in actuality, the river is five miles north of the battle site.)

He stationed the inexperienced irregular soldiers in the front line with instructions to fire two volleys and fall back behind the veteran troops. His cavalry was reserved for a counter attack. The plan worked perfectly. The bloody skirmish was over in an hour, with staggering British losses—110 dead, 200 wounded, and 500 captured—to only 12 patriot deaths.

A 1¼-mile walking trail and a three-mile auto tour road lead through the sloping battlefield. The Scruggs House, a one-room log cabin built in 1830, stands along the route of the British advance on the Green River Road. Major repairs on the house were made by the Park Service in the early 1980s.

The visitor center has a museum with artifacts and weapons representative of the type used by soldiers during the Revolutionary War; no original artifacts are exhibited. One British cannon is on display. An excellent slide show is presented hourly and lasts 20 minutes. The program, based on a poem by Greenville philanthropist Arthur Magill, is told through the eyes of a veteran who fought in the battle as a teenager.

On the weekend nearest January 17 each year, the park celebrates the battle with the firing of weapons and re-enactments of military drills. On the first weekend in October, the Over Mountain Marchers march from the Cowpens to the battleground at Kings Mountain.

Open: Visitor Center: 9 a.m. to 5 p.m. daily, with hours extended from Memorial Day to Labor Day. Closed Christmas Day.

Fees: None for the park, but there is a small charge for the slide presentation at the visitor center; $1.00 for ages 12 and above, $.50 for children.

Mailing Address: Cowpens National Battlefield, P.O. Box 308, Chesnee, SC 29323.

Telephone: 803-461-2828.

Getting There: The park is located in northwestern South Carolina, above Gaffney near the North Carolina border. From Greenville, take I-85 north in a northeasterly direction beyond Spartanburg. Turn north on Rt. 110, being careful not to be misled by signs to the town of Cowpens, and follow it to the intersection with Rt. 11. The park is on the right.

‖ Fort Sumter National Monument

In the early morning of April 12, 1861, the Confederates fired on Fort Sumter in Charleston Harbor. It was the first shot of the Civil War, and the beginning of a four-year siege of the fortress that would leave Fort Sumter reduced to little more than a pile of rubble.

A Confederate stronghold throughout the war, Fort Sumter was under constant bombardment by Union forces from July 1863 to February 1865. The evacuation of Charleston in 1865 brought an end to the 17-month ordeal. Fort Sumter National Monument includes the ruins of Fort Sumter and its counterpart, Fort Moultrie, which stands just across the harbor on Sullivans Island.

Fort Sumter was partially rebuilt by the army after the Civil War, and was used as a military post until 1947. The following year it was turned over to the National Park Service, which spent several years excavating the fort and stabilizing the Civil War ruins. Today, visitors can tour the old fort and listen to park rangers tell of its history.

Don't miss the museum, which has a scale model of the fort as it appeared in 1861 and numerous exhibits explaining its role in the Civil War. Artifacts include the sword of Captain George S. James, whose battery fired the war's first shot, the "Storm Flag," which flew over the fort during the 1861 bombardment, and the first Southern flag flown at the fort.

Fort Sumter cannot be reached by car. Fort Sumter Tours, Incorporated, operates daily excursions to the fort from the Charleston City Marina on Lockwood Boulevard and from Patriot's Point, just across the Cooper River from Charleston.

Fort Moultrie is located on Sullivans Island and can be reached by car. In 1776 patriot forces defending Fort Moultrie (or Fort Sullivan, as it was then called) defeated a British fleet, giving American forces one of their first victories in the Revolution. Since that time the fort has been rebuilt and modified several times.

It was last used as a military post by the army in 1947. Today its walls chronicle two centuries of American coastal defense. Francis Marion, the "Swamp Fox" of the Revolution, and George C. Marshall, the army chief of staff during World War II, both served at the fort, as did poet Edgar Allan Poe, who based his well-known short story "The Gold Bug" on his experiences on Sullivans Island.

A free film at the visitor center describes Fort Moultrie's history from 1776 to 1947. Guided tours are offered daily.

Open: Fort Sumter's hours vary with the season and boat schedules. Check at the visitor center for details. Fort Moultrie is open 9 a.m. to 5 p.m. daily, extended to 6 p.m. in summer. Closed Christmas Day.

Fees: None, but visitors using the concession must pay transportation to Fort Sumter, offered by Fort Sumter Tours, Inc. Fares: $7.50 adults, $3.75 children under 12, free for children under six. Contact Fort Sumter Tours, Inc., 205 King Street, Suite 204, Charleston, SC 29401. Telephone: 803-722-1691.

Mailing Address: Fort Sumter National Monument, 1214 Middle Street, Sullivans Island, SC 29482.

Telephone: 803-883-3123.

Getting There: The park is at the mouth of Charleston harbor, about halfway down the South Carolina coast. Fort Sumter is accessible only by boat. Tour boats to the fort leave from the Charleston City Marina on Lockwood Boulevard in Charleston and from Patriot's Point, a naval museum five minutes north of Charleston on Route 17. Fort Moultrie is accessible by car. To reach the fort, travel north on U.S. 17 (business) to Mt. Pleasant, then take Route 703 to Sullivans Island. Once you reach Sullivans Island, turn right onto Middle Street and proceed 1.2 miles to the fort.

‖ Historic Camden

In the mid-1730s, the colonial village established at Camden was known as Fredericksburg Township. It was re-named Camden in 1768 in honor of Charles Pratt, Lord Camden, who championed colonial rights in the British Parliament. The town is distinguished for having been the scene of two Revolutionary War battles, on August 16, 1780, and on April 25, 1781, and the site of a year-long occupation by the British under Lord Cornwallis, beginning May 1, 1780.

There are five historic houses in the historic Camden area, including the Cunningham House, the Drakeford House, and the reconstructed Kershaw-Cornwallis House, as well as a colonial powder magazine and redoubts.

There is also a craft show, the Historic Camden Exchange, where one can find unique handmade gifts, homemade jellies, and historic books.

For more information, contact Camden District Heritage Foundation, Camden Historical Commission, Box 710, Camden, SC 29020.

Telephone: 803-432-9841.

‖ Kings Mountain National Military Park

When Major Patrick Ferguson, the fiery-tempered British commander, took position at the top of Kings Mountain on October 7, 1780, he defied "God Almighty and all the rebels out of hell to overcome him." They did, and with a vengeance. Though outnumbered, the patriots moved up the rocky ridge tree by tree, encircling the British sympathizers and shooting those who did not surrender. The bold victory at Kings Mountain was a tonic to the tired patriots of the South, and gave the Continental Army fresh cause to keep fighting. Ferguson, the only Englishman to fight in the battle, is buried at the foot of the battlefield ridge.

An 18-minute film in the visitor center describes the action at Kings Mountain and a 1.5-mile trail through the battlefield contains explanatory markers and monuments. Rifles and musket balls are on display in the museum.

This 3,945-acre park in the Carolina Piedmont region has some of the most beautiful hiking and horseback trails in the region, especially in fall, when the pine and hardwood forests are dappled with color. There are 16 miles of hiking trails over easy terrain, and ten miles of horse trails. The longest trail is 4.7 miles from the visitor center to the horse stables near Lake York.

On October 7 each year, the park holds an anniversary celebration of the Battle of Kings Mountain. Check for details. There are two campgrounds in the park and others nearby.

Open: 9 a.m. to 5 p.m. daily, extended to 6 p.m. Memorial Day to Labor Day. Closed Christmas, New Year's, Thanksgiving Day.

Mailing Address: Kings Mountain National Military Park, P.O. Box 40, Kings Mountain, NC 28086. (The park is primarily in South

Carolina, but the visitor center receives mail from the nearest town, which is in North Carolina.)

Telephone: 803-936-7921.

Getting There: The park is in northwestern South Carolina near the North Carolina border. From Charlotte, NC, take I-85 south, in a southwesterly direction 30 miles. The exit to the park is marked by a green highway department sign.

‖ Ninety Six National Historic Site

This former frontier trading post and Revolutionary War stronghold played an important role in South Carolina's history.

Facilities at Ninety Six, which was added to the park system in 1976, are still being developed. The site is named for its location, 96 miles from the major Cherokee town of Keowee in the foothills of the Blue Ridge Mountains.

So far, the park consists of the underground remains of the frontier trading post and Indian fort, the colonial courthouse village, the Revolutionary War earthworks, and the post-war rural town. The visitor center has exhibits about Ninety Six, from its days as a backcountry trading post to its roles in the French and Indian War and Revolutionary War.

Pottery, buttons, clay pipes, cutlery, wine glasses, musket balls, and other artifacts from the 18th century are on display in the museum. An eight-minute videotape explains the importance of Ninety Six's unique history.

A mile-long trail leads to the reconstructed star-shaped earthworks of a Revolutionary War fort built by the British. Visitors can also walk along a remnant of the old Charlestown Road, which once led settlers from the cities of the East to the backcountry. The road was so heavily traveled by pioneers that it is sunken below ground level. Check for information about the park's special interpretive programs.

There is a 27-acre lake nearby for fishing. Fishermen need a valid state license.

Open: 8 a.m. to 5 p.m. daily. Closed Christmas and New Year's Day.

Fees: None.

Mailing Address: Ninety Six National Historic Site, P.O. Box 496, Ninety Six, SC 29666.

Telephone: 803-543-4068.

Getting There: The park is located in west central South Carolina, about 60 miles west of Columbia, near Greenwood, on Rt. 248. From Columbia, take I-26 north and then turn south onto Rt. 121. In Silverstreet, turn right at Rt. 34 and continue to Rt. 248 south.

SOUTH DAKOTA

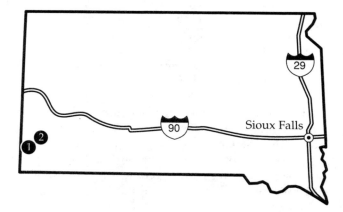

1. Jewel Cave National Monument
2. Mount Rushmore National Memorial

Ⅱ Jewel Cave National Monument

With multicolored crystal and stone formations spanning more than 79 miles of underground passages, Jewel Cave is truly a buried treasure.

Located in the Black Hills of South Dakota—so called because of the dark bark of the Ponderosa pines—Jewel Cave is the second longest cave in the country and the fourth longest in the world.

Jewel Cave was named for its spectacular jewel-like calcite crystals, called dogtooth spar, which resemble masses of interconnected prisms. The cave also has other mineral formations. Stalactites hang from the ceilings and stalagmites reach up from the floors. Tiny white formations, known as hydromagnesite balloons, grow on the walls, and coral-like formations called popcorn sparkle under the lights. The colors of these extraordinary encrustations range from black and white to brown, red, orange, yellow, green, and even lavender.

Three types of tours are available. There is the moderately strenuous Scenic Tour, the more rigorous Historic Tour, where visitors view the cave by candle lantern, and the Spelunking Tour for the truly adventurous.

The Scenic Tour, available from May through September, lasts about 1¼ hours and traverses one-half mile of cave passageways on a paved trail with handrails, taking visitors through some of the larger, electrically illuminated chambers. This tour involves some uphill walking and climbing of stairs. Scenic Tours are limited to 40 people and tickets are sold on a first-come, first served basis. Groups interested in tours should make special arrangements.

The Historic Tour enters and leaves the cave through a natural entrance in Hell Canyon and follows an unpaved trail with steep wooden steps and no electric lighting. Visitors carry candle lanterns. The tour, which lasts about 1¾ hours and covers one-half mile of cave passages, requires climbing, bending, stooping, and maneuvering through narrow spaces. Children under the age of six are not permitted on the tour. Historic tours, limited to 40 people, are conducted from late May to early September.

The Spelunking Tour is an introduction to caving for the physically fit. Sturdy, ankle-laced boots are required, and old clothing is recommended. The park provides hard hats and head lamps. This tour, which is given once daily from mid-June to mid-August, lasts about four hours and covers 3,000 feet of undeveloped passageway. Because the tour is limited to ten people a day, the park recommends advance registration. Contact the park for forms. Minimum age for this tour is 16 years.

Temperature in the caves remains 47 degrees year-round, with winds that can blow up to 30 miles an hour, so bring a sweater if you plan to go underground. People with heart trouble, respiratory ailments, or claustrophobia should not go on tours.

No one knows when Jewel Cave was discovered, but by 1900, Frank and Albert Michaud and Charles Bush laid claim to the cavern, mined it unsuccessfully, and later turned it into an equally unsuccessful tourist attraction. In 1908 President Theodore Roosevelt proclaimed it a national monument. However, it wasn't until the late 1950s that park rangers and spelunkers began to explore the cave in earnest. Exploration continues today.

Six species of bats and two types of rodents live in the cave. Mule deer, white-tailed deer, coyotes, bobcats, weasels, porcupines, marmots, and squirrels live in the rough and rocky terrain of nearby Hell and Lithograph canyons. In spring and summer, wildflowers bloom on the hillsides.

Open: 8 a.m. to 4:30 p.m. Oct. to April (Visitor Center only, no tours given). Hours are extended from mid-June to mid-Aug. Check park for precise closing times.

Fees: Scenic and Historic Tours: $3 for ages 16–61, $1 for ages 6–15, $1 for seniors with a Golden Age card. (Under 5 not admitted on Historic Tour). Spelunking Tour: $5 for ages 16 and up.

Mailing Address: Jewel Cave National Monument, Rural Route 1, Box 60AA 351, Custer, SD 57747.

Telephone: 605-673-2288

Getting There: There is no regularly scheduled public transportation to the park, which is located in southwestern South Dakota, near the Wyoming border. From Rapid City, take Rt. 16 southwest to Jewel Cave. The monument is on the left.

|| Mount Rushmore National Memorial

The faces of four great American presidents—George Washington, Thomas Jefferson, Abraham Lincoln, and Theodore Roosevelt—are immortalized in the granite of Mount Rushmore. Together, the figures of this well-known American icon symbolize the ideals on which the United States is based. Washington stands for independence, Jefferson for the democratic process, Lincoln for equality, and Roosevelt for prominence in world affairs.

Gutzon Borglum (actually John Gutzon de la Mothe Borglum), a sculptor of Danish descent, supervised the transformation of this 6,000-foot-high mountain into one of the most famous works of art in the world. The faces measure 60 feet from chin to crown; each nose is 20 feet long; the eyes are 11 feet across; the mouths are 18 feet long. If they were fully sculpted, they would stand taller than the Washington Monument in Washington, D.C.

Borglum was a colorful and controversial artist who was friendly with French sculptor Auguste Rodin. He traveled to the Black Hills of South Dakota to study the herculean task of carving presidents on the side of a mountain at the behest of South Dakota state historian Doane Robinson. Borglum picked Mount Rushmore because the rock was smooth-textured and faced the sun. He worked on this modern-day colossus from 1927 until his death in 1941. More than 360 people, laboring in 30-man crews, contributed to the construction. The tab came to $990,060.

Borglum deserves credit not only for his artistic achievement, but also for the engineering innovations that allowed him to turn mountain into monument. His technique started with the blasting of surface rock to reveal the granite below, then the precise removal of granite chunks with dynamite. Suspended over the side of the mountain in harnesses, carvers used jackhammers to flesh out the features. Workers removed the next layer by drilling holes three inches apart over the entire surface then using airhammers to bring out facial details. When the dust had settled, more than 450,000 tons of rock had been removed from the side of the mountain. Most of it lies in the heap of boulders below.

Mount Rushmore is one of the country's best-known memorials. Visitation is heavy, especially during the summer months, when

The faces of four American presidents—Washington, Jefferson, Lincoln, and Theodore Roosevelt—were carved to a scale of men 465-feet tall on Mount Rushmore.—*NPS photograph*

15,000 to 25,000 tourists a day troop through the park. The visitor center has a 15-minute audio-visual presentation that covers the history of the site. The main view terrace has a seven-minute audio presentation. A museum in the center displays tools and techniques used in construction. The sculptor's studio is open daily from mid-May to mid-September. It houses tools and models of the construction. From mid-May to mid-September, the National Park Service holds a free evening program at the amphitheater, with an introduction by a ranger and a movie, followed by the Star Spangled Banner and lighting of the sculpture.

The park has a great variety of wildlife, including mule deer and white-tailed deer, coyotes and bobcats, porcupines, and smaller mammals. A family of Rocky Mountain goats lives in the area and goats are occasionally seen scampering over the memorial.

There are no picnic facilities, but a concession sells gifts and operates a dining room. The park celebrates July 4 each year with afternoon concerts and speeches, but fireworks are prohibited because the area is prone to fires. For information about nearby campgrounds, contact the U.S. Forest Service, Black Hills National Forest, P.O. Box 792, Custer, SD 57730. Telephone: 605-673-2250.

Open: 8 a.m. to 10 p.m.from mid-May to mid-Sept., with hours reduced to 8 a.m. to 5 p.m. from Sept. to May.

Fees: None.

Mailing Address: Mount Rushmore National Memorial, P.O. Box 268, Keystone, SD 57751.

Telephone: 605-574-2523.

Getting There: The memorial is 25 miles southwest of Rapid City and three miles from Keystone, SD, on Rt. 244. Transcontinental buses and major airlines serve Rapid City.

TENNESSEE

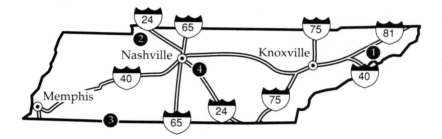

1. Andrew Johnson National Historic Site
2. Fort Donelson National Battlefield
3. Shiloh National Military Park
4. Stones River National Battlefield

|| Andrew Johnson National Historic Site

Andrew Johnson, the tailor who went on to become one of the most controversial presidents of the United States, lived in the quiet eastern Tennessee town of Greeneville. His two Greeneville residences, his tailor shop, and the grave where he was buried in 1875 are preserved at the Andrew Johnson National Historic Site.

Despite his early illiteracy, Johnson was an ambitious man who learned politics in the local and state government and worked his way up to U.S. Representative and Abraham Lincoln's vice president. After the Lincoln assassination in the spring of 1865, Johnson became president and the delicate task of reconstruction after the Civil War fell to him.

It was a difficult task, indeed. Try as he might, Johnson could not stitch the nation back together. Relations were strained between radical members of Congress, bent on treating the South as harshly as if it were conquered territory, and Johnson, who tried to carry out Lincoln's reconstruction plan "with malice towards none."

Matters came to a head when Johnson tried to fire his Secretary of War Edwin Stanton, a radical. This action was a violation of the Tenure of Office Act, which gave the legislature alone the power to approve and dismiss cabinet level officials. Infuriated by what members saw as a move to usurp congressional power, the House in 1868 drew up articles of impeachment, the formal accusation of presidential wrongdoing. But the case, tried in the Senate, was one vote shy of support by three-quarters of the majority, and impeachment proceedings stopped. The deciding vote was cast by Senator Edmund Ross of Kansas, who was never again elected to public office.

Johnson remained in office; Stanton resigned and was replaced by General John Scholfield. A few years later, Congress repealed the Tenure of Office Act, giving presidents free rein to hire and dismiss cabinet members. Despite the controversy surrounding his administration, Johnson maintained his public popularity and was re-elected to the Senate in 1875.

The little tailor shop where it all began is enclosed in the visitor center in downtown Greeneville, along with Johnson's tools and a wed-

The Andrew Johnson National Historic Site includes two homes and the tailor shop of the 17th president.—*NPS photograph*

ding coat he made. In this shop, Johnson's wife read to him while he worked. The brick house down the street, where he lived from 1851 to 1875, is furnished with many original and period pieces and is open to the public. Johnson's grave is located in the cemetery nearby.

Open: 9 a.m. to 5 p.m. daily. Closed Christmas Day.

Fees: $1 per person, ages 18–62 for entrance to the Johnson Homestead. The visitor center and gravesite are free.

Mailing Address: Andrew Johnson National Historic Site, Depot Street, P.O. Box 1088, Greeneville, TN 37744.

Telephone: 615-638-3551.

Getting There: The site is located in Greeneville in eastern Tennessee, 70 miles northeast of Knoxville and 26 miles southwest of Johnson City. From Knoxville, take I-81 north to Route 11 east to Greeneville, then follow Main Street to Depot Street. The visitor center and parking lot are located at the intersection of Depot St. and College St; the homestead is between Summer St. and McKee St. on Main Street.

Ⅱ Fort Donelson National Battlefield

Fort Donelson is forever remembered as the place where Ulysses S. Grant earned his moniker "Unconditional Surrender." Grant's victory on February 16, 1862, over Confederate troops at Fort Donelson was the first major Union victory in the Civil War. When Confederate Brigadier General Simon Buckner asked for terms, Grant replied with his now-famous phrase: "No terms except unconditional and immediate surrender can be accepted." Grant eventually assumed command of the Union army and under his leadership the North won the Civil War.

Fort Donelson is a 15-acre earthwork fort built by Confederate soldiers and slaves to guard the Cumberland River batteries from attack. Although the South managed to beat off an attack by Union gunboats on February 14, Grant and his troops surrounded the stronghold the next day and forced the Confederates to surrender.

The 543-acre park contains the site of the river battle, Fort Donelson's original earthen walls, several reconstructed log huts that served as winter quarters for the Confederate soldiers, and the Dover Hotel, where Buckner surrendered, unconditionally. The hotel, restored to look like a river tavern, has a short film on the surrender. The visitor center also has a presentation on the park's history.

During the summer, people dressed in period costume carry on typical activities of Civil War soldiers including musket firings. A self-guided auto tour leads through three miles of hilly park grounds. There is also a seven-mile Boy Scout Hike Trail, which is available to the public. Watch out for poisonous snakes; copperheads, rattlesnakes, and cottonmouths have been found in the park along with ticks. The river contains bass and catfish; a state license is required. Waterskiing and pleasure boating are popular activities and a boat ramp is available within a mile of the park.

Open: Buildings: 8 a.m. to 4:30 p.m. daily, extended until 5 p.m. in summer. The grounds are open until dark. Closed Christmas.

Fees: None.

Mailing Address: Fort Donelson National Battlefield, P.O. Box F, Dover, TN 37058.

Telephone: 615-232-5348.

Getting There: The park is in north central Tennessee along the

Cumberland River, one mile west of Dover and three miles east of Land Between the Lakes on Rt. 79. From Clarksville, take Rt. 79 west 35 miles to the fort, which is on the right side of the road.

‖ Shiloh National Military Park

Shiloh is a biblical word meaning "place of peace." It is also the name of the bloody Civil War battle fought along the Tennessee River on April 6 and 7, 1862. In this battle, Union forces under General Ulysses Grant held off Confederate troops commanded by General Albert Sidney Johnston. As a result, the rebels were forced to withdraw beyond the Tennessee border to Corinth, Mississippi.

Confederate soldiers surprised the Union Army during breakfast, creating an early advantage, and Rebel forces formed a three-mile-long front that pushed Union troops back to the Tennessee River. The tide turned for the Yankees during fighting at a place known as the "Hornet's Nest," northeast of Shiloh Church. Here, Northern soldiers held off 11 attacks. Johnston was mortally wounded east of Peach Orchard. The next morning, Grant's army, replenished with extra troops that arrived in the night, counterattacked and regained the field.

The fighting was intense. Bullets ripped through the peach blossoms in the orchards on the battlegrounds, and wounded and dead soldiers littered the fields. The small pond where soldiers would drink and bathe their wounds was called "Bloody Pond" for its blood-stained waters. Federal casualties totaled 13,000; the Confederates lost 10,700 men. Five times as many men died here as in the First Battle of Bull Run in Virginia, a hint of the many deaths the Civil War would bring.

Although many men died at Shiloh, many more were spared due to a centralized tent field hospital that was developed here. The makeshift hospital was set up by Union troops on the southeastern edge of the battlefield.

A tour road leads by the hospital site, by Bloody Pond, by the site of Shiloh Church—the one-room log church from which the battle takes its name—and by the Manse George cabin, the only remaining Civil War structure in the park. This rough log cabin was bought by the George family to replace a similar one that was destroyed during the battle.

In addition to the Civil War related sites, there are 35 prehistoric Indian mounds in the park, which were used as observation points during the battle and as burial grounds for Union solders. The dome-shaped mounds were probably Indian burial mounds, and the flat-topped mounds probably supported ceremonial buildings.

The visitor center has a 23-minute movie describing the battle and a museum with artifacts from the fighting. Shiloh National Cemetery has 3,761 interments, 2,370 of them unidentified.

Open: Visitor Center: 8 a.m. to 5 p.m., Labor Day to Memorial Day, extended to 6 p.m. in summer. Closed Christmas Day.

Fees: $1 ages 16–62.

Mailing Address: Shiloh National Military Park, Shiloh, TN 38376.

Telephone: 901-689-5275.

Getting There: The park is located along the Tennessee River, just north of the Mississippi border, along Rt. 22. From Memphis, take Rt. 57 east, turning left (north) on Rt. 22 into the park.

▌Stones River National Battlefield

The first Civil War clash at Stones River near Murfreesboro was one of song rather than gunfire. The Confederates crooned "Dixie" and "Bonnie Blue Flag " in the darkness, while Union troops countered with "Yankee Doodle" and "Hail Columbia." The next day, however, it was the clash of gunfire as bullets and artillery shells screeched through the corn and cotton fields. By the time the battle was over on January 2, 1863, the Confederates had lost 10,000 of their 38,000 men and had to retreat southward. The Union army, which lost 13,000 of 43,000 troops, was too weak to give chase.

Both Union General William Rosecrans and Confederate General Braxton Bragg planned attacks, but Bragg got the upper hand by attacking at dawn on December 31, 1862. By 10 a.m., the Union front (along McFadden Lane) had collapsed back to the Nashville Turnpike, and the Confederates took the field, skirmishing for the rest of the day. Fighting continued on the second day of the new year, when Union soldiers moved to high ground on the other side of the river. Seeing an opening, the Rebels rushed in, but they were repulsed by heavy fire from Union artillery. In less than an hour, 1,800 Confederates died at this spot.

Bragg's men were pushed back by Union counterattacks and his army was too weakened to withstand fire from Northern troops encamped on the other side of Stones River. Bragg had to retreat to Tullahoma, 40 miles away. Rosecrans knew his army was too devastated to give chase. By rousting the Confederates from Stones River, the Union army gained access to central Tennessee, the state's breadbasket of fertile farmland. It was a major blow to the South.

A self-guided tour leads by the major sites at the Stones River battlefield, including batteries, the defense lines of both armies, and the national cemetery, which has the graves of 6,100 Union soldiers. (The Confederates were buried in Evergreen Cemetery, at Greenland Drive and Highland Avenue in Murfreesboro.) A five-mile hiking trail circles the park.

The visitor center has an 18-minute film about the battle, and a short film on Civil War cannon. Four original cannon tubes and a Civil War cannon carriage with the original wood are on display. One of the most interesting monuments in the park is the Hazen Brigade Monument, the oldest Civil War memorial in the country. The large, squarish stone structure, built by Indiana troops in 1863, can be found on the field a mile from the visitor center.

During summer weekends, the park has a living history program with people in period costume demonstrating Civil War lifestyles and conducting historical tours. On July 4 each year, the park hosts a Civil War encampment with 75 to 100 soldiers and hourly cannon firings.

Open: 8 a.m. to 5 p.m. daily. Closed Christmas and New Year's Day.

Fees: None.

Mailing Address: Stones River National Battlefield, 3501 Old Nashville Highway, Murfreesboro, TN 37129.

Telephone: 615-893-9501.

Getting There: The park is located in central Tennessee, near Murfreesboro, 27 miles southeast of Nashville on Rt. 41/70 south.

TEXAS

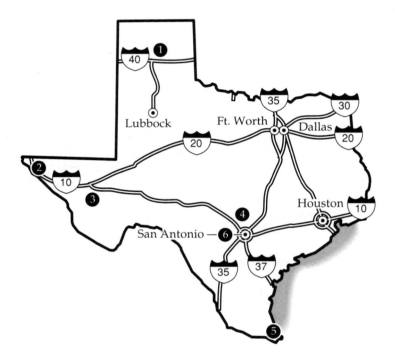

1. Alibates Flint Quarries National Monument
2. Chamizal National Memorial
3. Fort Davis National Historic Site
4. Lyndon B. Johnson National Historical Park
5. Palo Alto Battlefield National Historic Site
6. San Antonio Missions National Historical Park

|| Alibates Flint Quarries National Monument

Alibates flint is so hard and beautiful that it has been prized by Plains Indians for the past 12,000 years. Knives, arrowheads, spear points, awls, drills, and scrapers made of the flint were widely traded. Archeologists acquainted with the Alibates flint have found it in New Mexico, Texas, Oklahoma, Kansas, Colorado, Arizona, Arkansas, and Louisiana. Even today this stone, with its veins and splotches, rainbow stripes and crystalline filigree, is in demand by lapidarists. The park, just north of Amarillo, Texas, preserves more than 250 quarry pits and the rubble of 12 centuries of use.

The quarries themselves, located in the cap rock of the Canadian River breaks, look undistinguished. They are little more than shallow depressions in the ground, varying in width from four to eight feet wide and surrounded by rubble. Indians fashioned this flint into arrowheads and spear points by fracturing off chips using deer antler as tools.

Facilities here are rudimentary and the quarries are in their natural undeveloped state. Entry to the pits to is by guided tour only, with groups leaving daily in summer, and by reservation during the rest of the year. The half-mile trail to the quarries, which have been in use for the 12,000 years, is full of sharp pieces of stone. If time allows, rangers may demonstrate traditional flint chipping techniques.

Alibates also has the ruins of several dwellings built by the Plains Village Indians who lived here from 1100 to 1500. These consist of mostly single unit dwellings averaging 12 by 15 feet in size. In one location within the monument, the area has been used for so long that the ruins have contiguous walls, giving the appearance of a multi-room dwelling. These ruins, while interesting, are not as spectacular as other pueblos in the Southwest. A bluff near the ruins has Indian petroglyphs, drawings of turtles, bison, and human footprints pecked into the rock.

Alibates flint has been traded to distant areas and items brought from other areas are often found in the ruins. Among the most common imports are turquoise, obsidian, painted pottery from New Mexico, sea shells from the Gulf of Mexico and the Gulf of California, and pipestone from Minnesota.

Flint mining is prohibited at Alibates and discouraged by the local landowners, but visitors can take a free flint souvenir from the park headquarters. The park is covered with short prairie grasses. Wildlife includes both mule and white-tailed deer, coyotes, badgers, porcupines, skunks, raccoons, cottontail and jack rabbits, and a variety of birds and reptiles. One or two rattlesnakes are seen each year.

It is suggested that visitors wear sturdy shoes and long pants and carry water. The trail is not strenuous, but it is steep in places and visitors with medical problems should inform the guide before the tour begins.

Open: Tours run at 10 a.m. and 2 p.m. daily, from Memorial Day to Labor Day, and by appointment during the rest of the year. The site is open daily, weather permitting.

Fees: None.

Mailing Address: Alibates Flint Quarries National Monument, c/o Lake Meredith Recreation Area, P.O. Box 1438, Fitch, TX 79036.

Telephone: 806-857-3151.

Getting There: The site is located near Lake Meredith in the Texas Panhandle. From Amarillo, take Route 136 north, following white and brown park signs to the entrance.

‖ Chamizal National Memorial

This cultural arts park in downtown El Paso commemorates the peaceful and ingenious settlement of a thorny border dispute between the United States and Mexico. The territory in question was a detached part of Mexico's Chamizal plain that extended into U.S. territory when the Rio Grande changed its path between El Paso and Ciudad Juárez a century ago. The solution was to build a permanent, concrete-lined channel for the meandering river. The Treaty of Chamizal formalizing the solution was signed by Presidents John F. Kennedy and Alfonso López Mateos in 1962. It marked the final chapter in the 113-year effort to draw a boundary between the United States and Mexico.

Surveys started in 1851, when Major William Hemsley Emory and Major José Salazar y Larrequi set out to define the U.S.-Mexican border from the Pacific Ocean to the Gulf of Mexico. The expedition was ambitious, difficult, and dangerous. For six years cartographers

The Chamizal National Memorial celebrates Mexican and American cultures through the performing arts.—*J. Pfeffer, NPS photograph*

carried sensitive equipment over rough terrain and through hostile Indian country. The international border they mapped was 1,900 miles long, most of it meandering river frontier that created a problem only diplomacy and 20th-century technology would solve.

In celebration of the international cooperation represented by the Chamizal treaty, Congress set aside a portion of the land acquired from Mexico for the Chamizal Memorial, a performing arts park where festivals, shows, exhibitions, and workshops highlight the artistic achievements of the two countries.

A film in English and Spanish, "This Most Singular Country," tells the story of the boundary surveys. Paintings, photographs, crafts, and sculpture by Mexican and American artists in the park's art gallery promote friendship between the neighboring countries. Music, drama, and dance preformances are held regularly in the park's handsome 500-seat auditorium and in the outdoor amphitheater.

The park holds several special festivals, including a Golden Age of Spanish Drama Festival, with competitions of performing arts troops from the United States and Latin American countries. During the first week of July, the park holds its Fiesta of the Arts, with special performances, and a July 4th fireworks display. The annual Border Folk

Festival, a three day extravaganza of folk music, dance, and crafts, presents traditional Mexican, Native American, and regional American folk art. Check for dates. There are also performances and art exhibitions at the park throughout the year.

Mexico has established a companion park, with 700 acres of landscaped grounds and formal gardens, directly across the Rio Grande.

Open: 8 a.m. to 5 p.m. daily, and in the evenings for performances.
Fees: None, but there may be charges for some performances.
Mailing Address: Chamizal National Memorial, 700 E. san Antonio, Suite D-301, El Paso, TX 79901.
Telephone: 915-534-6277.
Getting There: The park is in El Paso, Texas, immediately adjacent to the international boundary, with entrances on San Marcial Street and Delta Drive.

‖ Fort Davis National Historic Site

The stone and adobe ruins of Fort Davis conjure all the romance and excitement of the western frontier, when Indians swooped down from the passes and canyons of the Davis Mountains to raid mail trains, stagecoaches, and travelers on the El Paso Road. From 1854 to 1891, Fort Davis was one of the most important military installations in western Texas. It was known as a center for campaigns against hostile Apache and Comanche Indians, a base from which the army tested camels in the western deserts, and one of the first posts in the West where black soldiers were stationed.

Fort Davis, named for Secretary of War Jefferson Davis (who later became president of the Confederacy), was originally a collection of pine-slab structures that housed the 8th Infantry. Camels were introduced between 1857 and 1860, and while experiments with camel transport proved successful, the project was abandoned during the Civil War. At its height in the 1880s, the fort had 50 buildings and 12 army companies, including the stalwart black units of the 9th and 10th Cavalry and the 24th and 25th Infantry. These soldiers were so highly regarded by the Indians that they were called the "Buffalo Soldiers." But controversy hit in 1881 when Lieutenant Henry Ossian Flipper, the first black graduate of West Point and the fort's Acting

Commissary of Subsistence, was accused of embezzling government funds and court-martialed. Flipper, who was acquitted but dismissed from the army for "unbecoming conduct," was exonerated in 1976.

The 460-acre park preserves the commanding officer's quarters, 14 officers' quarters, a small kitchen, a furnished commissary, and the enlisted men's barracks. The visitor center museum contains military mementos. Visitors can walk through the original hospital, which has plaques describing the rooms. The foundations of other buildings, including barracks, stables, and storehouses, are still visible. In summer the fort has an extensive living history program with interpreters in period costume. One hour before closing each day, a flag-raising ceremony is executed according to the traditions of the 9th and 10th Cavalry.

Spectacular peaks, rolling pastures, unusual rock formations, and impressive canyons make the surrounding mountain countryside an excellent side trip. Plants range from yucca and agave to range grass, oak, and pine trees. On the paved 74-mile scenic loop of the Davis Mountain Trail Ride there are antelope, deer, and other wild game.

At the summit of Mount Locke, 16 miles from the fort along Route 118, is the McDonald Observatory, one of the largest observatory complexes in the world. Visitors can tour the dome, which has a computer-operated, 107-inch telescope, between 8 a.m. and 5 p.m. weekdays and from 1 p.m. to 5 p.m. on weekends. The telescope is open for public viewing on the last Wednesday of each month. Advance written permission is necessary. For more information, send a self-addressed, stamped envelope to: McDonald Observatory, P.O. Box 1334, Fort Davis, TX 79734.

Davis Mountains State Park, also on Route 118, has camping facilities, hiking trails, and overnight accommodations at a concession called Indian Lodge. Contact: Superintendent, Davis Mountains State Park, Box 786, Fort Davis, TX 79734.

Open: 8 a.m. to 5 p.m. daily, from Labor Day to Memorial Day, extended to 6 p.m. in summer. Closed Christmas and New Year's Day.

Fees: $3 per car, or $1 per person.

Mailing Address: Fort Davis National Historic Site, P.O. Box 1456, Fort Davis, TX 79734.

Telephone: 915-426-3224.

Getting There: From El Paso take I-10 east, turning south onto Route 118 at Kent into Fort Davis.

|| Lyndon B. Johnson National Historical Park

This historic park in and near Johnson City, Texas, interprets the life of Lyndon Baines Johnson, 36th president of the United States. This is where the country boy in overalls who became a world leader spent his childhood, and where the wealthy liberal politician retired to his sprawling ranch house after 40 years of public service. The site in the Texas hill country represents all phases of Johnson's life, from his birth to his burial on the banks of the Pedernales River.

The son of a state legislator, Johnson was strongly influenced by his family's tradition of civil service and liberalism. He was elected to the Congress in 1937, where he served until he became vice president to John F. Kennedy. He became chief executive after the Kennedy assassination in November 1963, and was elected by a landslide to a full term in 1964. As president, Johnson expanded the Democratic social welfare programs of what he termed the "Great Society," expanded the space program, escalated American troop involvement in Vietnam, and pushed the Civil Rights Act of 1964 through Congress, guaranteeing minorities the right to equal opportunities in housing and employment.

In 1951 Johnson bought 2,000 acres of land 14 miles west of Johnson City. He remodeled and added to the eight-bedroom ranch house, with outbuildings and an airstrip, that became known as the "Texas White House." The ranch produced Hereford cattle, but it was more widely known as the retreat where President Johnson worked as president, vacationed, and received foreign dignitaries.

There are two sections to the park: the Johnson Settlement and Boyhood Home in Johnson City, and the LBJ Ranch 14 miles outside the town. The Johnson City visitor center has a slide show, family photographs, and exhibits about Johnson's life. Across the street is the original five-room Boyhood Home, a modest turn-of-the-century house furnished in period pieces. Here young Lyndon learned his politics as he listened to his father's legislative cronies debate policy.

A walking tour leads from the Boyhood Home to the nearby Johnson Settlement, where the family lived from 1865 to 1872. The original two-room log cabin belonged to Sam Ealy Johnson Sr., the president's grandfather. Like many people who lived in this part of Texas, the Johnsons were open range cattle farmers who took their herds to the railheads in Abilene, Kansas. A few longhorns at the settlement recall the early days of Texas cattle ranching. In summer, costumed interpreters demonstrate domestic ranch arts while cowboys in Stetson hats and leather chaps cook range-style from an authentic chuck wagon.

The LBJ Ranch on Route 290 west is open to tours only. There is no access to the main ranch house, where Mrs. Johnson still lives, but bus tours go by the front of the ranch every day except Christmas. The Johnson Family cemetery, where the president is buried, and the reconstructed LBJ Birth House, furnished with period pieces, are open to visitors.

Free tours leave from the visitor center at the state park directly across from the ranch. The state park is a great place to spend the rest of the day. It offers a swimming pool, picnic areas, tennis courts, a baseball field, hiking trails, and the historically re-created Sauer-Beckmann farm, which interprets the life of a turn-of-the-century German immigrant farm.

Open: 9 a.m. to 5 p.m. daily. Tours run all day. Closed Christmas and New Year's Day.

Fees: None.

Mailing Address: Lyndon B. Johnson National Historical Park, P.O. Box 329, Johnson City, TX 78636.

Telephone: 512-868-7128.

Getting There: From Austin take Route 290 west to Johnson City. The visitor center is at G Street and Ninth Street. To get to the LBJ Ranch, take Route 290 (Main Street) west 14 miles to the Lyndon B. Johnson State and National Historical Park.

‖ Palo Alto Battlefield National Historic Site

In the flat range land and chaparral of Palo Alto, the first major battle of the Mexican War of 1846 was fought. The victory by United States forces under General Zachary Taylor opened the way to the invasion of Mexico. The Treaty of Guadalupe-Hidalgo two years later extended the country's territory from the Gulf of Mexico to the Pacific coast. During the battle, Taylor gained advantage over his opponent General Mariano Arista at Palo Alto by using newly developed offensive artillery and maneuvers.

Other innovations tested at the Battle of Palo Alto include Samuel Colt's revolver, the use of ether as an anesthetic, combat photography, and the telegraph for military communications. Both Taylor and Arista went on to become president of their respective countries.

The site, which is currently fenced and under private ownership, is unavailable for visitor use. State and local government historic markers are at the intersection of Paredes Line Road and Route 511. The boundary of this site is not yet established and planning for visitor use and development has not been initiated. Facilities will not be developed for several years.

For further information, contact: Southwest Region, National Park Service, P.O. Box 728, Santa Fe, New Mexico 87504-0728.

‖ San Antonio Missions National Historical Park

The days of the 18th-century Spanish missions, when robed Franciscan "padres" rode up from Mexico to Christianize the Indians and anchor Spain's claim to North America, are interpreted at San Antonio Missions National Historical Park. This recently established addition to the Park Service preserves the sites of four missions along a seven-mile stretch of the San Antonio River. Each mission was a self-sufficient community, with churches, living quarters, workshops, fortifications, and farmlands.

The park has more than 40 original and reconstructed structures, most of them open to the public, making it one of the richest caches of Spanish colonial architecture and culture in the United States. Mission San José, established in 1724, is the largest and most heavily restored of the sites with a strikingly beautiful church adorned with an ornately sculpted facade and a "rose" window, named possibly for the sculptures that once adorned it. The site, which interprets missions as social and defense centers, preserves two corner bastions and tur-

Four Spanish frontier missions are preserved at San Antonio Missions National Historical Park.—*Fred E. Mang, Jr., NPS photograph*

rets from the fortification and has several re-created Indian quarters appointed with typical furniture of the time and displays of original pottery, housewares, and farming implements.

Mission Concepción, which dates from 1731, develops the concept of the mission as a religious center through exhibits, the church, priests' residences, and workshops. Mission San Juan, built in 1731, interprets the mission as an economic center for farming, trading, and ranching. This mission has two churches (one of them ruined), priests' quarters, a former school house, and a nature area along the San Antonio River. The Mission Espada has an original irrigation dam and aqueduct, the only remaining Spanish colonial stone aqueduct in the United States.

Another mission in the city, though not a part of the park, is the Mission San Antonio de Valero, popularly remembered as the Alamo. Here Davey Crockett, Jim Bowie, William Travis, and other Texas patriots were besieged, and finally overwhelmed, by the Spanish in 1836. Six weeks later, Sam Houston used the cry "Remember the Alamo!" to rally his forces to victory over General Santa Anna at San Jacinto. The Alamo is on Alamo Plaza along the river and is open from 9 a.m. to 5:30 p.m., Monday through Saturday, and 10 a.m. to 5:30 p.m. on Sunday. Telephone: 512-225-1391.

The missions host frequent festivals with lots of music, food, and color. Many of these are sponsored by the local churches rather than the Park Service. Contact the site for details. Religious festivities at the Missions may include Christmas activities, with special Spanish feasts, masses, cantatas, and las Posados, a re-creation of the journey Mary and Joseph took looking for a place to stay. Near Easter there may be traditional Living Stations of the Cross and Good Friday services. Also, local schools may hold cultural arts festivals with music, folk dancing, and crafts.

The first week in August is the annual Semana de las Missiones, the Week of the Missions, with lectures, demonstrations of mission life, and traditional performance arts. All four missions hold special parish festivals, with food booths, entertainment, folk and Indian dances, and crafts. Dates vary from site to site.

Open: 9 a.m. to 6 p.m. central daylight time and 8 a.m. to 5 p.m. central standard time. Closed Christmas and New Year's Day.

Fees: None, but donations accepted.

Mailing Address: San Antonio Missions National Historical Park, 2202 Roosevelt Avenue, San Antonio, TX 78210.

Telephone: 512-229-5701.

Getting There: The San Jose Mission is on Roosevelt Avenue in San Antonio two miles north of Southeast Military Drive. Get directions to other sites from here. The Alamo is at Alamo Plaza in downtown San Antonio.

UTAH

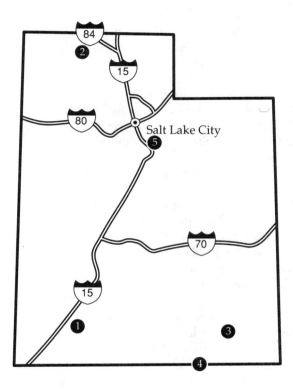

1. Cedar Breaks National Monument
2. Golden Spike National Historic Site
3. Natural Bridges National Monument
4. Rainbow Bridge National Monument
5. Timpanogos Cave National Monument

‖ Cedar Breaks National Monument

Cedar Breaks, with its green forests, wildflower meadows, and huge natural pink and purple limestone amphitheater, is a park with spectacular multi-colored scenery. A five-mile road along the rim of the monument offers views of the fantastic limestone formations in the "breaks"—the natural basin gouged out of the earth by water, wind, and frost. It takes little imagination to turn the outcroppings of this 2,500-foot-deep, 3-mile-wide canyon into the turrets and columns and crenelations of a surreal castle.

A counterpoint to these grotesque outcroppings are the surrounding Alpine forests that stand 10,000 feet above sea level. Fir and aspen trees attract a variety of birds and wildlife, from marmots and porcupines to the big-eared mule deer. In summer, fuchsia, purple, blue, and yellow wildflowers carpet the meadows.

The winters at Cedar Breaks are no less breathtaking than the summers. Starting as early as September, the entire area is covered with a blanket of pristine snow eight to ten feet deep. Facilities are closed for the winter, but visitors are welcome to use the park for cross-country skiing and other snow activities.

Clinging to the windswept ridges of Cedar Breaks are the bristlecone pines, the oldest living things on earth, some more than 1,600 years old. These gnarled and stunted trees, which rarely grow more than 20 feet in height, flourish in extremely harsh conditions. They are found only in Utah, Colorado, New Mexico, Arizona, California, and Nevada. The secret to the survival of the bristlecone pine is its evolved ability to limit the growth of tissue, which allows the tree to remain alive when nutrients are scarce.

No developed trails lead into the amphitheater, which covers 75 percent of the 6,154-acre monument. Along the rim are two trails, the two-mile Wasatch Ramparts trail in the south and the Alpine Pond trail, a two-mile self-guided nature tour. At such high elevations, these hikes are fairly strenuous and people with heart problems should be cautious.

The park has a campground with 30 sites, open from mid-June to mid-September, depending on the weather. There is a 14-day limit on stays and a small fee. There is no backcountry camping at Cedar

Breaks. From about June 20 through Labor Day, the park offers an evening program on the area and its offerings.

All roads into the monument are closed from November to May, depending on snow and weather conditions.

Open: Visitor Center: 8 a.m. to 6 p.m. in summer. Closed at 5 p.m. after Labor Day.

Fees: None.

Mailing Address: Cedar Breaks National Monument, P.O. Box 749, Cedar City, Utah 84720.

Telephone: 801-586-9451.

Getting There: The monument is located in the middle of Dixie National Forest in southwestern Utah. Approach the monument via Rt. 14 from I-15 at Cedar City or from Rt. 89 at Long Valley Junction. Another way is from Parowan via Rt. 143 or from Panguitch on a paved country road.

‖ Golden Spike National Historic Site

Golden Spike National Historic Site commemorates the completion of the transcontinental railroad across the United States. Located near Promontory, Utah, where the Union Pacific and Central Pacific railway lines were joined, the park contains 15.5 miles of original railroad grades. Here on May 10, 1869, railroad company representatives drove spikes of gold and silver into the ground, completing the task they started in 1863.

Using immigrant labor, mostly Irish and Chinese, the Union Pacific built westward from Omaha, while the Central Pacific worked eastward from Sacramento. This race of continental proportions culminated in a backbreaking competition between the two camps as they moved towards each other. The site contains the last four miles of a ten-mile stretch of rails that was completed in one day, an unheard of record at the time.

The Golden Spike site features full-scale, working replicas of the "Jupiter" and the "119"—the steam engines that met when the 1,800 miles of track were finally joined. A self-guided auto tour leads along the original railroad grade.

The first transcontinental railroad was completed here in 1869 with the meeting of the Central Pacific and the Union Pacific lines.—*Cecil W. Stroughton, NPS photograph*

A museum in the visitor center has replicas of the famous golden and silver spikes, tools, railroad equipment, a segment of original rail, and photographs documenting the progress of this immense undertaking. There are three films depicting various aspects of the construction of the transcontinental railroad and talks by park rangers on a variety of related topics.

Twice each summer the park holds special events associated with the building of the transcontinental railroad. On May 10, there is a re-enactment of the joining of the two railways. At noon, a troop of performers in period costume re-enact the speeches and testimonials from that famous day, and the audience is encouraged to toss hats and cheer. From a telegraph table set up at the site, telegraphers retype "Dot Dot Dot Done," the message that told the world about the project's completion. On the second Saturday in August, the site holds the annual Railroader's Festival with spike driving contests, hand-car races, and other railroad contests. This is a train lover's delight, a chance to swap stories and buy antique train pieces, model train sets, and other railroad memorabilia. There are two historic re-enactments during the day.

Open: Visitor Center: 8 a.m. to 4:30 p.m., extended to 6 p.m. from Memorial Day through Labor Day. Closed Thanksgiving, Christmas, and New Year's Day. The park is always open.

Fees: $1 per person, up to $3 per car.

Mailing Address: Golden Spike National Historic Site, P.O. Box W, Brigham City, UT 84302.

Telephone: 801-471-2209.

Getting There: The site is 32 miles west of Brigham City. From Salt Lake City, drive north along I-15, turn left and travel west along Rt. 83 to Promontory Junction, turn left and go two miles to the next junction, then turn right and go five miles to the park entrance.

| Natural Bridges National Monument

Three enormous stone bridges, carved by erosion out of the canyons of southeastern Utah, are the largest collection of natural bridges in the world. The yellow sandstone bridges illustrate different phases of development. Kachina bridge, a chunky, 93-foot-thick, 210-foot-high formation in the western corner of the park, is the youngest of the bridges. It is named for the prehistoric pictographs resembling masked Hopi Indian dancers, or kachinas, that decorate one of the abutments. Floodwaters are still enlarging the opening beneath the arch's 204-foot span.

The graceful Sipapu bridge, proportioned as evenly as a highway overpass, is considered a mature bridge. That is, groundwaters no longer shape the rocks below the span. This bridge is named for the sipapu—the passageway to the underworld in Hopi mythology—and stands 220 feet high with a span of 268 feet.

Owachomo bridge, the oldest of the three, resembles two banks connected by a felled tree. Owachomo is also the smallest of the bridges. It stands only 106 feet high, has a span of 180 feet, and is nine fragile feet thick across the arch. This formation may stand for centuries more, or an unseen crack could cause it to tumble down at any moment.

For a closer look at these extraordinary formations, take the eight-mile auto road or hike along the bed of the river that once scoured away the canyon's soft sandstone. Rivers create natural bridges by boring through soft rock below the bends they have created, whereas natural arches are formed by the slow erosion of wind and frost.

Scattered throughout the canyon are cliff dwellings, granaries, and ruins of the Anasazi Indians who lived in the region 650 to 2,000 years ago. For some mysterious reason, the Indians abandoned the area in 1300. The arid climate has helped to preserve their villages.

Interconnecting trails lead to the three bridges. It takes about six hours of hiking to make a complete circuit. Most visitors go only to one or two of the bridges and spend about two hours in the park. Because of the fragile nature of the landscape, backcountry camping is prohibited. The trails are hot, especially in summer, so bring plenty of water and protective clothing.

Wildlife includes deer, coyotes, bobcats, foxes, rabbits, and 160 species of birds, including prairie falcon, hawks, and flocks of jays, which swarm overhead in a noisy blue cloud.

There is a primitive, 13-site campground in the park. Water is available at the visitor center. However, there are no services, such as gasoline, food, or lodging in the park. The nearest source of supplies is in Fry Canyon, which has limited lodging, 26 miles west on U-95. Other overnight accommodations can be found in Blanding and Mexican Hat, both approximately 42 miles away.

Open: The park is always open. Visitor Center: 8 a.m. to 4:30 p.m. year-round. The visitor center is closed Thanksgiving, Christmas, and New Year's Day.

Fees: $3 per vehicle.

Mailing Address: Natural Bridges National Monument, Box 1, Lake Powell, Utah 84533.

Telephone: 801-259-7164.

Getting There: To arrive from Moab, U.S. 191 south, turn right on State Highway 95 west. The monument is on the right, near the junction of Utah 95 and Utah 275.

‖ Rainbow Bridge National Monument

This spectacular salmon-pink arch, standing 290 feet high and 278 feet long, is the largest natural bridge on earth and one of the seven natural wonders of the world. Nature carved Rainbow Bridge into the arid canyon lands of southeastern Utah by the waters of Bridge Creek. The bridge is as tall as the U.S. Capitol in Washington, D.C., and wide enough for a major highway, although no highways lead to this majestic monument.

The most popular way to visit Rainbow Bridge is by boat from Lake Powell. More intrepid visitors can hike a treacherous 13-mile trail through sheer-faced, sandstone canyons, or trek the canyon lands on horseback. Whatever the means, the trip is worth it.

In the afternoon sun, the pink sandstone, streaked red and brown by hematite deposits and underlain by purple and orange layers, gives the effect of a dazzling rainbow. (Unlike arches, which are created by wind erosion, natural bridges are formed when rivers undercut their own meandering paths by tunneling through the soft rock below the bed.)

The climate at Rainbow Bridge is extreme: Temperatures regularly reach 100 degrees on summer days and around 40 degrees in winter. You can visit the monument year-round. However, the best time to hike to the bridge is in April, May, or late September and October. From February through May, strong winds whip through the canyons, and in late summer, violent thunderstorms can cause flash floods. Exposure is the greatest hazard here, so make sure you carry enough water—at least a gallon per person per day. (You can refill your canteens at springs along the trails.) Sunglasses, sunscreens, and protective clothing are also helpful in fending off the summer sun. A hiking permit from the Navajo Nation is required.

Two trails lead overland from the Navajo Reservation to Rainbow Bridge, the 13-mile Rainbow Lodge Trail and the 14-mile Navajo Mountain Trail, which may require a four-wheel-drive vehicle. The hike to the bridge is strenuous and calls for sturdy shoes and backpacking experience. Although no rock climbing is involved, you'll be doing a lot of up-and-down walking with an elevation change of about 2,000 feet. You can make a round trip by trail or arrange with the park concessionaire for a boat trip at either end.

This salmon-pink sandstone bridge, the largest natural bridge in the world, rises 290 feet above the floor of Bridge Canyon, Utah.—*NPS photograph*

Do not attempt the trek without a topographical map purchased from the park service visitor center at Glen Canyon or from the U.S. Geological Survey. The map is entitled "Navajo Mountain Quadrangle Map" and can be ordered from the park by mail. At Glen Canyon you can also get a free brochure on camping and hiking in the Rainbow Bridge area.

There is a per person, per night charge for camping in the monument, payable to the Navajo Indians. For more information about a hiking or overnight permits, contact the Navajo Nation Recreation Department, P.O. Box 308, Window Rock, Arizona 86515. Telephone: 602-871-6645. Assume that you will stay at least one night on the trail if you hike to the bridge.

Another exciting way to see Rainbow Bridge is on horseback. J & N Enterprises in Tonealea, Arizona, may arrange private horseback trips with Navajo guides. Make reservations at least two weeks in advance with J & N Enterprises, Navajo Star Route Box A, Tonealea, Arizona. Telephone: 602-672-2852 or 602-672-2801.

Visitors with their own boats can launch at Wahweap, Halls Crossing, Bullfrog, and Hite marinas on Lake Powell. After boating across, a short canyon trail leads to the bridge. The nearest park service station is at Dangling Rope Marina, eight miles to the south of the monument. Visitors also can take tour boats that leave from Bullfrog, Halls Crossing, and Wahweap. For information contact ARA Leisure Services, Incorporated, 2916 No. 35th Avenue, Suite 8, Phoenix, Arizona 85017. Telephone: 800-528-6154 or 278-8888 in greater Phoenix. Yet another way to view the bridge is by air. Lake Powell Air Service runs 45-minute aerial trips over the canyon. Telephone: 602-645-2494.

Although plant life is scarce in the Colorado Plateau, cottonwood, ash, gamble oak, western redbud, tamarisk, arrowwood and serviceberry grow in the adjacent canyons. Animals in the area include snakes (rattlers are rarely seen), lizards, skunks, bobcats, and mountain lions.

Open: Visitor Center at Glen Canyon in Page, AZ, is open from 8 a.m. to 5 p.m. Labor Day to Memorial Day, extended from 7 a.m. to 7 p.m. in summer. Closed Christmas Day. The park itself is open year-round.

Fees: None.

Mailing Address: Rainbow Bridge National Monument, c/o Superintendent, Glen Canyon National Recreation Area, P.O. Box 1507, Page, AZ 86040.

Telephone: 602-645-2471.

Getting There: Glen Canyon National Recreational Area headquarters are located at the southern tip of Lake Powell in Page, Arizona, off U.S. 89. To get to the trail heads, take Rt. 98 towards Navajo Mountain Trading Post. Take the left fork to the 13-mile Rainbow Lodge Trail head, and the right fork to the 14-mile Navajo Mountain Trail head.

‖ Timpanogos Cave National Monument

Timpanogos Cave in the Wasatch Mountains of north central Utah is actually a system of three caves connected by man-made tunnels. They are famous for their stunning display of mineral formations called helictites, a rare formation with delicate fingerlike projections that twist and turn regardless of gravity. The caves are located on the north slope of Mount Timpanogos, a 11,750-foot snow-capped peak located between Salt Lake City and Provo.

Guided tours of the caves are provided by park rangers. The caves are a popular attraction, especially on weekends and holidays, so purchase tickets for the tours as early as possible. On Saturdays, visitors may have to wait as long as three hours for a tour. Only 20 people are allowed on a tour at a time.

A 1.5-mile asphalt trail leads up the side of the mountain from the visitor center to the entrance of the caves. Although the trail has benches and resting places, it is a strenuous climb and not recommended for people with heart or respiratory problems. Schedule about three hours for the entire tour, and take a sweater. The average year-round temperature in the cave is 42 degrees.

The visitor center has a 12-minute slide presentation about the caves, and an exhibit on the Timpanogos Mountain. This unusual site was discovered in 1887 by Martin Hansen, who followed cougar tracks to the entrance of the cave. But don't worry about meeting a cougar on your visit. Rangers say large cats are rarely sited.

Open: Visitor Center: 8 a.m. to 3 p.m. mid-May to Memorial Day, 7 a.m. to 5 p.m. Memorial Day to Labor Day, and 8 a.m. to 3 p.m. Labor Day to mid-October. The caves are closed from mid-Oct. to mid-May, but the Visitor Center remains open from 8 a.m. to 4:30 p.m. in winter.

Fees: Entry to the park is free. Cave tours cost $3 ages 16–61, $2 ages 6–15, free under 5, and $1.50 over 61.

Mailing Address: Timpanogos Cave National Monument, Route 3, Box 200, American Fork, UT 84003.

Telephone: 801-756-5239.

Getting There: If you are driving south from Salt Lake City, on I-15, turn east at S.R. 92 (exit 287). The monument is ten miles from the interstate. If you are driving north from Provo, turn east at Pleasant Grove or American Fork. Timpanogos Cave is seven miles from either town via a paved road.

VIRGINIA

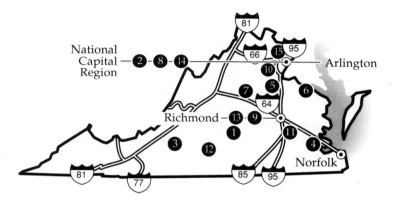

1. Appomattox Court House National Historical Park
2. Arlington House, The Robert E. Lee Memorial
3. Booker T. Washington National Monument
4. Colonial National Historical Park
5. Fredericksburg and Spotsylvania County Battlefields Memorial National Military Park
6. George Washington Birthplace National Monument
7. Green Springs Historic District
8. Lyndon Baines Johnson Memorial Grove on the Potomac
9. Maggie L. Walker National Historic Site
10. Manassas National Battlefield Park
11. Petersburg National Battlefield
12. Red Hill, The Patrick Henry National Memorial
13. Richmond National Battlefield Park
14. Theodore Roosevelt Island
15. Wolf Trap Farm Park for the Performing Arts

| Appomattox Court House National Historical Park

Wilmer McLean, a prosperous sugar merchant from Manassas, Virginia, lived in a house so close to the two Civil War battles of Bull Run that he could have watched from his front porch had he been present. In 1863, he decided to move to a more peaceful place, and installed his family in a two-story brick house in a quiet central Virginia village known as Appomattox Court House. McLean eventually found peace at Appomattox, or rather, peace found him. For in his house, General Robert E. Lee surrendered the Army of Northern Virginia to Union forces on April 9, 1865, ensuring an end to the Civil War.

Confederate General Robert E. Lee, in retreat after a nine-month siege at Petersburg, Virginia, with Federal General Ulysses S. Grant in hot pursuit, led his exhausted troops toward Appomattox Court House, where supplies would be waiting. The two armies converged there on April 8, 1865. Would Lee surrender the Army of Northern Virginia? Grant asked. Lee found all roads blocked and, realizing the futility of continuing to fight, consented. The two generals arranged to meet.

It was Palm Sunday, and since the municipal courthouse at Appomattox Court House was closed, the ceremony took place in a private home selected by Colonel Charles Marshall. He chose the finest house in the village, which belonged to Wilmer McLean, and that is where Grant and Lee exchanged formal documents of surrender on April 9.

On April 12, 28,000 Confederate soldiers furled their flags and laid down their weapons at Surrender Triangle in Appomattox. By the end of May, the last remaining Rebel holdouts west of the Mississippi River surrendered. The War Between the States was finally over.

The entire village of Appomattox Court House is now a park with 27 historic structures restored to their Civil War appearance, right down to the weathered shingles and white picket fences. The McLean House, which was completely dismantled in 1893 in an ill-fated plan to turn it into a museum in Washington, D.C., and then left to disintegrate, has been painstakingly reconstructed. The courthouse at Appomattox Court House (the village was named Court House because it was the county seat) is now a visitor center, with films and artifacts, including a pencil and a table from the surrender and maps explaining troop movements.

Other buildings in the park include the Clover Hill Tavern, the oldest structure in the village, Meek's Store, Woodson Law Office, and several smaller homes. All the buildings are within walking distance of the visitor center. Visitors can wander at leisure through the picturesque 19th-century country village. Rangers and costumed interpreters are on hand to answer questions.

There are no restaurants, campgrounds, or hotels in the park, but food and accommodations are available in the town of Appomattox, three miles away.

Other Civil War sites in the area include Lee's headquarters, a short drive northeast of the village on Route 24, and Grant's headquarters, just outside Appomattox Court House in the opposite direction. Check at the park for directions. There is a small Confederate cemetery just west of the village.

Open: 9 a.m. to 5 p.m. daily. Closed all federal holidays from November to February.

Fees: $1 per person, ages 17 through 61.

Mailing Address: Appomattox Court House National Historical Park, P.O. Box 218, Appomattox, VA 24522.

Telephone: 804-352-8987.

Getting There: The park is located in central Virginia, 90 miles west of Richmond, VA, on Route 24 off U.S. Route 460. Follow signs from Appomattox to the park.

‖ Arlington House, The Robert E. Lee Memorial

At night, the floodlit 140-foot façade of Arlington House, the former home of Confederate General Robert E. Lee, hovers over Washington, D.C., like an apparition from the American past. Arlington House is one of the premier historic houses in the country, a homestead so deeply enmeshed in America's past that it rivals George Washington's Mount Vernon home in importance. In fact, this antebellum mansion was built by George Washington's adopted son, George

Washington Parke Custis, and designed by the architect who constructed the Capitol, George Hadfield. The Marquis de Lafayette, Daniel Webster, and Andrew Jackson visited Arlington House. But the house is best known for Arlington National Cemetery, the military cemetery built on its grounds.

Robert E. Lee, the brilliant commander of Confederate Army, lived here with his wife Mary Randolph Custis and their seven children until he resigned his commission in the Federal Army on April 20, 1861, to avoid being forced to invade the South. The next day, the governor of Virginia asked Lee to take command of the state's force. Approximately a month later, Lee's wife and family left the property just ahead of the Union army, eventually moving to Richmond. The 1,100-acre estate overlooking the Potomac River was confiscated by the Federal government in 1864 after Mrs. Lee, who was suffering from arthritis, failed to appear in person to pay her taxes. As soon as the estate was confiscated, the government set aside a 200-acre section for the national cemetery that would later become the best-known burial ground in the country.

The 26-room mansion is being restored to its 1861 appearance. Although most of the original furniture, including some pieces that belonged to George Washington himself, are gone, several pieces survive. Period pieces and a few reproductions make up the rest of the furniture. Visitors can explore the grounds and the house, where paintings of battle scenes made by Mr. Custis decorate the walls, and original china and glassware are displayed in the family dining room. Park staff is on hand to answer questions and conduct occasional guided tours.

Each October, Arlington House has a candlelight tour. On June 30, the park commemorates Lee's wedding to Mary Custis with period music and refreshments.

Visitors can tour Arlington National Cemetery, which contains the Tomb of the Unknown Soldier, the graves of President John F. Kennedy and his brother Robert Kennedy, and the tombs of thousands of U.S. veterans. (Robert E. Lee is buried at Washington and Lee University in Lexington, Virginia.) Private tour groups offer guided tours. Contact the park for details.

Open: 9:30 a.m. to 6 p.m., daily, April 1–September 30. closing at 4:30 p.m. during the rest of the year. Closed Christmas and New Year's Day.

Fees: None.

Mailing Address: Arlington House, The Robert E. Lee Memorial, c/o George Washington Memorial Parkway, Turkey Run Park, McLean, VA 22101.

Telephone: 703-557-0613.

Getting There: The memorial is located in Arlington, VA just across the Potomac River from Washington D.C. From downtown Washington, take Memorial Bridge, behind the Lincoln Memorial, into Virginia. The bridge leads directly into the memorial grounds. Arlington House can also be reached by subway. Get off at the Arlington National Cemetery stop.

‖ Booker T. Washington National Monument

On this small tobacco farm in central Virginia, a young black slave fed the hogs, carried water, and fanned flies from the table while the master's family ate. From this early poverty, Booker T. Washington went on to become an educator, philosopher, advisor, and one of the most influential blacks of his time.

The Booker T. Washington birthplace is a re-creation of the modest mid-19th-century farm owned by the Burroughs family. Some of the cabins have been reconstructed; the sites of other buildings are indicated by markers. Fields are defined by split rail fences, as they were when Booker lived here.

Booker was only nine years old when the Civil War ended in 1865 and slaves were finally given their freedom. In his now famous autobiography *Up From Slavery*, he chronicles his early education, from the time he taught himself the alphabet to his years at the Hampton Institute in Virginia, one of the few schools in the country where ex-slaves could pursue higher education.

At Hampton, Washington so distinguished himself that he was recommended to head a new school for blacks, Tuskegee Institute in Alabama. Within a few years, the Tuskegee school that started in a dilapidated church with 30 pupils grew into a college with 1,500 students and a $2 million endowment.

The 224-acre birthplace park contains a replica of the 12-by-16-

foot kitchen cabin in which Booker was born. The interior has been re-created according to Washington's description in his autobiography, with dirt floor, whitewashed walls, a rough table and bench, crude shelves, pots, fireplace tools, and a "potatoe hole" (root cellar). Other buildings on the site include the corn crib, the horse barn, chicken lot, smokehouse, blacksmith shed, and tobacco barn.

The visitor center museum shows "Longing to Learn," an award-winning, 15-minute slide program on Washington's life. Several of Washington's original handwritten manuscripts of speeches are displayed. The Booker T. Washington Environmental Education and Cultural Center is available for special programs and meetings. Also at the site are several hiking trails: Plantation trail is a ¼-mile loop through the historic area; Jack-O-Lantern Branch Trail leads through the fields and woodlands for 1½ miles. Deer, fox, rabbit and other small animals can be seen on the trails. In spring the dogwood and redbud trees bloom along with wildflowers.

Near July 4 each year, the anniversary of the opening of Tuskegee Institute, the park hosts the two-day Booker T. Washington Farmlife Festival. In the past, this festival has included an extensive living history program, with conducted tours and costumed demonstrations of farm life. These activities have been suspended due to budget cuts.

Open: 8:30 a.m. to 5 p.m. daily. Closed Thanksgiving, Christmas, and New Year's Day.

Fees: $1, ages 17–61; $3 for family groups.

Mailing Address: Booker T. Washington National Monument, Route 3, Box 310, Hardy, VA 24101.

Telephone: 703-721-2094.

Getting There: The monument is located in central Virginia, 16 miles northeast of Rocky Mount. From Roanoke, take Route 116 south to Burnt Chimney and Route 122 north six miles to the monument.

‖ Colonial National Historical Park

On the banks of the James River in 1607, settlers landed to establish the colony that was the beginning of a vast British empire in the New World. On a battlefield some 20 miles away, this empire ended forever when the English surrendered to allied American and French forces at Yorktown in 1781. The birth site, and the grave, as it were, of Britain's Virginia colony in North America is preserved at Colonial National Historical Park.

This 9,833-acre park near Newport News, Virginia, is the site of Historic Jamestown Island and Yorktown Battlefield, connected by the 23-mile Colonial Parkway. (Although Jamestown was originally started on the river bank, 300 years of erosion washed away the narrow strip of land that connected the settlement to the mainland.) This waterside park now has the ruined foundations of historic houses and statues and monuments commemorating the people and events of the city's past. The only original building is the Old Church Tower, believed to have been built around 1639.

The Jamestown visitor center has a 15-minute film about the early settlement, and one of the most extensive collections of 17th-century artifacts in the country. Guided tours of the town are available, staffing and weather permitting. A five-mile car tour leads through the pine forest and the pitch and tar swamp behind the settlement, which attracts many birds and large herds of deer.

Don't miss the re-created glass factory near the park entrance where interpreters in period costume demonstrate glass making, one of the first industries in North America. Also near the park entrance, but not part of the park, is the Jamestown Festival Park featuring reconstructions of the Jamestown fort and the ships that brought colonists to the New World.

Yorktown, site of the last battle of the Revolutionary War, is on the north side of the Virginia peninsula. Here, on October 19, 1781, Lord Cornwallis' British and German forces surrendered to allied American and French forces commanded by General George Washington. British, American and French officers met at the house of Augustine Moore to work out the terms of the surrender. The actual surrender ceremony took place in an open field about two miles from Yorktown. (British soldiers were said to have thrown their arms to the ground, hoping to break their weapons. One colonel reportedly bit his sword in anger. And Lord Cornwallis did not even attend the surrender ceremony.) The Moore House, a two-story gray and white building surrounded by a picket fence, has been restored to its 18th-century appearance and is staffed with costumed interpreters.

Another house, the two-story brick house belonging to Thomas Nelson, Jr., commander of the Virginia Militia, signer of the Declaration of Independence, and Governor of Virginia at the time of the siege at Yorktown, is also open to the public. During the summer, a short drama on the history of the Nelson family is presented. Entrance to the house and the performance is free, but donations are accepted.

Earthworks and siege lines—some of them with colonial cannon —mark the positions and movements of the British, American, and French Armies during the Siege of Yorktown. A seven-mile tour road leads by the allied siege lines, Redoubts 9 and 10, that were taken by the French and Continental Army respectively on October 14, the turning point of the battle. The road also passes Surrender Field, where the British laid down their arms. The visitor center offers a 16-minute film, "The Siege at Yorktown," and displays field tents used by George Washington and a full-sized replica of a British warship's quarterdeck.

Located both geographically and historically between Jamestown and Yorktown is Colonial Williamsburg, which took over from James-town as the capital of Virginia. Though privately owned and not technically a part of the park, this restored village is a major tourist attraction that is worth visiting. It is an authentic reconstruction of the Virginia capital with hotels, restaurants, shops, and a hundred dem-onstrators practicing colonial crafts. An 18th-century drama troupe performs year-round, and the park sponsors special weekend events, such as the winter Antiques Forum and the Spring Garden Sympo-sium, as well as outdoor festivals on a regular basis. There is an entry fee for the park's 25 exhibits; check for details. The park is open 9 a.m. to 5 p.m. daily, closed all federal holidays. For further informa-tion, contact: Colonial Williamsburg, Box C, Williamsburg, Virginia 23187. Telephone: 804-229-1000.

The road running between these three sites is known as the Colo-nial Parkway, a scenic drive through typical tidewater countryside. The parkway, which does not follow any historic routes, was built especially for visitors to the Colonial Historical Park.

A third section of the park is the Cape Henry Memorial at the Fort Story military reservation in Virginia Beach, which marks the site where settlers first came ashore in North America.

On the weekend nearest May 13 each year, the park holds its annual Jamestown Day Celebration in commemoration of the first permanent British colony in North America. The festivities include special tours and demonstrations of 17th-century military life. Yorktown celebrates its historic battle annually on October 19 with parades, speeches, and a special luncheon of Brunswick stew, a local delicacy made with mixed vegetables and different kinds of game.

Open: Jamestown Visitor Center: 9 a.m. to 5 p.m. daily, in the winter, with extended hours during the rest of the year. Yorktown Visitor Center: 8:30 a.m. to 5 p.m. in winter, with extended hours during the rest of the year.

Fees: $5 a car for Jamestown; $2 a person. No fees for Yorktown. There is a $3 fee for commercial cars traveling on the Colonial Parkway between the two sites, good for a 1-day period. There is no fee for privately owned vehicles using the Colonial Parkway.

Mailing Address: Colonial National Historical Park, P.O. Box 210, Yorktown, VA 23690.

Telephone: 804-898-3400.

Getting There: To Yorktown, take I-64 east from Richmond to the exit for Rt. 199 East, Exit 57B. Follow Route 199 East to the Colonial Parkway, then follow the signs to Yorktown Battlefield. To Historic Jamestown Island, take I-64 east from Richmond to the intersection with Rt. 199 west, exit 57A. Follow Rt. 199 West to the Colonial Parkway, then follow the signs to Jamestown Island.

‖ Fredericksburg and Spotsylvania County Battlefields Memorial National Military Park

Between 1862 and 1864, four major battles took place in the Fredericksburg, Virginia, area. They include a famous confrontation between Union General Ulysses S. Grant and Confederate General Robert E. Lee, when the two commanders matched wits for control of this strategic territory halfway between the Union capital in Washington, D.C., and the Confederate capital in Richmond.

The first of the area's battles took place at Fredericksburg on December 11–13, 1862, when Union General Ambrose E. Burnside led his men in what amounted to a hopeless attack of Confederate positions at Marye's heights. (Burnside is known today for his unique whiskers, called "sideburns" in his honor; during the Civil War, Burnside was known as one of the less successful Union commanders.)

In preparing to take Fredericksburg, Burnside lost his advantage awaiting supplies and building six pontoon bridges across the Rappahannock River; Confederate General Robert E. Lee used the time to fortify his positions on the high ground around Marye's Heights. As the Union soldiers poured into Fredericksburg, Confederate sharpshooters behind a stone wall on Sunken Road mowed them down. Some 12,000 Federal troops were casualties in the battle.

From Sunken Road on Marye's Heights, you get a view of the route Burnside's men took on their ill-fated attack against Fredericksburg. The Confederate works along the road are in excellent condition. Prospect Hill to the south is the place where Federal forces briefly broke through the Confederate line before being repulsed.

On May 1–6, 1863, North and South clashed again at Chancellorsville. It was another spectacular victory for the Confederates as Lee outmaneuvered Union forces under General Joseph Hooker. Instead of meeting Hooker's army straight on, Lee sent troops under General "Stonewall" Jackson on a 12-mile march around Hooker's right flank. The Confederates bounded out of the heavy woods near Wilderness Church, surprising Union soldiers during dinner.

Jackson, on a reconnaissance mission in the thick woods after sundown, took a bullet from one of his own men that later killed him. He was taken to the Chandler plantation near Guinea Station, 27 miles to the south, where his left arm was amputated. Upon hearing the bad news, Lee was reported to have said: "He has lost his left arm, but I have lost my right." Jackson died of pneumonia on May 10. The Chandler plantation office building has been restored and is open to visitors weekends throughout the year, and on some weekdays. For more information, contact the park's main office.

The Battle of the Wilderness on May 5 and 6, 1864, and the fighting in Spotsylvania on May 8–21 marked the beginning of the classic confrontation between Grant and Lee. Grant's army, 100,000 strong, crossed the Rapidan River into the thick forests known as The Wilderness. Lee, outnumbered almost two-to-one, attacked first and used the heavy cover to his advantage. Fires raged in the forests during the two-day battle at Wilderness, and though no decisive winner emerged, the Union army lost 17,600 men to only 8,000 Confederate casualties.

Instead of retreating, Grant continued on to Spotsylvania Court House, which stood at the crossroads of the shortest route to Richmond. On May 12, Union forces struck against a projecting Confederate defense line known as the "mule-shoe salient." After 20 hours of intense hand-to-hand combat, Grant abandoned the field. The Confederate lines were intact, but both sides lost about a third of their men. A seven-mile hiking loop connects the most important sites at Spotsylvania.

Other sites in the battlefield park include Chatham, an elaborate Georgian mansion and estate located along the Rappahannock River just east of Fredericksburg. The house was a communications center, headquarters for Federal commanders, and a hospital that was visited by Clara Barton, founder of the American Red Cross, and poet Walt Whitman, who came to Virginia to nurse his wounded brother. Five rooms of the house and its delightfully landscaped grounds are open to the public.

Old Salem Church between Chancellorsville and Fredericksburg was a Baptist meeting house that served as a refugee center for the displaced residents of the region during fighting. Fredericksburg National Cemetery, dedicated in 1865, contains the remains of more than 15,000 veterans, most of them from the Civil War and many of them unknown. The cemetery is located in Fredericksburg near Sunken Road.

Chancellorsville and Fredericksburg battlefields both have visitor centers that offer guided and recorded tours of the grounds. The original trenches at Fredericksburg are also in excellent condition. During the summer, interpreters in period costume are on hand.

The eastern Virginia landscape ranges from rolling hills and fields to heavy forests of pine and scrub oak. The fall, when the days are crisp and the entire park bursts into color, is a particularly good time to visit Fredericksburg. Picnic tables are scattered throughout the battlefields and historic sites; there are no overnight camping facilities.

Open: Visitor Centers: 9 a.m. to 5 p.m. daily, extended hours in summer. Dates vary, check for details. Closed Christmas and New Year's Day.

Fees: None.

Mailing Address: Fredericksburg and Spotsylvania County Battlefields Memorial National Military Park, P.O. Box 679, Fredericksburg, VA 22404.

Telephone: 703-373-4461.

Getting There: The park is in four units in eastern Virginia, roughly halfway between Washington, D.C., and Richmond, VA, on

I-95. The main visitor center is located at 1013 Lafayette Blvd. in Fredericksburg. Get directions to the other sites from there.

| George Washington Birthplace National Monument

Tobacco ripens in the fields, flowers bloom in the gardens, and animals graze behind split-rail fences in this re-created plantation among the cedars of Pope's Creek in tidewater Virginia, the birthplace and boyhood home of the nation's first president, George Washington.

The birthplace house burned during the Revolutionary War and remains unreconstructed, but a 1½-story brick memorial house, typical of the home in which young George lived, has been built on the property. Its rooms are filled with period furniture. Outbuildings, including a kitchen and several other structures, have also been built. Excavations in the area have yielded 18th-century ceramics, jewelry, glassware, tools, and pipes.

George lived here as an infant and moved with his family in 1735, when he was 3½ years old, to Little Hunting Creek Plantation, better known as Mount Vernon. He returned here as an adolescent to live for a few years with his half-brother, Augustine.

The 538-acre park includes the homestead, a granite shaft memorial, the Washington family burial ground where 32 Washingtons are buried, and a short trail and picnic area. In February, in celebration of George Washington's birthday, there are refreshments and various special events. July 4 is another big day at Pope's Creek; check for details.

Open: 9 a.m. to 5 p.m. weekdays. Closed Christmas and New Year's Day.

Fees: $1, ages 17-61.

Mailing Address: George Washington Birthplace National Monument, Rural Route 1, Box 717, Washington's Birthplace, VA 22575.

Telephone: 804-224-1732.

Getting There: The park is along the Potomac River, 38 miles east of Fredericksburg, VA. From Fredericksburg, take Route 3 south to route 204 and continue into the park.

This reconstructed manor, standing on the site of Washington's birth, is surrounded by a farm operated with colonial methods.—*Richard Frear, NPS photograph*

‖ Green Springs Historic District

This 14,000-acre National Historic Landmark district in Louisa County, Virginia, contains a unique group of 35 historic farmhouses. They range from log cabins and corn cribs to grand estates. The houses are all privately owned and are not accessible to the public. However, they can be viewed from I-64 between Charlottesville and Richmond.

For more information, contact Fredericksburg and Spotsylvania National Military Park, P.O. Box 679, Fredericksburg, VA 22404.
Telephone: 707-373-4461.

‖ Lyndon Baines Johnson Memorial Grove on the Potomac

A 45-ton granite boulder surrounded by a grove of white pines forms this living memorial to Lyndon Baines Johnson, 36th U.S. president. The rough-hewn rock, which symbolizes Johnson's energy and strength, was quarried from the Texas hill country where Johnson was born. Surrounding it are granite plaques engraved with Johnson's philosophy on education, civil rights, environment, and the presidency. On civil rights, the following words are inscribed: "The promise of America is a simple promise. Every person shall share in the blessing of this land." It is a fitting passage for Johnson, who as president engineered the passage of the Civil Rights Act of 1964, which outlawed racial discrimination and guaranteed minorities equal opportunities in housing, education, and employment.

Johnson, the Texas senator who was John F. Kennedy's vice president, became president after Kennedy was assassinated in 1963. He served until 1969. Johnson was known as a classic Democratic liberal who implemented wide-ranging social programs to realize his vision of the "Great Society." Johnson is also known for escalating U.S. involvement in Vietnam, a policy that eventually forced him to withdraw as a presidential candidate in 1968. He retired from public life and returned to his ranch in Johnson City, Texas, where he lived until his death in 1973. His widow, Lady Bird Johnson, still resides there. (See Lyndon B. Johnson National Historical Park entry.)

The memorial grove is part of Lady Bird Johnson Park, a serene 150-acre site on Columbia Island in the Potomac River bordering Washington, D.C. The park, which is planted with daffodils, tulips, hyacinths, and other flowers, offers a beautiful, unobstructed view of the Washington skyline. Picnic tables and benches are available and parking is plentiful.

Open: Park is always open.

Fees: None.

Mailing Address: Lyndon B. Johnson Memorial Grove on the Potomac, c/o George Washington Memorial Parkway, Turkey Run Park, McLean, VA 22101.

Telephone: 703-285-2598.

Getting There: Take the Memorial Bridge from the Lincoln Memorial into Virginia and follow signs to the George Washington Memorial Parkway south. The grove is on the right, about one-third mile from the Memorial circle.

‖ Maggie L. Walker National Historic Site

In downtown Richmond, Virginia, the capital of the slave-holding Confederacy, stands the house of Maggie Walker, an early black businesswoman and leader of the women's movement. In 1903, Miss Walker became one of the first American women to establish a bank —the Saint Luke Penny Savings Bank. The bank, now called the Consolidated Bank and Trust Company, is located at the corner of First and Marshall streets in Richmond.

Miss Walker lived in the two-story, 22-room Victorian house at 110½ E. Leigh Street for 35 years until her death in 1934. The house is now restored and open to the public from Wednesday to Sunday. Currently, the house has Miss Walker's clothes, some oil painings and family photographs, and a figurine with grape clusters and a light bulb. Ninety percent of the furnishings are original.

Open: Wednesday through Sunday, 9 a.m. to 5 p.m.
Fees: None.
Mailing Address: Maggie L. Walker National Historic Site, c/o Richmond National Battlefield Park, Chimborazo Visitor Center, 3215 E. Broad Street, Richmond, VA 23223.
Telephone: 804-780-1380.
Getting There: The site is located at 110½ E. Leigh Street in Richmond, VA.

‖ Manassas National Battlefield Park

All of Washington, D.C., society turned out with their carriages and picnic baskets to watch the First Battle of Bull Run in Manassas, Virginia. Congressmen and socialites, journalists and tourists were eager to watch the opening volleys of the Civil War. Instead of pageantry, however, they found pandemonium.

At 5:30 a.m. on July 21, 1861, the first shot was fired. Federal commander General Irvin McDowell's troops, an undisciplined lot of "90-day volunteers," could not hold off the Southern forces. This was the battle in which Confederate General Thomas Jackson earned the moniker "Stonewall" for standing his ground so firmly that he rallied his fleeing brigades.

By 4 p.m. the South had won, and Federal forces, along with the audience that had gathered to watch them, were in chaotic retreat to the safety of Washington. The fields were littered with nearly 900 corpses, a hint of tragic things to come.

The second battle at Manassas, on August 29 and 30, was another victory for the South. Despite superiority in troop number, Union General John Pope was unable to gain the advantage over his experienced adversaries, Confederate Generals Thomas Jackson and James Longstreet. Pope made a major mistake when, believing the South was in retreat, he attacked. He then compounded this error by staging a frontal attack on the Confederate line, which stood perpendicular to Bull Run Creek just north of the Stone Bridge. Federal forces retreated towards Washington, D.C., when Longstreet's line, which ran parallel to the creek, began to close in. Although the Union Army conducted a good fighting retreat and the Confederates lost 16,000 men to Pope's 9,000 casualties, Pope was relieved of his command upon reaching Washington.

Manassas Battlefield, a 3,100-acre park in the rolling northern Virginia countryside, preserves the Civil War battlefield. The park includes a reconstructed Stone Bridge, where the opening shots of the first Battle of Bull Run were fired; the Stone House, restored to resemble the hospital it became during the battle; Dogan House, a log and frame building that has survived intact from the Civil War; and a Confederate cemetery. A self-guided tour takes about two hours.

Near the visitor center is the Henry House, a private home that stood in the middle of the fighting and the place where the first civilian was killed in the war. Here Judith Carter Henry, a bed-ridden elderly woman determined to stay in her home throughout the battle, was killed when Union soldiers opened fire on the house.

Re-enactments of both battles by private groups are held on Memorial Day weekend (for the First Battle) and in late August (for the second battle). Check the local papers and park for details.

Open: 8:30 a.m. to 5 p.m. daily, 8:30 a.m. to 6 p.m. in summer. Check for exact dates. Closed Christmas Day.

Fees: $1 for adults.

Mailing Address: Manassas National Battlefield Park, 6511 Sudley Road, Manassas, VA 22110.

Telephone: 703-754-7107.

Getting There: The park is located 26 miles southwest of Washington, DC, near the intersection of I-66 and Route 234.

‖ Petersburg National Battlefield

Union General Ulysses S. Grant attempted to slip in the back door of Richmond, Virginia, capital of the Confederacy, when he attacked Petersburg on June 15, 1864. But the city's southern flank was well protected by a 10-mile, 20-foot defense of dry moats and entanglements known as Dimmock Line. Intimidated, Federal forces fumbled their early advantage and settled in for a siege. The siege lasted nine months, and claimed 70,000 casualties. When it was over, General Robert E. Lee led his troops westward to Appomattox Court House, where the surrender took place that signaled the end of the Civil War.

Union soldiers lost a chance to end the Petersburg siege early on July 30, when the miners of the 48th Pennsylvania Infantry dug a tunnel under Pegram's Salient and blasted their way through the Confederate line. Instead of using the opening to overwhelm Southern troops, the attacking Federal soldiers became bogged down in the area of the crater and were either killed or captured by a well-directed Confederate counterattack.

Only after an assault against the Rebels' thin right flank on April 2, 1865, did Lee evacuate the city. In many ways, the fighting at Petersburg was a precursor of the trench warfare of World War I.

The grass has grown over the edges of the crater, and the bottom has filled in somewhat, but evidence of the ingenious attempt by Pennsylvania coal miners to cut short the fighting at Petersburg are still visible. The crater, and the tunnel leading to it, are at the last stop of an eight-site tour of Petersburg National Battlefield. Although there are trenches all the way from Petersburg to Richmond, you can only tour small sections of those in the Richmond National Battlefield area.

Elsewhere in the park, people in uniform re-create Union Camp and Confederate Cannon Crew life. There are demonstrations of Civil

War medicine and artillery. Firings of cannon and mortar occur five times daily, except Mondays and Tuesdays during the summer season, and musket and drill demonstrations are held on the weekends.

The visitor center has a 20-minute map show for orientation. The museum displays artifacts from the battle, including artillery, guns, swords, mortars, soup ladles, dominoes, and two bullets that collided in mid-air and fused together. Park employees lead 20-minute walking tours of Confederate Battery 5, where the fighting began.

In summer, an extensive living history program re-creates Civil War life, with soldiers drilling, running the sutler's store, and writing letters home. Poplar Grove National Cemetery is three miles south of the city on Route 675. The remains of more than 6,000 soldiers are buried there.

Open: 8 a.m. to 5 p.m. daily, late Aug. to late May, extended to 7 p.m. in summer. Closed Christmas and New Year's Day.

Fees: $3 per car, good for seven days.

Mailing Address: Petersburg National Battlefield, P.O. Box 549, Petersburg, VA 23804.

Telephone: 804-732-3531.

Getting There: The park is located in southeastern Virginia, 20 miles south of Richmond. From Petersburg take Route 36 east off I-95 to the site.

‖ Red Hill, The Patrick Henry National Memorial

Patrick Henry, plantation owner, patriot, and first governor of Virginia, is best known for his fiery words: "Give me liberty, or give me death," spoken in Richmond on March 23, 1775. Henry's last home and burial place, the Red Hill estate in Brookneal, Virginia, is preserved and interpreted in the memorial here, a recent addition to the National Park system.

At his death in 1799, Patrick Henry was one of the wealthiest landowners in Virginia, with vast holdings in Virginia, Kentucky, North Carolina, and Georgia. He had 17 children by two wives. His first wife, Sarah Shelton, died in 1775; his second, Dorothea Dandridge, survived him by 32 years and is buried beside him at Red Hill.

Of the places in Virginia that Patrick Henry lived during his life-time, Red Hill was one of his favorites. He called it "the garden spot of the world." The plantation grew tobacco, corn, and wheat on 2,920 acres and kept 21 horses, 167 cattle, 155 hogs, and 60 sheep.

The memorial consists of Patrick Henry's five-room plantation house, which has been reconstructed on its original site. The house contains a replica of the Chippendale corner chair in which Henry died, as well as his walnut clothes press. Other structures include the kitchen and outbuildings, a rebuilt two-story servant's cabin, Henry's law office and library, and a reconstructed carriage house with a hay-loft. In the cemetery is the grave where Henry was buried in 1799 at the age of 63.

The site may have a small celebration on May 29, in honor of Henry's birthday. On the Fourth of July there is a colonial re-enact-ment group at Red Hill, with soldiers, fife and drum corps, and fire-works.

Open: 9 a.m. to 4 p.m., November to March, extended to 5 p.m. March to October. Closed Thanksgiving, New Year's, and Christmas Day.

Fees: $3 adults, ages 18–62, $2 for seniors over 62, and $1 for ages 17 and under.

Mailing Address: Red Hill, The Patrick Henry Memorial, Route 2, Box 27, Brookneal, VA 24528.

Telephone: 804-376-2044.

Getting There: The memorial is located five miles east of Brook-neal on U.S. 501. Signs to the site are located at the traffic light in Brookneal.

‖ Richmond National Battlefield Park

Richmond, Virginia, was the capital of the Confederacy. The Union army made two major attempts to take this strategic city directly—the Seven Days Campaign in June and July, 1862, and the battle at Cold Harbor in May and June, 1864. Richmond National Battlefield Park remembers these two campaigns, and preserves ten sites associated with the defense of Richmond.

The sites are scattered throughout the city and three surrounding counties. They include the Confederate earthworks northeast of the city and the Rebel artillery works at Parker's Battery, which defended the city's southern flank until the final surrender in 1865. Visitors should start at the Chimborazo visitor center at 3215 E. Broad Street in downtown Richmond, which is located on the site of a famous southern military hospital. Here you can see an audio-visual presentation on the area's battles and get maps to Richmond's battlefields.

The first encounter of the Seven Days Battle took place at Beaver Dam Creek northeast of Richmond on June 26, 1862. Here Confederate General Robert E. Lee, who had only recently assumed command of the Army of Northern Viriginia, skirmished with Union General George B. McClellan. Due to lack of coordination, southern troops under General A.P. Hill led an unsupported attack against secure Union positions at Beaver Creek Dam. Although McClellan basically won this battle, he withdrew to Gaines Mill, where he aligned his troops in an arc along Boatswains Creek. Confederate troops, which outnumbered Union troops by 15,000, pushed through the left Federal flank at 4:30 p.m. and drove them south to Malvern Hill. It was Lee's first victory, and it cost him 8,000 men, twice the number of Union casualties. Visitors to the Gaines Mill Battlefield can tour the Watt House, used as headquarters by Union General Fitz-John Porter. The last of the battles was fought at Malvern Hill on July 1, when Confederate forces made a futile attempt to storm the Union battle line on the high ground. Lee lost 20,000 men in this battle, a quarter of his forces. But he managed to keep McClellan from Richmond.

Two years later, the North tried again to crack Richmond's defenses in the Battle of Cold Harbor. Here, in early June 1864, Yankees and Rebels lined up in a seven-mile front. Union General Ulysses S. Grant attacked at dawn on June 3, leading a suicidal charge against Confederate positions. For eight minutes, Rebel forces bombarded the Union forces from the front and flanks. Eight thousand Union soldiers fell in one of the bloodiest charges of the Civil War. Many of the soldiers, knowing they might not survive, had pinned names and addresses to their uniforms so their bodies could be identified.

The trenches and earthworks at Cold Harbor are preserved, and the Garthright House, a private residence on the battlefield, still stands. The house is closed to the public, but you can view it from the outside. Cold Harbor has an exhibit, shelter, restrooms, and picnic facilities.

Fort Harrison, where both North and South built earthworks, also has a visitor center. For more information about the specific sites, maps, guides, and special programs and events, contact rangers at the Chimborazo visitor center in Richmond.

Open: Chimborazo Visitor Center: 9 a.m. to 5 p.m. daily. Closed Christmas and New Year's Day.

Fees: None.

Mailing Address: Richmond National Battlefield Park, 3215 E. Broad Street, Richmond, VA 23223.

Telephone: 804-226-1981.

Getting There: The battlefield park is located in and around Richmond, Virginia. The main visitor center is in downtown Richmond, at 3215 E. Broad St., 15 blocks from the junction of I-95 and I-64.

‖ Theodore Roosevelt Island

Only the distant rumble of cars and the occasional passing airplane give any hint that this 88-acre island wilderness preserve in the Potomac River, dedicated to Theodore Roosevelt, the 26th president, is in the middle of the D.C. metropolitan area. Theodore Roosevelt Island is a fitting monument to the man who established the U.S. Forest Service, set aside five national parks, and established 51 bird and five game reserves.

A distinguished statesman and politician, Roosevelt was a robust outdoorsman, naturalist, and big game hunter who lived what he called the "strenuous life." His home in Sagamore Hill (see Sagamore Hill National Historic Site entry) on Long Island is filled with trophies from his many hunting expeditions; other trophies are on display at the Smithsonian's National Museum of Natural History on the National Mall in Washington, D.C. Roosevelt's love of the wilderness gave him an appreciation for the environment at a time when wildlife was wantonly hunted, timber and mineral reserves were being plundered with scant regard to the future, and erosion was fast reducing some of the most beautiful landscapes in the nation to wasteland.

One of Roosevelt's main objectives upon becoming president after William McKinley's assassination in 1901 was to make conservation a federal priority. "We have admitted the right of the individual to injure the future of the Republic for his present profit," he said. "The time has come for a change." Under his guidance, more than 234 million acres of American wilderness were reserved for conservation. Nearly extinct bison herds were protected, Roosevelt's Reclamation Act brought irrigated waters to the arid West, and the Antiquities Act authorized the preservation of cultural and historical landmarks.

Consistent with Roosevelt's belief in conservation and preservation, the island park that bears his name is almost as wild and undeveloped as it was in 1632, when Charles I granted the land to Lord Baltimore. The island has almost three miles of foot trails and a simple memorial in an oval terrace that is set off by a water-filled moat. Inside the terrace, which is accessible by footbridges, stands a 17-foot-high bronze statue of Roosevelt sculpted by Paul Manship. Roosevelt is surrounded by granite tablets inscribed with aspects of his philosophy. "I want to see you game, boys. I want to see you brave and manly, and I also want to see you gentle and tender."

At high tide, much of the island is a swampland where wrens, redwinged blackbirds, turtles, frogs, raccoons, and muskrats live. On higher ground toward the center of the island, squirrels, and chipmunks, and occasional red and gray foxes live among the elms, maples, and oaks. A ranger is on duty during daylight hours to answer questions. Guided walks are available on weekends. Tours for groups are available by advanced reservation.

Open: Daylight hours, daily.

Fees: None.

Mailing Address: Theodore Roosevelt Island, c/o George Washington Memorial Parkway, Turkey Run Park, McLean, VA 22101.

Telephone: 703-285-2598.

Getting There: The park is on Roosevelt Island across from the Kennedy Center. From Washington, take I-66 across the Theodore Roosevelt Bridge into Virginia, and take the George Washington Parkway north to the entrance. A footbridge leads from the parking area to the island.

|Wolf Trap Farm Park for the Performing Arts

This delightful complex of indoor and outdoor theaters set in the rolling green countryside of northern Virginia is the only national park dedicated solely to the performing arts. In summer, visitors can enjoy a romantic picnic dinner on the lawn while watching fine opera, theater, ballet, or concerts of classical and contemporary music at the Filene Center. Many well-known performers and groups such as the National Symphony Orchestra have appeared here.

Wolf Trap has three performance spaces: The Filene Center, an outdoor auditorium that seats 3,786 under cover and 3,000 on the lawn; the Theater-in-the-Woods, an outdoor theater in a rustic natural setting that seats approximately 750; and the Concert Shell, a stage used for special events and programs. A fourth theater, the privately owned The Barns of Wolf Trap Foundation, is located one-half mile past the park.

When the Dulles Airport Access Road divided her property in 1966, Mrs. Catherine Filene Shouse proposed to the United States government that she donate a portion (approximately 50 acres) of her Virginia farmland to create a park for the performing arts. In October 1966, Congress accepted her proposal. The Park Service acquired additional land for a total of 117 acres. In addition to donating land, Mrs. Shouse gave financial support to build and design the $2.3 million Filene Center. Mrs. Shouse still takes an active role in the programming and fund-raising activities of the Wolf Trap Foundation.

In 1982 a fire destroyed the Filene Center, which cost $23 million to rebuild. The rebuilt Filene Center is 13 stories (138 feet) high, three stories taller than the original structure. The stage area, 65 feet deep and 70 feet wide, is one of the largest in the United States. The backstage area, which is approximately 100 percent larger than the original Filene Center, includes dressing rooms, office space, and a large rehearsal hall. The entire center is accessible to disabled visitors.

Wolf Trap caters especially to children and sponsors a terrific series of youth programs designed to cultivate an appreciation for the performing arts. Programs for children of all ages are offered free of charge Monday through Friday from early July to late August in the

Theater-in-the-Woods. Although the programs are free, reservations are required. Telephone: 703-255-1827.

The International Children's Festival, a series of shows and workshops that draws 25,000 people over a three-day period, is traditionally held on Labor Day weekend. For additional information, contact the Fairfax County Council of the Arts by calling 703-642-0862.

Tours of the beautiful 117-acre site are given on request. Picnickers are welcome any time, although it may be necessary to reserve a favorite spot on performance nights. For more information, call 703-255-1800. Throughout the year, free classes in theater appreciation are given at irregular times. Tickets for the Filene Center, which holds performances during the summer, are available at the Box Office seven days a week starting the first week in May. For ticket information, call 703-255-1860. Tickets can also be charged by phone at 800-448-9009.

Open: The park is open until dusk all year except Thanksgiving and Christmas Day.

Fees: No entry fee; tickets for performances vary.

Mailing Address: Wolf Trap Farm Park, 1551 Wolf Trap Road, Vienna, Virginia, 22182.

Telephone: 703-255-1800 (TDD).

Getting There: The Wolf Trap Ramp off the Dulles Toll Road, Route 267 west, is open two hours before each Filene Center performance. Route 267 West is accessible from I-66, exit 20, or from the Capital Beltway (495), exit 12. Or, take Route 7, Leesburg Pike West, 2.5 miles and turn left onto Tolston Road, which is marked by a Wolf Trap Farm park sign. The park is one mile from this turn.

VIRGIN ISLANDS

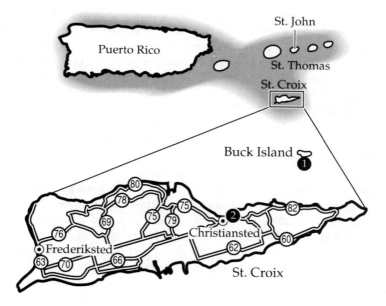

1. Buck Island Reef National Monument
2. Christiansted National Historic Site

‖ Buck Island Reef National Monument

Buck Island Reef, located 1.5 miles north of the coast of Saint Croix in the Virgin Islands, is a 175-acre tropical forest island surrounded by a coral barrier reef and marine gardens. Here beautiful reef fish—angels, butterflyfish, blue tang, and others—swim among magnificent coral formations and undulating sea fans. An underwater trail offers some of the best snorkeling and scuba diving in the Caribbean.

Coral reefs grow only in the warm, clear waters of the tropics, and only on the east coast of continents, where currents carry nutrients from as far away as the North and South poles. Layer upon layer of polyps—tiny tentacled marine invertebrates—form fantastically shaped colonies of coral: squiggly brain coral, branching elk and staghorn coral, and intricately patterned sea fans. From this living anchor, the reef habitat grows, and marine life forages and finds shelter and protection from passing predators like barracuda, snappers, and eagle rays.

Vacationers will find that Buck Island has a beautiful and exceptionally clean white sand beach, with picnic areas, changing rooms, and restrooms. However, no food or drinks are available. The island, currently uninhabited, was once farmed and used as a goat pasture. One can walk the beaches and take the overland hiking trail to the observation tower on the north shore, 200 feet above sea level. The overlook provides a spectacular view of the barrier reef, the turquoise waters of the Caribbean, and, on clear days, the island of Saint John.

Natural life on Buck Island includes the brown pelican and the least tern, both threatened species that nest here seasonally, hummingbirds, lizards, rats, and mongooses, which were brought in to keep the burgeoning rat population under control. The plan backfired—rats are nocturnal and mongooses are diurnal—and the Park Service now is trying to control both animal populations. Beware of the manchineel tree, which has irritating sap and poison applelike fruit. Three endangered species of sea turtle nest seasonally on Buck Island: the leatherback, the green, and the hawksbill. The nesting population of hawksbill sea turtles is being studied to better understand their nesting behavior and habitat requirements.

The weather is excellent from Christmas through March, when the days are a pleasant 70 to 80 degrees. Summers are hot and sticky, with

An underwater trail with coral grottoes, sea fans, and tropical fish make Buck Island Reef one of the finest marine gardens in the Caribbean. —*M. Woodbridge Williams, NPS photograph*

temperatures ranging from 78 to 92 degrees, but the snorkeling is best in summer when the seas are calm. There is no camping on the island, but private boats can anchor off the big beach for overnight stays of up to 14 consecutive days.

Watch out for fire coral, a smooth, leafy or encrusting, mustard-colored coral that causes a nasty burn when touched. Barracuda, tarpon, eagle rays and other predatory fish have been seen but rarely cause trouble. Sun and exertion are more dangerous. Snorkeling can be strenuous, especially for non-swimmers, and people with heart problems are advised to be cautious.

The only way to get to Buck Island is by boat from Saint Croix. At least nine concessions run full and half-day excursions to the park. Most trips include the 2 hour round-trip boat ride, snorkeling equipment, instruction, and a guided snorkel trip through the underwater trail. Scuba diving is limited to the area beyond the trail.

Open: Daylight hours.
Fees: None.
Mailing Address: Buck Island Reef National Monument, P.O. Box 160, Christiansted, Saint Croix, VI 00821.

Telephone: 809-773-1460.

Getting There: The monument is accessible only by boat from St. Croix. Fees range from about $18 for a half day to $30 for a full day. For more information, contact: Division of Tourism, Department of Commerce, Scale House, Christiansted, Saint Croix, VI 00820. Telephone: 809-773-0495.

‖ Christiansted National Historic Site

Christiansted's harbor-side historic park with the yellow-brick Fort Christiansvaern, customs house, scale house, and steepled former Lutheran church interprets two centuries of Danish colonial rule on Saint Croix. Discovered by Christopher Columbus in 1493, when he landed at Salt River, this 84-square-mile island was ruled first by Spain, and then Holland, England, the Knights of Malta, and France. The Danish influence lingers in Christiansted's picturesque arcades, courtyards, and plastered buildings with pastel wash.

In the 18th century, profits from cane sugar turned this island into a Caribbean paradise, a haven of lavish plantations and fancy homes. Saint Croix was so wealthy that its military officers here wore epaulets of gold thread and continued to wear them after the practice was forbidden in Denmark, when the national economy went bankrupt at the end of the Napoleonic Wars in 1814.

Alexander Hamilton, the U.S. statesman, was born on the island of Nevis and spent his formative boyhood years, from age nine to 17, on Christiansted.

The island's prosperity diminished in the early 19th century when beet sugar took over the cane sugar market after 1815. The economy further suffered when the slaves were freed in 1848, ending the supply of free labor. Because of its strategic position in the Caribbean, the United States had long wanted the island, but it was not until World War I that an agreement with the Danish government was reached and the U.S. bought Saint Croix for $25 million. Many plantations, now overgrown by the relentless forest, can be found on the island, along with some plantation houses that have survived intact and an impressive number of 18th- and 19th-century structures.

The park includes six buildings in seven acres along the waterfront. The cannon of Fort Christiansvaern, which was built of ballast bricks in 1738–1749, overlook the shimmering waters of the harbor. Tours of the fort, which is in excellent condition, are available by advance reservation. Duties were collected in the Danish Customs House, goods were weighed and measured in the Scale House nearby, and slaves were auctioned in the courtyard of the Danish and West India Company Warehouse.

The park's museum, located in the Steeple Building (originally a Danish Lutheran church) recalls the days of Saint Croix as a sugar capital and contains one of the largest archeological collections in the Caribbean.

Once there were 150 sugar plantations on Saint Croix. Today, only a few remain, in ruins. The best preserved is the Whim Plantation, run by the Saint Croix Landmark Society. For information, contact the group at P.O. Box 2855, Frederiksted, Saint Croix, VI 00840. Telephone: 809-772-0598. Other attractions include picturesque windmills, white sandy beaches, and snorkeling at Buck Island Reef. (See Buck Island Reef entry.)

Three Kings Day on January 5 is the island's carnival, a colorful festival with costumes, parades, floats, steel band orchestras, and "moco jumbies"—spirits on stilts. In February the island holds an agricultural fair with entertainment and such exotic local produce as mangoes, papayas, avocados, and soursop, which resembles breadfruit. Beware of crime and vandalism and keep possessions at a minimum while sightseeing.

Open: Visitor Center: 8:30 a.m. to 4:30 p.m. on weekdays, from 9 a.m. weekends. Closed Christmas Day.

Fees: $1 ages 16–62. All others free.

Mailing Address: Christiansted National Historic Site, P.O. Box 160, Christiansted, Saint Croix, VI 00820.

Telephone: 808-773-1460.

Getting There: The park is located in downtown Christiansted, St. Croix, U.S. Virgin Islands. The island is served by several major U.S. airlines as well as by commuter aircraft from San Juan, Puerto Rico, and from St. Thomas.

WASHINGTON

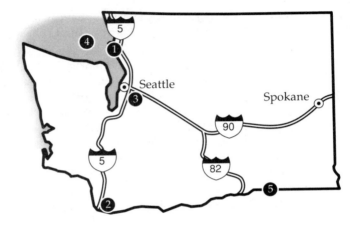

1. Ebey's Landing National Historical Reserve
2. Fort Vancouver National Historic Site
3. Klondike Gold Rush National Historical Park
4. San Juan Island National Historical Park
5. Whitman Mission National Historic Site

|| Ebey's Landing National Historical Reserve

This historic tract on Whidbey Island in Puget Sound preserves the sprawling Victorian houses and false-fronted shops of a 19th-century seafaring and farming community. It is named for Colonel Isaac N. Ebey, an early settler who was killed by Indians in 1857 during the struggles between the Indians and the white homesteaders in the northwest territory.

The 17,000-acre reserve includes the land Ebey claimed in 1850 and the claims of many other original settlers; the historic town of Coupeville, founded by Captain Thomas George Coupe in 1852; Fort Casey State Park recreation area, built at the site of a turn-of-the-century coastal fort; and Fort Ebey State Park, which offers excellent vistas of the Strait of Juan de Fuca.

Whidbey Island has a raw and rugged beauty, with craggy coasts, high cliffs, heavy pine forests, fields of rolling prairie grasses, sheltered lagoons, gentle beaches, and the deep harbor of Penn's Cove. Overlooks along the coast provide beautiful views of the water, where seals, gray whales, and killer whales are often seen.

There is a trail above the prairie from the cemetery to the bluff and Ebey's Landing, an easy walk with markers to follow. A self-guided walking tour, provided by the Island County Historical Society, leads by 27 historic buildings in Coupeville. Included in the tour is the 1854 home of Captain Thomas George Coupe, the sea captain after whom the town is named; Alexander's Blockhouse, built during the Indian hostilities and now containing a collection of Indian dugout canoes; and the Island County Historical Museum. The houses are privately owned and can be viewed from the outside only, but there are interesting shops in many of the historic buildings along the waterfront. Two miles to the south is Ebey's Landing where Ebey is buried.

Fort Casey State Park offers picnicking, surf fishing, an underwater reserve, and an unbroken stretch of beach to Ebey's Landing that makes an excellent day's hike. Fort Ebey State Park has a campground and hiking trails to the beaches. Wildlife includes black-tailed deer, foxes, sea otters, and bald eagles, which nest on the island. The fishing is excellent. Salmon, steelhead, halibut, and cod are common catches.

Hunting and fishing licenses are required. Charter fishing boats leave from Deception Pass at the north end of the island.

Open: The reserve is always open. A new museum is under construction; check for hours.

Fees: None for the reserve. A $2 card for recording the number of salmon caught, available in most hardware and tackle stores, is required for saltwater fishing. A three-day fishing license for non-residents costs $9.50.

Mailing Address: Ebey's Landing National Historical Reserve, P.O. Box 774, Coupeville, WA 98239.

Telephone: 206-618-6084.

Getting There: Whidbey Island is located in Puget Sound. By car: From Seattle, take I-5 north to Mukilteo, where ferries regularly depart on a scenic 20-minute ride to Clinton (about $6.50 each way for a car and passenger). The island can also be reached by car from the north. Take Mainland Drive, Route 20, from Mount Vernon to the Deception Pass Bridge. Route 525 goes to Coupeville. The town is also reachable by private boat or by air.

| Fort Vancouver National Historic Site

The wooden stockade and buildings of Fort Vancouver, erected along the tree-lined banks of the Columbia River by the Hudson's Bay Company in 1825, was the economic and cultural center of the Pacific Northwest during the early 19th century.

Brigades of pelt-ladened fur trappers congregated at Fort Vancouver after a winter of hunting. Here too, Indians came to trade.

Constructed under the direction of Dr. John McLoughlin, Fort Vancouver was intended to solidify Britain's claim to the fur-rich grounds of the Pacific Northwest. While McLoughlin made money for the Hudson's Bay Company, he also extended credit to American settlers in need, in direct contravention to company policy. Hudson's Bay Company influence declined in the area after 1846, when U.S. territory in Oregon was limited to the 49th parallel, and the doors of the fort were closed in 1960. (The United States was hoping to extend its claims all to the way to the 54th parallel, hence the slogan, "54-40 or Fight.") Today, McLoughlin is known as The Father of Oregon.

Fort Vancouver, built as the western headquarters of the Hudson's Bay Company's fur-trading operation, became the cultural, political, and commercial center of the Pacific Northwest.—*NPS photograph*

Seven reconstructed buildings, including a bakery, a blacksmith's shop, an Indian trade store, kitchen, and the Chief Factor's residence now stand on their original sites at the fort. The entire area is surrounded by a 15-foot-high stockade.

Interpreters lead visitors on hourly tours through the fort during the summer. Each year, on a day close to Queen Victoria's Birthday (May 24), the park holds a special celebration commemorating early British culture in the region. With "God Save the Queen" and other 19th-century tunes playing in the background, park staff and volunteers dressed in period costume, dance and toast the queen and royal family. The Union Jack flag is raised over the fort. Check for dates and activities.

Open: 9 a.m. to 4 p.m., Labor Day to April 1; 9:30 a.m. to 4:30 p.m. in summer. Closed Columbus Day, Veterans Day, Thanksgiving, Christmas, New Year's Day, Martin Luther King's Birthday, and Washington's Birthday.

Fees: $1 per person, ages 17 to 61.

Mailing Address: Fort Vancouver National Historic Site, 612 E. Reserve Street, Vancouver, WA 98661.

Telephone: 206-696-7655.

Getting There: The park is located in the city of Vancouver. To get there, turn off I-5 at the Mill Plain Blvd. exit and then follow the signs to the visitor center on East Evergreen Blvd. From I-205, exit at Rt. 14, go west on Rt. 14 about five miles, and turn right on Grand Blvd., and follow signs to park entrance.

‖ Klondike Gold Rush National Historical Park

The discovery of gold in the Canadian Klondike in 1897 turned Seattle into a boom town overnight, a place where prospectors made their final purchases before heading off to the Alaskan gold fields. Klondike Park in Seattle's historic Pioneer Square district commemorates the days of the Klondike Gold Rush, when money flowed freely and adventure was in the air.

Located near the waterfront, Pioneer Square has 27 turn-of-the-century buildings—once the hotels, restaurants, brothels, and general stores associated with the gold rush. During the height of gold fever, thousands of people flocked to Seattle on their way north to Skagway (Alaska) and Dawson City (Canada) in the Yukon Territory. At outfitters such as the one that used to be in the Schwabacher Building, they would buy a year's supply of food and equipment. (The Canadian Mounties would not let prospectors into the Northland unless they had adequate provisions.) Demand for goods was high among the gold-hungry men; outfitters could not stock the essentials fast enough and the streets overflowed with stock.

The visitor center in the Union Trust Annex at 117 S. Main Street tells the story of the days when Seattle was the gateway to adventure. There are displays of the food and clothing prospectors took into the wilderness, and a demonstration of panning for gold.

Half a dozen slide shows and films, some of them excellent, describe the gold-rush days of Seattle and the lives of the men who hoped to find their fortunes in the muck of the north. Don't miss the classic Charlie Chaplin film "The Gold Rush," a silent movie about one prospector's struggle with the harsh life of the Klondike. The film is shown on Saturday and Sunday. Check for schedules.

The region's first gold claim was staked along Rabbit Creek near the Klondike River on August 14, 1896. Almost a year later, a steamship landed in Seattle with almost two tons of gold that had been mined by 68 men.

But for every man who struck it rich, tens of thousands failed. An estimated 100,000 set off on the 1,500-mile journey to the gold fields, and perhaps a third of them made it to Dawson City. Of these, only an estimated 4,000 actually found gold, and only 300 of these, less than one in ten, made a fortune. In the end, only 50 walked away from the Klondike as wealthy men. If anyone made good, it was the people of Seattle who sold supplies to prospectors before their trips and provided luxuries upon their return.

A second section of Klondike park is in Skagway, Alaska, and includes the historic buildings of downtown Skagway, the ruins of nearby Dyea, and the Chilkoot and White trails that prospectors followed to the Yukon. Together, these two parks complete the 13,271-acre tribute to one of the most colorful and exciting chapters in American history. The National Park Service administers the trails only to the international boundary. At that point, Parks Canada administers the trails. For all intents and purposes, the White Pass Trail no longer exists as much of it was obliterated by the building of the White Pass and Yukon Route Railway in 1899.

Open: Visitor Center: 9 a.m. to 5 p.m. daily. Closed Thanksgiving, Christmas, and New Year's Day.

Fees: None.

Mailing Address: Klondike Gold Rush National Historical Park, 117 S. Main Street, Seattle, WA 98104.

Telephone: 206-442-7220.

Getting There: The visitor center is located at 117 South Main Street in the Union Trust Annex building. Parking is available at several nearby locations. Bus stops and the train station are within walking distance.

| San Juan Island National Historical Park

On this scenic island in Washington Sound the Americans and British almost went to war in 1859 over possession of a portion of the valuable Washington Territory. Anxious to lay claim to the region, the British established businesses on the island in the early 19th century while American settlers put down stakes. Tensions between the two groups ran high until they reached a crisis when one American killed a pig owned by a British citizen. The incident sparked the Pig War of 1859.

The remains of both British and American military encampments established during the hostilities on the island form the two sections of San Juan Island Historical Park. When hostilities were at a peak in August 1859, 461 American troops supported by 14 cannon opposed five British warships with 2,140 troops and 167 guns.

San Juan was occupied jointly while the standoff continued for the next 12 years, until Kaiser Wilhelm I of Germany settled the matter by ruling in favor of the United States. No shots had been fired, no one was injured, and the only casualty was the pig.

The British Camp, in the tree-sheltered cove of Garrison Bay at the northwest end of the island, has restored wooden barracks, a block-house, commissary, hospital, and formal garden. Trails lead from the parking lot to the British cemetery at Young Hill, and along the coast to Bell Point.

A barren, windswept peninsula on the island's southeastern tip was the site of the American Camp. Two original buildings, an officers' quarters and a laundress' quarters, survive. Nearby are the remains of the Redoubt, an earthwork defense. One trail leads in a loop past the historic buildings, the Redoubt, and the Belleview Farm. Another trail loops through the whispering Douglas-fir trees along Jakles's lagoon. Mount Finlayson in the middle of the loop, really only a 290-foot hill, offers magnificent vistas of Mount Rainier, Mount Baker, the Olympic Mountains, and British Columbia.

South Beach, a short drive from the park headquarters, is the largest public beach on the island and a good place to view shore birds and tidal life. Swimming in the cold waters and strong currents of the Strait of Juan de Fuca is not advisable.

There are no campgrounds in the park, but the island has two private campgrounds and a county-owned facility. Accommodations are available at Friday Harbor and Roche Harbor. Both camps have picnic areas.

From mid-June through Labor Day, the park occasionally features costumed interpreters demonstrating the daily activities of the soldiers who lived on San Juan Island during the Pig War.

Open: The park is open during daylight hours; the historic buildings are open 9 a.m. to 4:30 p.m. daily in the summers and on spring and fall weekends. Check for details. Closed Thanksgiving, Christmas, and New Year's Day, in winter and during inclement weather.

Fees: None.

Mailing Address: San Juan Island National Historical Park, P.O. Box 429, Friday Harbor, WA 98250.

Telephone: 206-378-2240.

Getting There: The island is located in Washington State and can be reached by ferries from Anacortes, WA, 83 miles north of Seattle, or from Sydney, British Columbia, 15 miles north of Victoria. The Washington State Ferry at Anacortes sails to San Juan Island at least five times daily, more often in summer. Trips on this scenic boat ride take about two hours each way, and round trips cost about $4.65 a person, $15.85 for cars. Private boats can dock at Friday and Roche Harbors. Commercial air flights leave from Seattle and Bellingham, WA, to the north. For more information about transportation, contact park headquarters.

‖ Whitman Mission National Historic Site

In the rolling grasslands of the Old Oregon Country, Dr. Marcus Whitman and his wife Narcissa built a mission in 1836 among the Cayuse Indians. The gathering of adobe buildings at Waiilatpu (which means "place of the people of the rye grass") was a welcome rest stop for settlers traveling the arduous Oregon Trail.

Whitman and his wife were murdered during an uprising 11 years after they arrived, and efforts to convert the Indians at Waiilatpu were abandoned. But in the brief time the mission was active, it was an important link in the early settlement of the American Northwest.

Today, the only reminder of the adobe mission where the Whitmans lived and worked are the stones in the lawn, marking the outline of the buildings and the restored millpond. But wayside exhibits at the site describe the buildings. Self-guided trails lead to the mission, the Whitmans' graves, and the Whitman monument, an obelisk on the hill where Narcissa would watch for her husband's return.

If the grounds leave the days of the Western frontier to the imagination, the visitor center has a rich cache of artifacts conveying a vivid impression of early 19th-century Oregon. The dishes used by the Whitmans, blacksmithing tools, buckskin clothes, and even the tomahawk believed to have been used by Cayuse Indian chief Tomahas to murder Marcus Whitman are on display.

On weekend afternoons in summer, there are demonstrations of pioneer life, with candle and soap making, open-fire cooking, and examples of Indian culture such as the preparation of deer hides.

Open: Visitor Center: 8 a.m. to 4:30 p.m. from Labor Day to Memorial Day, extended to 6 p.m. during the summer. Closed Thanksgiving, Christmas, and New Year's Day.

Fees: $1 per adult.

Mailing Address: Whitman Mission National Historic Site, Route 2, Box 247, Walla Walla, WA 99362.

Telephone: 509-529-2761.

Getting There: The monument is located in southeast Washington near Walla Walla. From Walla Walla, go west on Rt. 12 about five miles. The Whitman Mission is south of the highway.

WEST VIRGINIA

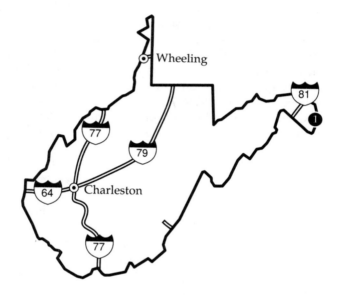

1. Harpers Ferry National Historical Park

|| Harpers Ferry National Historical Park

The picturesque town of Harpers Ferry, West Virginia, set in the Blue Ridge Mountains at the confluence of the Shenandoah and Potomac rivers, was the site of John Brown's famous raid. This ill-fated abolitionist insurrection of 1859 brought the issue of slavery to national prominence and forecast the bloody strife of the Civil War.

Brown was a religious fanatic who believed that he had been called by God to free the slaves. Intent on fomenting an anti-slavery revolution, he seized the federal armory at Harpers Ferry with a 22-man guerrilla force on October 16, 1959. Brown's men held the arsenal and armory for 36 hours until the group was overwhelmed by Marines led by Lieutenant Colonel Robert E. Lee. Sentenced to be hanged for treason, murder, and insurrection, Brown hoped his death would incite others to take up his cause. At any other time, such a revolt would have been quickly forgotten. But in the late 1850s, when the South was feeling increasingly alienated from the North, John Brown's raid stirred deep fears. The movement by southern states to secede was in part a reaction to Brown's incendiary message.

The armory attacked by John Brown was established in 1794 by President George Washington and the U.S. Congress. The strategic location of Harpers Ferry (60 miles northwest of Washington, D.C., at the mouth of the Shenandoah Valley, and along the Baltimore and Ohio Railroad and the Chesapeake and Ohio Canal) made the town a military prize throughout the Civil War. For nearly four years, Harpers Ferry was occupied by one army or the other.

In the fall of 1862, Confederate Stonewall Jackson captured the 12,500-man garrison here just before the Battle at Antietam. Two years later, Union General Philip Sheridan used Harpers Ferry as a supply depot in his campaign to destroy Confederate food sources in the Shenandoah Valley.

Martial law took its toll on the civilian population of Harpers Ferry. In her recollections, Annie Marmian, a doctor's daughter who was an adolescent during the war, described the nightly blackouts instituted because the occupying army thought lights were used to relay messages to the enemy. All metals, including doorknobs and hinges, were stripped from the houses and melted into military material. By the end of the war, only about 200 of the town's 3,000 people remained.

Those difficult days are recalled in the park's living-history program. In summer, staff in Civil War uniforms and period dress discuss the life of the shopkeepers and townspeople before and during the military occupation. Tours start at the visitor center, in the old Stagecoach Inn, where exhibits interpret the park's major themes: John Brown's raid, the Civil War, the early water-powered industry, and black history. (Until the 1950s, Harpers Ferry was the site of Storer College, an early normal school for freed blacks.)

The town has been restored to its 19th-century appearance. There is a working blacksmith shop, a dry-goods store stocked with typical provisions (including "souvenir" bits of the rope supposedly used to hang John Brown), a tavern, and the Harper House, built between 1775 and 1782 by Robert Harper, the town's namesake. This building, the oldest structure in the town, is furnished in the style of an 1850s tenant house. John Brown's Fort and the brick fire engine and guardhouse where Brown and his band were captured is open to the public. Across the street is the John Brown Museum, which has exhibits and an excellent film-and-slide show explaining the Brown raid. The Master Armor's House, built in 1858 as the home for the armory's chief gunsmith, has a museum about gun-making at Harpers Ferry. Cafés, restaurants, and craft and souvenir shops have opened up on the side streets adjoining the park.

History is not the only attraction here. Located on a bluff above the swirling waters of the Potomac and Shenandoah rivers, Harpers Ferry offers excellent opportunities for hiking, camping, rock climbing, fishing, and rafting. Several trails make particularly good hikes: the Appalachian Trail that runs through the park; the Grant Conway Trail, which leads by ruined forts and batteries; the trail up to the Civil War fortifications at Bolivar Heights; and the cliffs of Maryland Heights. (Register with the ranger before attempting this sheer climb.) For a less rigorous but equally beautiful walk, there is the Chesapeake and Ohio Canal towpath. This level gravel walkway parallels the Potomac River down to Washington, D.C. Hiking is best during the spring and in fall, when the leaves are awash in brilliant reds, oranges, and yellows. Indigenous wildlife includes deer, bobcat, rabbit, muskrat, and opossum.

Several private companies offer full- and half-day rafting trips, and in the heat of summer some outfitters lead floating caravans of inner tubes down the river. Check with the park for the names and numbers of local concessions. Bass, catfish, and carp are caught in the rivers. The water is turbulent and the currents swift; swimming is not recommended.

In fall, the park holds its annual "Election Day 1860," a weekend-long re-enactment of the presidential election of 1860. People in period dress make speeches and hold debates to illustrate the tremendous tensions that preceded the Civil War. On the first full weekend in December, there is an old fashioned Christmas celebration, with caroling, tree trimming, taffy pulls, and other period activities.

Open: 8 a.m. to 5 p.m. daily, extended to 6 p.m. in summer. Closed Christmas Day.

Fees: $5 per car or $2 per person on buses, bikes or for hikers.

Mailing Address: Harpers Ferry National Historical Park, P.O. Box 65, Harpers Ferry, WV 25425.

Telephone: 304-535-6371.

Getting There: From Washington, take I-270 north to Frederick, Maryland. From Frederick take Route 340 west to the entrance of the park. Harpers Ferry is about 20 miles from Frederick.

WYOMING

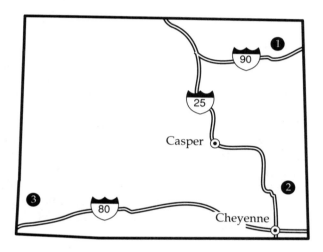

1. Devils Tower National Monument
2. Fort Laramie National Historic Site
3. Fossil Butte National Monument

‖ Devils Tower National Monument

The striking monolith of Devils Tower rises 867 craggy feet above the black pine forests and red soils of northeastern Wyoming and offers opportunities for mountain climbing, hiking, bird watching, and camping. The Indians called this extraordinary tower "Mateo Tepee," or "Bear Lodge." According to Indian myth, a boy-turned-bear created the tower when he clawed the base of a tree in which his sisters were hiding. The girls were thrust in the heavens, where they became the Big Dipper.

Geologists tell another story. Devils Tower was formed by molten rock that forced its way through the earth 60 million years ago. Eons of erosion then leveled the landscape, until all that remains today is the hardened rock of the volcanic intrusion.

Devils Tower may have been around for a long time, but it was only recently that hardy mountaineers—and wily entrepreneurs—attempted to scale the structure. William Rogers and Willard Ripley made the first ascent on July 4, 1893, using a 350-foot wooden ladder for the first leg of their climb. They raised a flag atop the tower, and their wives sold refreshments and pieces of Old Glory to the gawkers below.

There are over 120 routes to the summit. The climb is rough and demands proper gear. As a safety precaution, all mountaineers must register with the park ranger before and after their climb.

For the less adventurous, an hour-long, 1¼-mile trail around the base of the Devils Tower reveals some of the area's geology and wildlife. A prairie dog town, population 1,000, guards the tower. These creatures are skittish and usually dive into their holes when approached. White-tailed deer, mule deer, rabbits, chipmunks, and porcupines live in the park.

The museum in the park's visitor center has an extensive exhibit on the tower and on the ecology and geology of the area, as well as displays of climbing equipment and Indian tools. The park offers a junior ranger program for children.

Bird watching is rewarding. Located at the transition point between mountain and prairie, the park has a bird population of more than 90 species. These include bald and golden eagles, hawks, prairie falcons, and turkey vultures.

The nation's first national monument, Devils Tower, is an 865-foot monolith created by volcanic activity.—*NPS photograph*

The 1,300-acre park includes a 51-site campground nestled in a loop of the Belle Fourche River. Camping is allowed year-round with a 14-day limit. Water is turned off at the first hard freeze of the year, usually in late September. Showers, pay telephones, laundry, and food services are available outside the park.

From Memorial Day to Labor Day, the park service offers climbing demonstrations and evening programs about the region's geology and history.

Open: The park is open 24 hours daily. Visitor Center: 8 a.m. to 5 p.m. year-round, with hours extended to 7:45 p.m. in summer.

Fees: $3 per vehicle, $1 per person between the ages of 16 and 62, collected March through November.

Mailing Address: Devils Tower National Monument, Devils Tower, WY 82714.

Telephone: 307-467-5370.

Getting There: The park is located off Wyoming Rt. 24, seven miles north of Rt. 14. From Gillette, take I-90 (Rt. 14/60) to Moorcroft, exit North on Rt. 14. Continue north on this road to Rt. 24. Turn west on Rt. 110 into Devils Tower, which will take you to the park entrance.

‖ Fort Laramie National Historic Site

From the fur trapping days of the 1830s through the time of the Pony Express, Fort Laramie in eastern Wyoming was an important trading center and military base on the High Plains. Eleven original military structures have been restored and are open to the public, and the ruins and foundations of at least a dozen more historic buildings occupy the site.

Between June 1 and mid-August, the park offers a living history program that illustrates daily life at the fort, with staff in period clothing. The staff is well-versed in the life of a frontier fort and will answer questions. You might encounter a laundress, cavalry man, a surgeon, an officer's wife, or a mountain man. The Post Trader's store supplied the area with everything from woolens to weapons and housed the enlisted men's bar and officers' club. Bachelor officers lived in "Old Bedlam," a portion of which is furnished to look as it might have in the mid-1850s. The restored bakery, constructed in 1876, produced one 18-ounce loaf of bread each day for each soldier at the post. Outhouses have also been restored and are open for viewing.

Intending to exploit the region's abundant beaver population, two trappers built a fort on the banks of the Laramie and North Platte rivers in 1834, then sold it to the American Fur Company two years later. Sioux, Cheyenne, and Arapaho Indians set up trading camps nearby, attracted by the influx of manufactured goods from the East.

Covered wagons carrying the Marcus Whitman party, which settled in Oregon, the Mormons, who landed in Utah, and countless other Americans on their way west stopped at Fort Laramie for repairs and supplies. The U.S. army bought the fort in 1849, using it as a base of operations against the Plains Indians. As the ranks of the Indians diminished and the region became more settled, the outpost lost its importance. It was abandoned in 1890.

The visitor's center, through artifacts, text, and photographs, will introduce you to the story of Fort Laramie. Picnic areas are available, but open fires and hunting are prohibited on the 832-acre park. Fishing is allowed with a state license.

Open: 8 a.m. to 4:30 p.m. from Labor Day to Memorial Day, 7 a.m. to 7 p.m. during the rest of the year. Closed Thanksgiving, Christmas, and New Year's Day.

Fees: $1 per vehicle.

Mailing Address: Fort Laramie National Historic Site, Fort Laramie, WY 82212.

Telephone: 307-837-2221.

Getting There: The park is located in southeast Wyoming, about three miles southwest of the town of Fort Laramie on State Highway 160. From Cheyenne, take I-25 north to State Highway 160.

‖ Fossil Butte National Monument

Fifty million years ago, this dry grassland in southwestern Wyoming was a lake teeming with prehistoric life. The primitive perch and herring, paddlefish and stingray that swam here are preserved at Fossil Butte, an 8,198-acre park containing the most extensive record of fossilized fresh-water fish in North America.

The base of Fossil Butte, laid bare by erosion, is a palette of brightly colored rock beds—red, purple, yellow, gray, and white. In the 18-inch layer of Green River limestone at Fossil Butte, paleontologists have found spectacular fossils of whole fish and insects, and fragments of birds that are 48 to 52 million years old. Other layers have yielded bits of fossilized horses, monkeys, snakes, and crocodiles.

As of June 2, 1990, a permanent visitor center will be open year-round containing displays of exquisite fossils quarried in the area. Visitors are encouraged to participate in fossil preparation.

The park is best seen by foot. The 1½-mile historic quarry trail takes visitors to the old quarries on the butte. Markers help to explain the terrain and fossils. A second trail, the Fossil Quarry Look

Trail, approximately 1½ miles in length, takes the visitor to a quarry where fossils may be viewed in the field. Rangers give guided tours on request—write ahead to make sure there is room—and can provide more specific directions and topographical maps to those desiring more extended hikes.

Fossil Butte abounds in wildlife as well as fossils. Deer, antelope, and elk graze on the grasslands; coyote and bobcat can be found at higher elevations. Many birds, including bald and golden eagles, can be sighted in the area. Cross-country skiing and snowshoeing are excellent in winter.

Open: Visitor Center: 8:30 a.m. to 5:30 p.m. daily. The park's administrative offices are open Monday through Friday, from 7:30 a.m. to 4:30 p.m. year-round. Closed on government holidays.

Fees: None.

Mailing Address: Fossil Butte National Monument, Box 527, Kemmerer, WY 83101.

Telephone: 307-877-3450 or 307-877-5500.

Getting There: Located in southwestern Wyoming, about 11 miles west of Kemmerer, just north of Rt. 30 N and the Union Pacific Railroad. From Rock Springs, take I-80 west to Rt. 30 north through Kemmerer to the monument.

INDEX

Jill MacNeice is a Washington, D.C.-based writer and editor who has written and contributed to six books.